Executive Editor: Shi Gaoxiang 施高翔
Cover&Illustrations: Dr.William N.Brown Xia Lin 潘维廉 夏 林

中英对照

Discover Quanzhou

by Dr. Bill Brown

魅力老潘

魅力泉州

〔美〕潘维廉 著　　潘文功 等 译

厦门大学出版社
XIAMEN UNIVERSITY PRESS

Ancient Garden City

(These 4 pages of photos compliments of master photographer Chen Sizhe)

Garden Community

Twin Pagodas

Prized Miniature Landscapes

East Lake Park

West Lake (the "Western Ocean")

Photographer Chen Sizhe

Hui'an Maiden

Traditional Minnan (S. Fujian) Village

300-year-old Bridge

Confucian Literary Temple

Quanzhou's "Great Wall"

Marco

Historic Zhongshan Rd. Restoration Project

Bamboo Rafting in Dehua

Art in the Park

Fowl Play

Nightscape

One of 407 Protected Ancient Trees

Ancient Canal

UNESCO's "Excellent Relic Protection in Asia-Pacific Area, 2001"

Ancient Zaytun's
Rich and Diverse Heritage

Origin of Anxi Tea and Tea Ceremony

Ancient Biological Engineering!

Home of S. Chinese Music

Start of the Maritime Silk Road

Source of Legendary Porcelain

Birthplace of S. Shaolin Kung Fu

Home of Chinese Puppetry

UNESCO
"World Museum of Religion"

Judaism

Nestorian

Hinduism

Taoism

Confucianism

Manichaeanism

Christianity

Tibetan Buddhism

Islam

Quanzhou
Cuisine
Shark lips!
Fish 'n crispy
rice
泉州市财贸委员会编

Ancient "Academy Upon the Sea" with Pioneers like Quanzhou #7 School

Visionary Leadership

International Faculty

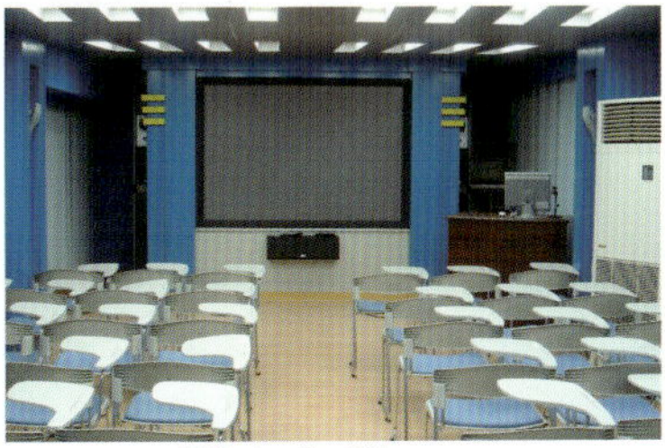

Hi-tech Classrooms

Nat'l Chemistry Competition Gold Medalist

RoboFish Explorer (Int'l Gold Medal)

Broadcast Studio

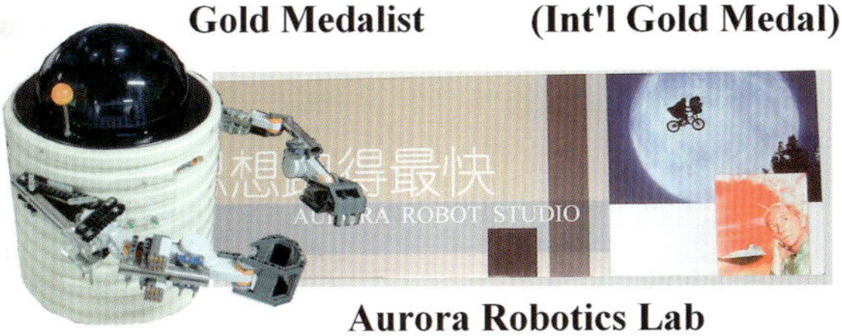

Aurora Robotics Lab

10 Nat'l and 60 Provincial Awards

Gold Medal in Thailand

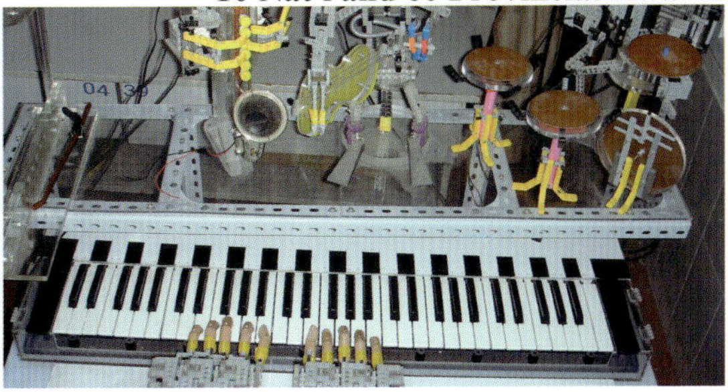

Gold-Medal "2061 RoboBand"

World-Class Hotels
such as the 5-Star Quanzhou Mandarin

★★★★★ (Page 338)

Executive Floor

Elegant Dining

Fujian's Best Pastry Chef!

Home Away From Home

Quanzhou's Best Heated Pool

State-of-the-Art Gym

Mandarin Garden Cafeteria and Lounge

Ancient Zaytun -- City Upon the Sea

Book in Overseas Chinese Museum

Anhai Bridge (world's longest stone bridge)

Foot-powered Irrigation

Graceful Quanzhou Junk

Another view of Anhai Bridge

Quanzhou Harbor

Quanzhou Plain

Confucian Temple (1902)

Kaiyuan Temple

Village Life (1902)

Quanzhou City Wall

Quanzhou Skyline (about 1900)

Zaytun People

"Brother Ba"

School Matron, Mrs. Tsa

Mandarin and Son

Ringing the Church Bell

Street Barber

Lunchtime

Girl Students

Bridal Palanquin

Children at Play

Basket Kids

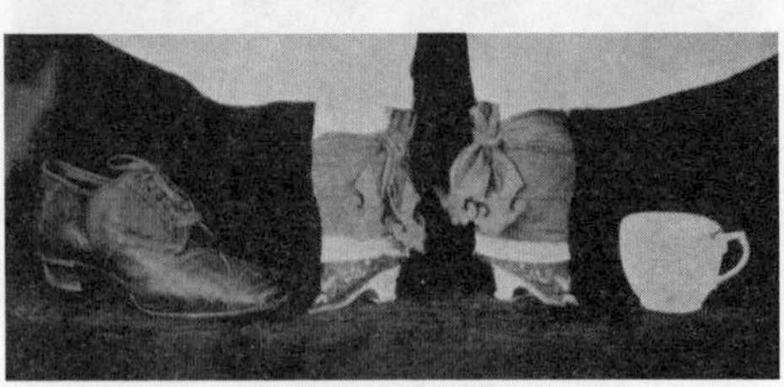

"Golden Lilies"

Kids and Grannies

Fruit Sellers

Pigging Out

Girl and Little Brother

Discover Quanzhou

(Former Mystic Quanzhou)

魅力泉州

Zaytun's True Wealth Marco Polo was impressed by Zaytun' s gems, pearls, porcelain, and silk, but he overlooked the true wealth of this mythic port—the place and the people! Zaytun was blessed with an unparalleled natural wealth and beauty that the enlightened inhabitants maintained as meticulously as their miniature landscapes, which have been famous throughout Asia for 1000 years...

刺桐真正的财富 马可·波罗对古泉州的玉石、珍珠、陶瓷和丝绸印象深刻，但他却没注意到这个神秘古港的真正财富——这一方水土和这一方人！上苍赋予泉州无与伦比的天然财富和美景。

Discover Quanzhou City of Light![1]

(Former *Mystic Quanzhou*)

Comments, suggestions, questions, or requests for copies of Discover Quanzhou at bulk corporate and educational discounts?

E-mail: Amoybill@gmail.com

Snail mail:
Dr. Bill Brown,
Box 1288, Xiamen University
Xiamen, Fujian, PRC 361005

Complaints? Write my wife, Susan Marie!
And check her website:
http://www.amoymagic.com (outside China)
http://www.amoymagic.mts.cn (within China)

Also visit: http://www.xiamenguide.com (by www.mts.cn)

Quanzhou International Club 泉州国际俱乐部网址
http://www.qzintlclub.com/
E-mail: qzintlclub@hotmail.com. David: 1379-9503010

[1] *The City of Lights* is the title of Selbourne's alleged translation of the memoirs of Jacob D'Ancona, a Jewish merchant who supposedly visited China 4 years before Marco Polo. True or not (and I doubt it), it's a great read, and I like the name "City of Light" for several reasons: Quanzhou, start of the Maritime Silk Road, was a commercial and cultural crossroads, a great melting pot, with people of all nations and faiths living together peacefully—a true light in that era, and one that I hope to see rekindled.

魅力泉州[①]

——新光明城

Aren't horns banned within city limits?

市内禁鸣喇叭？

如有疑问、意见、建议和指正，或需要购买《魅力泉州——新光明城》，请发电子邮件至Amoybill@gmail.com。

写信请寄福建省厦门市厦门大学1288信箱 潘维廉博士，邮编：361005。

投诉信件，请直接寄给我的妻子苏珊·玛丽女士！

亦可上她创办的网站，了解最新资讯：

http://www.amoymagic.com
http://www.amoymagic.mts.cn
http://www.xiamenguide.com

① 《光明城》系塞尔伯恩根据雅各布·德·安科纳的回忆录翻译而成的。据说，这位犹太商人到中国的时间比马可·波罗还早四年。无论真实与否，这个故事确实动人。我喜欢《光明城》这个书名有以下理由：泉州是古代海上“丝绸之路”的起点，商业与文化曾经在这里交汇；泉州还是一个大熔炉——来自世界各国和拥有不同宗教信仰的人民在这里和平共处。在那个时代，她给人们带来了光明。如今，我希望看到光明再现泉州。

Table of Contents

	Page
Preface	vi
Quanzhou at a Glance	xii
Supplement China Fujian-Taiwan Relationship Museum	xiv
Supplement Quanzhou Wins the Gold!	xvi
Chapter 1 Introduction	2
Supplement On The City & Great Haven of Zayton	24
Chapter 2 Quanzhou Maritime Museum	28
Supplement Zaytun's Openness to Foreign Religions	48
Chapter 3 Downtown Zayton Sites	58
Supplement Down in the Dumps?	98
Chapter 4 Quanzhou Puppets !	102
Chapter 5 Academy Upon the Sea	112
#7 School—a Window on the Future	118
Chapter 6 Quanzhou Outskirts	130
Chapter 7 Quanzhou Gardens & Parks	146
Supplement Ancient Garden City	152
Chapter 8 Quanzhou Bridges	154
Chapter 9 Hui'an	170
Supplement Professor Wu Shinong —Hui'an Entrepreneur	202
Chapter 10 Nan An—Home of Koxinga	208
Supplement 1 Legend of the "Made in Japan" Chinese Hero Koxinga	226
Supplement 2 General Shilang	228
Supplement 3 Tomb Raiders	230
Chapter 11 Jinjiang and Shishi	234
Supplement 1 Getting Your Foot in the Door with AIDER, Ltd	252
Supplement 2 The Quanzhou Tiger	254
Supplement 3 Strike Gold at CIFIT	258
Chapter 12 Anxi—Oolong Tea Capital of China	260
Supplement 1 Huaxiangyuan Tea	278
Supplement 2 The Book of Tea	282
Chapter 13 Dehua—Porcelain Paradise, and Yongchun	286
Chapter 14 Quanzhou Cuisine	302
Chapter 15 Chinese-English Menu	320
Chapter 16 Quanzhou Specialties	330
Chapter 17 Quanzhou Hotels & Travel Agencies	336
Emergency Phone Numbers	344

目 录

序 …… vii
泉州一瞥 …… xiii
附录 中国闽台缘博物馆 …… xv
附录 泉州夺金！ …… xvii
第一章 导言 …… 3
附录 关于泉州及其宏伟的刺桐港 …… 25
第二章 泉州海外交通史博物馆 …… 29
附录 刺桐城对外国宗教的开放 …… 49
第三章 刺桐市区风景点 …… 59
附录 身在垃圾场？ …… 99
第四章 泉州木偶 …… 103
第五章 泉州——"海滨邹鲁" …… 113
魅力七中—未来之窗 …… 119
第六章 泉州市郊 …… 131
第七章 泉州花园与公园 …… 147
附录 古老的花园城市 …… 153
第八章 泉州的桥梁 …… 155
第九章 惠安 …… 171
附录 吴世农教授——惠安籍企业家 …… 203
第十章 郑成功的故乡——南安市 …… 209
附录 1 驱逐荷寇的爱国者——郑成功传奇 …… 227
附录 2 施琅将军 …… 229
附录 3 盗墓贼 …… 231
第十一章 晋江和石狮 …… 235
附录 1 走进艾德鞋业有限公司 …… 253
附录 2 泉州虎 …… 255
附录 3 中国国际投资贸易洽谈会 …… 259
第十二章 安溪——中国乌龙茶之都 …… 261
附录 1 华祥苑茗茶 …… 279
附录 2《茶书》 …… 283
第十三章 德化——瓷器的天堂，永春 …… 287
第十四章 泉州美食 …… 303
第十五章 中英对照菜谱 …… 321
第十六章 泉州特产 …… 331
第十七章 泉州酒店和旅行社 …… 336
应急电话 …… 345

Preface

Quanzhou—My 3rd Home!

When former Fujian Governor Xi Jinping saw *Amoy Magic*, he suggested I also write about my "3rd Home" as well (Xiamen being my 2nd, and I'm not sure where my 1st is). I wrote *Mystic Quanzhou* in only six weeks, between semesters, and it probably shows it, but we were rushed to prepare for Quanzhou's entry to the international Livcom Awards in Holland (Quanzhou won the gold! See page xvi). In spite of the shortcomings, I hope it helps you better appreciate and enjoy, one of China's most fascinating cities—especially for foreigners.

Quanzhou, the ancient start of the Maritime Silk Road, has changed dramatically since my first visit in January, 1989. In fact, during a two decade period, Quanzhou was #3 in economic growth amongst China's biggest 212 cities. But happily, perhaps more than any other Chinese city, Quanzhou balanced phenomenal growth with preservation and enhancement of an unparalleled historical, cultural and natural heritage.

Quanzhou did not just save (store away!) her heritage but actually incorporated it into the new city. For example, all new architecture, whether apartment buildings, banks or shopping malls, must follow codes that insure the historical and cultural aesthetics of each district. The result is a uniquely modern, comfortable city that embraces the future while preserving a colorful past—a feat that has won the city kudos from UNESCO's Relic Protection Campaign, as well as honors for environmental protection. Quite a city!

While Quanzhou seems to change constantly, it manages to retain and even strengthen that identity that so enthralled Marco Polo and others. And the more I understand Quanzhou, the more I suspect that both Columbus and Marco Polo totally overlooked the true wealth of this beautiful place and people…

Dr. Bill Brown
Xiamen, China
June, 2007

Zaytun Treasures

序

泉州——我第三故乡！

Planting Trees

原福建省省长习近平看到《魅力厦门》一书的时候，他建议我应该写写我的"第三故乡"——泉州（厦门是我的第二故乡。至于第一故乡在哪里，我还没搞清）。利用暑假写《魅力泉州》，我只用了六周的时间，结果可想而知。不过，我们当时是为泉州参加"国际花园城市大赛"而匆忙写就本书的（泉州获得了金奖！详见第XVII页）。尽管书中难免出现各种错误，我希望本书能够帮助您更好地欣赏并爱上泉州——中国最迷人的城市之一（特别是对外国人而言）。还有，别忘了跟以前那样，把你发现的错误、建议和新的资料信息电邮给我。

自1989年1月我首次造访至今，中国古代海上丝绸之路的起点泉州已经发生了巨大的变化。事实上，在过去二十年里，泉州的经济增长速度在中国212个大城市中名列第三。令人欣慰的是，跟中国其他城市相比，泉州市在经济快速增长的同时，较好地保存并弘扬了她独有的历史、文化和自然遗产。

对于这些历史文化遗产，泉州市不只是保存，而是真正地把它们融入这座新城市。例如，在泉州，所有的新建筑，不管是公寓楼房、银行，还是购物中心，都必须遵循各街区所特有的历史和文化审美准则。其结果是催生了一座非常现代且又舒适的城市，拥有美好的未来，同时也保存了她多姿多彩的历史。这一壮举为泉州赢得了联合国教科文组织的遗产保护优秀奖（2001年）以及环境保护的诸多荣誉。相当地不简单啊！

泉州的变化堪称日新月异。不过，她还是想方设法保存，甚至强化了她让马可·波罗和其他老外着迷的那种魅力。随着对泉州了解的进一步深入，我越来越确信：哥伦布和马可·波罗都没看到这座美丽城市及其人民的真正价值……

潘维廉博士

中国厦门（2007年6月）

Many Thanks to

Quanzhou art from Lin Yingming

My family—Susan Marie and sons Shannon and Matthew, for their patience as I dragged them through the same museums for the dozenth time.

Translation Team: Pan Wengong, Xie Youfu, Huang Huaifei, Wen Jinhui, and Xu Haibin.

Quanzhou Party Secretary Mr. Zheng Daoxi (郑道溪): thanks for providing the cover calligraphy.

Quanzhou Evening News Vice Chief Editor Lin YingMing and reporter Wu Zehua for their encouragement, guidance, and support. Mr. Wu Zehua opened many doors. Thank you!

Quanzhou Tourism Dept. Mr. Wen 温锦辉, for his guidance.

Mr. Wang Guoliang, Quanzhou Landscape Administration Office.

Mr. Harry Chen (陈喜), of Quanzhou Foreign Affairs, for providing insights on history and culture, invaluable books and literature, and unwavering moral support.

Master Translation Service was a great support and helped with some translation. Visit their website:
http://www.mts.cn
Tel: 595 28000791

Miss Robin (Fei Fei) helped proofread the final draft.

Enjoy Quanzhou!

Bill Brown

鸣 谢

感谢我妻子苏珊和两个儿子神能和马太，尤其是当我硬拉着你们往同样的博物馆跑几十趟的时候，谢谢你们的耐心。

感谢《魅力泉州》翻译人员：谢友福、黄怀飞、潘文功、温锦辉、许海斌。

感谢泉州市委书记郑道溪为本书题写书名。

感谢泉州晚报副总编林英明和吴泽华记者的支持和指导。

Mr. Wu Zehua and Wife

感谢泉州旅游局温锦辉。

衷心感谢泉州园林局王国良先生。

非常感谢泉州外办精力旺盛的陈喜先生。他陪我开着我家的丰田面包车多次往返于泉州乡野，并为我提供了不少珍贵的书籍和文学作品，道义上的坚定支持以及关于泉州历史、文化的诸多见解。

感谢泉州精艺达翻译服务有限公司的支持。电话：0595-28000791，手机：13859907696，www.mts.cn。

感谢费菲，她为本书做了最后修改。

请欣赏魅力泉州！

潘维廉博士

A Brief Intro to Quanzhou Evening Newspaper Agency

(Provided by *Quanzhou Evening News*)

Since its founding in 1985, the Quanzhou Evening Newspaper Agency (QENA) has developed the *Quanzhou Evening Newspaper* (domestic and overseas edition), *Southeast Morning Newspaper*, the *Quannan Culture* monthly, and Fujian Province's oldest newsweb: www.qzwb.com. It is #1 in newpaper circulation and gross advertisement revenues, and enjoys prestige in news circles throughout the country.

Quanzhou Evening News (QEN), for years Fujian's top selling regional paper and Quanzhou's most authoritative news medium, is both an official paper and an evening paper. It reports on life and society while also promulgating justice on many fronts. Devoted to its readers, the strongly humanist paper offers rich and colorful content with an authority, timeliness, readability and practicability well suited to the history and culture of this legendary port city. QEN is the main channel for Quanzhou's news, and of Fujian Province's most important medias, with extensive influence not only throughout Fujian but also in Hongkong, Macau and Southeast Asia.

Southeast Morning Newspaper, Quanzhou's 2nd most infuential new medium, has the largest circulation of civic newspapers in south Fujian.

For the past two years, QENA has been honored as a national advanced unit in administration in regional newspapers by the State News and Publication Bureau. This highly effective agency has strategically expanded on many fronts and now has more than ten modern corporate entities, including a printing company, Southeast Travel Agency, Southeast Real Estate Company, Southeast Morning Newspaper Circulation Company, and Southeast Property Management Company.

QENA also leads Fujian's regional newspapers in hi-tech media coverage, utilizing a comprehensive digital operation and management system from collection, processing, editing, and revision of news information to computerized direct plate making.

Quanzhou Evening Newspaper Agency—South Fujian's guardian of the past, reporter of the present, and herald for the future!

泉州晚报社简介

泉州晚报社成立于1985年，目前拥有《泉州晚报》、《泉州晚报·海外版》、《东南早报》三报和福建省创办最早的新闻网站“泉州网”（www.qzwb.com）、文化生活月刊《泉南文化》，反映报社实力的报纸发行量和广告收入均居全国地市报前列。

泉州晚报社旗下的《泉州晚报》兼具机关报和晚报特色，以多视角反映民生民情、传播社会正义为己任，具浓郁的人文气息，内容丰富多彩，具有权威性和时效性、可读性和实用性，与泉州历史文化名城内涵相得益彰，是泉州市新闻传播的主要渠道、福建省的重要媒体，并且在海内外和省内有一定的影响力，在东南亚华侨居住区和港澳地区拥有众多的读者，发行量连年遥居福建省地市报首位，是泉州市最具权威的第一媒体；《东南早报》为泉州第二大媒体，为闽南地区发行量最大的市民报。

泉州晚报社连续两年被国家新闻出版总署评为全国地方报纸管理先进单位。报社开展多种经营，建立多元经营体系，按照现代企业制度组建投资经营公司，现拥有印务公司、东南旅行社、东南房地产公司、东南早报发行公司、东南物业管理公司等十多个经济实体。

泉州晚报社报业技术水平在福建省新闻界和中国地市报中位居前列，实现从新闻信息采集、加工、编组、审校，到计算机直接制版全程数字化运作和管理。

Quanzhou at a Glance

Climate
Subtropical marine monsoon climate
Annual avg. temperature 20.7°C; annual avg. precipitation 1235mm.
Latitude: N. 24°30′ ~25°56′ ; longitude E. 117°25′ ~119°05′
Demographics
Size: 538.74 square kilometers
Coastline of 16.6 km; 2,700 ha of beaches; sea area of 4,200 ha
Developed area: 49 square km in 2002 (from 12.5 in 1992)
Population 830,000 (in urban area, 360,000, up from 196,000 in 1992).
GDP avg. increase 1993-2002: 26 % (#3 among top 212 Chinese cities)
Urban Greening
Urban green coverage: 31.2% (16.1% in 1992).
Residential zone greenery 33.8% (167.21 ha—from 15.54% in 1992).
Industrial zone greenery 189.27 ha,
Green area per capita: 8.65 sq. m. (2.6 sq. m. in 1992).
Gardens and Scenic Areas
23 Public Parks and Squares, (486.38 ha)
Gardens and Green Belts: 1532.29 ha (201 ha in 1992)
Public green belts, 311.38 ha, Road green belts, 99.39 ha
Ecological Defense (anti-flood/erosion) Greenbelts, 284.75 ha,
Industrial zone green belts 102.29 ha
Forestation
Urban Forestation 43.2% (from 21.1% in '92)
Total forest coverage 58.45% (31,489 ha, incl. 378 ha of Scenic Forests)
Natural Heritage
1,127 species wild plants, including 35 endangered species.
4,000 species wild animals, including 31 endangered species.
407 protected ancient trees (27 kinds). 416.38 ha mangrove forest
Chinese white dolphin habitat 21 Lakes (2,983 ha).
Historical Heritage
Spent almost 1 Billion Yuan between 1992-2002 on 135 Protected Cultural and Historical Relics incl. 20 churches & temples (the 1700-yr-old Yanfu Temple is Fujian's oldest.).
6 City Museums (including 27.5 million Yuan Maritime Museum (China's best), and a 60 Million Yuan City Museum under construction).
Folk Culture
Home to many treasured crafts and traditions such as acrobatic hand puppets, paper lanterns, bamboo weaving, porcelain, wood sculpture, tree-root carving, miniature flour carvings, paper weaving, lacquer ware, clay work, and a 1700-year-old stone-carving tradition, etc. Also home to S. Shaolin Kung Fu and the Minnan Tea Ceremony (precursor to the Japanese Tea Ceremony). Special arts schools train youngsters to perpetuate these.

泉州一瞥

气候

亚热带海洋季风气候，年平均气温20.7℃，年平均降雨量1235毫米。北纬24°30′～25°56′，东经117°25′～119°05′

相关统计数字

市区面积538.74平方公里，海岸线16.6公里，海滩面积2700公顷，海域面积4200公顷，城区开发面积：49平方公里（2002年，1992年为12.5平方公里）城区人口：83万（1992年为36万）

城区绿化

城区绿化覆盖率：31.2%（1992年为16.1%）

住宅区绿化率：33.8%（1992年为15.54%）

工业区绿化面积：189.27公顷

人均绿地面积：8.65平方米（1992年为2.6平方米）

公园与风景区

23个公园、广场（486.38公顷）

花园与绿化带：1532.29公顷（1992年为201公顷）

公共绿化带：311.38公顷，公路绿化带：99.39公顷

生态防护(防洪、防风)林带：284.75公顷

工业区绿化面积：102.29公顷

森林覆盖率

城区森林覆盖率：43.2%（1992年为21.1%）

全市森林覆盖率：58.45%，31489公顷，包括378公顷的风景区林地

自然遗产资源

1127个植物物种，包括35个濒危物种

4000个动物物种，包括31个濒危物种

27种、407棵珍贵保护古树，416.38公顷红树林

中国白海豚栖息地，21个湖泊（2983公顷）

历史遗产资源

1992年至2002年间，投入近10亿元，保护135个历史、文化遗产，包括20个教堂和寺庙（有1700年历史的延福寺是福建省历史最久远的寺庙）。

6个城市博物馆（包括投资2750万元建设的中国最好的海外交通史博物馆和耗资6000万、正在建设中的城市博物馆）

民间文化

泉州是提线木偶、花灯、竹编、陶瓷、木雕、根雕、捏面人、纸织画、漆器、泥人以及具有1700多年历史的石雕等众多珍贵民间文化艺术的故乡，同时也是南少林、闽南茶艺（日本茶道的祖宗）的发源地。这里有专门的艺术学校，培养年轻一代，传承并发扬这些传统文化。

Supplement

China Fujian-Taiwan Relationship Museum
中国闽台缘博物馆

Quanzhou has many fine museums, ranging from the excellent UNESCO-sponsored Maritime Museum to the Quanzhou South China Architectural Style Museum, but one of the most significant, for me at least, is the China Fujian-Taiwan Relationship Museum.

I fell in love with Taiwan and her people while serving there in the U.S. Air Force from 1976 to 1978. I'd have never imagined back then that a decade later I'd move across the Straits and become Fujian's first foreign permanent resident. I fell in love with the Fujianese as easily as with the Taiwanese, but that's no surprise because ¾ of Taiwanese came from Fujian. Both sides of the Strait share not only the same blood but the same language, customs, religious beliefs, traditions, and architecture.

And thankfully, the Taiwan Strait is narrower today than ever. Twenty ships a day ferry over 50,000 passengers a month between Taiwan-controlled Jinmen and Xiamen (where 15% of Jinmen households own apartments). Taiwanese are not only investing in all areas of enterprise but making themselves at home in Fujian, and donating generously to their motherland's education, rural infrastructure, social development, etc.

To learn more about Taiwan and Fujian's historic and intimate ties, spend a day at this 180 million Yuan, 23,332m^2 museum. And bring the kid; they'll love the 3-D videos projected onto lifelike miniature dioramas, as well as the endless rooms and halls of exhibits covering every aspect of Fujian-Taiwan relations, from opera and puppets to pottery.

I'll write about this fascinating museum in greater detail in this book's next edition. For now, please visit their website: http://www.mty.org.con/

附录　中国闽台缘博物馆

费　菲　译

泉州有包括联合国教科文组织赞助的海外交通史博物馆、泉州南中国建筑风格博物馆等众多极其出色的博物馆。但是意义最深的，至少是对我来说，要属中国闽台缘博物馆了。

1976 年至 1978 年我在美国空军驻台湾基地当兵期间，爱上了台湾这片土地和人民。那时我根本不曾想到，10 年之后我会来到海峡彼岸的福建成为了本省第一个取得永久居住权的老外。我很快便像爱上台湾人那样爱上了福建人，当然这一点儿都不奇怪，因为台湾人口的四分之三来自福建，海峡两岸拥有共同的祖先、语言、习俗、宗教信仰、传统甚至建筑。

让人高兴的是，台湾海峡变得越来越“窄”了：厦门和台湾管辖的金门之间每天有 20 班客轮往来，每月载客量达 50000 人次（15%的金门家庭在厦门拥有住房）。台湾人不仅投资于福建各行业，而且将福建视作自己的家，慷慨解囊，捐资于教育、乡村基础设施、社会发展等项目。

想了解更多关于台湾和福建的历史渊源，何不花一天时间游览一下这座投资 1.8 亿、占地 23332 平方米的博物馆呢。别忘了把小孩子也带来，他们会很快喜欢上 3D 制作的微缩画馆和数不尽的把闽台戏曲、木偶到陶器等方面的渊源介绍得极其全面的展览厅。

本书再版时，我将会更加深入地介绍这座魅力无穷的博物馆。在此之前，请您访问网站：http://www.mty.org.cn/

地址：西湖北侧　电话：28986366　邮箱: xieqinghai2008@sina.com

Taiwanese tourists explore their roots

Supplement

Alan Smith, Sue and Bill Brown

Quanzhou Wins the Gold! (Livcom, 2003, Holland)

In 2003, I was honored to prepare and deliver Quanzhou's presentation for the Livcom Competition (formerly "Nations in Bloom") in Holland, and thrilled when we won both the Gold Medal (against cities like The Hague and Seattle) and the Heritage Management Award. So imagine my surprise when I returned to have even Quanzhou people ask me, "How could we have won?" They obviously understood neither the scope of the competition nor the magnitude of Quanzhou's accomplishments over the past two decades.

Livcom is about much more than gardens and landscaping. To bring home the gold in this "Oscar of Livable Communities" a city must excel in all six categories, and after eight months of research to prepare for Quanzhou's presentation, I had no doubt the city deserved the gold.

Three Golds—One Lesson! I was fortunate to represent Xiamen in Germany in 2002, Quanzhou in Holland in 2003, and Shanghai Songjiang in Spain in 2005—and all three cities got the gold, beating such stiff competitors as Hague and Seattle. Each of these three Chinese cities was very different, but each won the gold because of their commitment to creating prosperous yet livable communities. And I've seen many other Chinese cities, large and small, that exemplify Livcom's ideals.

An Invitation I hope that even more Chinese cities will enter events like Livcom, not just to win a gold medal, which in the end will sit upon some shelf gathering dust, but to learn from the rest of the world, and just as importantly, to share with the rest of the world the invaluable lessons that Chinese cities have learned during the past 20 years of phenomenal reforms.

And to that end, I'm happy to end this chapter with a description of Livcom written by founder Mr. Alan Smith.

附录　泉州夺金！

（国际花园城市大赛 2003年，荷兰）

Quanzhou get the Gold—Twice!
Aperdoon, Netherlands, 2003
"Nations in Bloom"

2003年，我有幸帮助泉州为参加在荷兰举办的国际花园城市大赛（现更名为“人居大赛”）做准备，并在大赛上发表参赛陈述。当泉州战胜海牙和西雅图等城市，获得国际花园城市大赛的金奖和遗产管理大奖时，我欣喜若狂。凯旋归来，甚至连泉州人也问我：“我们为什么会赢？”想想，这种疑问让我感到吃惊。很显然，他们不理解国际花园城市大赛的性质，也不懂得泉州在过去20多年里所取得的伟大成就。

国际花园城市大赛远远不是花园和园林那么简单。为了获得“人居大赛奥斯卡”金奖，参赛城市必须在所有的六个方面胜出。为了参赛陈述，我调查研究8个月，毫无疑问，泉州当之无愧。

三块金牌，一条经验！ 我感到十分幸运，因为2002年在德国代表厦门，2003年在荷兰代表泉州，2005年在西班牙代表上海松江——我所代表的三座城市战胜了诸如海牙和西雅图这样的强劲对手，胜出了。三座中国城市各不相同，但每一个城市都获得了金奖，因为这些城市都致力于创造繁荣且适合人类居住的环境。在中国，我也注意到，许多城市，无论大小，均堪称人居理想典范。

参赛邀请　我希望更多的中国城市加入到诸如“人居大赛”这样的竞赛活动。参赛不仅仅是为了获得金奖（奖杯最终总是被放在某个架子上长灰尘），而是为了向世界其他城市学习。在过去20多年的改革巨变中，中国吸取了许多宝贵的经验。与世界其他城市分享这些经验，也同样是相当重要的。

为此，在本章节的结尾，我收入了国际花园城市大赛创始人阿兰·史密斯撰写的有关人居大赛的内容。

International Awards for Livable Communities

(Formerly "Nations in Bloom")
By Mr. Alan Smith, Founder and Director

Despite the possible interpretations of the name Nations in Bloom [now "LivCom—International Awards for Livable Communities], it is NOT a flower show, but a unique international initiative concerned with all aspects of the local environment.

The objective of LivCom is the improvement in the quality of life through the creation of livable, viable communities, encouraged through international exchange of best practice. The international media has named LivCom as the International Benchmark for management of the local environment.

Reasons for Creating LivCom: There is a long history of international meetings attended by world leaders and experts that have sought to reach agreement on environmental issues. But despite these meetings and good intentions, too often the outcomes have been diluted to enable acceptance in many different political cultures. In the end, they often have little real impact on real communities.

There is no way of imposing penalties when countries break from previously made agreements, and there is no lasting ongoing commitment. The USA walked away from the Kyoto Agreement because the previously agreed terms of this agreement did not suit the current Administration's political and financial aspirations.

Increasingly, local communities have sought to improve their environment, but have not had the essential network through which they could seek and exchange the best international practice.

LivCom was created to involve the main partners in the management of the local environment, including local politicians, local experts and the community.

Management: LivCom is managed by a non profit-distributing Company that is a UK Registered Charity. LivCom is endorsed by the United Nations Environment Program.

Participation: LivCom was piloted in 1996 and launched internationally in 1997. Each year new countries are represented in the Competition. Over 50 countries are now in the LivCom family.

Structure: Participants compete in six Population Categories.
Communities are required to submit a 4,000 word report, which an international Panel of Judges assess against six criteria: Enhancement of the Landscape, Heritage Management, Use of environmentally Sensitive Practices, Community Involvement, Healthy Lifestyles, and Planning for the Future.

The Judges invite a number of communities from each Population Category to compete in the Final, where they are required to make a verbal Presentation supported by slides and a video. Following the Presentation, communities face a series of questions from the Judges. The Judges then assess each community against the above criteria.

国际花园城市大赛

虽然对大赛名称的翻译可能会让人误以为它是一个鲜花展，但它确实是一个国际化的先进性的考虑到地区环境方方面面的比赛。

大赛的主题是通过创建花园城市提高生活质量，通过国际化的交流加强经验。国际媒体都将大赛称为城市环境管理的国际性评定。

举办国际花园城市大赛的原因：长久以来，各国的领导人及专家一直在开会讨论，以达成一个关于城市环境标准的协议。但是即使这些会议的目标很好，由于各国不同的政治文化体系，会议的结论就经常被弱化，最后的结果往往是对城市的发展影响甚小。

如果有城市违反了最初制定的规则，是没有任何办法对其进行惩罚的，也无法形成长期的承诺。美国就因最初的协议不适应现行的行政及金融规则而退出了协议。

各国城市都越来越关注城市环境的改善，但是他们都没有找寻及交换其他国家经验的联络途径。

因此，国际花园城市大赛就产生了，它使城市环境的管理因素，包括政府官员、当地专家及整个城市很好地结合起来。

New Apartment; Classic Minnan Style

管理：大赛是由一个在英国注册的非营利慈善机构进行管理，并由联合国环境规划署认可。

参赛：1996年，国际花园城市大赛通过试行，并在1997年正式举办。每一年都有不同的城市参赛，现在已经有50多个城市参加过大赛。

分组：参赛城市按照人口数量分成六组。

参赛城市需递交一份4000字的报告，由国际评委通过六个方面进行评判：城市景观的改进，历史遗产的管理，环境实践的运用，健康的生活方式，城市社区的参与及未来的展望。

评委从每一个参赛组中挑选一些城市进入最后的决赛。决赛中，选手需通过幻灯片及影像资料作口头陈述。陈述后回答评委提问，随后评委按标准进行评定。

Benefits:
The writing of the Initial Report is a self-audit process, and highlights to municipal authorities both what the community is doing and is not doing. This initial Report has often been used as the basis for a community's long-term plan.

Management of the environment has more international implications than possibly any other community responsibility. No community faces unique challenges, and no community has all the answers. It is essential that anyone responsible for environmental management maintain an awareness of how communities in other parts of the world respond to similar challenges.

Environmental challenges have no national or cultural borders. LivCom is non political and therefore offers the only opportunity for communities to meet other communities from all parts of the world that are seeking an improved local environment.

There are many examples of communities meeting through LivCom that have formed agreements to exchange best practice, to exchange technical visits, or work together to address a common challenge. These partnerships have produced accelerated technical advances and significant financial savings.

The community has never before been better informed, had a greater desire to become involved, or had greater expectations regarding the improvement of their local environment. This increases the pressure on those responsible for the local environment to seek out international best practices.

LivCom is the only initiative through which communities can become aware of international best practices.

For full details, visit http://www.livcomawards.com For Registration Forms and general enquiries, please contact info@livcomawards.com, or phone +44 118 946 1680. Closing date for annual competitions is May 31st.

LivCom, Globe House, Crispin Close, Caversham
Reading, Berkshire, RG4 7JS, England
Tel/Fax: +44 (0)1189461680

收获：

写陈述报告是一个自我剖析的过程，它使城市当局明确什么正在做而什么还没开始。很多城市把这份报告作为长期规划的基础。

环境的管理相对于其他的城市职责来说更具国际影响性。没有一个城市会面对独特的问题，没有一个城市知道所有的解决方案。负责城市环境的任何人都应该时刻注意其他国家的城市如何面对这些相似的问题。

环境问题没有国家或文化的界限。国际花园城市大赛不是政治性的，它为那些找寻改善城市环境方法的各国城市提供了一个相互接触的机会。

因此，许多在大赛上交流的城市都签订了协议，相互交流经验，进行技术性访问或共同工作。这种伙伴关系不仅促进了技术发展，更带来了经济实惠。

参与者们从未像今天这样渴望参与进来，也从未像今天这样得到如此多的有效信息，更从未像今天这样对自身环境的改善充满期待。这对负责环境管理的人员提出了更加严格的要求，促使他们主动找寻国际经验。

国际花园城市大赛是唯一一个让城市了解国际上优秀实践经验重要性的比赛。

Chapter 1

Introduction

"There is no people in the world
wealthier than the Chinese"
Ibn Battuta[1] (Arab Traveler, 1304-1358)

Columbus Meets Zhenghe!

Columbus may have ended up in a "New" World but he was seeking an ancient one. He had devoured Marco Polo's accounts of the legendary wealth of Quanzhou, from which the Venetian vagabond sailed for home.

Zaytun (the Arab's name—a homonym for "olive," symbol of peace), was the largest port on earth, rivaling Alexandria in Egypt. Start of the Silk Road of the Sea, this was the legendary port of call for Ibn Battuta, Sinbad, and Admiral Zheng He, who 70 years before Columbus sailed the seas in 440 foot treasure ships that would have dwarfed Columbus' little 85' Santa Maria.

Columbus never made it to Zaytun, but I have. That mystic "City of Light" is just a 90 minute drive up the coast from my adopted home of Xiamen (which a few centuries ago was part of Quanzhou).

Marco Polo

"At this city you must know is the Haven of Zayton, frequented by all the ships of India, which bring thither spicery and all other kinds of costly wares. It is the port also that is frequented by all the merchants of Manzi, for hither is imported the most astonishing quantity of goods and of precious stones and pearls, and from this they are distributed all over Manzi. And I assure you that for one shipload of pepper that goes to Alexandria or elsewhere, destined for Christendom, there come a hundred such, aye and more too, to this haven of Zayton; for it is one of the greatest havens in the world for commerce."

Marco Polo (Venetian vagabond)

第一章

导 言

Columbus

“在这个世界上，没有人比中国人更富有。”

——伊本·贝图塔（威尼斯旅行家，1304—1358）

哥伦布或许最终找到了“新大陆”，不过他实际上寻找的是一片古老的土地，因为他曾经如饥似渴地阅读过《马可·波罗游记》。在游记中，马可·波罗记录了泉州不可思议的富裕程度。也正是从中国泉州，这位威尼斯浪子启航回国。

当时，泉州是世界上最大的港口，可与埃及的亚历山大媲美。阿拉伯人把泉州叫做刺桐（意为橄榄树，和平的象征）。作为“海上丝绸之路”的起点，泉州这个神奇的地方接纳过阿拉伯旅行家伊本·贝图塔、水手辛巴德和郑和。郑和率领的船队比哥伦布早70年出海。跟440英尺的郑和宝船相比，哥伦布小小 85 英尺的“圣·玛利亚号”肯定会显得相形见绌。

哥伦布没能把船开到泉州，我却做到了！这座神秘的光明城就在我的第二故乡厦门以北的滨海，开车只要 90 分钟。数百年前，厦门还只是泉州的一部分。

> “在这座城市，你应该知道刺桐港。印度商船经常造访，带来了那边的香料和其他各种贵重的器皿。‘蛮子’（马可·波罗称南方的中国人为‘蛮子’）也经常来泉州做生意，因为这里进口的货物、宝石和珍珠数量惊人，并已分销到整个中国南方。我敢向你保证，假若有一艘船通过亚历山大港进入基督国家的话，就会有100艘，甚至更多的船只进入刺桐港。对商界来说，刺桐港是世界上最伟大的天堂之一。”
>
> ——马可·波罗（旅行家）

Zaytun's True Wealth Marco Polo was impressed by Zaytun's gems, pearls, porcelain, and silk, but he overlooked the true wealth of this mythic port—the place and the people! Zaytun was blessed with an unparalleled natural wealth and beauty that the enlightened inhabitants maintained as meticulously as their miniature landscapes, which have been famous throughout Asia for 1000 years.

Zayton was a city of gardens, lakes and forests, ringed by mountains, facing the sea, and nestled between two great rivers. Zaytun, with its three great concentric city walls, had a storybook setting that has inspired over 1,000 years of Chinese poets and philosophers.

It is no wonder that the great Arab traveler Ibn Battuta remarked upon Quanzhou folks' love of gardens. The entire city was indeed like a miniature garden but on a gigantic scale, with each citizen playing their part—even as they do today.

5,019 Years of Balance For 1,000 years, Quanzhou folks have crafted their prize-winning miniature landscapes not to win prizes but for the sheer beauty of it. And even as they revel in the judicial juxtaposition of stone and miniature trees, so they have adapted their city to the confines of their unique topography to create not just family gardens but neighborhood gardens, public parks and city forests that reinforce rather than destroy their environment. I suspect this uniquely Chinese sense of balance and long-term perspective explains how China has survived for 5,019 years (a Chinese professor told me China was 5,000 years old—and that was 19 years ago).

"Land is Life" is an old Chinese adage that proved true in Quanzhou. Both land and inhabitants thrived, and the City of Light became a global commercial and cultural crossroads—a **melting pot** where merchants, diplomats, philosophers and missionaries from all over the world coexisted peacefully, inter-married, and most importantly, learned from one another.

刺桐真正的财富 马可·波罗对古泉州的玉石、珍珠、陶瓷和丝绸印象深刻，但他却没注意到这个神秘古港的真正财富——这一方水土和这一方人！上苍赋予泉州无与伦比的天然财富和美景。聪明的泉州人千百年来像伺候盆景一样小心谨慎地维护着这些财富，使其在全亚洲闻名已逾1000年。

古泉州坐落在福建两条大河之间，东临大海，三面环山，花园、湖泊、森林不计其数。刺桐古城有三道雄伟的同轴城墙。这种传奇的景致在过去1000多年的历史中给了中国诗人和哲学家创作的灵感。

难怪阿拉伯伟大的旅行家伊本·贝图塔会注意到泉州人对花园的迷恋。实际上，泉州整座城市就一座规模巨大的花园。直到现在，市民们还在这座花园里扮演着各自的角色。

5019年的平衡 上千年来，泉州人一直用手工制作精美的盆景。他们的目的不是为了获奖，而是纯粹为了美。尽管热衷于工整地摆弄石头和盆景，他们还是按照城市独特的地形、地貌创建私家花园、社区花圃、公园和城市森林，以保护而非破坏环境。我想，中国人独特的平衡感和长远的眼光足以说明中国得以生生不息5019年的原因（一名中国教授曾经告诉我，中国有5000年的历史——那是19年前的事情了）。

“土地就是生命” 这句中国古话在泉州显得尤为真切。这里土地肥沃，人丁兴旺。光明城变成了全球的商业和文化中心。在这个“大熔炉”里，来自世界各地的商人、外交官、哲学家和传教士和平共处，相互通婚。最重要的是，他们互相学习。

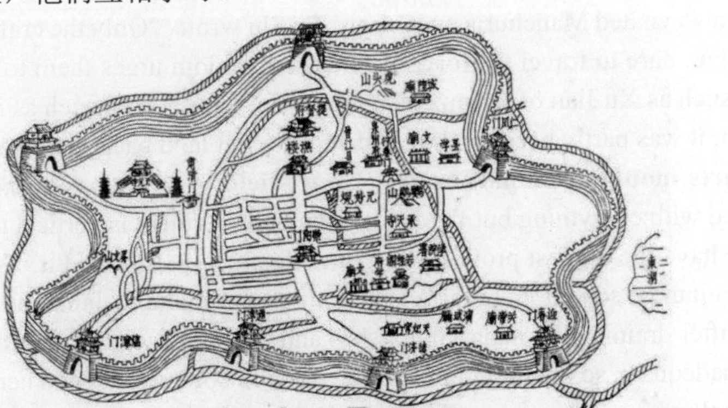

Ancient Zaytun

Jerusalem of Asia[2] UNESCO dubbed Quanzhou a "World Museum of Religion" because the city hosted every major religion, from Nestorian Christianity and Tibetan Buddhism to Islam. Quanzhou's Muslim community supposedly dates back to the day of Mohammed himself, and the Persian Manichean religion survives today only in Quanzhou. Quanzhou people not only did not lack diversity of religion or philosophy, they were also well grounded academically. Called the **Academy Upon the Sea**, Quanzhou produced 2,473 successful candidates in the highest imperial examinations, twenty prime ministers, and 950 nationally acclaimed scholars.

World Citizens Broad exposure to world philosophies, religions and academics helped nurture the uniquely global outlook that insured Quanzhou folks' prosperity both at home and abroad. Today, over 5 million Overseas Chinese, and 40% of Taiwan's Han Chinese, trace their roots to Quanzhou. But Fujianese were a force to be reckoned with long before the City of Light became a beacon for the world.

The Fujian Flame As we'll see in China's best Maritime Museum (next chapter), China's great maritime tradition was born right here in Fujian over 2,000 years ago when King Fuchai built a shipyard near Fuzhou. Our province is named after King Fuchai, as are the great Fujian boats (fuchuan), with their prows' painted "dragon eyes" that enabled boats to see where they were going—which too often was straight into the mouth of a watery hell.

Guang Sima claimed that during the 10th century, fully 40% to 50% of ships traveling from Fujian to North China were lost at sea! So it was with some awe that Koreans recorded the arrival of Quanzhou merchants as early as 1017 A.D. They also visited Manchuria and Japan. Su Shi wrote, "Only the crafty merchants of Fujian dare to travel to Koryo where the kingdom urges them to seek profits. Men such as Xu Jian of Quanzhou are legion." But if men such as Xu Jian were legion, it was partly because they had so little flat land back home to hang onto.

"8 parts mountain, 1 part water, 1 part field" 八山一水一分田 Fujian is blessed with everything but flat land. So much of Fujian is vertical that we could easily have the biggest province in China if someone flattened it. A millennium ago, Fujianese sought more farm land with massive land reclamation projects, but even after draining the malarial marshes and pushing back the sea, farm land was still inadequate, so the intrepid Fujianese took to commerce—and here they found their calling.

亚洲的耶路撒冷 联合国教科文组织授予泉州"世界宗教博物馆"的称号，因为这里容纳了世界上几乎所有的主要宗教：从景教、藏传佛教到伊斯兰教。泉州的伊斯兰社区据说可以追溯到穆罕默德时代。来自波斯的摩尼教如今只在泉州得以幸存。泉州人不仅拥有多种多样的宗教和哲学，而且在学术方面也颇有建树。泉州有 2473 人参加过殿试，出过 20 位相国，950 位全国知名文人，被誉为"海滨邹鲁"。

世界公民 泉州人广泛接触世界各国的哲学、宗教和学术理论，形成了自己独特的全球观，确保了泉州人在海内外的发展。今天，500 多万海外华侨，40%的台湾汉族同胞在泉州找到了自己的根。早在光明城成为世界文明的灯塔之前，福建人就已经是一支不可忽视的力量了。

福建人的激情 在下一章，我们将访问中国最好的海事博物馆。你会发现，2000 多年前，吴王夫差在福州附近建造了一个造船厂，中国伟大的海事传统就诞生在福建。吴王夫差给福建省命名，并把高大的福建船称为"福船"。福船的船首描有"龙的双眼"，直视它们行进的方向——常常直逼水狱的大门。

From "City of Springs"

司马光称，公元 11 世纪，航行在福建至中国北方的海船，40%～50%葬身海底！因此，韩国人在公元 1017 年就有了泉州商人来访的记载，实在是令人敬畏。这些商人还到过中国东北和日本。苏轼曾写道，朝廷极力鼓动商人前往高丽经商，但只有精明的福建人胆敢冒险，其中不乏像徐戬这样的泉州商人。如果说，像徐戬这样的泉州商人不计其数，那其中一部分原因是，他们的老家可以立足的平地太小。

八山一水一分田 福建物产丰富，独缺平地。福建大部分地区山高壁峭。要是摊平的话，肯定会变成中国面积最大的省份。1000 多年前，福建人为了拥有更多的耕地展开了大规模的造地运动。在开发毒气频发的沼泽地和填海垦荒之后，耕地仍然不够。因此，勇猛的福建人做起了生意，并找到了自己的强项。

Fujianese Integrity Over the centuries, Fujianese developed a reputation not only for business prowess but also for unimpeachable integrity. In 1912, Reverend Pitcher wrote in *In and About Amoy*:

> "...what shall we say of them [Fujianese]? They are a part of a wonderful people...
> "One hears all kinds of comment upon the deceptiveness of the Chinese and yet in business circles, the commercial world, they have the reputation of being the most straightforward and conscientious merchants in the whole Eastern hemisphere. This holds true here in Amoy...You may always depend upon the man with whom you may be dealing to deliver the goods. No matter how much they may lose in the transaction the Chinese have the reputation of fulfilling their contracts every time to the letter."

It was the people, as much as the place, which made Zaytun the natural start of the Silk Road of the Sea. And, of course, there was also Zaytun's silk…

> "The first city which we reached after our sea voyage was the city of Zaytun... Zaytun is an immense city. In it are woven the damask silk and satin fabrics which go by its name, and which are superior to the fabrics of Khansa and Khan-Baliq. The port of Zaytun is one of the largest in the world, or perhaps the very largest. I saw in it about a hundred large junks; as for small junks, they could not be counted for multitude."
>
> Ibn Battuta, Arab Traveler (1304-1358)

Silk Road of the Sea "Silk Road" evokes images of deserts and camels, but the Maritime Silk Road accounted for much of the trade because one ship carried as much as 700 camels (and ships didn't spit at you). While Fujianese sailed the seven seas, the rest of the world sailed to Zaytun for tropical fruits, agricultural products, Chinese medicines, and Fujian's famous porcelain and silks (our English word 'satin' comes from "Zaytun").

Over 3,000 years ago, silk was worth its weight in gold in the West. The Roman poet Horace (65-8 B.C.) wrote about silk, and Lucan (39-65 A.D.) wrote of "Cleopatra's white breasts...revealed by the fabric... close-woven by the shuttle of the Seres [Chinese]."

The Secret of Silk For centuries, Westerners beguiled by visions of Cleopatra's silky undies sought to discover silk's origin. Pliny (A.D.23-79), in *Natural History*, wrote that silk grew on trees!

福建人的诚信　数百年来，福建人不仅在经商能力方面获得了声誉，诚信方面也是无懈可击的。1912年，皮彻牧师在《厦门内外》一书中写道：

> "……我们应该怎么评价他们（福建人）呢？他们是一个伟大民族的一部分……
>
> "你也许听说过关于中国人不可靠的各种传言。但是，在实业界，在商界，他们拥有东半球最正直、最尽责商人的名声。在厦门也是这样的……你完全可以信任给你送货的生意人。交易中，无论亏掉多少，中国人每次都会不折不扣地履行合同。"

正是这样的人民、这样的地方使得刺桐成为海上丝绸之路的起点。当然，还有刺桐的丝绸……

> "我们海上航行抵达的第一座城市就是刺桐……刺桐是一座大城市。城里编织的绸缎及其织物以刺桐为名，质地高过杭州和北京。刺桐港是世界上最大的港口之一，或许就是最大的！在这里，我看到了大约一百艘大船；至于小船，不可计数。"
>
> ——伊本·贝图塔 (1304–1358)

海上丝绸之路　丝绸之路令人想起沙漠和骆驼的景象，海上丝绸之路却承担了大部分的贸易，因为一艘船可以装载的货物相当于700只骆驼运载的量（而且海船不会像骆驼那样朝你吐口水）。福建人扬起风帆漂洋过海，而世界各国的商人却纷纷坐船到刺桐采购热带水果、农产品、中药材和福建著名的瓷器和丝绸。英语单词"satin"(绸缎) 源自"刺桐"（Zaytun）。

三千多年前，在西方，丝绸的价钱与同等重量的黄金相同。古罗马诗人贺拉斯（公元前65年—公元前8年）曾经描述过丝绸。鲁坎（公元39年—65年）曾写道："克利奥帕特拉雪白的双乳……在赛利斯人（中国人）编织的锦绣文绮下……若隐若现。"

丝绸的秘密　数百年来，西方人在克利奥帕特拉柔滑内衣的诱惑下追寻丝绸的发源地。普林尼（公元23年—79年）在《自然史》中写道："丝绸长在树上！"

"The first race encountered are the Seres, so famous for the fleecy product of their forests. This pale floss, which they find growing on the leaves, they wet with water, and then comb out, furnishing thus a double task to our womenkind in first dressing the threads, and then again of weaving them into silk fabrics. So has toil to be multiplied; so have the ends of the earth to be traversed: and all that a Roman dame may exhibit her charms in transparent gauze."

To safeguard silk's secret, China forbade the export of raw silk. Silk fabric was sent through Constantinople to the Island of Cos, where it was unwoven and used to produce Roman nobility's ethereal garments. Silk's secret was discovered only in 550 A.D., when Nestorian monks secreted silkworms in bamboo tubes and smuggled them out of China. But the production of porcelain was a tougher nut to crack.

Zaytun Porcelain Even more desirable than Zayton's silk was her porcelain. One of China's top porcelain centers, Quanzhou's delicate wares so bewitched Western rulers that some monarchs bankrupted national treasuries to amass their vast collections (see Dehua chapter).

Fujian—Established Happiness With her silk, porcelain, and other treasures, this province well deserved the name of "Fujian (福建, Fukien in old Romanization):"

"The name Fukien, which means 'established happiness,' in a large measure characterizes the people of this district. I think we may safely go further and say that this is true of the whole province. What we mean is this: they are not antagonistic to foreigners... With the exception of a few occasions, the Chinese in these parts have never exhibited any opposition to the stranger within their gates."

Pitcher, *In and About Amoy*, 1912, p.96

Unfortunately, that happiness was soon to be disestablished…

Rise and Fall Zayton was bustling by the early 7th century when Mohammed's two disciples supposedly arrived, followed closely by Nestorian Christians, Manicheans, and adherents of virtually every other religion and philosophy. By the 13th century, Quanzhou was a magnificent city with three concentric walls encircling the central government area, inner city, and foreigner's quarters.

China and India together accounted for over half of the world's gross national product (and Angus Madison, a British economic historian, claims China accounted for 29% of the globe's GNP as late as 1820!). But within a century of Zheng He's day the legendary City of Light was extinguished.

> “塞里斯以树林中出产的细丝著名。这种灰色的乱丝在树上生长。他们先将丝用水浸湿，再加以梳拢，于是妇女们将丝整理，再织成丝织品。因此，商人开始了艰苦的跋涉，横穿地球的东西两端：罗马贵族的夫人娇嫒方得以穿上薄纱，施展魅力。”

为了保守丝绸的秘密，中国严禁生丝出口。丝绸织物通过君士坦丁堡输往科思岛，重新编织并制成罗马贵族轻薄的衣物。直到公元550年，丝绸的秘密才被基督教传道士破解。他们将桑蚕藏在竹管里，偷偷地运出中国。至于瓷器的生产，那是一个更难搞清楚的问题。

刺桐瓷器 比刺桐丝绸更吸引人的是刺桐的瓷器。泉州是中国最好的瓷器生产中心之一。西方国家的统治者对刺桐的精美瓷器如此着迷，以至于有些君主不惜亏空国库，大量收集。

福建——已经建成的幸福 有了丝绸、瓷器和其他珍宝，福建的确名副其实。

> “福建，意思是‘已经建成的幸福’，在很大程度上体现了本地老百姓的性格。我们，我们完全可以再进一步说，这对这个省份来讲也是对的。我们的意思是：他们对外国人并无敌意……除了极个别几次例外，这个地区的中国人对陌生者进入他们的国门从未表现出敌意。”
>
> ——皮彻（《厦门内外》，1912年，第96页）

不幸的是，他们的幸福不久之后就被毁了。

兴与衰 公元7世纪初，穆罕默德的两个门徒到来之时，刺桐就已经相当繁荣。紧跟而来的是，基督教信徒、摩尼教徒以及世界上几乎所有其他宗教、学派的追随者。到了公元13世纪，泉州已经是一座拥有三道城墙、规模宏大的城市，从里到外，分别守卫着官府机构、内城和番区。

到了郑和时代，中国和印度的国民生产总值之和占据了世界GNP的半壁江山。（英国的经济史学家安格斯·麦迪逊称，直到1820年，中国还占有全球GNP的29%！）然而，郑和时代之后不到一百年，传说中的光明之城已经黯然无光。

Before his seventh voyage in 1432, Zheng He erected a tablet in Changle (near Fuzhou), in which he claimed to have "unified seas and continents" and "the countries beyond the horizons from the ends of the earth have all become subjects." But his great expeditions had taken a heavy toll on the land—especially on the common folk, who received nothing in return for their sacrifices to build the fleets.

While Westerners made a killing at commerce (Magellan's crew once sold 26 tons of cloves for 10,000 times the cost!), the Emperor's fleet was built primarily to impress the world with the glories of China (and, of course, her Emperor). And the ships returned not with practical commodities but cargoes of exotic gifts and luxuries for the imperial court (primarily the corrupt eunuchs).

The Emperor decried the waste, saying, "I do not care for foreign things. I accept them because they come from far away and show the sincerity of distant peoples, but we should not celebrate this." His sentiments echoed those of Chinese 1500 years earlier, whom Pliny wrote were,

> "…inoffensive in their manners indeed; but, like the beasts of the forest, they eschew the contact of mankind; and, though ready to engage in trade, wait for it to come to them instead of seeking it out."

Dousing the City of Light Not long after Zheng He's death, China closed her doors and destroyed the greatest navy the world had ever seen. Whereas the Ming navy had 3,500 ships in the early 1400s, within decades it was a capital offense to build boats with more than two masts.

In 1525, the emperor ordered the destruction of all seafaring ships, and the arrest of the merchants who sailed them. By 1551, it was a crime to sail the seas in a ship with more than one mast.

Rekindling the City of Light Zaytun had so captured the imagination of foreigners that some thought it was China's capital! In 1515, Giovanni d'Empoli wrote, "The Grand Can is the King of China, and he dwells at Zaytun." But trade ceased, the ports silted up, and that mystic City of Light was snuffed out. But thanks to a couple of decades of dramatic reform and opening up, Quanzhou's new generation is as excited about their future as they are proud of their past, and Quanzhou is becoming once again a global commercial and cultural crossroads.

#3! Quanzhou people still have their age-old knack for business! Over the past decade, this resurrected city's annual GDP grew an average of 26%—#3 amongst China's top 212 cities. And Quanzhou is using this newfound wealth to make the place a better place to live.

1432年，第七次下西洋之前，郑和在福州附近的长乐立下了一块石碑，称："皇明混一海宇"，"际天极地，罔不臣妾"。然而，郑和的远征对国家，特别是普通百姓来说是致命的，因为他们为建造船队所付出的代价并没有得到任何补偿。

当西方人在生意上大赚一笔的时候（麦哲伦的船队曾经以高出成本价一万倍的价格出售26吨的香料），中国的皇帝建造船队却主要是为了向世界展示中国（当然还有她的皇帝）的伟大。船队返航时并没有带回实用的商品，而是为皇廷（主要是腐败的太监们）运回大量奇珍异宝。

皇上谴责这样的浪费说："寡人不在乎外番的贡品。寡人接受它们是因为它们远道而来，展示了远方客人的诚意。但我们不能因此庆幸。"他的观点回应了1500年前普林尼所描述的中国人：

> "行为方面一点也不伤人；但是，像森林中的野兽，他们逃避与人类的接触；而且，尽管也随时准备参与交易，但守株待兔而非积极进取。"

毁灭光明城 郑和去世不久，中国关闭了国门，拆毁了史无前例的伟大船队。15世纪早期，明朝海军拥有3500艘战船。此后数十年，建造超过两根桅杆的海船就是死罪。

1525年，明朝皇帝下旨销毁所有的远洋海船，拘捕出海的商人。到了1551年，把超过一根桅杆的船开到海上也算犯罪。

再现光明城 刺桐如此诱发老外的想象力以至于有些外国人曾误以为她就是中国的首府。1515年，意大利人焦万尼·达·埃姆波里写道，"大汗即国王，他住在刺桐"。但是，贸易被禁，港口淤泥堆积，神秘的光明之城被毁灭。得益于20多年来的改革开放，泉州年轻一代对自己的未来无比憧憬，对自己的历史无比自豪。泉州已经再一次成为全球商贸和文化的中心。

位居第三！ 泉州仍然掌握世代相传的商业诀窍！在过去十多年里，这座崛起的古城GDP增长年均保持在26%，在中国前212座城市中位居第三！现在，泉州人正在利用新创造的财富，把这个城市建设得更美好。

Return to the Garden City Quanzhou people are once again managing their city with the same meticulous care as they lavish upon their gardens and miniature landscapes. And Quanzhou gardening is grass-roots, not a top down affair begun by bureaucrats spouting "One earth" slogans. For example, from 1998 to 2002, Quanzhou youth spent 1.3 million man hours planting over six million trees.

From family gardens to neighborhood gardens, city parks, forests, and lakes, Quanzhou people are again molding their city to their unique environment, rather than wrecking that environment to accommodate urban sprawl.

Off The Wall Quanzhou, once famous for its city walls, now has a new wall. This one billion Yuan project, with its grand battlements, towers and gates, recaptures the feel of old Zaytun—but it has many practical uses. The wall shields the city from floods, offers beautiful roadside gardens and forests for recreation, and the parallel ring road deflects traffic around the city and lessens congestion and pollution. Even the wall's interior is put to use. The endless row of rooms will accommodate Quanzhou folks' entrepreneurial bent as they rent them out for shops, work areas, cafes.

Endless Cultural Traditions Quanzhou is also resurrecting and breathing new life into its numerous cultural sites and traditions. This ancient city of traders, educators, philosophers, and adherents of virtually all major religions, also gave birth to Chinese marionettes, S. Shaolin Kung fu, and Southern Chinese music and opera. Quanzhou produced the prized blanc' de Chine porcelain now displayed proudly in museums around the world. Hui'an's 1700 year tradition of stonework attracts admirers and buyers from all over the planet.

Mr. Xia, Puppet Master
Amoymagic.com

再说花园城市 眼下，泉州人正在小心翼翼地管理着他们的城市，就像他们在花园和盆景上下足工夫那样。而且，泉州的园林工作是群众自发的，而不是自上而下、由政府官员发出的“我们只有一个地球”的生硬口号。比如说，从1998年到2002年，泉州的青年人投入了130万工时，种下了600多万棵树。

从庭院花园到社区绿地，到城市公园、森林公园和人造湖，泉州人正在根据这里独特的自然环境塑造他们自己的城市，而不是破坏环境以谋求城区的拓展。

城墙 泉州一度因城墙闻名。新近修筑的新城墙表明这里的人民思想比以前更为超前且注重实效。投资 10 亿元，新城墙拥有壮观的城垛、塔楼和城门，让人重新找到了刺桐古城的感觉——而且它还有许多非常实际的用途。新城墙防洪护城，有美丽的路边绿地和防护林可供人们休闲娱乐。平行的环城路分导了车流，避免了交通堵塞和环境污染。甚至连城墙内的空间也派上了用场。里面多排的店面租出后，可以开商店、办工厂、设餐馆，满足泉州人对生意的爱好。

无数的文化传统 泉州正在重建并给其无数的文化遗址和传统注入新的生命。这是一座商人之城，一座教育家之城，一座学者之城，一座包容了几乎天下所有宗教信仰者之城，同时也孕育了中国的提线木偶、南少林功夫、南音和民间戏剧。泉州生产的乳白釉瓷器如今自豪地展示在世界各国的博物馆里。惠安具有 1700 年传统历史的石雕工艺也吸引了来自全球各地的景慕者和买主。

Dozens of architectural relics include one of Islam's top ten mosques, the last temple to the Persian Mani, and engineering marvels like the ancient Luoyang and Anping stone bridges (longest in the world). Quanzhou is also famous for its unique cuisines, and, of course, the Anxi tea that sparked the Boston Tea Party.

S. Shaolin Kung Fu

Above ground, not below Some experts claim that modern Quanzhou has more archaeological artifacts than any Chinese city but Beijing or Xi'an,[3] but as Quanzhou people quickly point out, "Xi'an's heritage is below ground--ours is above!"

Touring Zaytun – a Sample Itinerary

An official Quanzhou brochure boasts "2,000 tourist sites famous at home and abroad," so where on earth (or China) do you start? With a few dozen trips to Quanzhou under my belt (eat your heart out, Columbus!), I suggest the following simple itinerary. For updates, check out my wife Susan Marie's website, **http://www.Amoymagic.com.**

1. Maritime Museum The first stop in Zaytun should be the UNESCO-sponsored Maritime Museum—China's biggest and best! After enjoying these eye-opening bilingual exhibits you'll have a better handle on not only ancient China's marvelous maritime achievements but also ancient Quanzhou's pivotal role in both domestic and international affairs. And after the museum, head downtown.

2. Zhongshan Rd. Historic District, was so abuzz with activity 1,000 years ago that one visitor said it was "intoxicating." Treasure Street had more gems, jewels, and gold than any place on the planet (today, the best buy is a granny's sausage-on-a-stick).

The Zhongshan Road restoration and preservation project was awarded the "Excellent Relic Protection in Asian-Pacific Area" in UNESCO's Relic Protection Campaign. After a stroll along this delightfully shaded street, enjoy a dozen major sites all within walking distance (or catch a pedicab if you can wake the operator). With a good 3 dozen tours of Quanzhou under my belt (and excellent Quanzhou cuisine hanging over it!), I suggest this simple itinerary:

数以十计的建筑遗迹包括伊斯兰世界顶尖的十大清真寺之一，波斯摩尼教的最后一座神殿以及诸如洛阳桥和安平桥（世界上最长的石板桥）这样的古代工程奇迹。泉州独特的美食也很有名气。当然，还有那引发了波士顿倾茶事件的安溪茶叶。

地面，不是地下 有些专家称，泉州考古发现的历史遗物仅次于北京和西安，超过中国的其他城市。不过，泉州人马上回应说，“西安的文物在地下，我们的文物在地面！”

泉州旅游——推荐线路

一份官方手册称，“泉州拥有 2000 个海内外闻名的旅游景点”。如此看来，到底应该从哪里开始呢？有数十次的泉州之行为基础（伤心吧，哥伦布！），我推荐下面简单的行程。要想了解最新资讯，或者跟大家分享你自己的新发现，请查询苏珊·玛丽的网站（www.Amoymagic.com）。

海上交通博物馆 刺桐之行第一站应该是联合国教科文组织资助的泉州海交馆——中国规模最大、最好的！馆内展品有双语注释，看过后令你大开眼界，并使你更好地了解古代中国非凡的海事成就以及泉州在中国国内和国际事务中的关键作用。看过海交馆，进市区。

中山路历史街区 1000 年前商业活动就已经相当活跃，一位游客说它“令人陶醉”。曾几何时，珠宝街上的宝石、珍珠和黄金比这个星球上的任何地方都要多。（如今，你能买到的最好东西是老奶奶棒极了的香肠串）

泉州中山路修复保护工程曾获得过“联合国亚太地区遗产保护优秀奖”。漫步在绿树成荫、赏心悦目的大街上，你徒步即可欣赏十来处主要的景点（要是你能叫醒车夫，也可以叫部三轮车）。以我本人 30 多次的泉州之行为基础（加上饱尝泉州精美绝伦的美食），我推荐下列简单的行程：

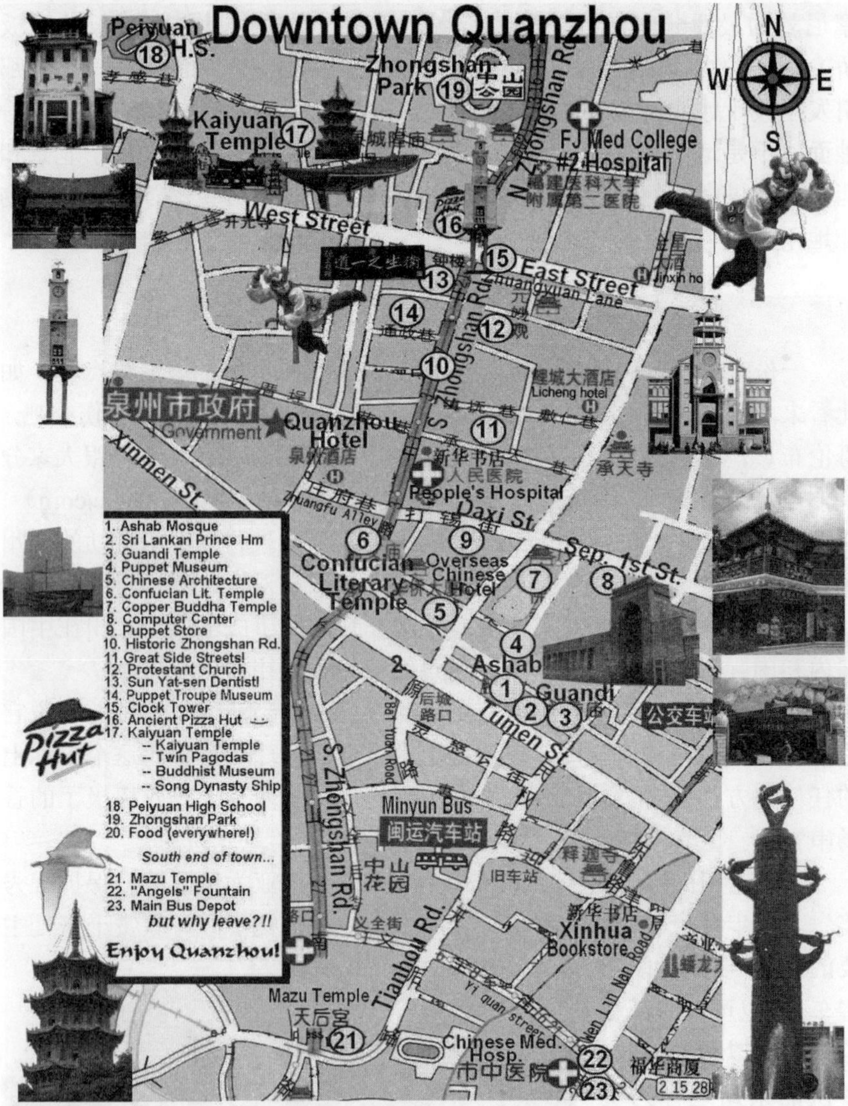
Downtown Quanzhou
N
W
E
S
Peiyuan H.S.
18
Zhongshan Park
19
中山公园
Kaiyuan Temple
17
FJ Med College #2 Hospital
福建医科大学附属第二医院
N. Zhongshan Rd.
West Street
开元寺
16
15
East Street
13
钟楼
Zhuangyuan Lane
14
12
10
S. Zhongshan Rd.
Licheng hotel
鲤城大酒店
泉州市政府
Government
Quanzhou Hotel
泉州酒店
11
新华书店
人民医院
People's Hospital
承天寺
Xinmen St.
Zhuangfu Alley
Daxi St.
6
9
Confucian Literary Temple
Overseas Chinese Hotel
7
8
Sep. 1st St.
5
4
Ashab
2
1
Guandi
3
Tumen St.
公交车站
1. Ashab Mosque
2. Sri Lankan Prince Hm
3. Guandi Temple
4. Puppet Museum
5. Chinese Architecture
6. Confucian Lit. Temple
7. Copper Buddha Temple
8. Computer Center
9. Puppet Store
10. Historic Zhongshan Rd.
11. Great Side Streets!
12. Protestant Church
13. Sun Yat-sen Dentist!
14. Puppet Troupe Museum
15. Clock Tower
16. Ancient Pizza Hut
17. Kaiyuan Temple
-- Kaiyuan Temple
-- Twin Pagodas
-- Buddhist Museum
-- Song Dynasty Ship
18. Peiyuan High School
19. Zhongshan Park
20. Food (everywhere!)
South end of town...
21. Mazu Temple
22. "Angels" Fountain
23. Main Bus Depot
but why leave?!!
Enjoy Quanzhou!
Pizza Hut
Bai Yuan Road
S. Zhongshan Rd.
Minyun Bus
闽运汽车站
中山花园
旧车站
Tianhou Rd.
新华书店
Xinhua Bookstore
Wen Lin Nan Road
Yi quan street
Mazu Temple
天后宫
21
Chinese Med. Hosp.
市中医院
22
23
福华商厦

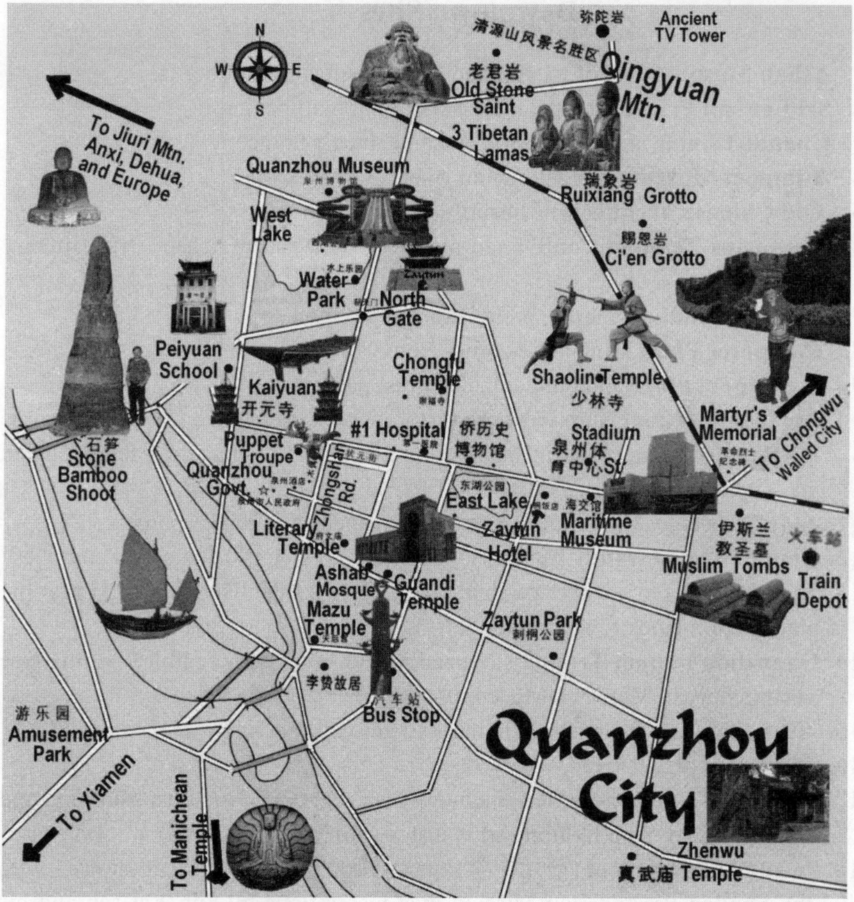
N
W
E
S
To Jiuri Mtn. Anxi, Dehua, and Europe
弥陀岩
Ancient TV Tower
清源山风景名胜区
老君岩
Old Stone Saint
Qingyuan Mtn.
3 Tibetan Lamas
Quanzhou Museum
泉州博物馆
瑞象岩
Ruixiang Grotto
West Lake
赐恩岩
Ci'en Grotto
水上乐园
Water Park
North Gate
Peiyuan School
Chongfu Temple
崇福寺
Shaolin Temple
少林寺
Kaiyuan
开元寺
Martyr's Memorial
革命烈士纪念碑
To Chongwu Walled City
石笋
Stone Bamboo Shoot
Puppet Troupe
#1 Hospital
侨历史博物馆
Stadium
泉州体育中心
Quanzhou Govt.
Zhongshan Rd.
东湖公园
East Lake
海交馆
Maritime Museum
Literary Temple
Zaytun Hotel
伊斯兰教圣墓
Muslim Tombs
火车站
Train Depot
Ashab Mosque
Guandi Temple
Mazu Temple
Zaytun Park
刺桐公园
李贽故居
汽车站
Bus Stop
游乐园
Amusement Park
To Xiamen
To Manichean Temple
Quanzhou City
Zhenwu
真武庙 Temple

Downtown Sites

1. **Ashab Mosque** One of Islam's top 10 holy sites. Next door is…
2. **Sri Lankan Prince's** home, tourist shopping mall behind it.
3. **Guandi Temple** adjoins the Sri Lankan Prince's home.
4. **A Puppet Museum** is right behind Ashab Mosque.
5. **Old Chinese Architecture** beautifully rebuilt as shops.
6. **Confucius Temple** is only a ten minute walk west of Ashab. Nice literary museum.
7. **Copper Buddha Temple**, park, lake and pavilion
8. **Computer Plaza** around the corner from Copper Buddha
9. **The Puppet Store** and puppet makers just past the KFC.
10. **At Historic Zhongshan Rd**—the restoration project won a UNESCO award! As you stroll, sample local snacks, and exotic West China delicacies pedaled by Xinjiang Muslim vendors.
11. **Side Streets** lead to hidden treasures like ancient official's homes.
12. **Quannan Protestant Church** Quanzhou has over 170 Protestant churches.
13. **Sun Yat-sen** left an inscription in, of all places, a dentist office! It's near the intersection clock tower, on the left.

14 **Quanzhou Puppet Troupe's Museum** is absolutely incredible—a **must-see** second only to Maritime Museum.

15. **Clock Tower** – a Timely Landmark to get your bearings
16. **Pizza Hut** –has moved.
17. **Kaiyuan Temple Complex** (includes Twin Pagodas, Buddhist Museum, and Song Dynasty Ship Exhibition) is just west of the clock tower.
18. **Peiyuan High School (培元中学)**, started 100 years ago by a missionary with the London Presbyterian Mission, has inscriptions by Sun Yat-sen and his wife Soong Ling Qing.
19. **Zhongshan Park** is nice for a break; great shops in vicinity, including an extensive art supply shop by the south gate.
20. **Food!** I moved to China primarily because Chinese food is too expensive in America—and Quanzhou cuisine fits the bill perfectly. Review the chapter on Quanzhou Cuisine, then try any of the hundreds of fine restaurants, or try out the "Delicacy Street" just east of the puppet store about a 15 minute walk.

市区景点

1 艾苏哈卜清真寺，伊斯兰世界十大圣地之一，隔壁就是……

2 斯里兰卡王子的府宅，背后有旅游商品市场。

3 关帝庙以斯里兰卡王子的府宅为邻。

4 木偶博物馆就在艾苏哈卜清真寺背后。

5 古中国建筑修葺一新成为商店。

6 文庙在艾苏哈卜清真寺西边，走路只要十分钟，不错的文学博物馆。

7 铜佛寺，内有公园、池塘和亭阁。

8 电脑城，在铜佛寺拐角附近。

9 木偶店和木偶工匠就在肯德基旁边。

10 中山路历史街区——修复工程曾获得联合国教科文组织的奖励！漫步街头，品尝当地小吃及新疆回族商贩装在三轮车上的西部风味。

11 僻静的小巷通向古代政府官员私宅等珍贵的景点。

12 泉南新教教堂 泉州的新教教堂超过170座！

13 不会吧？孙中山先生竟然会为一个牙科诊所题词！就在十字路口钟楼附近，靠左边。

14 泉州木偶剧团的博物馆绝对令人难以置信——仅次于海交馆的第二必看地。

15 钟楼——一个及时的标志，可帮助你弄清方向。

16 必胜客已迁址。

17 开元寺（院内包括双塔、佛教博物馆和宋代古船）位于钟楼正西。

18 培元中学，100年前由伦敦长老会的一位传教士设立，内有孙中山先生及其夫人宋庆龄女士的题词。

19 中山公园，稍作休息的好地方，附近商店都不错，其中有一个在公园南门入口处，专卖各种各样的艺术品。

20 美食！我移居中国主要是美国的中餐太贵了——泉州的美食正合我意！参阅第十四章“泉州美食”，然后从泉州数百家好餐馆中随便选一家试试，或者到木偶店东边的“美食街”试试，走路大约十五分钟。

Quanzhou's South Side

21. **Mazu Temple**, very south of town.
22. **Quanzhou Angel sculpture** /dancing fountain (in intersection)
23. **Quanzhou Main Bus Station**

City Outskirts

1. **Muslim Holy Tombs** (just east of the Maritime Museum)
2. **Overseas Chinese Museum**. Most Overseas Chinese are from Fujian, and most of them from Quanzhou, hence the museum.
3. **Qingyuan Mountain** to the north (many sites, including China's largest Taoist statues, and carvings of the three Tibetan lamas)
4. **S. Shaolin Temple** – home of Southern Shaolin Kung fu, the young abbot Master Shi is putting Quanzhou's martial arts back on the map.
5. **Luoyang Bridge**, one of my favorite sites, is just to the north.
6. **Jiuri Mountain**, official start of the Silk Road, is a few kilometers west of the city.
7. **Stone Bamboo Shoot**—a fertility totem (we'll leave that for later).
8. **Wenling Delicacy Street**—a lane dedicated to fine local cuisine.
9. **Parks and Gardens**—endless parks and gardens.
   Also note the famous miniature landscapes.
10. **Well**… explore for yourself, and e-mail us your discoveries!

Hit the Road! Quanzhou's Counties

1. **Hui'an** (ancient walled city, Hui'an girls, extraterrestrial beaches, and China's best stone masons)
2. **Nan' an** (birthplace of Koxinga, Cai's Minnan Village, and Anping Bridge—our planet's longest stone bridge)
3. **Jinjiang** (our planet's last Manichaean temple, Muslim Ancestral Hall of Chendai, ancient kilns)
4. **Anxi** (home of the tea that sparked the Boston Tea Party)
5. **Dehua** (ancient porcelain center, and origin of the blanc de chine porcelain coveted by collectors and museums worldwide)
6. **Yongchun** (incense capital, and dongguan bridge)
7. **Shishi** (garment capital of China, Sisters-in-law tower, and China's largest ocean theme park).

Whether ancient Zaytun or modern Quanzhou, there's plenty to see, but to appreciate both, start your visit with China's best Maritime Museum.

城 南

21 后宫，泉州的妈祖庙，在城市的最南端。
22 泉州城雕、喷泉，在标号 23 的十字路口。
23 泉州汽车总站

市 郊

1 **伊斯兰圣墓**（就在海外交通史博物馆以东）
2 **华侨博物馆** 许多中国华侨来自福建，福建的华侨多数来自泉州，因此才有这个博物馆。
3 **城北清源山**（景点很多，包括中国最大的道教雕像和三个西藏喇嘛的雕刻）
4 **南少林寺**——南少林功夫的故乡，年轻的住持释师傅正在努力复兴泉州的武术。
5 **洛阳桥**，我最喜欢的景点之一，在市区的东北边。
6 **九日山**，海上丝绸之路的正式起点，在城西数公里处。
7 **石笋**——这座高高耸起的细长石柱是崇拜多产的图腾。嗯，我们还是以后再讲吧！
8 **温陵美食街**——专门提供当地美食的小巷。
9 **公园和花园**，泉州有许多漂亮的公园和花园。
10 嗯……自己摸索，然后把你的新发现通过电子邮件发给我们！

走出泉州城外！

1 **惠安**（崇武古城，惠安女，世外桃源般的海滩和中国最好的石匠）
2 **南安**（郑成功的故乡，闽南蔡氏古民居，安平桥——全球最长的石板桥）
3 **晋江**（地球上最后的摩尼庵，陈埭伊斯兰祖祠，古瓷窑）
4 **安溪**（茶叶的故乡，此地茶叶曾引发波士顿倾茶事件）
5 **德化**（古代陶瓷制造中心，乳白釉瓷器的发源地，世界各国的收藏家和博物馆对乳白釉瓷器特别钟爱）
6 **永春**（神香之都和东关桥）
7 **石狮**（中国服装之都，姑嫂塔和中国最大的海洋主题公园）

无论是古刺桐，还是现代的泉州城，都有许多值得一看的地方。但要品尝到古今两种风格，建议你从中国最好的海上交通史博物馆开始。

Supplement

On The City & Great Haven of Zayton

By Marco Polo

(Yule-Cordier Edition, Volume II, 1903 edition & 1920 addenda)

"Now when you quit Fuju and cross the River, you travel for five days south-east through a fine country, meeting with a constant succession of flourishing cities, towns, and villages, rich in every product. You travel by mountains and valleys and plains, and in some places by great forests in which are many of the trees which give Camphor. There is plenty of game on the road, both of bird and beast. The people are all traders and craftsmen of Fuju. When you have accomplished those five days journey you arrive at the very great and noble city of ZAYTON, which is also subject to Fuju.

"At this city you must know is the Haven of Zayton, frequented by all the ships of India, which bring thither spicery and all other kinds of costly wares. It is the port also that is frequented by all the merchants of Manzi, for hither is imported the most astonishing quantity of goods and of precious stones and pearls, and from this they are distributed all over Manzi. And I assure you that for one shipload of pepper that goes to Alexandria or elsewhere, destined for Christendom, there come a hundred such, aye and more too, to this haven of Zayton; for it is one of the greatest havens in the world for commerce.

"The Great Kaan derives a very large revenue from the duties paid in this city and haven; for you must know that on all the merchandise imported, including precious stones and pearls, he levies a duty of ten per cent, or in other words takes tithe of everything. Then again the ship's charge for freight on small wares is 30 per cent, on pepper 44 per cent, and on lignaloes, sandalwood, and other bulky goods 40 per cent, so that between freight and the Kaan's duties the merchant has to pay a good half the value of his investment [though on the other half he makes such a profit that he is always glad to come back with a new supply of merchandize]. But you may well believe from what I have said that the Kaan hath a vast revenue from this city.

"There is a great abundance here of all provision for every necessity of man's life. [It is a charming country, and the people are very quiet, and fond of an easy life. Many come hither from Upper India to have their bodies painted with the needle in the way we have elsewhere described, there being many adepts at this craft in the city.]

附录 关于泉州及其宏伟的刺桐港

——马可·波罗

"离开福州，渡过这条河（译注：指闽江），往东南方向（译注：应为西南方向）行走五天，穿过一个人口稠密的地区。途中，繁荣的都市、城镇和乡村连绵不断，物产丰富。一路上，你翻山越岭，穿林过川。在一些地方，森林茂密，灌木丛生，盛产樟脑树。在路上，禽兽出没，猎物颇多。这里的居民都是福州的商人和工匠。五日的行程既过，你即抵达宏伟秀丽的刺桐城（行政上隶属福州管辖）。

"在这座城市（泉州），你应该知道刺桐港。印度商船频繁出入，带来了香料和其他各种贵重的货物。蛮子（指中国南方）的商人也经常造访，因为这里（指刺桐港）进口了数量惊人的货物、宝石和珍珠。然后，从这里分销到蛮子各地。我可以向你保证，假若有一艘船通过亚历山大港进入西方基督国家的话，就会有100艘，甚至更多的船只进入刺桐港。在贸易界，刺桐港是世界上最大的海港之一。

"从这座城市（泉州）及其港口，大汗获得了大量的海关关税和巨额的财政收入，因为你必须知道，他（大汗）对所有的进口商品，包括宝石和珍珠，征收了10%的关税。换句话说，也就是对所有的货物课征了什一税。然后，加上这些商船的运费（体积小的货物是30%；胡椒粉44%，沉香、檀香和其他笨重货物是40%），商人必须付出相当于货物价值的一半。[然而，就是从这余下的一半，他们也能获利颇丰，并乐于再次返回（泉州），带来另一批的商品。]从我刚才所说的，你可以确信，大汗从这座城市获取了巨额的收入。

"在这里，人们生活的各种必需品都非常充足。[这是一个风景迷人的地方，百姓性情平和，爱好安逸的生活。有许多人从上印度（即印度斯坦及其邻近国家）来到这里，目的是为了文身。用针文身的习惯，我们在前面的章节里已经讲过。在这座城市（泉州）里，有许多擅长此艺的老手。]

"Let me tell you, and also that in this province there is a town called TYUNJU where they make vessels of porcelain of all sizes, the finest that can be imagined. They make it nowhere but in that city, and thence it is exported all over the world. Here is abundant and very cheap, insomuch that for a Venice groat you can buy three dishes so fine that you could not imagine better.

"I should tell you that in this city (i.e. of Zayton} they have a peculiar language. [For you must know that throughout all Manzi they employ one speech and one kind of writing only, but yet there are local differences of dialect, as you might say of Genoese, Milanese, Florentines, and Neapolitans, who though they speak different dialects can understand one another.]

"And I assure you that the Great Kaan has as large customs and revenues from this kingdom of Chonka [Fujian?] as from Kinsay, aye and more too.

"We have now spoken of but three out of the nine kingdoms of Manzi, to wit Yanju and Kinsay and Fuju. We could tell you about the other six, but it would be too long a business; so we will say no more about them.

"And now you have heard all the truth about Cathay and Manzi and many other countries, as has been set down in this book...."

NOTES

[1] Ibn Battuta, the "Prince of Travelers," was born in Tangier on 24th February, 1304, and after a stay in India was dispatched by the Sultan Muhammad Thugluq to China. After many adventures, he returned home in 1349, having traveled, according to Yule's estimate, over 75,000 miles by land and sea. "The Traveler of Islam" died twenty years later—but fortunately not before dictating his travels (which many disbelieved at the time) to a royal secretary, Ibn Juzayyat Fes.

[2] Jerusalem of Asia: Arabs called Quanzhou "Zayton," and Jerusalem "Zaytoniyah"

[3] "Learning About Quanzhou; the Archaeology of a Medieval Port in Fujian, China." Richard Pearson, Li Min, and Li Guo, Department of Anthropology and Sociology, University of British Columbia

“让我告诉你，这个省里还有一个镇叫“迪云州”，制作各种规格的陶瓷器皿，属于你想象得到的极品。别的地方没有，就在那个镇里生产，然后从那里出口到世界各地。这里盛产陶瓷，且价格便宜。这么说吧，用一个四便士的威尼斯银币，就能买到三个精美的盘子，天下还有比这更好的吗！

“我要告诉你，在这座城市（即刺桐），他们使用一种奇特的语言。[因为，你要知道，蛮子各地只用一种语言和统一的文字，但还是有方言的差别。你可以说，与热那亚人、米兰人、佛罗伦萨人和那不勒斯人的情形相似，尽管他们说的方言不一样，但彼此之间还是能听得懂的。]

“我敢向你保证，大汗从楚伽（即福建）这个地方收取的进口税和财政收入跟行在（即杭州）一样多。是的，也许更多。

“蛮子省的九个地区，我们现在只谈到其中的三个，也就是扬州、行在（杭州）和福州。我们可以跟你讲其他六个，不过那会耗费太长时间，因此我们就不再讲了。

“现在，你已经听说了关于震旦（或称契丹省，指中国北方）和蛮子省以及许多其他国家的真实故事。这些故事都已经记录在这本书里……”

注释：

1. 伊本·巴图塔，1304年2月24日生于摩洛哥北部的丹吉尔港。在印度稍做停留之后，他受命于穆罕默德·思格拉格苏丹，前往中国。历经重重艰险，他于1349年回国。据尤尔估计，伊本·巴图塔陆地和海上的行程超过75000英里。两年后，这位“伊斯兰旅行家”去世。值得庆幸的是，他去世前把他的旅行（当时很多人不相信）口述给一位名叫伊本·贾扎亚特·费思的皇室秘书。

2. 亚洲的耶路撒冷：阿拉伯人称泉州为“刺桐”，耶路撒冷为“刺桐尼亚”。

3. 理查德·皮尔逊，李闽（音译）、李过（音译）：《认识泉州：中国福建中世纪古港的考古学研究》，加拿大不列颠哥伦比亚大学人类与社会学系。

Chapter 2

Quanzhou Maritime Museum

The sign in the foyer of Quanzhou's UNESCO-sponsored maritime museum (China's best!) well summarizes Quanzhou folks' aspirations: "UNESCO, Peace and Friendship, Cultural Dialogue, Looking Back on the Past, Looking Forward to the Future."

Quanzhou Maritime Museum

The more I look back on the past, the more I appreciate that the Chinese were a peaceful people (at least outside their own borders). Had Chinese been more inclined to conquering than commerce, they could have easily dominated our planet 1,000 years ago, and today the world would be wielding chopsticks at McRice outlets.

A millennium ago, China had a vast navy armed to the teeth with weapons the West had never imagined. They had cannon, giant crossbows, and even land and sea mines.

Advanced shipbuilding features like watertight compartments weren't used by Westerners until the mid-1800s! And even 2,000 years ago they had battleships with paddlewheels that could just about walk right up onto land. China's shipbuilding greatness continued right into the 19th century…

> "In February, 1822, Captain Pearl, of the English ship Indiana, coming through Gaspar Straits, fell in with the cargo and crew of a wrecked junk, and saved 198 persons out of 1600, with whom she had left Amoy, whom he landed at Pontianak." [1]

Imagine a junk, almost 200 years ago, with 1600 passengers. Yet even that ship was dwarfed by the treasure ships of Zheng He's day, as you'll learn in Quanzhou's Maritime Museum. Famous Arab traveler Ibn Battuta described the magnificent "Zaytun Ships":

第二章

泉州海外交通史博物馆

由联合国教科文组织资助兴建的海外交通史博物馆（中国最棒的！）大厅里的标志精辟地概括了泉州人民的心声：“联合国教科文组织，和平和友谊，文化对话，回首过去，展望未来。”

回顾过去，我越发觉得中华民族是爱好和平的民族（至少在他们自己的国境之外）。要是中国人以前更倾向于征服而不是贸易的话，那么 1000 年前他们就可以轻而易举地统治我们的星球了，“麦当米(McRice，仿拟 McDonald[麦当劳]——译者注)”连锁店里挥动的就该是筷子了。

1000 多年前，中国就拥有了一支庞大的海军，其武器装备之精良是西方未曾想象过的，有加农炮、弩弓，还有海陆地雷。

先进的造船方法，如水密舱，西方人直到 19 世纪中叶才开始应用！甚至在 2000 年前他们就有了带蹼轮的战舰，可以长驱直入登上陆地！中国造船业的宏伟一直持续到 19 世纪……

> “1822 年 2 月，英国印第安纳号船珀尔船长在穿越加斯帕海峡（今属印尼——译者注）时，帆船失事，船上的货物和船员一同沉没，1600 人中有 198 人获救，她和这些获救人员一起离开厦门，在庞提纳克（又名坤甸，今属印尼——译者注）登陆。”

想象一下，约 200 年前的一艘平底帆船竟能承载 1600 多人！然而，从泉州海外交通史博物馆您可以了解到，那艘船与郑和时代的宝船相比却相形见绌。阿拉伯著名的旅行家伊本·贝图塔是这样描述那艘宏伟的“刺桐船”的：

Zaytun Ships

"The large ships have anything from twelve down to three sails, which are made of bamboo rods plaited like mats. A ship carries a complement of a thousand men, six hundred of whom are sailors and four hundred men-at-arms, including archers, men with shields and arbalists, who throw naphtha [flaming petroleum]. These vessels are built **only in the towns of Zaytun** [Quanzhou] and Sin-Kalan [Guangzhou]. The vessel has four decks and contains rooms, cabins, and saloons for merchants; a cabin has chambers and a lavatory, and can be locked by its occupant, who takes along with him slave girls and wives. Often a man will live in his cabin unknown to any of the others on board until they meet on reaching some town... Some of the Chinese own large numbers of ships on which their factors are sent to foreign countries." Ibn Battuta

The World of China's Ships (2/F, to the right). The history of shipbuilding begins with a video of how the ancients went from flotation (hollow gourds tied to their waists) to bamboo rafts, dugout canoes, animal hide coracles, boats, and large ships. I was surprised to see a 2,000-year-old drawing of a Dragon Boat Race (2,000 years, and they haven't beaten the dragon yet).

"Stealth Junk"
Ancient hi-tech

Stealth Junk? I showed some guests the epitome of ancient China's maritime hi-tech. When they complained it was just an empty glass case, I said, "That just shows how well it works."

Tibetan yak skin coracle was nothing to yak about, but to its left was a beautifully painted canoe used by natives of a small island off Taiwan's east coast; it reminded me of ceremonial Native American canoes.

刺桐船

“该大船(刺桐船)有着3~12面不等的帆板，帆板由竹杆席状编制而成。一艘船足可承载1000人，其中600人为水手，400人为武士，包括弓箭手、手执盾牌和劲弩的兵卒，专司投掷石脑油（燃烧的汽油）。这些船仅在刺桐城（泉州）和新迦蓝（广州）制造。该船有四个甲板，设有房间、船舱和商人会客室；船舱内设有若干个房间和一间厕所，携带妻妾和丫鬟的住客房门可上锁。通常，住在船舱的人们在抵达某个陆上城镇碰面之前彼此都互不相识。有些中国人拥有大量的船只，随船的商人被派往国外各地。”

中国船的天地　博物馆二楼的右侧展厅叙述着造船的历史。开头是一段录像，记述了古人是如何发现浮选（将空心葫芦系在船腰上），如何造成竹筏、掏空的独木舟、兽皮小圆舟（西藏）、小船和大船。我惊奇地发现一幅2000多年前绘制的赛龙舟古画（已经2000多年了，而他们还没有打败这条龙）。

隐形船？　我向一些客人展示了中国古代的海上高科技。当他们抱怨说那只不过是一个空玻璃柜时，我说，“瞧，这高科技多棒啊！”

西藏牦牛皮小圆舟　并没有什么可吹牛的，但是在它右边的却是一条台湾东海岸一个小岛的原住民使用过的漆工精美的独木舟；它让我想起美洲印第安人的独木舟。

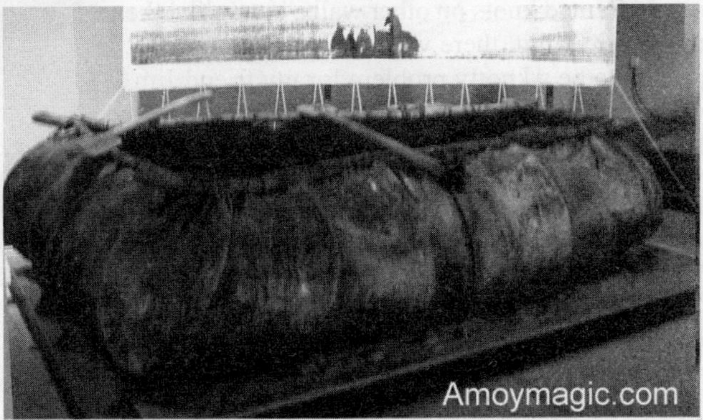

Yakskin Coracle—a holey boat for holymen?

Does this get your goat?

Getting my goat. My friends thought I was kidding when I said Chinese made rafts from inflated goatskins. A photo on the wall behind the model shows a gigantic river raft made of over 700 goatskins!

Miniature Boat Models A vast array of intricately detailed boat models show the sheer diversity and sophistication of Chinese ship building. Boats were designed according to use, climate, and water conditions (rough or smooth seas, hot or cold climes). My favorite is the crooked bow boat. I've no idea why a ship would be designed with a crooked bow. I asked if it was used by crooked bureaucrats on vacation but that didn't go over very well.

Grand Houseboats, owned by foreigners and wealthy Chinese, used to ply Fujian's rivers during the hot summers. As I write this in a sweltering Amoy July, I wish I was on one.

Tying the Knot! The museum used to have an excellent knot-tying station but it was removed. Maybe too many lasses were tying the knot. Months later, someone made a half-hearted attempt to resurrect the exhibit by dangling a few frayed bits of rope on a pole, and hanging a few nicely framed knots on other walls, but unlike the previous exhibit, there were no instructions, so it proved to be a knotty problem for my friend Jim, who was soon at the end of his rope. He should have been more resourceful, like the string...①

"South Pointing Needles" Chinese, probably on pure principal, insist that compasses point south, not north, but since they invented compasses (and almost everything else), I guess they've a right to say so. Westerners were so ignorant of compasses that when they finally came into use in Europe, captains forbade sailors from eating onions lest they interfere with the cunning device's powers!

---

① The bartender kicked out a string, saying, "This is a 'rope only' bar." The resourceful string simply unraveled one end, tied himself in a knot, and reentered the bar. The bartender demanded, "Aren't you the same string I just kicked out?" The string replied, "I'm a frayed knot."

我的羊！ 我提到中国人用充气羊皮造筏时，我的朋友以为我在开玩笑。模型背后墙上挂着一张巨大的由700多张羊皮制成的筏的照片！

Paddlewheel Battleship

微缩船模 一大排花纹复杂的船模显示了中国造船术的多样性和复杂性。船只是根据用途、气候和水况（汹涌或平静的大海，冷热气候）来设计的。我最喜欢的是船首呈弯弓状的船只。我不晓得船头为什么设计成弯弓状。我询问说这船是不是供不诚实的官僚度假所用的，但这句话并不很受欢迎。

Chinese Houseboat

大房船 由外国人或中国富人所拥有，用于炎热季节时往返于福建的河流上。当我在 7 月的厦门汗流浃背地撰写这本书时，我多么希望自己就坐在这样的船上！

打绳结！ 该博物馆曾经设有一个很不错的结绳展台，但已经迁走了。也许太多女人在编绳结。几个月后，有人曾尝试着复办这种展览，将一些磨损的绳段垂悬在一个柱子上，然后将一些打好的绳结精致地装框，悬挂在其他墙面上，但是，与以往展览不同的是，由于缺乏指导，这次展览对吉姆来说是个难解的“绳结”，所以不久他就黔驴技穷了。足智多谋些，就像绳子一样。

指南针 另外一项展览展示了各种中国的“指南针”。当然，中国人坚持说指南针是指向南方而不是北方的。但是，既然中国人发明了指南针（还有其他东西），他们爱怎么取名都行。我们西方人曾对指南针一无所知，以至于欧洲人首次使用指南针时，船长竟然禁止水手吃洋葱，唯恐洋葱干扰这种精密设备的灵敏度！

South Pointing Needles

Koxinga, the pirate-cum-patriot born in Japan of a Japanese mother and Quanzhou Chinese father, was well represented with paintings, ship models, clips from the Koxinga TV series (I played the last Dutch governor of Taiwan), and a diorama with lights, sound and action of the great battle in which he wrested control of Taiwan from the "greedy grasp of the Dutch invaders."

Flagging Exhibit For the record, however, the two Dutch ships' flags are French, not Dutch! Both nations' flags have red, white and blue stripes, but the Dutch flag's stripes are horizontal, the French stripes are vertical. Though perhaps such details are too trivial to matter…

I mentioned the flag issue several times to the museum staff. One finally said, "Dutch, French—six of one and half dozen of the other.① They're both foreign." She paused, and added for good measure, "Koxinga fought them 300 years ago. Maybe the Dutch and French have switched flags by now."

Dioramas & Displays The East side of the museum's upper floor has delightful dioramas detailing the construction of wooden ships, which hasn't changed much in centuries. Dozens of models of fishing junks, treasure ships and warships help convey the complexity of ancient Chinese ship making. The sails were so stable that during the past decade many designers have begun to adapt them to Western yachts and sailing ships.

① 半斤八两, bànjīn bā liǎng—half a jin (1.1 lbs.) or 8 ounces. A Chinese jin used to be sixteen ounces; nowadays it's ten, but they still use the same expression.

郑成功 这位海盗和爱国者，出生于日本，母亲是日本人，父亲是中国泉州人。绘画、船模、国姓爷电视连续剧剪辑（我饰演过最后一任台湾的荷兰总督！）以及一个带声、光和动作的立体模型生动地描述了他从“贪婪的荷兰侵略者手中”夺回台湾的伟大战役。

旗帜飘扬的展览 然而，那两艘荷兰船只飘扬着法国国旗，而不是荷兰国旗！两国的国旗的确都有红、白、蓝条纹，但是荷兰国旗上的条纹是横向的，而法国国旗的条纹是纵向的。然而这样的细节也许是无关痛痒……

我几次向博物馆工作人员提过国旗的问题，有一个人终于说：“荷兰、法国——半斤八两，都是外国。”她略作停顿，接着说出一个好的解释办法，“郑成功300年前就打过他们。也许荷兰和法国如今已经互换了国旗。”妙哉！

立体模型与陈列 博物馆往上一层的东侧陈列着赏心悦目的立体模型，详细地记述了历经多个世纪仍保留完好的木船的建造情况。许多渔船、宝船和战船的模型反映了中国古代造船的复杂工艺。这些船帆是如此平稳，以至于在过去的十年里许多设计师已经开始将它们应用于西方的快艇和帆船上。

Koxinga fights the Dutch, or French, or—whatever

Thanks to innovative ships, navigational techniques, mastery of mapmaking, and the compass, Chinese seafarers like Admiral Zheng He sailed pretty much around the globe. In fact, Gavin Menzie, former submarine commander in the British Navy, claims that Zheng He's fleet, not Columbus, discovered America. While his claims seem to me a bit farfetched, his book, *1421—The Year China Discovered America*, has at least gotten Westerners' attention.

Admiral Zheng He, 1421
(Adapted from *Amoy Magic*)

The eunuch admiral and his female admirers

Zheng He, China's most illustrious adventurer, was a Muslim descendant of the King of Bukhara (southern Uzbekistan), and the governor of Yunnan, who was the last Mongol to hold out against the Ming. After the Ming defeated Yunnan in 1381, they castrated thousands of youths, including Zheng He—a cruel punishment for a Muslim boy dreaming of adulthood and four wives. But Zheng He proved to be an excellent scholar and linguist, and his skills in court (if not courting) got the attention of the prince who overthrew the emperor, and made Zheng He an admiral.
Over his 28-year career, Zheng He commanded at least 317 ships and 37,000 men. He sailed from Korea to Antarctica and around Africa into the Atlantic. His navigational charts remained unsurpassed for centuries (though his geographical knowledge was not perfect; Zheng He wrote that both Christ and Mohammed were from Western India, which he assumed included all of the Middle East).

During his first voyage, in 1405, Zheng He commanded 62 ships and 27,800 men. The first voyage passed peaceably enough, but during the second voyage of 1409, Zheng He had differences with the King of Ceylon and hauled him back to China. Even today, a Sri Lankan prince's home stands to the east of Quanzhou's Ashab Mosque (adjoining the ancient temple).

随着船只的创新、航海技术的进步、地图绘制方法的掌握以及指南针的发明，郑和将军等中国的航海家几乎行遍了整个世界。实际上，英国海军前司令官加文·孟席宣称美洲是郑和的船队而不是哥伦布发现的。尽管有些说法至少在我看来显得有点牵强附会，可他写的一本名叫《1421 年——中国发现美洲》的书至少已经引起了西方人的关注。

郑和将军，1421 年（节选自《魅力厦门》）

郑和是中国历史上最卓越的探险家，南乌兹别克斯坦布哈拉国王传袭的穆斯林后裔，统领过云南，也是最后一个与明朝对抗的蒙古人。1381年，明朝占领云南后，阉割了成千上万年轻人，其中也包括郑和。这对于那些梦想成年后娶四房媳妇的穆斯林小伙儿来说，是一项极为残酷的刑罚。然而，郑和后来却成了一位杰出的学者和语言学家。他在宫廷里的权术(如非“追女生”之术的话)得到了推翻当时皇帝的王子的重用，被册封为海军大将军。

Columbus' Santa Maria vs. Zheng He's ship

在他 28 年的职业生涯中，郑和手下至少有 317 艘船只和 37000 人。他从高丽国航行至南极洲，绕过非洲进入大西洋。几个世纪以来无人能超越他航海所及的范围（然而他的地理知识却不尽如人意，郑和曾写过基督和穆罕默德同源于西印度。他认为，西印度包括了中东所有地区）。

1405年，郑和第一次下西洋，指挥了62艘船和27800人。首次航行非常顺利，但在1409年的第二次航行期间，他与锡兰国（今斯里兰卡——译者注）国王起了争执，把国王带回了中国。时至今日，锡兰王子的一处住宅仍矗立在泉州艾苏哈卜清真寺东侧（毗邻古庙）。

Alas, Zheng He's 7th voyage was his last. The Emperor decided that the rest of the world had nothing China needed, and after Zheng He died, international trade declined as well. Decades later, all records of Zheng He's exploits were destroyed, Chinese were forbidden to travel abroad, and the members of Zayton's Islamic community, facing increasing persecution, adopted Chinese surnames and melded right into Han society--so well, in fact, that in the 1990s some Hui had no idea their ancestors were Middle Eastern Arabs until researchers informed them.

A UNESCO "World Museum of Religion" It's no wonder that UNESCO calls Quanzhou a World Museum of Religion. Today, tens of thousands of Quanzhou people are descended from Zayton's early foreign settlers, and they brought with them not only Islam but every other religion imaginable, as we shall see in the museum's fascinating collection of foreign religious artifacts.

Nestorian Tombstone

The foreigners who flocked to ancient Zaytun exchanged not just commodities but cultures, philosophies, and religions. The Maritime Museum's hundreds of ancient religious relics help us realize that, at one time, Zayton was indeed the "Jerusalem of Asia," with representatives of most religions.

The ground floor hall to the left of the foyer displays many of religious artifacts unearthed over recent decades. There are so many, in fact, that they are even scattered about the field behind the museum (hence the present construction of the large Islamic Heritage Center).

Over 150 Islamic tombstones and carved stone fragments were recovered during the dismantling of the city walls during the first part of the 20th century. While most were from cities scattered across Persia, some were from Yemen, Hamdan, al Malf in Turkestan, and Khalat in Armenia.

唉，郑和的第七次航行成了他的最后一次航行。皇帝认为世界的其他地方没有中国所需要的东西，而且郑和去世后，中国的对外贸易也开始走下坡路。几十年后，所有关于郑和航海功勋的记录都被销毁了，中国人被禁止到国外旅行。刺桐城的伊斯兰群体由于面临日益加剧的迫害，遂改姓中国姓氏并直接融入汉族社会——实际上，这种融入非常完美，以至于20世纪90年代当研究人员告知一些回民说他们的祖先是中东阿拉伯人时，他们才如梦初醒。

一座联合国教科文组织任命的“世界宗教博物馆” 难怪联合国教科文组织把泉州称为世界宗教博物馆。如今，有好几万泉州人是刺桐城早期外来定居者的后裔，他们不仅带来伊斯兰教，还有其他的宗教。这一点从博物馆那些奇妙的外国人制造的宗教物品中可见一斑。

聚集古刺桐城的外国人所交换的不仅仅是商品，还有文化、哲学和宗教。海外交通史博物馆成千上万的古代宗教遗址让我们认识到，刺桐城的确曾是“亚洲的耶路撒冷”，代表着每一种宗教。

大厅左侧的第一层展示着近几十年来出土的宗教人造物品。出土文物数目庞大，以至于不得不将它们散置在博物馆后边的空地上（因此也就有了伊斯兰文化遗产中心）。

在20世纪初期拆除城墙期间，发掘出了150多块伊斯兰墓碑和石刻断片。其中大部分来自波斯一带的不同城市，还有一些来自也门、哈姆丹、土耳其斯坦的阿尔玛法和亚美尼亚的喀尔兰。

Over 150 Islamic relics

The Arab Connection

China's rulers valued Muslims' business skills so highly that they appointed them to high municipal and provincial level posts. Mr. Pu Chongqing (蒲重庆), who runs an incense factory in Yongchun (永春) and is a descendant of Muslims who came to Quanzhou about 1200 A.D., said one of his ancestors was Pu Shougen (蒲寿更), the Quanzhou Maritime Commissioner, and later assistant to the governor. Another ancestor was governor of Chongqing in Sichuan, in W. China. But foreigners' power went to their heads and when they tried to take charge, the incensed Han Chinese put them in their place, and many hightailed it to some other place.

Persian ship (painted 1240 a.d.)

Muslim Chinese Muslims are still in Zaytun, but they've blended into the woodwork. After their failed coup, Zaytun's Laowai avoided trouble with increasingly xenophobic Chinese neighbors by adopting Chinese names. Baiqi Island now has over 10,000 descendants of Arabs, all surnamed Guo. They did not even know they had Arab blood until historians told them recently, and the Bu and Huang people of Yunlu Village learned that they were descendants of Pu Shougeng, the ancient Arab customs officer.

Triangles and Calculators Muslims also traded in knowledge. Much of Western science and mathematics we owe to Arab traders who sailed from ancient Zayton with storehouses of mathematical and scientific knowledge more precious than their cargoes of silk, porcelain and pearls.

Pascal's triangle, for instance, was not invented by the great French philosopher Blaise Pascal (1623-1662) but by Chinese centuries earlier. Pascal is also credited with inventing the adding machine, but centuries earlier Chinese had been ciphering with the abacus, which in the hands of a Chinese merchant or tax collector was deadly accurate. (I've never understood the devilish device, which some say was invented in ancient Persia. I'm not surprised. Who but Saddam's ancestors would have dared?)

阿拉伯人的亲戚 中国的统治者非常看重穆斯林的经商能力，任命他们为县级或省级官员。蒲重庆先生的祖先是公元1200年前后迁入泉州的穆斯林。蒲先生在永春经营了一家制香厂。他说，他的一个祖上叫蒲寿更，主管过泉州的市舶司，后来当上了州府的助理。另一个祖上任中国西部城市四川重庆的“市长”。但当异域人的权力驾驭汉人权力之上并试图掌权时，气愤的中国汉人便对他们进行管制以使其安分，有些穆斯林人则仓皇逃往其他地方。

穆斯林中国人 穆斯林仍居住在刺桐城，但是他们已经融入当地了。政变未遂后，在刺桐城的老外们怕惹那些日益憎恶外国人的中国邻居，遂改姓中国姓氏。现在的百崎岛有10000多阿拉伯人的后裔，都姓郭。直到近来历史学家告诉他们，他们才知道自己有阿拉伯人的血统，云鹿村的卜姓和黄姓的人也才知道他们是古代阿拉伯海关官员蒲寿更的后裔。

三角和计算器 穆斯林也做知识贸易。许多西方的自然科学和数学都归功于阿拉伯商人，他们带着比丝绸、陶瓷和珍珠等货物更为珍贵的大量数学和自然科学知识，从刺桐城启航。

比如说，帕斯卡三角尺就不是法国伟大的哲学家布莱兹·帕斯卡（1623－1662）发明的，而是几世纪以前由中国人发明的。帕斯卡还享有发明加码测量器的美名，但是，早在几个世纪以前中国人就已经用算盘来加码，这算盘在中国商人或征税者手中运用起来可是精确至极。（我从来都弄不懂这小魔方，有人说是波斯人发明的。对此，我也没什么可惊讶，除了萨达姆的祖先还有谁有如此的胆量呢？）

Christian inscription in Phags-pa (Tibetan/Chinese)

The museum's barely legible Muslim relics are in Chinese and Arabic. The Arabic often has quotes from the Koran, or poetry, but the Chinese translation are much more straightforward—like "Dead Foreigner."

A Yuan Dynasty stone quotes the Koran in Arabic but in Chinese simply reads, "General Kang died on 1st day of the 4th month." (April 1st?!)

My favorites include a stone found outside the southwest city gate in 1978. It reads, "The arrow of death has hit!" Another stone, excavated from the South City gate in 1946, has quotes from the Koran (9:21-22 and 55:26), and a Sufi poem, "Death is a cup from which all men drink." It just proves you should boil the water before drinking it.

Christian Artifacts The museum has over 40 Christian relics, with nearly 1,000 lines of inscriptions—the largest collection of its kind. Many Yuan Dynasty headstones were unearthed from the wall foundation of the east gate in 1947. The languages include Chinese, Latin, Syro-Turkic (Turkish written in Syriac script), and even the unusual Phags-pa (script based on Tibetan and Chinese).

Quanzhou discovered that its heritage included Tibetan Buddhism when the outer layer of three "Buddhist" monks on Qingyuan Mountain was removed to discover that, underneath, they were Tibetan lamas! Perhaps Nestorians and Tibetans arrived together!

博物馆的穆斯林遗迹几乎难以辨认，是用中文和阿拉伯文写的。阿拉伯文通常引用《古兰经》或诗歌中的诗句，而汉语的解释则直截了当得多，如“死板的外国人”一样。

一块元朝的石碑上用阿拉伯语镌刻着引自《古兰经》的语句，而用汉语只是简单地写着“康将军卒于第四个月的第一天”（4 月 1 日？！）。

我最喜欢的东西包括 1978 年在西南城门发现的一块石头。上面写着“死亡之箭已射出”。另一块石头 1946 年出土于西城门，刻有引自《古兰经》的语句（第 9 章第 21 至 22 节和第 55 章第 26 节）和一首苏菲派诗：“死亡如同水杯，世人皆饮水其中。”

首先必须把水烧开。

Syrian inscription: On the earth under the Holy Father in the name of the Holy Father and Holy Son.
Chinese inscription on the reverse side

基督教的人造物品 该博物馆收藏着 40 多件基督教遗迹，有近 1000 行题字——同类中最大的藏品。1947 年在东城门墙基出土了许多元代基石。基石上的语言包括汉语、拉丁语、叙利亚－土耳其语（用叙利亚手迹书写的土耳其语），甚至还有与众不同的八思巴文（基于藏文和汉文的一种语言）。人们不禁要问：西藏是怎么掺和到其中来的。

当清源山上的三个“佛教”和尚的外层被掀开时，人们发现他们竟是西藏喇嘛！由此泉州发现的遗产还包括藏传佛教。也许景教教徒和藏族人一起到过这里！

Nestorians were a millennium ahead of their time. Their advanced medical skills opened doors everywhere, and wherever they went they established language centers and translated their scriptures into the local tongues.

Nestorians had missions in Tibet, and some historians believe the Tibetans actually adapted their rites for worshipping the dead from Nestorian practices (who expanded upon ancestor worship to please an Emperor anxious to please his extinguished forebears). Nestorian syncretism (which in the end proved their doom, not their salvation) is seen in the tombstones with a four-winged angel beneath the Christian cross in a Buddhist lotus position before a lotus.

At one time, hundreds of thousands of Nestorians were scattered throughout China, and a Nestorian metropolitan set up a center right here in Zayton. And then the Nestorians vanished almost without a trace.
Some tombstones are of Franciscan Catholics, like Bishop Antonius, or Bishop Bar Solomon, who died in 1313. I was amazed at how far afield Franciscans roamed within a mere century of Francis' death, and after reading so much about the 3rd Franciscan Bishop of Zayton, Andrew of Perugia (who supervised construction of the Franciscan Cathedral outside of the East Gate), I was excited to see his headstone on display. Though I did wonder where the Bishop now rests his head.

Andrew's headstone was unearthed in 1946 at the foundation of the city wall, near the Dragon Temple. The Latin inscription reads, "Here lies at rest the Catholic priest Andrew of Perugia, follower of Jesus Christ."

Hindu Relics The Maritime Museum displays some of the 300+ Hindu architectural and sculptural fragments discovered in Quanzhou. Many were found in the vicinity of the Tonghuai Gate, indicating there was probably a Hindu temple in the southeastern part of the city.

景教教派领先于他们所处的时代有一千年。他们先进的医药技术遍地开花，他们走到哪儿，就在哪儿建语言中心，将他们的经文翻译成本地语。

景教教派在西藏有其使命。有些历史学家认为藏族人事实上从景教教派惯例（该教派信徒沿袭拜祖先习俗以满足一位渴望取悦其已故祖先的帝王）中沿袭了拜祭死人的仪式。从墓碑里，我们可以看到景教教派的综摄现象（到头来证实他们的毁灭而不是他们的得救）。在这些墓碑里，佛教的莲花位置上，有一个基督教十字架，十字架下方是一位长着四个翅膀的天使。

曾有一时，无数景教信徒分布在中国各地，而有个景教大主教就在刺桐城建立了一个中心。接着，景教信徒消失得无影无踪。有些墓碑是天主教的，如安东尼斯主教，或者是死于 1313 年的巴尔·所罗门主教的。令我惊讶的是，在弗兰西斯之死仅一个世纪之内，圣芳济会信徒是如何背井离乡、四处漂泊的，阅读了许多关于刺桐城的圣芳济会主教、佩鲁贾的安德鲁的有关史料之后，我兴奋地看到了他的墓石展出。尽管我的确很想知道这个主教如今长眠何处。

安德鲁的墓石于 1946 年在龙山寺附近的城垣墙基处出土。拉丁语的碑文写道：“这里长眠的是耶稣基督的信徒、天主教牧师佩鲁贾的安德鲁。”

印度教遗迹　博物馆展出了在泉州发现的 300 多件印度教建筑和雕塑断片。许多断片是在通淮门附近发现的，表明该城市东南地带可能曾经有过某个印度教寺庙。

Over 300 Hindu stone fragments...

In 1933, an elephant presenting a lotus to Shiva lingam was discovered in a small temple on Xianlei street. In 1934, workers at the drill grounds excavated the 4-armed Protector of Hinduism, with upper two arms holding the chakra and sangra. Even the ancient Kaiyuan Buddhist temple has a couple of Hindu columns added during reconstruction. Hinduism was strong in Quanzhou because of the close ties between Quanzhou merchants and Tamil guilds in India.

Inscribed with Manichean Scriptures (found in Hanjiang, Putian)

Manichaean Relics The last section of the religious relics display is devoted to Persian's Manicheanism. A legend beside some strange dog-like carvings say they resemble Assyrian art, so I'm guessing they are Manichaean. The carved granite Buddha-like Mani, by the way, is a reproduction. The real McCoy is in our planet's last Mani temple (southeast of the city in Jinjiang).

Quanzhou's Sole Jewish Relic? On October 10th, 2001, Xinhua News Agency reported that workers had unearthed from beneath the ancient Deji Gate what some thought was the first archaeological proof of the ancient Jewish community. It is probably not Jewish. Jews weren't the first to use a six-pointed star. Hindus also use it, with the Tamil "Om" in the center. But an excavated synagogue in Roman era Capernaum had a "Star of David" architectural motif, so the Quanzhou stone may prove to be of Jewish origin as well—if it survives the elements. After months of searching, I finally found it lying unprotected in the open courtyard of the Mazu Tianfei Temple.[①]

① Reach Tianfei temple on #24 bus or special tourist bus #601. Hours: 8:00 to 17:30 Phone: 2220-3731

1933年，在县后街的一座小寺庙里发现了一座大象向湿婆教派男性生殖器献莲花的石雕像。1934年，南校场的工人们挖掘出一尊四臂印度教保护神的雕像，上面的两个手臂握着光轮和莲花。即使是古老的开元寺在重建时也加上几根印度教圆柱。印度教在泉州很强大，因为泉州商人和印度泰米尔行会之间有着密切的关系。

摩尼教遗迹　宗教遗迹展览的最后部分是波斯的摩尼教。在一些犬状的怪异石雕旁的铭文说这些雕刻类似亚述艺术（亚述，公元前 7—公元前 8 世纪亚洲西南部古国——译者注），因此，我猜想它们是摩尼教的。顺便提一下，佛像状的花岗岩摩尼石刻是地球上仅存的摩尼寺庙（位于晋江市东南部）的真品（或者说是真品摩尼？）的复制品。

B.B.

泉州唯一的犹太遗迹？

2001 年 10 月 10 日，新华社报道，工人们在古德济门下出土了可能是首次从考古学上证明古犹太群落的遗迹。这大概不是犹太人的，犹太人并非第一个使用六角星（印度教徒也使用它，中间是泰米尔功绩勋章）。但是在罗马纪元迦百农的一座犹太教会堂也发掘出带有“大卫之星”的建筑图形，因此泉州的这块石刻也许会被证实是同源于犹太教——如果它能经受风吹雨打的话。经过几个月的寻找，我终于发现它被搁置在妈祖天妃庙的露天庭院里，没有得到任何保护。[①]

① 乘24路公交车或者601路旅游专线车即可抵达天后宫。开放时间：8：00—17：30，电话：22203731。

That Zayton had a large Jewish community is confirmed by many sources, from Arab traders to Bishop Andrew of Perugia, who in January, 1326, lamented in a letter that Zayton's Jews obstinately refused to undergo Christian baptism.

In the controversial book "City of Light," which purports to be a translation of the journal of a Jewish traveler who reached Zayton before Marco Polo, Jacob d'Ancona wrote that Zayton had 2,000 Jews, and many tens of thousands were scattered around the rest of China, their ancestors having arrived during the days of the patriarchs. Some say that the Lost Tribes of Israel are in China. Though given the maps they use here, I can see how they got lost.

In the next chapter we'll visit sites in the UNESCO award-winning downtown area—and I'll even give you a map so you don't end up with the Lost Tribes.

Supplement
Zaytun's Openness to Foreign Religions

> "As for the doctrine of the Occident which exalts I'ien Chiu [天主, Lord of Heaven—Christian God], it is … contrary to the orthodoxy [of China's Classics], and it is only because Christians are thoroughly versed in mathematical sciences that the State uses them. Beware, lest you forget that."
>
> Emperor Kangxi

> "Passing through many cities and towns, I came to a certain noble city which is called Zayton, where we Friars Minor have two Houses…The city is twice as great as Bologna, and in it are many monasteries of devotees, idol-worshippers every man of them. In one of those monasteries which I visited there were 3,000 monks. The place is one of the best in the world.
>
> Friar Odoric[2] (in China from 1323-1327)

All but one of Zayton's 7 mosques have vanished, and Ashab has but a shell of its former grandeur—but Christians don't even have a shell left standing. Not a trace is left of the great Franciscan cathedral that Bishop Andrew built with the Emperor's funding, or of the other Catholic churches and monasteries, or of the Nestorian churches. All that remains today are a few dozen tombstones (which survived thanks to the efforts of local historian, Wu Linliang). But we also have Bishop Andrew's letter home.

许多资料证实刺桐城曾经住过大量的犹太人。在1326年1月的一封信中，从阿拉伯商人到佩鲁贾的安德鲁主教，都抱怨说刺桐城的犹太人非常固执，拒绝接受基督教的洗礼。

《光明之城》是一本颇有争议的书籍。据说，该书是一位比马可·波罗更早到过刺桐城的犹太旅行家游记的译本，作者雅各布·德安科纳写道，刺桐城有 2000 名犹太人，还有好几万散居在中国其他地区。这些犹太人的祖先早在中国父权制社会时期就到过这里了。有人说以色列“走失的部落”就在中国！不过看了这里使用的地图，我能明白他们是如何走失的。

下一章我们将参观获得过联合国教科文组织奖的市区——我甚至会给你一张地图，这样你就不会落得像“走失的部落”那样的下场！

附录　刺桐城对外国宗教的开放

“欧美人信奉天主教（天上之神——基督教的神），这与中国正统的教义是相悖的，国家任用这些基督教徒，乃是因为他们深谙数理。切记勿忘。”（由文言文翻译而来——译者注）

——康熙皇帝

“走过许多城镇之后，我来到了一座名叫刺桐城的尊贵的城市，在这里，我们的小修道士有两座寺院……刺桐城有博洛尼亚的两倍大，城中有许多信徒僧侣，他们每个人都是偶像崇拜者。我去过其中的一座修道院，那里有 3000 名修士……这里是世界上最美好的地方之一。”

——奥多力克修道士（1323-1327年间在中国）

在刺桐城的七座清真寺只剩下一座，而艾苏哈卜清真寺仅是原先宏伟建筑的一个空壳——然而基督教甚至连一个空壳子也没有留下。无论是安德鲁主教用帝王的钱建造的圣芳济会大教堂，还是其他天主教堂和修道院，或者是景教教堂，如今都已无迹可寻了，今天所剩的只是一些墓碑（这些墓碑多亏当地历史学家吴林良的努力才得以保存下来）。但是，我们还存有安德鲁主教写的家书！

3rd Bishop of Zayton Andrew of Perugia, 3rd Bishop of Zayton presided over one of Zayton's Franciscan convents (while Peter of Florence supervised the other. Andrew also supervised construction of the east gate Catholic Cathedral, which the emperor not only allowed but actually financed! Following are excerpts from Andrew's fascinating letter home (written in 1326) in which he shed much light on the size of the foreign community, the vast wealth of his Chinese hosts, and the openness of Chinese to foreign trade, philosophy and religion.

Headstone of Andrew 3rd Bishop of Zayton (Quanzhou Maritime Museum)

Bishop Andrew's Letter Home

"Friar Andrew of Perugia, of the Order of Minor Friars, by Divine permission to the Bishop, to the revered father the Friar Warden of the Convent of Perugia, health and peace in the Lord for ever!

"…through much fatigue and sickness and want, through sundry grievous sufferings and perils by land and sea, plundered even of our habits and tunics, we got at last by God's grace to the city of Camballech, which is the seat of the Emperor the Great Chan, in the year of our Lord's incarnation 1308, as well as I can reckon.

"There, after the Archbishop was consecrated…we obtained an Alafa from the emperor for our food and clothing. An Alafa is an allowance for expenses which the emperor grants to the envoys of princes, to orators, warriors, different kinds of artists, jongleurs, paupers, and all sorts of people of all sorts of conditions. And the sum total of these allowances surpasses the revenue and expenditure of several of the kings of the Latin countries.

"As to the wealth, splendor, and glory of this great emperor, the vastness of his dominion, the multitudes of people subject to him, the number and greatness of his cities, and the constitution of the empire, within which no man dares to draw a sword against his neighbor, I will say nothing, because it would be a long matter to write, and would seem incredible to those who heard it. Even I who am here in the country do hear things averred of it that I can scarcely believe…

刺桐城第三主教 佩鲁贾的安德鲁是刺桐城的第三任主教，主持刺桐城的一座圣芳济会女修道院（而佛罗伦萨的彼得主管另一座）。安德鲁还监管东门天主教堂的修建，这座教堂的修建不仅得到皇帝的恩准，而且还得到皇帝的资助！以下是安德鲁所写的家书（写于1326年）的摘录。在信中他谈了许多关于外国人群落的规模、他的中国主人的富有以及中国人对外贸易、哲学和宗教的开放程度。

安德鲁主教的一封家书

“佩鲁贾的安德鲁，代表所有的神职人员，在主教的神圣授权下，祝愿佩鲁贾的修道院神父沃尔登修士在主的保佑下，永远健康、安宁！

“……尽管在旅途中经历了无数次海上、陆路的疲劳、疾病、苦难和危险，甚至连我们的法服和外袍也被人抢走，在主的保佑下，我们终于在上帝化身之年 1308 年到达了元大都，也就是伟大的可汗的所在地。

“在那里，给大主教祝圣以后，我们得到了帝王馈赠给我们的用来买衣服和食物的阿拉法(Alafa)。阿拉法是帝王赐予诸侯国使节、演说家、勇士、各类艺术家、吟游诗人、叫花子以及各种不同境况不同人士的薪俸。这些薪俸的总额超过了好几个拉丁国家君主的税收和开支。

“这位伟大帝王的财富、智慧和荣耀是无可争议的，他权倾四野，万人归顺。在他的国度里，城镇无数，繁华无比。在他的帝国范围内，没人敢和他的邻居拔刀相见，我无法说什么，如果要写下来的话，那将会是非常冗长的故事，而且听到这些事情的人可能会觉得难以置信。就连身处该王国的我听到一些说法，都几乎不敢相信……

"There is a great city on the shores of the Ocean Sea, which is called in the Persian tongue Zayton; and in this city a rich Armenian lady did build a large and fine enough church, which was erected into a cathedral by the Archbishop himself of his own free-will. The lady assigned it, with a competent endowment which she provided during her life and secured by her will at her death, to Friar Gerard the Bishop, and the friars who were with him, and he became accordingly the first occupant of the cathedral."

The cathedral was taken over by Friar and Bishop Peregrine, who died July 7th, 1322, and was succeeded by Andrew, who continues:

"I caused a convenient and handsome church to be built in a certain grove, quarter of a mile outside the city, with all the offices sufficient for twenty-two friars, and with four apartments such that any one of them is good enough for a church dignitary of any rank. In this place I continue to dwell, living upon the imperial dole before-mentioned… Of this allowance I have spent the greatest part in the construction of the church; and I know none among all the convents of our province to be compared to it in elegance and all other amenities…

"'Tis a fact that in this vast empire there are people of every nation under heaven, and every sect, and all and sundry are allowed to live freely according to their creed. For they hold this opinion, or rather this erroneous view, that everyone can find salvation in their own religion. Howbeit we are at liberty to preach without let or hindrance. Of the Jews and Saracens there are indeed no converts, but many of the idolators are baptized; though in sooth many of the baptized walk not rightly in the path of Christianity….

"Farewell in the Lord, father, now and ever. Dated at Zayton, A.D. 1326, in the month of January."

For Whom the Bells Toll Of course, the many religions occasionally had their squabbles. One of the most amusing weapons that the Catholics wielded against Muslims was bells!

For some reason, Muslims abhorred bells. Even intrepid Arab traveler Ibn Battuta, who seemingly feared nothing, recounted his "terror and dismay" at the clangor of bells in Caffa. So of course our Saintly Marignolli[3] delighted in letting the Saracens know for whom the bells tolled. In his "Recollections of Travel in the East", he wrote,

"在大洋海岸边有一个波斯语称作Zaytun（刺桐）的大城市。在这个城市里，有一个富裕的亚美尼亚女士修建了一座大而美的教堂，大主教按照自己的意志将其建成了大教堂。那位女士在其有生之年以及临终前立下的遗嘱中将教堂以及大部分东西捐赠给了主教杰拉德修士和那些跟随他的修士，因此他成了教堂的第一个所有人。"

教堂由修士兼主教佩里格林接管。他卒于1322年7月7日。此后教堂由安德鲁继承下来。安德鲁接着写道：

"我筹建了这么一座方便而美观的教堂，它建在一个小树林里，离城里大约四分之一英里。这座教堂的所有办公室都可容纳22名修士，四间公寓的任何一间都能很好地满足教堂里任何等级高僧的需要。我继续住在这里，靠帝王馈赠的津贴过日子。这份津贴的大部分我用来修建教堂；我知道，教堂是如此的雅致和宜人，以至于我们教区内没有任何一座修道院可与之相媲美……

"实际上，在这个庞大的帝国，各个民族、各种教派的人都可以按照自己的教义自由地生存。因为他们持有这种观点，或者说是错误的观点，认为每个人都可以从自己的宗教中获得拯救。尽管我们可以不受限制地自由传教。然而，犹太人和撒拉逊人很少改变宗教，但其中很多崇拜者都接受了洗礼。不过，事实上很多受过洗礼的人都没有走上正确的基督教之路……

"再见了，父亲。以上帝的名义，从今日到永远。公元1326年1月于刺桐城。"

钟声为谁而鸣？ 当然，这么多的宗教偶尔也会发生口角。天主教徒用一种非常有趣的武器——钟，来对抗穆斯林教徒。

由于某种原因，穆斯林教徒憎恨钟。就连看起来无所畏惧的勇敢的阿拉伯旅行家伊本·贝图塔说起他在加法听到钟的叮当声时竟感到"惊慌和恐怖"。当然，我们圣洁的马里诺利[3]以能让撒拉逊人（阿拉伯人的古称——译者注）知道钟声为谁而鸣而开心。在《东方之旅回忆录》中，他写道：

"There is Zaytun also, a wondrous fine seaport and a city of incredible size, where our Minors Friars have three very fine churches, passing rich and elegant; and they have a bath also…

John Marignolli proudly wrote of the Franciscan's "fine bells of the best quality, two of which were made to my order, and set up with all due form in the *very middle* of the Muslim community."

Maybe the Catholics used the bells to call the Muslims on the prayer carpet for waking them at dawn with the Muslim call to prayer?

The Catholics', Nestorians' and Muslims' keen interest in Chinese souls is not surprising, given that ancient Western tradition claims Chinese are descendents of Noah's son Shem, ancestor of Abraham, patriarch Islam, Judaism, and Christianity. John Marignolli wrote,

"Shem was anxious to maintain the worship of the true God, and his history we shall now follow. In the second year after the flood he begat Arfaxat, who … at the age of thirty-five begat Sela or Sale, by whom India was peopled and divided into three kingdoms. The first of these is called Manzi, the greatest and noblest province in the world, having no paragon in beauty, pleasantness, and extent. In it is that noble city of Campsay, besides Zaytun, Cynkalan [Canton], Janci, and many other cities."

Ancient Zayton

“刺桐城也是一个令人惊叹的良港、一个规模极大的城市。在那儿，我们的小修士有着三个非常不错的教堂，历经了繁盛和典雅；他们也有浴室……他们还有几口高质量的好钟，其中有两口是按我的要求去做的，以预期的形状设立于撒拉逊教区中心。”

也许这些钟是对每天五次大声祷告的吵闹声的一种回击吧？

考虑到古代西方传统曾断言说诺亚的儿子闪是中国人的祖先，是伊斯兰教、犹太教和基督教之父亚伯拉罕的祖先，天主教徒、基督教徒和穆斯林教徒对中国人产生浓厚的兴趣就不足为奇了。约翰·马里诺利写道：

“闪非常希望保持对真主的崇拜，而我们现在应该理解他的历史。在洪灾过后的第二年，他成为阿法扎特之父，阿法扎特在35岁时成为西拉或撒利之父，而印度就是通过他繁衍并分割成三个王国的。第一个王国名叫曼齐，它是世界上最大、最高贵的教区，其美丽、愉悦程度和地域并非尽善尽美。在这个王国里，除了刺桐城、新迦兰（旧时的广州）、监兹及其他许多城市外，还有那高贵的城市坎赛。”

Notes

[1] Williams, in *Chinese Repository*, VI. 149, quote in *The Travels of Marco Polo*, V. II. P.252

[2] Friar Odoric: arrived in Canton in 1322 with Friar James (Ireland) and traveled on foot to Zayton. Legend has it that he brought the bones of four missionaries martyred in India to Zaytun, where he buried them. During the voyage, he stilled a storm by tossing one of the bones into the sea. (Evidently the martyr didn't complain of such ill treatment; if he had, he would not have had a leg to stand on). He landed in Canton and traveled overland on foot to Zayton.

[3] John Marignolli: Giovanni di Marignolli , Franciscan missionary in China from 1342 to 1346, Giovanni di Marignolli . Born in Florence, Italy, 1290, became a Franciscan and held the chair of theology in the University of Bologna. Because of a Chinese embassy that arrived in Avignon in 1338, Pope Benedict XII sent Marignolli and other Franciscans to China. At the end of 1341, he crossed the Gobi Desert and was received with honors in the court at Peking. After 3 years in Peking, he traveled through Southern China, and Southeast Asian countries, and arrived back in Italy 15 years after his departure. Years later he wrote of his eastern travels in his *Chronicon Bohemiae*.

Manichean bowls (Maritime Museum)

注释：

1. 威廉著：《中国的宝库》，第六章，第 149 页，引自《马可·波罗游记》第七章，第 252 页。

2. 奥多力克修道士：1322 年与詹姆斯修士（爱尔兰）一同来到广州，然后步行来到刺桐城。传说他将四位在印度殉教的传教士的遗骸带到了刺桐城并安葬在那儿。在一次航行中，他把其中的一根骨头抛入海里，平息了一场风暴。（显然，那位殉教者并没有抱怨如此糟糕的待遇。如果真有的话，他就不会有一条腿继续航行下去了）。他在广州登陆，然后在陆地上步行至刺桐城。

3. 约翰·马里诺利：吉奥凡尼·迪·马里诺利，1342—1346 年旅居中国的圣芳济会传教士。他于 1290 年出生于意大利的佛罗伦萨，之后成为圣芳济会修道士并在博洛尼亚大学担任神学教授。由于一位中国使节在 1338 年到了阿维尼翁（今法国东南部城市——译者注），本尼迪克特教皇十二世也派遣了马里诺利和其他圣芳济会修道士到中国。1341 年底，马里诺利穿过戈壁滩，在大都（今北京——译者注）受到隆重接见。在大都待了 3 年后，他游历了中国南部，以及东南亚国家，在阔别十五年后，他回到了意大利。几年后，他在其《波希米亚录》一书中描述了他的东方之旅。

Chapter 3

Downtown Zayton Sites

Ashab Mosque 清净寺 is the perfect place to start your downtown tour because it is a convenient walk from the Mosque to half a dozen other key sites. Ashab is not only one of China's ten most famous temples but also, I'm told, one of Islam's top ten holy places.

Zayton once had at least 7 mosques, like the Qingjing Mosque at the southern gate (built by a Muslim from Shiraf, on the Persian Gulf), but Ashab is the only Mosque still standing.

The 2500m^2 Ashab Mosque (also called "Kylin," for Chinese unicorn, or Shenyou Mosque), was built in 1009 A.D., (year 400 of the Muslim calendar). The beautiful imitation of a Damascus was built of blue and white granite, and has a Fengtian altar, Mingshan Chamber, and Prayer Hall. The mosque was renovated in 1310 (Yuan Dynasty) by Ihamed B. Muhammed Gudeish, from Iran.

The dome above Fengtian Altar collapsed during a 1607 earthquake, but the magnificent 20m. high vaulted entrance and four walls remain.

Ashab Mosque's portal has four large pointed arches that create three compartments. The second compartment has 99 small pointed arches, which symbolize Allah's 99 appellations of excellence. Above the portal is a square tower with battlements (great spot for taking photos if you can get them to unlock it for you).

第三章

刺桐市区风景点

艾苏哈卜清真寺（清净寺）　艾苏哈卜清真寺（清净寺）是市区观光的最佳出发点，因为从清净寺到其他几个主景点走路便可到达，非常方便。清净寺不仅是中国十大名刹之一，据说，它还是十大伊斯兰圣地之一。

刺桐城曾经有过至少七座清真寺，如位于南门的清净寺（由波斯湾设拉子城的一名穆斯林所建），但是，清净寺是目前仅存的一座。

面积 2500 平方米的清净寺（也称“麒麟”——中国的独角兽，又名神游寺）建于公元 1009 年（回历 400 年）。这座美丽的寺院仿造大马士革清真寺，由蓝白花岗岩砌成，设有奉天坛、明善堂和礼拜殿。清净寺曾于 1310 年（元朝）由来自伊朗的艾哈默德·本·穆罕默德·贾德斯重新扩建。

在 1607 年的一次地震中，奉天坛的穹顶倒塌，然而，20 米高的宏伟的拱形正门和四堵围墙却残存下来。

艾苏哈卜清真寺的入口有四个大的尖拱门，分为三层。第二层有 99 个尖拱门，象征安拉的 99 个雅称。入口的上方有一个筑有垛子的方塔（如果你能找人开锁的话，此处是一个不错的拍照点）。

An Arabic inscription engraved in the stone lintel of the archway reads,

> "God is witness that there is no God but He, and the angels and all those possessing knowledge stand up for justice. There is no God but He, the mighty, the wise. Verily, in God's sight the true religion is Islam."

To the west of the portal is the former 600 sq. m. worship hall, once covered by a large Islamic dome. A 15th century Chinese record describes the worship hall:

> "The halls on the west stand in rows supremely. Their design is different from that of other earthly monasteries, yet swelling and floating, as if emulating a heavenly pavilion."

A minaret once towered between the portal and worship hall but it collapsed, and was replaced with a wooden tower. And then a typhoon blew the tower down in 1687—eighty years after an earthquake knocked down the dome. In the northwest corner of the Mosque are the Ming-shan Hall, Ablution Pavilion and Sermon Hall.

Ashab's 1,000-year-old well

Well Kept The 1,000-year-old-well is said to never run dry, and to always have clean, pure water. It did have a plant growing in its dark depths, but I'm sure it was a clean, pure plant.

A Buddhist nun demanded to know why Ashab Mosque had a stone incense burner, since Muslim worship doesn't use incense. Worse yet, the burner has a lotus leaf motif, suggesting Buddhist influence—and I found a duplicated incense burner in Fuzhou's mosque as well. When I suggested the lotus suggested Buddhist influence, an incensed Muslim said, "Buddhists have no monopoly on the lotus! All religions use them." But another Muslim confided that incense burners were adopted because Chinese converts felt Islam wasn't a bona fide religion without incense. (And, of course, Muslims also had strong vested interests in the incense trade).

Two steles in the Mosque's eastern grounds record the Yuan Dynasty and Ming Dynasty renovations, and on the north wall is engraved a 1407 imperial edict protecting Islam.

门楼正额横嵌阿拉伯文浮雕石刻，写着：

“真主秉公作证，除他外，绝无应受崇拜的；众天神和一般学者，也这样作证，除他外，绝无应受崇拜的，他是万能的，是至睿的，真主所喜悦的宗教，确是伊斯兰教。”

自入口往西是600平方米的前礼拜殿，曾经盖有一个大的伊斯兰风格的穹顶。有一个15世纪中文档案对礼拜殿作过这样的描述：

“门以南为向，堂以西为尊。叠叠重重，规制异人间之庙宇，昂昂哙哙，翚革仿天上之楼台。”

在入口和礼拜殿之间曾屹立着一座尖塔，但却坍塌了，取而代之的是一座木塔。1687年的一次台风将这座塔吹倒，80年后的一次地震又将其穹顶震塌。寺院的西北角是明善堂、净身亭和讲经堂。

存留的古井 据说这口千年古井从未枯竭，且井水清澈纯净。古井的暗深处长着一棵植物，但我相信这棵植物一定是洁净的。

有一个尼姑很想知道为什么艾苏哈卜清真寺会有石香炉，因为穆斯林是不烧香的。更绝的是，香炉上竟然有莲叶图案，这表明是受佛教的影响——我在福州的清真寺也见过同样的莲花香炉。当我提出这是受佛教影响的看法时，一位穆斯林愠怒地说：“莲叶并非佛教徒的专利啊！所有的宗教都用它。”但是另一位穆斯林坦言说他们采用香炉是因为中国信徒觉得没有薰香伊斯兰教就不成为真正的宗教了。（当然，穆斯林对薰香交易也是兴趣浓厚哦！）

清真寺东侧立有两块元、明朝重修清净寺的碑记。北墙立有1407年颁发的关于保护伊斯兰教的《敕谕》石刻一方。

During the state-funded reconstruction of Ashab Mosque in 1983, workers found several tombs, including that of the son of the Persian prime minister whose father was killed in 1312. Other tombstones belonged to Muslims from Tabriz, a Khan (elite muslim) from Khorazm, and a woman from Nabrus in the Eastern Mediterranean.

Proposed New Mosque

New "Islamic" architecture across the street from ancient Ashab Mosque

Restoration Today, Quanzhou Muslims are not only restoring the place but also plan to build a new Mosque. In addition, the city has a large Islamic Cultural Heritage Center adjoining Maritime Museum.

Ashab's lotus incense burner

Quanzhou's comprehensive development plan insures cultural and historic integrity of new architecture by requiring new construction in "Muslim" areas to retain at least a stylized Islamic flavor. The shopping area across the street from Ashab has an Islamic gate, and even the signboard behind the Mosque has a Middle Eastern flavor!

Buses to Ashab: 3,4,5,6,7,16,18,19,26
Hours: 8:00—17:30
Phone: 219-3553

在1983年由国家出资重建艾苏哈卜清真寺的过程中，工人们发现了几处坟冢，其中包括遇害于1312年的波斯国首相的儿子。其他墓碑属于大不里士(伊朗西北部城市——译者注)的穆斯林，来自花拉子模的一个可汗(穆斯林的精粹)和来自地中海东部那不勒斯的一位女士。

修复工作 如今，泉州的穆斯林不仅对旧址进行修复，而且还正在建造一座新的清真寺。此外，该城市有一座伊斯兰文化遗产中心（靠近海上交通史博物馆）。

Quanzhou Islamic Cultural Center

泉州综合发展计划中要求“穆斯林”地区的新建筑物至少要保留某种固定格式的伊斯兰风味，确保了新建筑的文化和历史的完整性。清净寺对面的购物区有一道伊斯兰特色的门，就连清净寺后面的招牌也带有中东风格！

乘车：搭乘 3、4、5、6、7、16、18、19 和 26 路车均可到达艾苏哈卜清真寺。

开放时间：8：00—17：30 **电话：**22193553

Guandi Temple 关帝庙 Just east of Ashab Mosque is the ancient temple dedicated to heroic generals Guan Yu and Yue Fei. This "general" purpose temple seems to sprawl forever, incense smoke wafting through the dark recesses hosting a myriad of idols for 24 other famous generals, as well as enlisted heroes for those who have more "private" needs. Cultural relics include Zhu Xi's inscription, "Righteousness" and Zhang Ruitu's, "Heaven and Earth Imbue the Valiant Spirit." (For a contemporary insight on how such worship begins, visit Hui'an's "PLA Temple" in the walled city of Chongwu).
Buses: #3, 4, 5, 6, 7, 8, 9, 16, 18, 19, 26 **Hours**: 6:00-19:00 **Phone**: 228-6613

A "General" Purpose Temple

Houcheng Tourist Culture Street 泉州后城旅游文化街 Quanzhou's official tourist shopping area, Houcheng Street intersects Tumen Street just east of the mosque and temple, and offers a variety of tourist services and products. Between Ashab Mosque and the temple is a winding Tourist Shopping Center with vendors offering everything from replica antique coins and copper bowls to jade jewelry, gramophones, and 60s era Chairman Mao alarm clocks and watches (which are increasingly popular, so don't expect to land a real Mao clock for only a few mao). After emptying your pockets, walk west a block to the Confucian Hall.

关帝庙 清净寺的东边是一座古庙，纪念英勇的将军关羽和岳飞。关帝庙似乎永远香火缭绕,香的烟在供奉着另外24位著名将军和有“个人需要”的英雄们的壁龛间飘荡，文化遗迹则包括朱熹的题字“正义”和张瑞图的“充塞天地”。(如欲以当代的眼光去探究这种崇拜是如何开始的,可参观惠安崇武古城的“解放军庙”)

乘车：乘3、4、5、6、7、8、9、16、18、19和26路车均可到达关帝庙。

开放时间：6：00—19：00 **电话**：22286613

后城旅游文化街 泉州的官方旅游购物区后城街，与涂门街相交叉，位于清净寺和古庙的东边，提供各种各样的旅游服务和各式商品。清净寺和古庙之间是一条弯弯曲曲的旅游商品街，这里出售的物品有仿古钱币、铜碗到翡翠项链、留声机和20世纪60年代毛泽东时代的闹钟和手表(现在正逐渐流行, 因此别想用几“毛”钱就能淘到一件“毛”时代闹钟的真品)。掏空口袋之后,向西走过一个街区就到了文庙。

Mao Memorabilia Shop

Historic Zhongshan Rd (中山路) From the Puppet Shop, head west and turn north on the ancient Zhongshan Rd, with its endless shops and the leafy canopy of trees that make a stroll pleasant on the sultriest days. Notice the Islamic architecture.

Zhongshan Rd.

I particularly like the building with Islamic windows above and a "Fun" clothing store with "Life in U.S." motto below. The city is almost as cosmopolitan as ancient Zaytun.

Muslim Chinese Life in U.S.!

Hidden Treasures Head down almost any narrow side street and you'll come upon hidden treasures like the home of the Qing Dynasty Minister of Defense, Huang Zonghan (黄宗汉,1803-1864 A.D.) who succeeded the famous Opium era Commissioner, Lin Zexu.

Home of Huang Zonghan 黄宗汉 (Sufficient Benevolence Lane, 敷仁巷). According to Qu Weiwei, a tourism student at Overseas Chinese University, Huang Zonghan was born in Quanzhou, and was governor of Guangdong and Guangxi provinces (两广总督) from 1856-1861. Huang fought so "bravely" against the Taiping rebels that Emperor Xianfeng (咸丰) personally inscribed a stele with 忠勤正直—"Loyal, Diligent, Honest". It was a great honor. Unfortunately, the Emperor stole the stele back when his hero became embroiled in a political scandal, and the stele is probably gravel by now.

沧桑中山路 从木偶店出来，朝西走，然后向北转就是古老的中山路，这里有着望不到尽头的商店和郁郁葱葱的树木，这些树木为我们在闷热的日子里漫步街头平添了惬意。有很多伊斯兰式的建筑物。

我特别喜欢那座上面有伊斯兰式的窗户、下面写着“美国的生活”标语的“FUN”服装店的建筑物。这城市正变得和古刺桐城一样有大都市味道。

隐藏的财富 沿着任何狭窄的小街道走下去，你会发现一些隐藏的财宝，像清朝防务大臣黄宗汉（公元1803—1864）的故居，他接替鸦片战争时期的著名的钦差大臣林则徐。

黄宗汉故居（位于鲤城区镇抚巷内北侧51号） 在华侨大学读旅游专业的曲微微同学给我当了几天的导游。她介绍说，黄宗汉出生于泉州，1856—1861年间任两广（广东和广西）总督，由于他“勇敢”地镇压了太平天国运动，咸丰皇帝特赐“忠勤正直”匾额勉之。这是个莫大的荣誉。不幸的是，当这位英雄卷入政治丑闻时，皇帝收回了那面匾额，现在那个匾额可能已经变成沙砾了。

Overseas Chinese University Professor Cheng Lichu (程立初), Huang Zonghan's descendant, gave us a tour. He pointed out the granite stele engraved, right to left, with Da Si Ma (大司马) and said, "Written by the Emperor himself! Only the Emperors could write that well."

1 Million Yuan Restoration! Professor Cheng said the restoration, which received no government funding, cost his family one million Yuan. I could not imagine how they could pour that much money in fixing up such an old house until he showed me the intricately carved woodwork, and the granite columns in the courtyard. "The originals were wood," he said, "But trees don't come that big nowadays."

Professor Cheng claimed he could easily earn the million Yuan back if he needed it. (If he doesn't need it, Quanzhou Overseas Chinese University must pay a lot more than we get at Xiamen University!). Professor Cheng claimed that he was offered 10,000 Yuan for just one potted tree—and refused. Maybe he's saving it for when he's really up a tree?

Prof. Cheng also said he could get one million Yuan just by selling the painting of a matriarch that hangs above the family ancestral shelf. It didn't look that hot to me, but I can't tell a black velvet Elvis from a Van Gogh. According to the professor, this dour dowager was painted by none other than renowned Chinese artist Xu Beihong (徐悲鸿).

Xu, Beihong (1895-1953), most famous for his horse paintings, studied in France and adapted his techniques to Chinese painting. He survived his early years in part by painting portraits of wealthy clients, so the painting in Huang Zonghan's house may indeed be a genuine Xu Beihong piece.

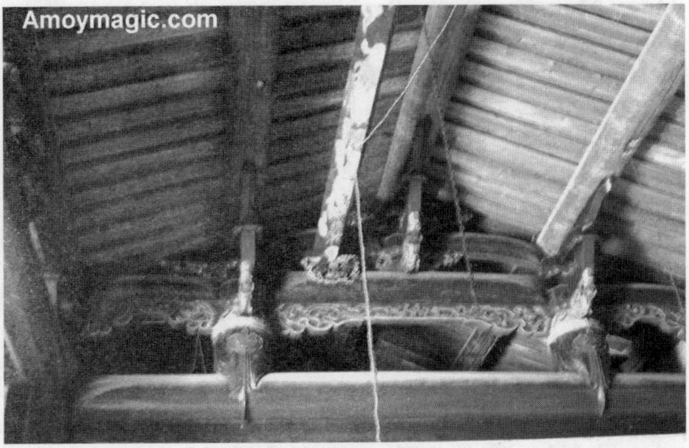

黄宗汉的后裔、华侨大学教授程立初带我们游了一圈，他从右向左指出那面花岗岩匾额中的“大司马”三个字，说道：“这可是皇帝的亲笔御书啊！只有皇帝才能写得那么好！”

耗资一百万元的修缮！ 程教授说，修缮费用花了他们家族一百万元，没拿政府的任何资金。我难以想象修缮这样的旧房子要花他们那么多的钱，直到他让我看了那些精雕细琢的木制品和庭院里的那些花岗岩柱。“这些原先都是木头柱子”，他说，“但今天的树木无法长得那么大。”

程教授声称他要是需要钱的话，他可以很轻松地赚回这一百万。（如果他不需要这笔钱的话，泉州华侨大学的工资一定比厦门大学高得多！）程教授称，有人曾出10000元高价想买走一棵盆栽树，但被他拒绝了。或许他留下这棵树是为了有朝一日他真的骑“树”难下，陷入困境时用得着吧？

程教授还说，他只要卖掉悬挂在他们家供奉祖先的神龛上的那幅高雅的老妇人的油画，就能拿到一百万元。我觉得它并没有那么抢手，但我是连黑色天鹅绒的埃尔维斯和梵高都无法辨别出的。据这位教授说，画这位冷峻贵妇的不是别人，正是中国著名的艺术家徐悲鸿！

徐悲鸿 (1895－1953)，以擅长画马而著名，他留学于法国，并将他的绘画技巧应用于中国画。他早年曾靠给有钱的顾客画肖像谋生。因此，黄宗汉家的画很有可能是徐悲鸿的真品。

"The straight and narrow"

Many Mansions As Professor Cheng showed us some more of Huang Zonghan's 14 mansions (lots of wives, probably), we came upon several ladies having tea in a tight lane between two beautiful brick buildings. A great photo op, you can enter that picturesque lane at #22 Jade Rhinoceros Lane—Yuxi Lane, 玉犀巷—which is north of and parallel to Furen Xiang). We exited the north end, and then entered the next doorway on the left to find a delightful courtyard that was refreshingly cool, in spite of the oppressive heat. "Beats air conditioning!" the Professor said.

Tie Who? A man was scooping leaves from a spring fed carp pond with a net on a long bamboo pole. The carp looked old enough (and complacent enough) to have lived there since the days of Huang Zonghen himself. Towards the back of the courtyard was a massive jumble of outlandish stones. Professor Cheng said, "Taihu Stone!"

"Tie who?" I said. (Maybe a relative of Sharon Stone?)

"That's right!" he said. "Taihu (太湖) stones, of Jiangsu Province's Tai Lake [Taihu] are prized by miniature landscape artists throughout China. These are sold by the pound now. Imagine what this is worth!" Given what he is asking for his paintings and trees, I did not want to ask.

Taihu Stone Story

By Miss Qu Weiwei (曲微微)

"Taihu Lake's Taihu Stones, also called Dongting Stones, come in two kinds: those from water and those from land. Water stones are of course better because the water has carved it into more elegant shapes. While Taihu Stone is usually white, black and green stones have also been found.

"Taihu stones became popular in the Tang Dynasty, and from the Song Dynasty have been widely used in rich people's gardens. Even the emperor asked that Taihu stones be shipped to his palace.

"The famous novel Shui Hu Zhuan (Outlaws of the Marsh) mentions Taihu stones in some chapters. Today, the most valuable Taihu Stone is in Shanghai's Yu Garden. It is named Yu Linglong (exquisite jade,玉玲珑).

"Chinese think Taihu Stones are beautiful precisely because they are so crinkled, thin, holey--downright ugly. This reflects the Taoist philosophy in which when something reaches the peak it crosses over. So Taihu stones are so ugly they are beautiful."

[So maybe there is hope for Bill Brown yet!]

Taihu Stone

许多官邸 当程教授带我们看黄宗汉 14 座官邸（他应该是妻妾成群吧）中的另外一些时，我们遇见几个妇女在两座漂亮的砖楼之间那狭窄的小巷中泡茶。想要拍照的话，你可以进入那别具一格的小巷——玉犀巷 22 号（玉犀巷在敷仁巷北边并与之平行）。我们从北端走出来，然后进入左边的下一个门道，才发现那里有一个宜人的庭院，尽管天气闷热，可这里的空气却是清新凉爽。“胜过空调制冷！”这位教授调侃道。

绑谁？（太湖） 一个男人正在鲤鱼池塘中用绑在竹竿上的网打捞着落叶。那条鲤鱼自从黄宗汉那个年代起就生活在那里，因此看上去足够老了（也是足够自满的了）。庭院后面是一大堆杂乱的稀奇古怪的石头。

“太湖石！”程教授说道。

“绑谁？”（“太湖”的汉语拼音近似英文“tie who?[绑谁？]”——译者注）我说道。（也许是莎朗·斯通的一个亲戚吧？）

“对了！”他说，“江苏省的太湖石，深受全中国盆景艺术家的青睐。这些石头是按重量卖的，想想这有多值钱啊！”想到他在自己家的画和树上要的价钱，我就不想去问了。

太湖石的故事

（曲微微小姐讲述）

太湖的太湖石，又名洞庭石，分为两种：来自水里的和来自陆地的。水石头当然比较好，因为它由水冲刷形成优美的形状。太湖石通常是白色的，但也有看到黑色的和绿色的。

太湖石在唐朝就开始盛行了，而从宋朝开始已经被广泛用于装饰富人的花园。就连皇帝也下令将太湖石运送到他的皇宫里。

著名的小说《水浒传》在某些章回中也提到太湖石。今天，最有价值的太湖石在上海的豫园，名叫玉玲珑（精致的宝玉）。

中国人认为太湖石非常美丽，就是因为它们有皱纹、质地薄，多孔——十足的难看。这反映了道教的哲理：当某事到达鼎盛的时候就会开始衰落。因此，太湖石虽丑犹美。

[我暗想，自己仍有希望!]

National Treasure The professor pointed out a glistening cave stone and exclaimed, "This is a priceless National Level Treasure! Look closely and you can see that the natural design resembles snow on winter plums--like a Chinese abstract painting."

I guess I'll never paint Chinese abstracts, because I saw neither snow nor plums, but I did appreciate the stones natural beauty (I've collected minerals and stones since I was six, and our apartment is crammed with a few hundred pounds of specimens). But it didn't appear that local residents were so enamored of the stone. They were using it as a mop rack. When I aimed my camera, Miss Qu Weiwei started to remove the mops, but the professor said, "Leave them there so people can see how we care for such treasures!"

Getting to Huang Zonghan's Home: it's but a 5 minute walk from the Copper Buddha Temple (Tongfo Si, 同佛寺),on Furen Lane (Furen Xiang, 敷仁巷), between Zhongshan Rd. and Nanjun Xiang (南俊巷)—just north of Fengze St. (丰泽街).

Zhongshan Shopping Quanzhou is shopper's heaven, with wall-to-wall shops—and name brands at that! Stores that don't hawk name brands make up for it with grandiloquent names—like the sports shop called "Standard Physical Culture Stores."

Sue can happily spend half a day sifting through cotton slippers or tea towels, whereas I can make it even through the sprawling Mall of America in minutes—with wallet intact. But I do enjoy meeting people in Chinese shops. They're friendly, and invariably invite you in for tea before getting down to business. And bargaining can be a real eye-opener…

One Size Fits All!

(Adapted from "Amoy Magic")

My wife Susan Marie rummaged through a pile of sweaters in a Longyan City street stall. She finally found one she liked, but it was too small. "Bu yao jin!" [不要紧! No problem!] the lady said. "It stretches when you wear it!"

"I don't know," Sue said. She eventually found another sweater she liked, but it was far too large.

"Bu yao jin!" the same lady said. "It shrinks when you wash it!"

国宝 教授指着一块闪光的石头喊道："这是一块国宝啊！仔细看看，你会看见它天生犹如冬天梅花上的雪——好似一幅抽象的国画。"

我想我将不会画中国的抽象画，因为我既看不出雪也看不出梅花，但是我确实欣赏石头那自然的美。（从六岁开始，我就喜欢收集矿物和石头，我的公寓里已经塞满了数百磅的石头标本）。但是，当地的居民似乎并不怎么喜爱石头。他们拿它当拖把架用。当我拿着照相机要拍照时，曲微微小姐想把拖把挪掉，但是教授说："就让它放在那里吧，让人们看看我们是如何'爱护'宝物的！"

黄宗汉故居参观路线 位于敷仁巷，在中山路和南俊巷之间、丰泽街的北面。从铜佛寺步行仅5分钟即到。

中山路购物街 泉州是购物者的天堂，一间紧挨一间的商店——还有那些招牌！没有招牌的商店则起些夸张的名字，例如，一家体育用品商店叫做"一流体育文化店"。

我无法像苏珊·玛丽那样投入地购物。苏珊可以花上大半天的时间去细看那些棉拖鞋和茶巾，而我却可以在几分钟内穿过美国的商店钱夹安然无恙。但是我喜欢在中国商店里与中国人相识。他们友好，在谈正事前总会热情地邀请你喝点茶。而讨价还价真让我开了眼界……

一样尺码，人人合身

（节选自《魅力厦门》）

我的妻子苏珊·玛丽在龙岩市街道的一个货摊上翻着一些毛衣。她最后发现一件她喜欢的，但是却太小了。"不要紧！"那位卖衣服的妇女说。"你穿了以后，它会伸展的！"

"我不知道。"苏说。她最后找到另一件她喜欢的，但是却太大了。

"不要紧！"那位妇女说，"洗了以后，它会缩水的!"

Happy Shoppers

Fortunately, even the die-hard "one size fits all" types are good natured about it, and will laugh as they hit you with, "I'm losing money, but hey! We're friends!" (Though you met only ten minutes earlier). Or they toss out a line common in many countries, "I'll sell to you at a loss because it is bad luck if the 1st customer of the day doesn't buy something" (and this at 3 p.m.).

The one that really gets to me is, "Chinese New Year is coming up so I'm selling everything at a loss or I won't make enough to return home to my family." How do I know what's a "line" and what isn't? One Yuan means much more to them than me, but I dicker anyway, on pure principle. And kindly shopkeepers have often laughed and sold their wares for less than I asked—or given me something in addition for free!

So yes, bargaining *can* be fun. Even my little friend Emma got caught up in bargaining for a bear, and just bearly got them down to her budget (and that's the bear truth).

Pastor Su Weiyuan 苏伟垣

Quannan Protestant Church (Zhongshan Rd) Zaytun's Nestorian Christianity and Franciscan Catholic cathedrals and monasteries vanished, and while Islam did keep a toehold, many Hui's sole claim to orthodoxy is their refusal to eat pork. But churches have reentered the scene over the past 140 years, and Quanzhou now has Catholic churches and over 170 Protestant Churches.

Pastor Su Weiyuan 苏伟垣, of the South Street Church (泉南堂, on historic Zhongshan Rd.), kindly gave me an outline of the history of Protestantism in Quanzhou, and also allowed me to use information and photos from *Unforgettable Journey—Fifty Years for Fujian Christian Churches on the Three-Self,*[1] for which Pastor Su was Editor-in-Chief.

幸运的是,即使坚持说“一样尺码，人人合身”之类的人也是和善的,而且会对你报以会心的微笑，说“我亏本呢,嘿，但我们是朋友嘛!”(尽管你们见面才 10 分钟)要么他们会抛出一句在许多国家常说的话，“我亏本卖给你，因为如果当天第一个顾客什么也不买的话，就意味着商家会倒霉”(可现在却是下午 3 点)。

给我印象最深的一句话是：“春节就要到了，我亏本出售所有的商品，不然就挣不到钱回家过年了。”但是我又怎么知道哪句话是“台词”，哪句话才是真的。此外,一元钱对于他们来说，其意义远远超过了对我，但我仍然和他们讨价还价,纯粹是出自原则。好几次,和善的店主笑了笑，然后以低于我出的价格把东西卖给了我，或者送我一些免费的小礼品!

因此，讨价还价可以成为一种乐趣。甚至我的小朋友艾玛为了一只玩具熊而进行讨价还价，而且是在预算的价格内把它买下(那确实是事实)。

泉南教堂（中山路） 刺桐的基督教和天主教的大教堂、修道院都荡然无存了,只有伊斯兰教还有自己的立足点,许多回族人唯一信奉正统的主张就是拒绝吃猪肉。但是在过去的 140 年里教堂再次登上舞台,泉州现今有天主教教堂和 170 多所基督教堂!

泉南堂牧师苏伟垣（泉南堂，位于中山路）, 热情地给我概述了泉州基督教的历史, 允许我使用《难忘的旅程——福建基督教三自爱国运动的五十年》的资料和图片, 苏牧师担任该书的主编。

The first Opium War opened five treaty ports, including Amoy and Fuzhou, but Quanzhou remained off limits to foreigners. So in 1856, Rev. Carstairs Douglas, a Scottish minister in the English Presbyterian Mission who had arrived in Amoy in July, 1955, sailed in secret (Stealth Junk?) to southern Quanzhou's Anhai Town.

In 1863, he moved on to Quanzhou, and in 1866, they opened the first Protestant church right across from Kaiyuan Temple, where they preached right in the temple gates. Infuriated scholars burned the church down, whereupon the Christians took a gamble on a gambling den's location a few blocks away on Zhongshan Rd.

General Shilang, the Chinese hero (see Nan'an chapter), had a house and rockery on the church's new site, but it had fallen to ruins and become a gambling den. The Christians bought Shilang's land and set up shop again, but once again the scholars burned the church down. And here is where being a foreigner during the Opium Era came in handy. Complaints were registered with the British forces in nearby Amoy, and in 1876, the compensation extracted from the perpetrators was used to help build a new church of brick and timber, as well as a parsonage for the foreign pastor (the first Chinese pastor was Chen Xuanling 陈宣令, from Zhangzhou, in 1886).

Quannan Church was renovated in the 1890s, and rebuilt in 1927, but by the 90s it had deteriorated so badly that it was razed to the ground in 2002. A $1.5 million USD church seating 3,000 was finished in December, 2003.

Minnan Dialect and Missions Our vertical province has more dialects than any place else in China. In some places, villagers cannot understand neighbors only 3 km away! Yet ironically, instead of hindering Christian work this actually worked out to their advantage. Before missionaries could get into China, they worked in other Southeast Asian countries, most of which had large populations of overseas Chinese.

第一次鸦片战争打开了中国五个通商口岸,包括厦门和福州,但是泉州仍然是限制对外开放的。英国长老会教区的一位苏格兰牧师雷夫·卡斯泰尔斯·道格拉斯1855年7月就来到了厦门, 1856年,他秘密地(乘文物隐形船?)来到泉州南部的安海镇。

1863年，他继续前进，来到了泉州。1866年，他们在开元寺正对面建了第一座基督教教堂，而他就在寺庙的大门里宣讲教义，被激怒了的学者烧毁了教堂，因此基督徒只好在几个街区外的中山路的一个赌窝冒险安顿下来。

施琅将军 我们将会在“南安”这章讲到这位中国英雄,他在教堂的新址建有一座房子和假山花园,但是它已经变为废墟，成了一个聚赌的地方。基督教徒买下了施琅的土地，重建了商店，学者们再一次烧毁了教堂。作为一个鸦片战争期间的外国人此时就占到了便宜。申诉由驻扎在厦门附近的英国军队记录在案。在 1876 年的时候，从犯人那儿缴来的赔偿金用于修建一座新的砖木结构的教堂,以及一幢外国牧师住宅(首位中国牧师是陈宣令,1886 年来自漳州)。

泉南教堂 于19世纪90年代翻新,1927年重建,但是到90年代它已经严重破损，因而2002年被推平。一座花费1500万美元、可容纳3000人的崭新教堂在2003年底前建成。

闽南方言和传教士 我们省从北至南有各种方言,比中国任何其他地方都要多。在一些地方，3公里开外，村民们已无法沟通。然而具有讽刺意味的是,这非但没有阻碍基督教的传播，反而对它有利。传教士进入中国之前,已经在东南亚其他国家从事此类活动,大多数国家都有大量的华侨。

THE ABOVE PHOTOGRAPH IS COPIED FROM ONE TAKEN WHEN HE WAS ABOUT 42 YEARS OF AGE.

your loving brother
Carstairs Douglas

Most overseas Chinese, of course, were from southern Fujian, and so the missionaries learned Minnan dialect. Once China opened up, foreign missionaries converged upon southern Fujian because they already knew the language. Faced with widespread illiteracy, they developed romanization schemes and Minnan language dictionaries and references. Rev. Carstairs Douglas' "Dictionary of the Vernacular or Spoken Language of Amoy," published in 1873, remains a standard reference work even today. Unfortunately, he died only 4 years later of cholera at the age of 46 (having spent 22 of his years in China).[2] But these early foreigners' legacy in education continues at places like Peiyuan High School…

Dr. Sun Yat-sen & the Dentist This Zhongshan Rd. dental clinic (鲤中卫生院，二楼), south of the clock tower, proves that in ancient Zayton, virtually every corner has something of interest if you know what to look for.

The modern second floor clinic of Dr. Sheng Mingjie (盛明捷) has a plaque inscribed by Dr. Sun Yat-sen. It was written for his grandfather, Sheng Jiuchang (盛九昌). Elder Mr. Sheng, also a dentist, was one of Dr. Sun's soldiers-in-arms. Dr. Sun's inscription reads, right to left, 卫生之一道. Weisheng Zhi Yi Dao. I think it roughly means that the mouth is an important part of sanitation. A copy of the inscription is on the outside of the building, near the roof (the original, by the way, is in a Beijing museum).

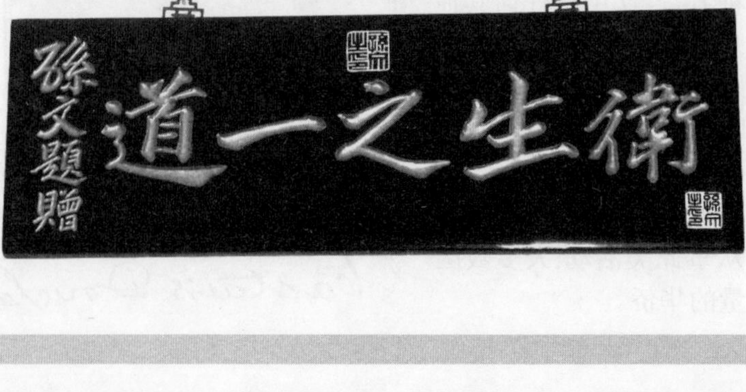

这些华侨大部分来自福建南部,因此传教士学了闽南话。中国门户一开放，外国传教士便纷纷涌入闽南，因为他们已经懂得闽南话。面对普遍的文盲,他们开发了古罗马化图解和闽南语字典以及参考书。牧师卡斯泰尔斯·道格拉斯编撰的《本地语暨厦门话词典》于1873年出版, 至今仍作为标准的参考用书使用。不幸的是，四年后他死于霍乱，时年46岁(他在中国22年)。

但是这些早期的外国人在教育方面留下的遗产在培元中学等地继续得到发扬光大……

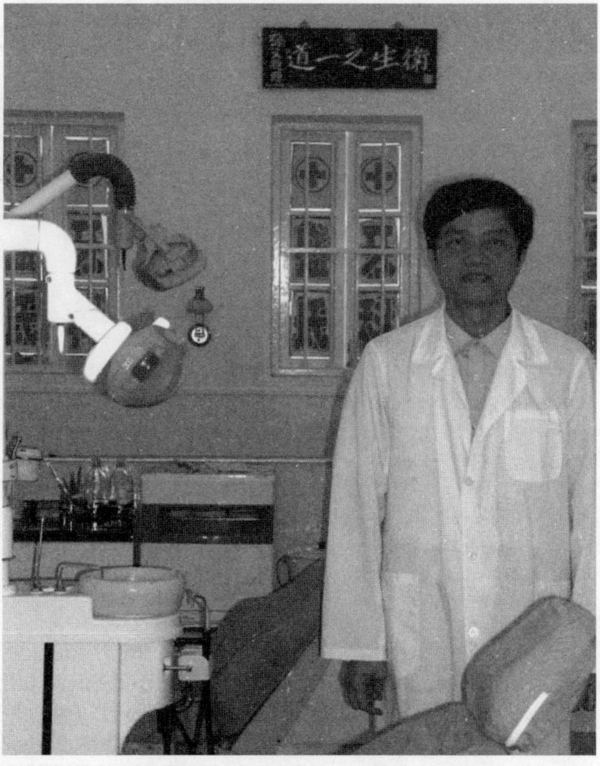

孙中山先生和牙科医生　中山街的牙科诊所（鲤中卫生院二楼），位于钟楼南部。这家诊所证明了在刺桐古城，假如你知道要寻找什么东西的话，那么事实上每个角落都会有一些有趣的东西。

盛明捷医生现在的二楼诊所墙壁上，有孙中山先生的题词！这是孙中山先生为他的祖父盛九昌题写的。盛老先生也是一名牙科医生，他曾经是孙中山先生的卫兵之一。孙先生的题词从右到左写着“卫生之一道”。我想意思大概是口腔是卫生的一个重要部位。在楼房外靠屋顶处有一幅仿制的题匾（顺便说一下，原题匾收藏在北京的一个博物馆内）。

Kaiyuan Temple

> "...there were three thousand monks and eleven thousand idols…All the dishes which they offer to be eaten are piping hot so that the smoke riseth up in the face of the idols… But all else they keep for themselves and gobble up. And after such fashion as this they reckon that they feed their gods well." Friar Odoric

Take a left at the Zhongshan Rd. clock tower and you'll come to Kaiyuan Temple (circa 686 A.D.), one of China's most important temples and, at 78,000 sq.m., Fujian's largest religious center. Kaiyuan's inexpensive entry ticket gains you access to half a dozen other famous sites, including a tree that's a bloomin' miracle.

Miraculous Mulberry-Lotus Tree
According to legend, Mr. Huang Shougong, owner of a mulberry field, dreamed that a Buddhist monk asked him to donate land for a temple. Mr. Huang threw out a fleece. "I'll donate the land if this mulberry tree blossoms with white lotus flowers."

Three days later, white lotus flowers bloomed on the mulberry tree. Mr. Huang said, "It's a bloomin' miracle!" and ceded the land. (Though given Quanzhou folk's prowess at making silk flowers, I wonder if Mr. Huang thought to make sure the lotus blossoms were real?)

Key Kaiyuan Sites Kaiyuan's main areas include "Purple Clouds Screen," "Hall of Heavenly Devarajas," "Great Buddhist Hall," "Sweet Dew Altar of Precepts," and "Depository of Buddhist Texts" (which has over 37,000 volumes of rare Buddhist scriptures and relics). Other sites include "Sanders Shade Temple," "Mini-Kaiyuan Temple," "Hall of Benifence," "Triumph Temple," "Land and Water Temple," and the five level, octagonal "Ganlujie Altar," where Buddhists underwent rites to become monks and nuns. Ganlujie Altar is the largest and best preserved altar of its kind in China, with the Supreme Buddha Losana sitting on a lotus platform of 1,000 lotus leaves, each having a six centimeter engraved Buddha.

开元寺

"……这里曾经有3000个僧侣和11000尊神像。寺里用来供人们吃的斋饭都是滚烫的，好让烟能够弥散到佛像上。但是其他东西他们都自己留着吃掉。通过这样的方式，人们认为已经把神佛供奉得很好了。"

——奥多力克修道士

从中山路钟楼向左拐，你就来到了开元寺（约建于公元686年）。开元寺是中国最重要的寺庙之一，占地面积为7.8万平方米，是福建省最大的宗教中心。但这还不是全部！开元寺廉价的门票可以让你参观其他六个著名景点，包括一棵开花的奇树。

神奇的桑莲古树 据传说，桑园主黄守恭先生梦见有一位僧人向他募地建寺，黄先生扔了一片羊毛回答道："如果桑树会开出白色莲花的话，我就把地捐出去。"

三天后，满园桑树都开了雪白的莲花。黄先生说"这真是奇妙"，并将土地捐了出去。（然而考虑到泉州人在制作丝绢花方面很厉害，我不知道黄先生是否曾想过要弄清那些莲花是不是真的。）

重要景点开元寺 开元寺的主要景区包括"紫云屏"、"天王殿"、"大雄宝殿"、"甘露戒坛"和"藏经阁"（藏经阁中有37000多卷珍贵的佛经和文物）。其他景点还有"檀樾祠"、"小开元寺"（即"准提禅院"）、"功德堂"、"尊胜院"、"水陆寺"以及分为五级、呈八角状的"甘露戒坛"。佛教徒都是在甘露戒坛接受戒礼成为和尚或尼姑的。甘露戒坛是中国最大的、保存最完好的圣坛。坛上最上层供奉着卢舍那佛，其所坐的莲花台座有1000叶莲花瓣，每片莲叶上各刻一尊6厘米大小的佛像。

Barbarian-befuddling Dates, Mus, Li way, & Other Taels

An English brochure claimed Kaiyuan Temple was built in the 2nd year of Chuigong in the Tang Dynasty. This is the Chinese" singularly barbarian-befuddling way of saying "686 A.D." Why they persist in such dating I'm not sure, since even many Chinese can't remember the years of different dynasties, much less the reigns within them.

I don't give a fig for Chinese dates, but weights and measures are worse. For example, Xiamen's Huli Hill cannon cost 60,000 taels (tael= 38 grams) of silver, and Quanzhou's Luoyang Bridge, built in 1059, cost 1.4 million liang of silver. But what did silver cost in the 1800s, or in 1059?

If the MBA Center starts paying me in taels or liangs I'm quitting.

Another pet peeve is the "mu," which is not cow talk but a unit of land measure. The Chinese dictionary said, "100 mu = 1 qing, currently called shimu, 1 shimu = 60 sq. zhang or 666.7 sq. m."

I don't want to have a cow over mus, but sometimes they're enough to make me bleat. As for lengths and distances... An English brochure boasts Anping Bridge is 8,110 chi long and 16 chi wide--but what's a chi? And a Quanzhou sign says, "Shaolin Temple 600 m." but I measured it and it's 1.1 km. Granted, the road winds a lot, and the Kungfu kicking monks probably fly direct, but I'm not the first to go the extra mile when tackling Chinese distances. In 1912, Rev. Philip Pitcher[3] wrote in *In and About Amoy*:,

"These distances may not be accepted as entirely accurate. They are only approximate. When one comes to calculating distances in this part of China he meets with difficulties at once, chief among them being the difference in the length of the li (lee) [about 1/3 of a mile] in different parts of this district. There are long li and short li; there are mandarin li and the common ordinary country li. The difference between these two is considerable, a mandarin li being one fourth shorter."

A Chinese boasted that Anping Bridge is 5 li long. Did he mean long li, short li, mandarin li or country li? I guess I'll just have to give him a little li way.

The Buddhist Scripture Library boasts over 37,000 volumes of rare Buddhist scriptures and relics. Two carved stone poles bear carvings of Shiva the Destroyer, a member of the Hindu trinity (which includes Brahma and Vishnu). The poles were transported to Quanzhou from a collapsed Indian temple. But no one seems to mind the mixed motifs. In fact, Chinese temples often have Buddhist, Confucian and Taoist idols and rites in the same temple, as if the more the merrier (or perhaps they are just covering all of their bases).

落后、玄奥的日期、亩、里路和银两

一份英语手册称开元寺是在唐朝垂拱二年建造的。这是中国人以其独特的落后、玄奥的方式来表达“公元 686 年”。我不确定为什么他们要坚持这种记载日期的方法。很多中国人就连不同朝代的年份都记不起，更不用说是各个朝代里的统治时期了。

我对中国的日期毫无概念，重量和度量衡就更糟了。比如，厦门胡里山的大炮花费了 6 万两银子（1 两=38 克），而建于 1059 年的泉州洛阳桥花费了 140 万两银子。但是在 19 世纪或者 1059 年，银子又值多少钱？

如果 MBA 中心开始用银两付钱给我的话，我会辞职不干的。

另一个令人讨厌的是“亩”，这并不是牛的叫声而是土地丈量单位。汉语字典是这样解释的：“100 亩=1 顷，现在叫市亩，1 市亩=60 平方丈或 666.7 平方米。”

我不想生“亩”的气，但是这些东西有时候足以让我叫苦不迭。说到长度和距离，一份英语手册夸口说安平桥是 8110 尺长、16 尺宽。可是，什么是尺？泉州有一个路标写着“少林寺 600 米”，但是我测量了一下是 1.1 千米。就算这条道路蜿蜒曲折，有功夫的和尚可能直飞，但在对付中国的距离问题上，我并不是第一个走冤枉路的人。1912 年，菲利普·皮彻牧师在《厦门内外》中这样写道：

> “这些距离的说法并不能视作完全准确的距离丈量而让人接受，它们只是一个大概的说法。当有人到中国这地方来测量距离的时候，他立刻就会觉得犯难，最主要的原因在于‘里’（大约 1/3 英里）这个长度单位在这个地区的不同角落有不同的算法。‘里’有长里和短里之分、官方中的里和普通地方的里之分。这两种区分之间的差异是相当大的，官方中的里要短 1/4。”

最近，一个中国的朋友夸口说安平桥有 5 里长。我不知道他指的是长里还是短里，是官方中的里还是普通地方的里。我想我得让他几里路。

佛经图书馆（藏经阁） 拥有 37000 多卷珍奇的佛经和文物。两根石雕柱上雕刻着婆罗神，是印度教的圣三主节中的一员（包括梵天和护持神）。这两根石柱是从一所倒塌的印度婆罗教寺院搬运过来的。但是，似乎没有介意这些混杂的图形。事实上，中国寺庙通常在同一所寺庙里同时供奉着佛教、儒教和道教的神像和教派，好像多多益善（或者可能是他们只是想要填满他们的地方）。

Ring a bell?

Lugang Iron Bell was cast in 1837 and presented to Kaiyuan Temple by 46 companies of Lugang, Taiwan. Supposedly, the bell is so loud it can be heard all the way to Luoyang Bridge on the coast.

Purple Haze and Buddhist Angels Purple clouds surrounded Kaiyuan's 1,387 sq. m. main hall while under construction, so it was dubbed Purple Cloud Hall (which inspired Jimi Hendrix' *Purple Haze*?). The great hall had 100 granite pillars, so also called 100-Pillar-Hall. But the hall's most unique feature is its 24 flying bat-winged angels (apsaras)--one for each division of the traditional Chinese solar year.

Bats symbolize evil and death for Westerners, but Chinese think they are lucky because "bat" (fu, 蚨）and "fortune"（fu,福) are homonyms. The batty angels (or "wonderful music birds") protrude from pillar brackets and help support the uniquely complicated beam structure. Their outstretched arms bear fruit, scholars' "four treasures" (writing brush, ink slab, ink stick and paper), and traditional Chinese musical instruments.

Kaiyuan's angels can't be photographed without written permission from the provincial Religious Affairs Bureau, so I applied and waited to see what would develop. I just got negatives. But Quanzhou does have other angels—at the musical fountain across from the Quanzhou long distance bus station.

Hindu Influence The Hindu relics scattered throughout the Kaiyuan temple are reminders of Zaytun's extensive early contacts with India—largely because of commerce with Tamil merchants. The unusual Indian sphinx in the temple's base was added early on, but the columns with Indian carvings behind Kaiyuan's main hall were scavenged from an Indian temple about four centuries ago when the father of Koxinga (Nan'an chapter) helped rebuild the temple. The Twin Pagodas also show Indian influence, in part because an Indian monk supervised one of the renovations.

鹿港铁钟 铸造于1837年，是由台湾鹿港的46家公司联合赠予开元寺的。据称，这口钟声音洪亮，可传到洛阳桥沿岸一带。

I thought horns were forbidden within city limits?

紫云和飞天乐伎 在兴建面积1378平方米的主殿之时，紫色祥云笼罩开元寺上空，故此殿又名紫云殿（这激发了吉米·亨德瑞克斯创作《紫雾》的灵感？）。大殿内有一百根花岗岩柱子，所以又叫百柱殿。然而大殿最具特色的还是那二十四尊蝠翼飞天神像，分别代表中国传统的二十四节气。

对西方人而言，蝙蝠象征邪恶与死亡，而中国人却认为蝙蝠象征吉祥，因为“蝠”与“福”同音。蝠翼飞天神像（或称“妙音鸟”）从柱榫里露出身来，支撑着独特而复杂的斗拱结构。她们双臂伸展，手捧文房四宝（笔、墨、纸、砚）、瓜果点心和丝竹管弦。

若没有省宗教事务局的批文，开元寺的神像不允许拍照。因此，我提交了申请并静候佳音，但还是被拒绝了。然而，泉州还有其他的飞天乐伎——伫立于泉州长途汽车站旁的“飞天迎宾”。

印度教的影响 印度教的遗迹遍布整个开元寺，见证了早期泉州人民与印度的广泛联系——主要是与塔米尔商人接触。寺中奇特的印度狮身人面像早就加在寺院的底座了，然而在400年前郑成功（见“南安”一章）的父亲帮助重建寺庙时，位于开元寺主殿后面那些带有印度雕刻的立柱却是从一座废弃的印度寺庙搬过来的。东西塔也显示了印度教的影响，部分原因是一位印度和尚曾监管过寺庙的修缮工作。

East and West Pagodas The East and West Pagodas flanking Kaiyuan Temple are the best preserved stone pagodas in China. They were first built of wood and stone, then brick, and later stone. Modeled after the great wooden pavilions of the Central Plains, they have withstood 1,000 years of earthquakes and tourists, thanks to their Song Dynasty reconstruction, which took 22 years.

The East Pagoda (Zhenguo—"nation-protecting"), a brochure says, was built of wood in 670 A.D. (I thought of writing "1st Year of Xianheng in the Tang Dynasty"—just to see if my Chinese readers could figure it out!]. It was later rebuilt as a 48.24m stone pagoda.

The West Pagoda (Renshou—"merit and longevity") was built in 916. Both of the five story octagonal structures are carved top to bottom with vivid relief sculptures, and warriors are carved into the niches of each story. Legend has it that when the East Pagoda had been built up to the fourth level, abbot Faquan died, and the remaining construction was supervised by Tianxi, a monk from India who had come to Quanzhou to preach Buddhist scriptures. This resulted in an unusual marriage of Chinese and Indian motifs, and a bit of monkey business as well.

Bearded Beauty The West Pagoda has two highly unusual carvings. One is of the Monkey King, and the other is of a moustached Goddess of Mercy. Maybe she was related to Guanyin, goddess of mercy and compassion? Guanyin was originally a man, but Chinese woman needed a female to pray to, and male gods were not seen as compassionate or merciful; just look at their expressions).

东西塔　开元寺两侧的东西塔是中国保存最为完好的石塔。最初它们是由木头和石头建造的，之后改用砖，最后用石头建造。以中原地区的大木亭为原型，东西塔经受住了千余年来的地震和游客的考验。这多亏了宋代历时22年的重建。

East Pagoda

东塔（镇国塔——保护国家的塔） 据载，东塔初为木塔，始建于公元670年（我想过改用“唐朝咸亨元年”，看看中国读者是否能明白！），之后，东塔被重建为高48.24米的石塔。

Twin Pagodas of Old Quanzhou

西塔（仁寿塔——仁义和长寿之塔） 建于公元916年。从上到下五层八角结构刻有栩栩如生的浮雕，每一层的神龛内也刻有武士。相传，当东塔建到第四层时，法权法师圆寂，剩余的工程由一名来泉讲经、名叫天锡的印度和尚主持。这导致了中印间独特的图形结合，也引发了一些关于“猴子”的故事。

Bearded Bodhisattva

长胡子的美人 西塔有两尊非比寻常的浮雕，一个是孙行者，另一个则是长胡子的菩萨。也许她和观音有关，是慈善同情之佛？观音原先是男性，但是中国妇女需要一位女性来祈祷（人们认为男性神明不够慈悲为怀，看他们的表情就知道了！）。加利福尼亚有这么多宗教，但为何这尊男扮女装的神没有流行起来呢？

Monkey King

Monkey Business Some folks go ape over the West Pagoda's Monkey King carvings, claiming they are the origin of the Monkey King story since they predate, by hundreds of year, the 16th century epic "Journey to the West," which popularized the simian saint. In all likelihood, this monkey business began with the monkey-god Hanuman in the Indian epic, Ramayana. After all, an Indian monk oversaw the pagodas' renovations.

Incensed Trader's Unsinkable Ship

Song Dynasty Ship To the right of Kaiyuan, past the Buddhist museum, is the display for the Song Dynasty (960-1279) ship unearthed in Houzhu Harbor in 1974. . The 24.2 m by 9.15 m. ship had 13 separate watertight compartments, which made the ship virtually unsinkable—at least until it sunk. A typhoon snapped off the mast and the ship went down 100 meters offshore, fully laden with Southeast Asian products, as well as 2350 kg of incense wood—which no doubt incensed the Muslim owners to no end.

Westerners didn't use watertight compartments until the 19th century. This innovative technique was used on the unsinkable Titanic, which of course promptly sunk. "Oh, Jack!" For more about the Muslim incense trade, and to actually meet a descendant of the incensed Muslim's who owned the unsinkable Song Dynasty sunken ship, turn to the Dehua/Yongchun chapter.

Overseas Chinese History Museum 华侨历史博物馆 Given that most overseas Chinese hail from Southern Fujian (especially Quanzhou), it is no surprise the city has an extensive museum chronicling their history and their contributions to the motherland. The upper floor has an extensive photo display of overseas Chinese' contributions to virtually every area of Quanzhou.

The Southern Shaolin Temple, for example, was rebuilt with the aid of 1 million Yuan from a Filipino Chinese and a Singaporean martial arts organization, and a Singaporean Chinese, Mr. Lin, gave 500,000 Yuan to build the Buddhist museum at Kaiyuan Temple. Overseas Chinese endless contributions have gone towards new schools, universities (like Yang En, New China's first private university), hospitals (Li Guo Xing gave 3 million Yuan for the emergency center), temples, churches, and perhaps most importantly in my eyes, roads.

孙行者事件　有人根据西塔上的孙行者浮雕，称孙猴王的故事源于这些浮雕，因为这些石雕的时间比 16 世纪小说《西游记》早几百年，使得这位猴圣声名大噪。因此很有可能孙行者事件源于印度叙事诗《摩罗衍那》中的圣猴。毕竟西塔的重建是在印度僧人的主持下进行的。

宋代古船　在开元寺右侧，过了佛教博物馆，陈列着一艘于 1974 年在后渚港出土的宋代船只（960—1279）。这艘船长 24.2 米，宽 9.15 米，13 个分开的水密舱令这艘船几乎不会沉没——至少在沉没之前是这样的。一次台风把船上的桅杆刮断了，船也沉入近海 100 多米深处。船上满载着从东南亚运来的商品，还有 2350 千克的香木。毫无疑问，这件事激怒了那些穆斯林物主。

直到 19 世纪，西方造船者才采用了水密舱，20 世纪早期这项创新技术才被应用于永不沉没的泰坦尼克号上，可是这艘船却很快沉没了。“噢，杰克！”更多有关穆斯林的香料贸易，以及如何与拥有这艘宋代不沉之船的穆斯林后人见上一面，请翻至第十三章：“德化和永春”。

华侨历史博物馆　考虑到绝大多数的海外华侨都是来自闽南（尤其是泉州），这座城市建有一座大型博物馆记录他们的历史和他们对祖国做出的贡献，就没什么值得奇怪的了。博物馆的最上层是一个大型的图片展览，展示了海外华侨对泉州各界所做的贡献，尤其是捐资修缮或建设学校、医院、教会、寺庙、桥梁——不管是什么，都倾注了海外华侨的心血。

例如，南少林寺就是在一位菲律宾华人和一个新加坡武术组织 100 万元的捐助下重建的。新加坡华侨林先生捐资 50 万元在开元寺里建立了佛教博物馆。海外华侨不断捐资兴建学校、大学（比如新中国的第一所私立大学仰恩大学）、医院（李国兴捐赠了 300 万元建立了急救中心）、寺庙、教会以及我认为最重要的道路。

Fish or Hook? "Better to give a man a hook and line than a fish," goes the saying, and the best hooks nowadays are new roads. A young friend of mine from Anxi lived a hard life of heavy labor in Xiamen for a decade, but saved enough money that he was able to plant fruit trees back home. The fruit would not have been worth harvesting a decade ago when poor mountain roads meant markets were four times as far. A couple years ago my friend said, "I'm going back home, Professor. Now I can make more money there than in Xiamen!"

Pigs 'n Poison The Overseas Chinese Museum also sheds light on a very dark subject—the notorious "Piggy Trade" (trafficking in coolies, which comes from the Chinese *kuli*,苦力, for "bitter labor.") Exhibits explain how we dastardly foreigners kidnapped Chinese and forced them to labor in inhuman conditions abroad. And, unfortunately, it is all too true. But…having said that, I think the museum should also note that the kidnapping itself was carried out by corrupt Chinese, who in turn sold them to dastardly foreigners. In the wax figure exhibit (below), the boss beating the coolie was Chinese, not a foreigner. Granted, foreigners paid him—but that's my point.

Without the connivance of corrupt officials, the opium and coolie trades could never have survived—hence the article I wrote in *People's Daily* a few years ago pointing out that the biggest threat to China's sovereignty has always been not direct foreign aggression but the domestic corruption that allowed us wily barbarians to get a foothold and then a stranglehold.

Hopefully, Laowai and Laonei alike will learn some lessons from the Poison 'n Piggy trades.

Getting There: Just west of Stadium, and East of Pizza Hut, near Maritime Museum.
Hours: Inquire
Phone: 22987593

鱼，还是钩？　有句俗语说："授之以鱼不如授之以渔"，如今最好的鱼钩是新路。我的一个年轻的安溪朋友，在厦门做了十年艰苦的重活，已经攒够钱回家种植果树了。十年前，水果并不像现在这么好卖，因为那时崎岖的山路意味着市场距离遥远。几年前，我朋友说："教授，我打算回家去。现在，我在老家可以比在厦门赚更多的钱！"

猪仔与毒害　华侨博物馆还突出了一个很黑暗的主题——臭名昭著的"猪仔贸易"（贩卖劳工，它来源于汉语的"苦力"）。展览品说明了我们这些卑鄙的外国人是如何拐骗中国人，如何迫使他们在国外毫无人性的环境下劳动。很不幸的是这些都是完全真实的。但是……既然如此，我觉得博物馆还应该注意到拐骗行为本身是由腐败的中国人干的，然后再把这些苦力转而贩卖给卑鄙的外国人的。在蜡像的左边，那个正在抽打劳工的老板是中国人而不是外国人。有可能是外国人付钱让他这样做的——但那不是我想说明的。

如果没有腐败官员的纵容，那么鸦片和苦力贸易就不能生存——因此几年前我写给《人民日报》的文章被退回了。中国最大的威胁，现在和当时一样，并不是外国的直接侵略，而是国内的腐败势力让我们这些狡猾的野蛮人有了可乘之机，紧接着便是压制。

但愿，"老外"和"老内"都能够从"猪仔"贸易毒害中吸取一些教训。

地　　址：（体育馆的正西面，比萨店的东面）海上交通史博物馆
开放时间：请询问：22987593

Coolies packed for shipment

Other Miscellaneous City Sites

Tianhou Temple 天后宫 Both Chinese and foreign government officials and merchants used to seek smooth sailing by offering sacrifices to the Sea Goddess in Tianfei Temple (circa 1196). Tianhou's nationally protected "History Museum for Fujian-Taiwan Relations" has a large collection of cultural relics, including the purported "Star of David" (lying in the courtyard by a pile of assorted relics).

Getting there: bus #24, or tourist bus #601
Hours: 8:00-17:30 **Phone**: 2220-3731

Two "General" Purpose Mazu Tales

Admiral Zheng He and the "Queen of Heaven" According to legend, when the Muslim admiral Zheng He encountered a violent storm at sea, he calmed his passengers by telling them the story of Miss Mazu. The storm abated, and upon his return to China he asked the emperor to honor Mazu with a royal title, whereupon the emperor declared her the "Queen of Heaven," and built a temple for her.

General Shilang and Mazu When the Qing Dynasty General Shilang (in Nan' An chapter) sailed to Taiwan to oust Koxinga's descendants, he took a Mazu idol, which he left behind after his victory. When he reported to the Emperor how Miss Mazu had helped him gain victory, the Emperor gave her the title "Imperial Concubine," and ordered Shilang to expand her temple on Meizhou island. As for the idol left behind in Taiwan, over the centuries the smoke from countless worshippers' incense has turned Miss Mazu's face black, so they've nicknamed her "Black-faced Mazu" (easier nicknaming her than keeping her face clean, I suppose).

The Quanzhou Museum for Ancient Architecture 泉州古建筑博物馆 Conveniently located downtown on the corner of Huxin St. and Wenling St., this museum is built on the site of the Hong Clan Ancestral Hall. While you're in the area, stop at the Huxin Hotel for some of award-winning Chef Zhong's mouth-watering Quanzhou cuisine (check out the Quanzhou Cuisine chapter).

市区其他各景点

天后宫　中国和外国政府官员常常到天后宫（约建于公元1196年）祭祀海神祈求出航平安。建置于寺内、受国家保护的“闽台缘博物馆”收藏有大量的文物，包括传说中的“大卫之星”（于庭院一堆碎石中）。

乘车路线：24路车或者601路旅游公车
开放时间：8：00—17：30
联系电话：22203731

妈祖和军人的两则故事

郑和将军和“天后”　传说，穆斯林将军郑和在海上遭遇大风浪时，他讲述了妈祖的故事，安慰船上人员。果然，风浪平息了。郑和回国后，奏报朝廷为妈祖封号。随后，皇帝封她为“天后”并为其立庙。

Miss Mazu
Sea goddess

施琅大将军和妈祖　清朝大将军施琅（见“南安”篇）前往台湾攻打郑成功后裔时，他带上妈祖神像，胜利后，神像留在了台湾。他上奏朝廷声称妈祖显灵助阵。皇上封她为“天妃”并命令施琅在湄州岛扩建寺庙。留在台湾的妈祖神像，被无数香客焚香的烟熏黑了脸部。因此，人们给她起名“黑脸妈祖”。（我想，称她为“黑脸妈祖”总比保持神像脸部清洁更省事吧。）

泉州古建筑博物馆　坐落于泉州市区温陵路与湖心街交汇处，交通便利。该馆以洪氏宗祠为馆址。到此处，您可以在湖心大酒店歇歇脚，品尝一下钟厨师所做的一流的美味可口的泉州菜（详见第十四章：泉州美食）。

Chengtian Temple (承天寺), on Nanjunxiang Lane (南俊巷), is one of Quanzhou's three greatest Buddhist Temples (the other two being Kaiyuan and Chongfu). It was first built in the Tang Dynasty, and renovated in the 30th year of Emperor Kangxi in the Qing Dynasty. (That's 1691 A.D., for us foreigners). The brochure says it used to have "ten wonderful views" but was renovated and returned to its original condition (which means, I suppose, that the original did not have the 10 wonderful views?).

Getting there: Bus # 19, Bus # 16, Bus # 18, Bus # 25.
Hours: 6:00-17:30 **Phone**: 2227-6917

Chongfu Temple (崇福寺) This recently renovated temple on Chongfu Road (崇福路) is a provincial level protected cultural relic, and where Shaolin Kungfu was taught after Quanzhou's Shaolin Temple was destroyed. Be sure and visit the reconstructed Southern Shaolin Temple on the hill behind the Sports Stadium.

Getting there: Bus #15 **Hours**: 6:00 - 17:30 **Phone**: 2278-4046

承天寺　位于南俊巷，与开元寺和崇福寺并称为“泉州三大禅寺”。它始建于唐代，修建于清朝康熙三十年（对我们外国人来讲是公元1691年）。据手册上介绍，过去承天寺曾有“十大奇景”，但是经过重修恢复原貌。（我想这意思是说原来的承天寺并没有这十大奇景？）

乘车路线：19 路、16 路、18 路、25 路公车均可

开放时间：6：00—17：30

联系电话：22276917

崇福寺　位于崇福路，是福建省文物保护单位。在泉州少林寺被毁后，此地成为传授少林武功的地方。为了探个究竟可到体育场后位于山上的重建后的南少林寺。

乘车路线：15 路公车

开放时间：6：00—17：30

联系电话：22784046

Zaytun Street Life

> "Many come hither from Upper India to have their bodies painted with the needle in the way we have elsewhere described, there being many adepts at this craft in the city (Zaytun]" Marco Polo

It's no wonder that medieval travelers claimed Zaytun was intoxicating. If you wanted it, Quanzhou had it—everything from silken tapestries to tattoos. While Quanzhou is tamer nowadays, there's still enough to keep you busy--especially at night, when bright lights are strung through the trees, and across buildings and pagodas.

Night markets are a shopper's paradise (and her husband's nightmare), offering everything imaginable and a few things that aren't. And street vendors' endlessly diverse offerings of snacks are guaranteed to please your stomach as well as your wallet.

> "His music isn't as bad as it sounds."
> Mark Twain (of Wagner).

Streetside Opera Each evening, rain or shine, local artists perform music or drama on stages set up by intersections. Others sketch charcoal caricatures, or transform names into beautiful works of calligraphy. And there is always a fellow who weaves amazingly realistic flowers and insects from leaves, and sells them for a pittance to locals and tourists alike. The streets are one unending delightful performance. And if in spite of all this revelry you find yourself down in the dumps—try visiting the dumps…

Nightly streetside performances

刺桐的街头生活

Pavilion by Night

“许多印度上层人士来到了这里，用针自己在身上做彩绘，这种方式我们在别处已经描述过，在刺桐这个城市，有不少人擅长这一手艺。”

——马可·波罗

难怪中世纪时期的旅行者们称刺桐是个醉人的城市，从织锦画到文身，你想要的东西，泉州应有尽有。如今，泉州貌似平淡，仍有东西让你忙个够。尤其在晚上，当缠绕在树上、建筑物上和塔上的夜灯开启的时候。

夜市是女士的购物天堂（也是她丈夫的“地狱”）。那里有你想象得到的和想象不到的东西。街上各种各样的小吃足够让你大快朵颐和狂掏钱包。

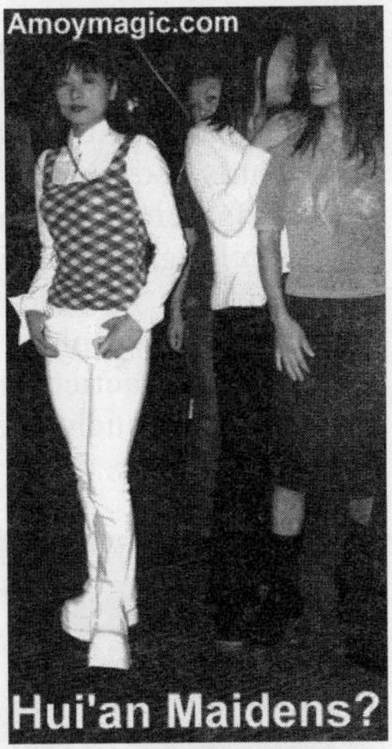

Hui'an Maidens?

“他的音乐听起来并不赖。”

——马克·吐温评音乐家瓦格纳

街头表演　无论是雨天还是晴天，每个晚上，当地艺人在交叉搭建成的舞台上唱歌或演戏。有的画素描或者把名字画成美丽的书法作品。你常常可以看到一个艺人，他会把叶子编织成形象逼真的花朵或昆虫，卖给当地人或者旅行者们以赚取一些小钱。这里的街道充满无尽欢乐的节目。除去所有这些欢闹，你会发现自己置身垃圾堆里——试着去看看这些垃圾场……

Supplement

Down in the Dumps?

No, I'm not really suggesting you visit the city dump or sightsee the sewage treatment center, but they are in fact remarkable, and part of the reason that Quanzhou has been able to balance mushrooming economic growth with preservation of its historical, cultural and natural heritage. And in an age when environmental problems loom large over us (especially in China, with 1.3 billion consumers/disposers), it's encouraging to see cities like Quanzhou that make preservation of their environment a priority.

Passing Water[①] Quanzhou treats only 30% of its daily sewage, but that's better than 0% a decade ago, and new plants should get the city to 80% by 2010. The 133 million Yuan Baozhou Sewage Treatment Plant is state-of-the art, and treated water is pure enough that it can be used for irrigation or to raise fish!

Down in the Dumps Quanzhou has one of China's most advanced volume-reduced, harmless sanitary landfills. It easily meets present needs, and a new plant is being built for future demands. The plant not only uses the most cutting edge imported technology and practices but also employs some good old Chinese ingenuity—like lining the dumping grounds with inert waste from the shoe industry. This gets rid of the waste, and also forms an additional protection against percolating liquids. (Fascinating, eh? Or maybe not—but it's these kinds of practices behind-the-scenes that make the Quanzhou that tourists see such a beautiful, clean and healthy place to visit). And its getting better.

① Sign in restaurant of Acapulco, Mexico's 5-Star Princess Hotel: "The manager has personally passed all of the water."

附录　身在垃圾场？

不，我并不是真的劝你去参观一下市垃圾处理场，或者去游览一下污水处理中心，不过它们确实做得不错，这也是泉州在飞速发展经济的同时能够兼顾历史、文化和自然遗产的保护的原因之一。在环境问题日益严峻的时代（在拥有 13 亿消费者和垃圾制造者的中国尤为突出），像泉州这样的城市能优先考虑环境保护，这令人感到鼓舞。

排水　目前泉州只能处理 30%的日常污水，但比起十年前的零处理能力要好多了。新的污水处理厂将在 2010 年前将城市污水处理能力提高到 80%。投资 1.33 亿元兴建的宝州污水处理厂技术一流，经它处理过的水，纯净得可以用来灌溉，还可以用来养鱼！（见照片）

Treated Sewage used in waterfall and fish pond

在垃圾堆下面　泉州有全国最先进的占地小、无害的卫生垃圾填埋场，能满足目前的需要。一个新的填埋场正在兴建，以满足未来的需要。填埋场不仅使用最尖端的进口技术和运作方式，还运用了一些古老的变通办法——比如，用鞋厂的填充料作为填埋场的边缘隔离带。这样既处理了废料，又能防止液体的渗漏，可谓一举两得。（意想不到吧？或许没有我说的那么神奇——但正是这些后台工作使泉州成为一个美丽、清洁、健康的旅游胜地。）而且她还变得更加美丽。

Phase Two will improve recycling, and allow conversion of some waste into fertilizer. This, combined with extensive campaigns to encourage citizens to reduce, reuse and recycle, and to presort garbage, are all part of Quanzhou's holistic planning, and a good reason why the City of Light may still be around when less enlightened cities have gone the way of the dodo bird.

Notes

---

[1] *Unforgettable Journey—Fifty Years for Fujian Christian Churches on the Three-Self*, published by "The Three Self-Patriotic Movement Committee of Christian Churches in Fujian and the Fujian Christian Council."

[2] Rev. Carstairs Douglas, who did more for Westerner's understanding of the Minnan Dialect than perhaps any other man, was in excellent health one day and dead of virulent cholera the next. Talmadge wrote of Douglas,

> "By overwork he had worn himself out, and made himself an old man while he was yet comparatively young in years. He came to China quite young and at the time of his death was only about forty-six years of age, and yet men who had recently become acquainted with him thought him over sixty… he did more work during the twenty-two years of his missionary life than the most of men accomplish in twice that time…"
>
> "Recently, especially during the last year, it was manifest, at least to others, that his physical strength was fast giving way. Yet he could not be prevailed upon to leave his field for a season for temporary rest, or even to lessen the amount of his work."
>
> "I never knew a more incessant worker. He was a man of most extensive general information. I think I have never met with his equal in this respect. He was acquainted with several modern European languages and was a thorough student of the original languages of Holy Scripture, as witness the fact of his study of the Hebrew Bible, even after his last sickness had commenced. As regards the Chinese language, he was already taking his place among the first sinologues of the land."

[3] Pitcher, Rev. Philip Wilson, *In and About Amoy*, Methodist Publishing House in China, Shanghai and Foochow, 1912., p. 283

第二个阶段中泉州将改进回收过程，将一些废品转化成肥料。与此同时，将会开展一系列活动来鼓励市民减少垃圾排放、重新利用垃圾、循环利用垃圾以及分拣垃圾。这一切均纳入泉州整体规划。泉州这座“光明之城”为什么在许多不开明的城市纷纷走向衰落时，仍屹立于城市之林，原因即在于此。

注释：

1．《难忘的旅程——“三自”方针指导下福建基督教的50年》，由福建基督教三自爱国会和福建基督教协会出版。

2．雷夫·卡斯泰尔斯·道格拉斯致力于让西方人了解闽南语，做出了卓著的贡献，死前一天还好好的，次日便死于急性霍乱。塔尔梅奇提到道格拉斯时这样说：“由于过度劳累，他把自己的身体拖垮了，因而尽管自己还比较年轻，却显得老态龙钟。他到中国的时候还很年轻，去世时年仅46岁，但刚刚认识他的人都以为他已年过花甲了……在22年的传教生涯中，他做的工作远远超过了其他人两倍时间能够取得的成果……”

“最近，尤其在他临终那一年，至少其他人看来，他的体力明显衰弱。但没人能说服他离开岗位休息片刻，或是减少工作量。”

“我从未见过像他这样有毅力的人，他广识博学。我想在这方面没人能与他相比了。他熟谙几种现代欧洲语言，还通晓圣经的源语言，这可以从他对希伯来圣经的研究看出来，甚至在他最后一次犯病后也是如此。至于汉语，他已经跻身本土一流的汉学家之列了。”

3．菲利普·威尔逊·皮彻著：《厦门内外》，中国上海、福州卫理公会教派出版社1912年版，第283页。

Chapter 4

Quanzhou Puppets!

International Puppet Festivals Quanzhou was perfect for hosting the International Puppet Festivals in 1986, 1990 and 2000 because this ancient center of commerce, philosophy and religion is also the home of Chinese marionette, with more puppets than Parliament.

Of course, Quanzhou has many unique crafts, including exquisite paper lanterns, bamboo weaving, porcelain, wood sculpture, tree root carving, paper weaving, lacquer ware, clay sculptures, miniature flour carvings, and 1700 years of Hui'an stone carving, but the icing on the cultural cake is puppets, which stand camphor heads and shoulders above the rest.

Quanzhou Marionette Troupe (泉州木偶剧团) has thrilled audiences in over 30 countries and regions, including performances in London's Royal Festival Hall. Over 30 puppeteers manipulate the puppets while singing to the background of a full Chinese orchestra. Unfortunately, it's hard to catch their acts at home, but you can arrange a once-in-a-lifetime command performance for only 2,000 Yuan. Contact the Vice Director of Performers, Mr. Xia Rong Feng (夏荣峰), at 2237-5497 Mobile Phone: 13959798518 He can also arrange for a tour of the marvelous Puppet Troupe's museum.

Mr. Xia Rong Feng

Chinese puppetry dates back at least to the Han Dynasty 2000 years ago, though legend has it the art began 3000 years with King Mu of the Zhou Dynasty. While returning from hunting in the Kunlun mountains, he saw a carpenter, Yanshi, giving a song and dance performance with his wooden dolls.

第四章

泉州木偶

国际木偶节　泉州于 1986 年、1990 年和 2000 年三次主办国际木偶节,这理所当然:泉州这个古代贸易、哲学和宗教中心,也是中国木偶的发源地。

当然，泉州拥有许多独特的工艺品，包括精美的纸灯、竹编、瓷器、木雕、根雕、纸织画、漆器、泥塑、面人以及有着 1700 年历史的惠安石雕，但是最为重要的文化瑰宝是木偶。这些樟脑木偶远远胜过其他艺术。

泉州木偶剧团　他们的表演打动了 30 多个国家和地区的观众，其中包括在伦敦皇家节庆表演厅的表演。30 多名木偶表演者在操作木偶的同时，还得跟着后台中国乐队演唱。可惜的是，在国内很难看到他们的表演，但是你只需花 2000 元，就可以安排一场独一无二的专场演出。您可以联系表演团的副团长夏荣峰先生，电话：22375497，手机：13959798518。他还可以为您安排一次奇妙的木偶剧团博物馆之行。

中国的木偶至少可追溯到 2000 年前的汉朝时期，传说木偶艺术始于 3000 年前周穆王时期。在昆仑山打猎返回途中，穆王看到一个名叫偃师的木匠用他的木制玩偶表演。

The art evolved over the past two to three thousand years, and reached its epitome in Quanzhou, which has the only Chinese puppets that boast their own musical repertoire performed on unique musical instruments, with over 300 songs and tunes written for the 700+ traditional puppet shows.

These miraculous marionettes have more strings attached than a henpecked husband. When deftly wielded by a master puppeteer, 14 to 36 strings bring the wooden folk to life as they strut and fret with abandon across intricate Chinese stages.

Unlike Western puppeteers, who work mainly with the control, Chinese puppeteers also manipulate groups of strings with their fingers. The longer the strings (up to 2 meters!), the more difficult to operate, but the more expressive the puppets can become as they portray men and women of all ages and professions—or even spirits or wild animals.

Puppets make love and war, bicker and barter, dance, jog and somersault. Their deft hands even retrieve objects from the stage floor! Maybe their lips move too, because Jimmy sure fell for this fellow (who robs cradles too). But everything hinges on puppeteers like Mr. Xia Rong Feng (夏荣峰), Quanzhou Puppet Troupe's Vice Director of Performers (who kindly gave us a tour and a delightful demonstration).

Puppeteers, who often begin training as children, may take 5 years to learn the basics, and over 20 years to completely master the 30+ strings! The sheer complexity of marionettes is amazing. They have a torso, limbs, strings and a hollow wooden head (usually camphor or willow) with internal mechanisms to move the lips and eyes. They have civilians hold pens and cups or swing fans, and military hands to brandish swords, spears, and other weapons. There are even three types of feet: bare, booted, and womanly.

No wonder modern youth aren't keen on devoting their lives to mastering puppetry, and the camphor creatures are getting more complex by the year.

Quanzhou Marionettes

这项艺术在过去的两三千年间得到了发展，在泉州达到鼎盛。只有在泉州，木偶是通过演奏者用独特的乐器演奏出自己的音乐节目，为700多种传统木偶表演而谱写的曲调达300多首。

这些神奇的木偶身上配置的线比一个“妻管严”的丈夫的还要多。在木偶表演大师的熟练操作下，这些木偶趾高气扬地在舞台上走来走去，这14～36条线会把这些木头人演绎得栩栩如生。

西方木偶表演者主要是通过控制器来表演的，和他们不同的是，中国木偶表演者还要用他们的手指操纵若干组线。越长的线（长达2米）越难操纵，但是越具有表现力，因为它们能扮演出不同年龄、不同职业的男女，甚至是精灵或野生动物。

木偶能演绎爱情与战争，斗嘴与交易，舞蹈、跑步以及翻跟斗。它们灵活的双手甚至可以从地板上捡起东西！或许它们的嘴唇也可以动，因为吉米·苏爱上了这个家伙（这家伙还搞姐弟恋呢）。然而一切都要由操纵木偶的人来掌控，比如泉州木偶剧团副团长夏荣峰先生（他很热心地带我们参观了一下并为我们作了演示）。

木偶表演者通常需要从小开始训练，先学习五年的基础知识，若想完全掌握30根以上的线则需要20年以上的时间。木偶的复杂令人惊叹。这些木偶由身躯、四肢、线和一个中空的木制偶头（通常是樟木或柳木制成的）组成，内部设有机械装置用来移动嘴唇和眼睛。木偶中文官的手用来握笔杆、拿杯子或摇扇子；武将的手则用来挥动刀剑、长矛和其他武器。就连它们的脚也分为三种：光脚的、穿靴子的和女人的脚。

怪不得现在的年轻人并不热衷于致力掌握木偶艺术，而这些由樟木做成的木偶也一年年变得更为复杂。

Modern Puppetry Master Puppeteers of the late Qing Dynasty, like Lin Chengchi, could make their puppets draw swords and open umbrellas, but modern puppeteers are as good, or better. And for all their skill, they are continuing to perfect their craft to create utterly breathtaking puppets and performances. Modern stages are deeper, allowing the puppets greater freedom of movement, and allowing the use of different types of puppets simultaneously. For example, the Iron-fan Princess in "Flaming Mountain" is manipulated with strings, poles and fingers.

Camphor wood comes to life!

In *Taming the Monkey*, the simian puppet monkeys about doing everything from riding a bicycle to playing a guitar. In *Drunken Zhong Kui*, Kui fails the imperial examination simply because he is so ugly. After he commits suicide, the King of Hell appoints him "Master demon chaser," but he is so overwhelmed by the number of wicked demons and ghosts that he turns to drink. But in the end he goes on the wagon, and then devotes himself to an eternal battle against wickedness. It's a hell of a story.

Carrying the Tradition Abroad The Quanzhou Puppet Troupe held a workshop for eleven British puppeteers and puppet lovers in London's Little Angel. Puppeteer Christopher Leith had worked with marionettes for over 35 years but still found the training tough. The Chinese said they'd done well in such a short time, and should be up to snuff in a couple of years (a long time for us Westerners, but nothing for Chinese who spend decades at it).

现代木偶艺术 晚清时期，像林承池这样的木偶表演者已经可以让木偶拔出刀剑、撑开雨伞。然而当今的木偶艺术家一样出色甚至技艺更加精湛。尽管如此，他们仍不断完善自己的技艺，以创造出令人惊叹的木偶和表演。现代的木偶表演台比以前更大，这给予木偶更大的移动空间，也允许许多不同的木偶同时在台上表演。比如说，《火焰山》中的铁扇公主就是由线、杆和手指一起操作表演的。

在《驯猴》中，猴子木偶可以表演从骑自行车到弹吉他的各种动作。在《钟馗醉酒》中，钟馗只因人长得丑而在科举考试中名落孙山。在他自杀后，阎罗王封他为判官，但是由于妖魔鬼怪数目众多，他寡不敌众，于是开始借酒浇愁。不过最后他戒了酒，与邪恶势力展开了一场持久战。这是一个很棒的故事。

让传统文化走出国门 在伦敦的小天使木偶剧院，泉州木偶剧团为 11 名英国木偶表演者和木偶爱好者举办了一次小型研习班。克里斯多夫·利思已经做了 35 年多的木偶工作了，但是他仍然觉得训练很难。然而，中国人还是认为在这么短的时间内，这些英国木偶表演者已经做得很好了，相信再经过几年的训练，他们会相当出色的（对西方人来说几年很长，但对花了几十年时间研究木偶的中国人来说几年并不算什么）。

Over 30 countries and regions!

Crafting Puppet Heads Crafting quality camphor wood puppet heads is a vanishing art. People just aren't patient enough nowadays to spend 10 to 15 years mastering this exacting craft. Of the few dozen puppet head makers left in Quanzhou, only ten to twenty make quality puppets. The rest churn out mass produced heads (or, worse yet, press out plastic heads, which may look the same but don't have the soul of the genuine wooden folk).

Puppet heads begin life as a block of camphor wood which is cut to a rough form, sanded, then carved with finer detail. After a coat of paint, and then gloss, further details and hair are added. Cheap heads are churned out in only 3 to 4 days, but it takes Master carver Wang Yique a couple of weeks to give birth to his master-pieces…

The article *Heads Up*, in Dragon Air's in-flight magazine, *The Silk Road*, (September 1988) was about Quanzhou puppet master, Wang Yique, who at the time had made puppets for 60 years. Master Wang said, "I've done this since I was 13 years old. I can't give it up now. Besides, I want to leave something behind after I'm gone." He also noted that none of his children or grandchildren had chosen to make puppet heads.

Wang Yique spends up to half a month carving a head with the exaggerated features that can be seen from a distance. Some puppets have four heads, 4 mouths and 8 eyes—all controllable by one finger!

Glove puppets appear simpler to use than marionettes, but these require years of training. With the forefinger in the head and thumb and middle finger operating the arms, the puppeteer can perform astonishing feats. The puppets pour tea into tiny pots, wield fans, change clothes, brandish swords, or perform somersaults while juggling barrels and dishes on poles balanced on their head. Quite literally breathtaking.

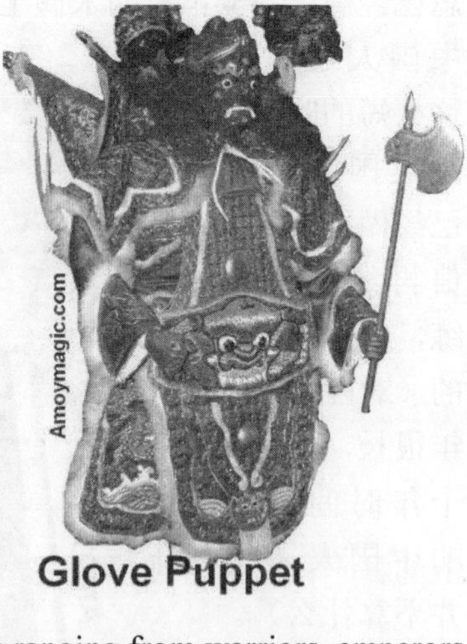

Glove Puppet

Quanzhou Puppet Troupe Museum. I could spend an entire day going through the endless displays of ancient and modern puppets ranging from warriors, emperors and the Monkey King and his entourage, to heroes of the Liberation, foreign villains, and musician puppets that play violins.

Address: No. 24 Tongzheng Lane, Quanzhou （通政巷24号泉州）

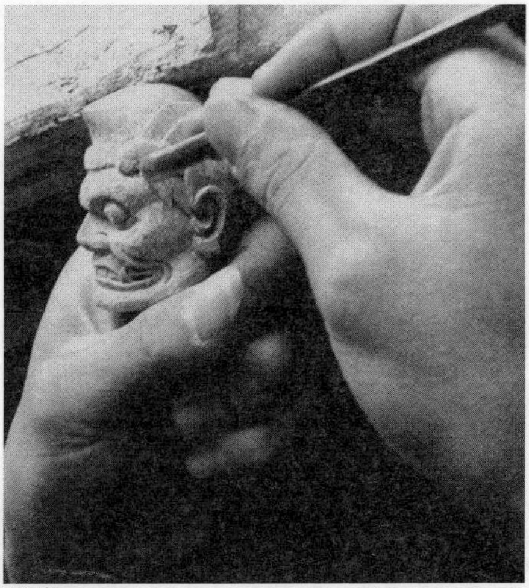

雕刻木偶头　雕刻品质优良的樟脑木偶头这项艺术正在逐渐失传。现在的人们没耐心花费10～15年的时间来掌握这门精细的手艺。泉州仅有的几十个木偶头制作者中，只有10～20个能够做出高质量的木偶头，其余的只是粗制滥造（或者更糟的是，生产出塑料偶头，虽然看起来并无二致，但却丧失了真木偶人的灵魂）。

木偶头的制作首先要选择一块樟木，把樟木切成一个粗坯，磨光，然后再精雕细琢。接着上漆、上光，然后再进一步修饰和添加头发。便宜的木偶头只要 3～4 天就能完成了，但是雕刻大师王奕缺却会花上几个星期来完成他的杰作。

香港港龙航空公司的航空杂志《丝绸之路》（1988 年 9 月）在《抬起头》一文中介绍了泉州木偶艺术大师王奕缺。当时他制作木偶已经有 60 多年。王大师说："我 13 岁就干这一行了，现在我不能放弃，而且我想在我走后能给后人留点东西。"他还提到他的子孙没有人选择制作木偶头这一行当。

王奕缺花了长达半个月的时间来制作一个木偶头，从远处就能让人看到木偶头那夸张或挤眉弄眼的表情。有些木偶有四个头、四张嘴和八只眼睛——却只用一只手指头来操作！

掌中木偶（布袋木偶）比起傀儡来说，掌中木偶看起来更容易操纵些，但是也是需要经过多年的训练才行。用食指撑起头，大拇指和中指操纵双手，这样表演者就可以演绎出令人赞叹的技艺。掌中木偶能将茶倒入小茶壶里、摇扇子、换衣服、舞刀弄剑，还会表演翻跟斗，同时用头部上的杆子顶着盘子或桶表演杂耍。真是令人击节叫好！

泉州木偶剧团博物馆　我可以花上整整一天的时间参观无尽的古代和现代木偶展品，这些木偶从战士、帝王、孙猴王及他的手下，到解放军英雄、外国鬼子和拉小提琴的乐师，　应有尽有。

泉州木偶剧团博物馆地址：泉州市通政巷24号

Puppet Museum Sign

"Quanzhou puppet art has a long history and has been inherited for generations. It is well known at home and abroad as a bright pearl in the treasure house of Quanzhou. On display are master puppet pieces, rich contented articles and photographs, which vividly present the exquisite carved puppet heads and the unique craftsmanship of the puppetmaking, and also shows you the puppeteer's high skill of the string and glove puppet manipulation, as well as the Quanzhou puppet arts' influence in Taiwan and abroad. All of these will present to you a splendid picture of this art. Please step into the gallery of Quanzhou puppet art. Enjoy its magic."

Chen Family Puppet Museum. One of my favorite stops, this topnotch museum is right behind the Ashab Mosque.

Puppet Museum (behind Ashab Mosque)

The display includes marionettes, Jinjiang hand puppets, and many other forms of puppetry. Nicely laid out displays show how the wooden creatures are crafted lovingly from blocks of camphor wood until, in the hands of a master, they spring to life with more gusto than Pinocchio on the trail of the Blue Fairy.

After the museum, walk north (towards the mountains) past the Overseas Chinese hotel, and at Fengze St. (丰泽街—the Copper Buddha Temple and lake will be on your right), turn left. About 100 meters past the KFC is the puppet shop, with a broad assortment of puppets, Chinese souvenirs, full-sized Chinese costumes, and a broad array of silk cloth. In the alley behind are other shops with classical Chinese musical instruments.

Mr. David Zeng (曾国恒), when he's not pulling other strings, can arrange for you to watch artisans carving camphor puppet heads or creating beautifully embroidered puppet costumes. Contact Mr. David Zeng.
E-mail: aghzeng@hotmail.com Mobile: 13799503010
Ofc: 0595-22989432 Fax: 0595-22989431

木偶博物馆标志

“泉州木偶艺术历史悠久，代代相传。它作为泉州宝库中的一颗璀璨的明珠而享誉国内外。这里展览的木偶的杰作、内容丰富的文章和图片生动地表现了木偶头的精雕细琢和木偶制作的独特工艺，同时向您展示了木偶艺人操纵提线木偶和布袋木偶的高超技巧，以及泉州木偶艺术在台湾和海外的影响。所有的这一切将呈现给您一幅优美的木偶艺术画卷。请步入泉州木偶艺术画廊，来享受这神奇的艺术吧！”

Puppet Shop

陈氏木偶馆 是我最喜欢驻足的地方。这家一流的木偶馆在清真寺正后面。

这个精美的博物馆展品丰富，不仅有泉州著名的提线木偶，还有晋江市掌中木偶和其他许多形式的木偶。布局精美的木偶展品展示了那些可爱的木头生灵是如何从一块块樟脑木中雕刻出来，然后在大师手中是怎么变得活蹦乱跳，这比匹诺曹跟踪蓝色仙女更具趣味性。

走出博物馆，向北走（朝着山的方向），过了华侨大厦，到丰泽街（你右边是铜佛庙和湖）后向左拐，肯德基过后 100 米就是木偶店，有各种各样的木偶、各种中国纪念品、各种尺码的中国服装，还有一排排的丝绸。后面的小巷有中国古典乐器店。

曾国恒先生，在泉州电视台工作。不忙的时候，他会安排你参观工匠雕刻樟脑木偶头或制作精美刺绣的木偶服装。

电邮：aghzeng@hotmail.com 手机：13799503010

电话：0595-22989432 传真：0595-22989431

Chapter 5

Academy Upon the Sea

"THE city of Chinchew, in South China, lies a short distance inland from the port of Amoy, opposite the north corner of Formosa. It is about the size of Edinburgh, and, like Edinburgh, is devoted to learning…"
City of Springs, 1902

Overseas Chinese University

Quanzhou Confucian Literary Temple, a block West of Ashab Mosque, on the north side of Tumen Street, showcases Quanzhou's educational legacy, with life-size wax sculptures of Quanzhou's literati.

Dubbed "Seashore Zhoulu" ("Academy/Scholar Upon the Sea") Quanzhou has been a wellspring of literary talent and leadership. From the Tang to the Qing Dynasty (about 1,100 years), Quanzhou churned out 2,473 successful candidates in the highest imperial exams, and 950 famous scholars produced 2,083 influential works. Quanzhou also produced twenty prime ministers.

Famous Quanzhou intellectuals have included writers Ou'yang Zhan, Wang Shenzhong and Huang Kehui, historians Xiaqing, Liang Kejia, Huang Fengxiang and He Qiaoyuan, and philosophers Li Zhi, Cai Qing, Chen Chen and Cai Ding. Quanzhou military talents have included Ding Gongchen, Zeng Gongliang, Yu Daqin, Zheng Chengyong, Su Song, Li Guangdi, etc.

Confucius would have been proud!

Getting There: Buses #1, 3, 18 **Hours:** 8:00-17:30 **Phone**: 2228-3914

Ancient Confucian Education

"Failure to obtain a coveted prize never baffles or discourages the indefatigable competitor. In some cases the contest continues a lifetime with the prize never won. For example at a single prefecture 10,000 candidates presented themselves, under the old regime, at the regular examination. Among them were found the grandfathers, sons, and grandsons, all competing for the same prize, i.e., the same degree. In 1889 the Governor General of Fukien reported that at the autumnal examination in Foochow there were nine candidates over eighty, and one over ninety years old. At still another, thirty five competitors were over eighty and eighteen over ninety. Such indomitable perseverance along educational lines...has been seldom witnessed outside of China. If ever her educational methods conform to Western ideas...Chinese scholarship is destined to take first rank."

Rev. Pitcher (*In and about Amoy*, 1912, p.84)

第五章

泉州——“海滨邹鲁”

“中国南部的泉州城，位于距厦门港不远的内地，与台湾岛的北部遥相呼应。泉州的面积大小与爱丁堡差不多，而且与爱丁堡一样，它也致力于追求学问……”

——《泉之城》（1902年）

Confucian Literary Temple

泉州儒家文庙 位于清净寺的西边，过一个街区，涂门街的北侧就是泉州的教育遗迹文庙,里面陈列着一些与实物大小一样的泉州文人的蜡像。

号称“海滨邹鲁”（类似“海边的学堂”）的泉州是文人和领袖的发源地。从唐代至清朝(大约1100年)，泉州走出的学子有2473人参加了殿试，出过著名文人950位、写述有影响力的著作2083篇。泉州还出过20位宰相。

泉州著名的文人包括作家欧阳詹、王慎中和黄克晦，历史学家吕夏卿、梁克家、黄凤翔和何乔远，哲学家李贽、蔡青、陈琛和蔡鼎。泉州的军事家包括丁拱辰、曾公亮、俞大猷、郑成功、苏颂、李光地等等。

孔子会为此而感到骄傲的!

乘车路线： 乘1、3、18路车均可到达泉州文庙。

开放时间： 8：00—17：30 **电话：** 22283914

古代孔子教育

“不屈不挠的挑战者从未因未能获取令人垂涎的功名而被击退或吓倒过，有些时候，人们甚至用尽一生来夺取功名，到头来却还是两手空空。例如，在旧有的政治制度下，光一个辖区参加常规考试的人就有10000名。他们中，祖父、儿子和孙子同场竞争，争夺同一功名，即同一个级别。1889年，福建总督上报说，在秋季福州考场中，有9位考生超过80岁，有1位超过了90岁。还有另一个考场,有35位考生超过80岁,18位超过90岁.他们在教育行列中如此执著与不屈……这在中国之外是难以看到的。如果中国教育方法与西方观念相一致的话……中国的学者必将是世界第一的。”

——皮彻牧师（《厦门内外》，1912年，第84页）

Anxi Confusion Temple? Anxi also has a famous Confucius Temple (安溪文庙), built in 1001 A.D. Or is it a Confusion Temple? A Quanzhou English map has designated it the "Anxi Confusion Temple." I'm not absolutely certain it is a typo.

Given that Taoism and Confucianism, two of China's main religions, are 180 degrees apart in philosophy, it is surprising that in some temples, people worship both. Unlike Confucianism, which emphasizes absolute obedience, conformity, standards, and education to preserve them, Taoism is the Montessori approach to enlightenment. Taoism means "The Way" (as New Testament Christianity also meant "The Way"), and is based on the teachings of Lao Tzu in 6th Century B.C. China. But with Taoism the way is relative for there are no standards for proper behavior or right and wrong. All is relative. The emphasis is individual freedom, loose government, and mystical experience.

Not surprisingly, the powers that be preferred Confucius to Lao Tzu—though not in the sage's own lifetime….

A Brief Bio of Confucius

(Adapted from *Amoy Magic*)

As a youth, Confucius mastered poetry and history classics, and the six arts (ritual, music, archery, charioteering, calligraphy and arithmetic). In his 30s, he became a teacher and devoted his life to insuring that Chinese for the next 2000 years followed suit.

Confucius humbly claimed to be a common man of ordinary intellect, so anyone could follow his lead in seeking perfection through study and conformity to society. But few wanted to follow Confucius' lead because he was usually jobless, homeless, and half-starved.

Confucius' failures ate at him. He said, "It is these things that cause me concern: failure to cultivate virtue, failure to explore in depth what I have learned, inability to do what I know is right, and inability to reform myself when I have defects."

I think what really ate at him was his wife, who was also homeless and half-starved – not choice ingredients in the elixir of marital bliss.

While claiming to be just one of the boys, the unemployed Confucius said he was unstoppable and immortal until his heavenly mandate was completed. "If Heaven does not intend this culture to be destroyed, then what can the men of K'uang do to me?"

安溪“混乱”的寺庙？ 安溪也有一座著名的文庙,建于公元1001年。或者它是一座“混乱的”庙?（译注：作者在下文中提到那张泉州英文版地图中，将“安溪文庙”的英文误写成“Anxi Confusion Temple”，因为confusion的意思是“混乱”，故有此疑问。）一张泉州英文版地图上标有“Anxi Confusion Temple（安溪混乱的寺庙）”英文字样（正确的写法应该是“Anxi Confucian Literary Temple”——译者注）。但我不能绝对确定它是打字错误。

作为中国两大宗教，道教和儒教在哲学思想上完全相左，然而令人惊讶的是，在一些寺庙中人们往往两者都崇拜。不同于儒教强调绝对的服从、一致、标准和通过教育来保护他们,道教是蒙台梭利(1870—1952，意大利女医师及教育家——译者注)式的教化。道教意为“方法”（正如基督教新约意思也是“方法”）,是建立在公元前6世纪老子的教义的基础上的。但是在道教看来，方法是相对的，因为没有既定的标准来衡量行为是否得当以及事物的对错。一切都是相对的。它强调的是个性的自由、宽松的统治和神秘的经验。

不足为奇的是，当权者推崇的是孔子而不是老子——尽管这位圣人在有生之年没有得到重视……

孔子简介

（节选自《魅力厦门》）

早在年轻的时候，孔子已熟读了大量的诗歌和历史典籍，并精通六艺（礼、乐、射、御、书、数）。30岁的时候，他成为一名老师，毕生致力于教育，中国后来2000多年的教育都以他为榜样。

孔子谦称自己是一名才智一般的普通人，因此，任何人都可以跟随他通过学习和顺应社会来寻求完美。但是很少有人愿意跟随他，因为他总是无业可从、无家可归、半饥半饱。

孔子的失败让他感到困扰。他说：“正是这些事情让我担忧:没能培养德行,没能更加深入地探究我的所学,无法去做我认为是正确的事情,而当我有缺点时我也无法改正它们。”

我想让他真正感到困扰的是他的妻子，她也是无家可归、半饥半饱——在美满婚姻的万能药中缺乏首选的成分。

在宣称自己仅是这些男子中的一员时,失业的孔子说他是不可阻挡、流芳百世的，直至他完成上天赋予自己的使命。“如果上天无意让这种文化毁灭,狂人又能奈我如何?”

Confucius

Not much, except keep him unemployed. So at age 56 he left the inhospitable leaders of Lu, who still weren't hiring, and spent 12 years traveling about with a slowly growing following. He returned home at age 67 and died 6 years later, leaving behind 3,000 disciples who were usually jobless, homeless and half-starved. But they kept alive the teachings that would become dear to 2400 years of imperial hearts.

Confucians taught a grassroots philosophy that the foundation of society is filial piety. Obedience to father and elders and magistrates and emperor guarantees social order, stability, and peace. Deviations, of any kind (like preferring coffee over tea) insure anarchy.

Emperors loved Confucius's emphasis on obedience, but his warning that unjust governments would be overthrown did not go over as well. In 231 B.C., the emperor tried to eliminate Confucius' influence by destroying every book in China, but someone missed a few volumes. Confucians crawled back out of the woodwork, regained the upper hand, and have been stacking China's deck ever since (while being careful to remove all the wild cards).

My Favorite Confucian Quotes

Fishy Fishing, "子钓而不纲." "Confucius fished but didn't use a net." (No wonder he was poor)

On Women: 子曰：唯女子与小人为难养也，近之则不孙，远之则怨 "Girls are the most impossible; too close and they lose their humility; keep your distance and they're disgruntled." (Lesson: You can't win!)

"Aspire to the principle, behave with virtue, abide by benevolence, and immerse yourself in the arts."

除了失业之外，他并没有尝到多少苦头。因此在56岁时他离开了冷漠无情的鲁国国君，依旧是无业可从，花了12年的时间去游历各个地方，逐渐有了一些个门徒。67岁时他回到了家，6年后便去世了，留下了3000名常常是无业可从、无家可归、半饥半饱的弟子。然而他们使这种教育发扬光大，令2400年来帝王们深感珍惜。

孔子所传授的基本哲学思想认为，社会的基础在于子女的孝行。对父亲、长者、长官和帝王的服从能保证社会的有序、安定与和平。任何背离(比如偏爱咖啡而不是茶)将导致无政府状态。

帝王们偏爱孔子所强调的服从，但是对孔子不公平的政府会被推翻的这一警告并不欢迎。公元前231年，秦始皇为了消除儒家思想的影响而焚毁了中国民间所有的儒家典籍，但是有人偷偷藏留了几册。儒家学者经历这场浩劫后重新恢复了它的主导地位，儒家思想从此以后深深地影响着中国（同时非常小心地去除其所有的异见）。

我最喜欢的儒家名言

关于钓鱼——子钓而不纲。“孔子只钓鱼，但不撒渔网。”（难怪他穷困）

关于女人——子曰：“唯女子与小人为难养也，近之则不孙，远之则怨。”（切记：你赢不了。）

“志于道，据于德，依于仁，游于艺。”

Confucian Temple (1902)

#7 School – a Window on the Future

When Quanzhou Evening News reporter Wu Zehua (吴泽华) heard I was giving three Americans a tour of Quanzhou, he invited us to visit a school. I was hesitant because our schedule was tight and, frankly, my friends didn't fly 12,000 miles to China to see a school—especially when one was a teacher himself. But we did visit the school, which was tucked away on a small street opposite Mazu Temple—and that tour turned out to be the highlight of our day.

I've long studied Quanzhou's rich history, but #7 offers a glimpse into Quanzhou's even richer future. After our visit I could well understand how #7 shot from relative obscurity in the early '90s to become one of the nation's most innovative schools today. In 2007, Qinghua University chose #7 as one of the country's top six schools, with national and international recognition in everything from traditional academic and athletic pursuits to robotics innovation!

#7 School began on the premises of Mazu Temple in May, 1937, as the private "Huiming Middle School"私立晦鸣中学"[1]. The high school was added in 1948, and in 1956 the school went public, was moved across the street to its present location, and renamed #7. But it wasn't until the 90s that the school underwent its radical metamorphosis, thanks primarily to radical and visionary leadership.

① The name is from a phrase in Confucius' Analects: "When wind and rain howls darkly, birds cry unceasingly"《论语》"风雨如晦，鸡鸣不已").

魅力七中——未来之窗

当泉州晚报社记者吴泽华听说我正带着三位美国朋友游览泉州时，他邀请我去参观一所学校。我当时有些犹豫，因为我们的行程很紧张，坦白地讲，我的朋友可不是飞越一万二千英里到中国来参观一所学校，何况其中一位也是一名老师。我最后同意到这所深藏在妈祖庙对面一条小街里的学校，出乎意料，这次参观竟成为当天最大的亮点。

对于泉州悠久的历史我一直都在研究，但七中却展示了这个城市更加辉煌的未来。参观后我也明白了为什么七中能从 90 年代初期一所默默无闻的学校迅速成为今天中国最富有创新意识的一所学校。正是全国乃至世界对七中在拔尖和全面素质人才的培养、科技创新以及学校发展潜力等方面的认可，2007 年，清华大学将七中排名为全国前六。

泉州七中的前身“私立晦鸣中学”成立于 1937 年，位于今天的妈祖庙。1948 年设立高中部，1956 年成为公办学校并且搬迁到街对面今天的校址，更名为泉州七中。紧跟改革开放的步伐，在富有拼搏精神和远见的学校领导的带领下，七中开始了她翻天覆地的变革。

1948 Grad Photo 1948 年秋，初中毕业生与教职员合影

Leadership #7's Party Secretary, Lin Peihua 林培华, has a Master's in Education and is a Provincial Model Worker. Headmaster and Vice Party Secretary, Lu Qingshan (卢清山), has Masters' degrees in both Education and Management Science, and has received awards such as the Provincial "May 1st" Workers' award. And teachers, age 33 years on average, are all graduates of some of the nation's top teacher's colleges; 28 have post-graduate work.

Visionary Leadership

Global Mission #7 School's mission is to "Nurture Modern Chinese, Healthy in Body, Spirit, Mind, and Morals" (培养身心健康的现代中国人). "Modern" implies suitable knowledge and competitiveness for modern global society—graduates who are cooperative and innovative. But the school aims not just for "Modern Chinese" but responsible *global* citizens by developing excellent English and communication skills through an international curriculum.

An International School In 2002, #7 School was Fujian's first middle school to offer a joint program with a foreign school. The school has several Canadian teachers, and graduates of 2005 and 2006, recipients of dual Chinese and Canadian diplomas, were qualified to study abroad in an English-speaking country. The school further promotes communication skills with activities such as English corners and competitions, an English cultural festival, English arts performances, Christmas parties, etc. Students with exceptional promise can further hone their talents at the school's modern broadcast and recording studio.

10 National and 60 Provincial Awards

The Pay Off #7 went from 3rd level in 1990 to 2nd level in 1993, and 1st level in 1995. Today, the school is one of Fujian's 12 model high schools and a provincial 1st-level middle school. In 2001, the school's management received ISO9002 certification, and in 2003 it became one of Fujian's first schools to be designated a National Model school The school has received 10 national and 60 provincial awards in everything from athletics and linguistics to science and environmentalism.

领导班子 泉州七中党总支书记林培华是教育硕士、省劳模；校长兼党总支副书记卢清山拥有教育学和管理学双硕士学位，省“五一”劳动奖章获得者。全校教师平均年龄 33 岁，全部毕业于全国知名师范大学，其中有 28 位研究生。

全球眼光 泉州七中的使命是培养身心健康的现代中国人；“现代”意味着掌握全球化社会的知识和竞争能力——培养富有合作和创新意识的人才。学校的定位不仅仅局限在“现代中国人”，还瞄准了培养负责任的国际公民——七中正通过国际合作办学提高学生的英语水平和沟通能力。

国际学校 2002 年，泉州七中通过与海外学校合作成为福建省首家推出合作办学的中学。学校里有好几位加拿大籍教师，该项目 2005 年、2006 年的毕业生获得中国和加拿大的双文凭，顺利进入英语国家就读大学。

Foreign Faculty

为进一步促进学生的语言交流技能，学校还举办英语角、英语竞赛、英语文化节、英语才艺表演、圣诞晚会等等。有能力的同学还可以进入学校现代化的广播和电视工作室发展个人才能。

春华秋实 泉州七中从 1990 年三级达标到 1993 年二级达标，1995 年晋升为省一级达标中学；今天七中是福建省 12 所示范性高中之一；2001 年学校的管理通过了 ISO 9002 的认证，2003 年被认定为福建省首批国家级示范性高中；同时学校在体育、语言、科学和环保等方面获得 10 项国家级、60 项省级奖励。

Academic Excellence In 2005, 64 students scored over 600 on the college entrance exams, with 8 gaining entrance to Qinghua and Beijing University and 38 entering the Top Ten. In 2006, student Ceng Chunming (曾春明) scored 673, highest in the province, and 164 students scored over 600; 11 students entered Qinghua and Beijing Univ., and 42 entered China's Top Ten.

Nat'l Chemistry Competition Gold Medalist Shi Qiulong

Students have won numerous national and international academic and scientific competitions, including 18 national and international gold medals during the first few months of 2007. Since the Robotics Lab was built in 2003, alumni have won 45 gold medals in robotics. In October, 2006, three #7 students were China's only students to land gold medals in the International Youth Robotics Competition in Thailand.

Fine Tuning the "2061 RoboBand"

The **Year 2061 RoboBand** (2061 星空乐队) won China's only gold medal for middle school students at the International Youth Robotics Competition. The robotic ensemble is fully programmable, or it will play along to music played on a CD, fingers, hands and bodies moving with the music!

RoboFish Explorer (水下观察者) not only won a gold medal in the 2006 Int'l Youth Robotics Competition, but also the prize for "Most Innovative Technology." Whereas most underwater devices disturb the environment, churning sediment with propellers, this remote-controlled fish propels itself gracefully and naturally with fins and tail as it uses GPS or pre-programmed guidance to analyze its environment and transmit video from the fish head's camera. I asked Vice Principal Chen if the robotic fish was good to eat and he said, "No. Too many bones!"

#7 is also developing a Genetics Lab 基因工作室) overseen by 4 graduate biology researchers of Zhongshan University's Genetics Lab.

Zeng Chunming, Fujian Top Score
2006 College Entrance Exam

一流成绩 2005年，七中有64位学生高考成绩总分超过600分，其中8名学生被清华、北大录取，38名进入全国排名前十的大学；2006年该校曾春明同学高考673分获福建省文科状元，164位学生高考成绩总分超过600分，11名同学进入清华、北大，42名同学进入全国排名前十的大学。

七中学子还在许多国家级和国际级的学术、科学竞赛中获奖：其中2007年头几个月18位学生获全国或国际金牌；从2003年建立机器人工作室至今，该校学生获得45枚金牌。2006年10月，3名七中学生成为在泰国举办的国际青少年机器人比赛中唯一获金牌的中国学生。

他们的代表作“2061星空乐队”是中学生组唯一获金奖的作品。这组机器人完全是程序化控制，可以通过电子眼扫描乐谱，转化为电子信号指挥机器人合奏，也可以重复人的演奏，手指、手和身体随音乐摆动。

2007年，机器人“水下观察者”荣获一枚“最佳技术奖” 金牌。大部分的水下工具会干扰环境，卷起沉积物，可是这个鱼型机器人可以优雅、自然地摆动它的鳍和尾巴，同时GPS定位和预装的程序可以分析环境和通过头上的摄像机传输图像。（我问陈副校长这条机器鱼是否好吃，他说不好吃，骨头太多了。）

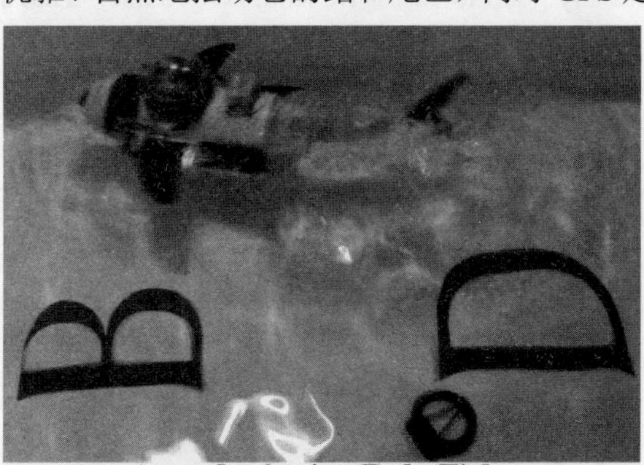

Award-winning RoboFish

七中正在组建一个基因工作室，由四位中山大学毕业的研究生负责指导。

Enthusiastic Alumni #7's metamorphosis has of course excited its alumni, who are proudly pouring funds in to their alma mater. Alumni donations have helped build the state-of-the-art gymnasium (Fujian's best), the

HK Alumni Bldg.

library, the Hong Kong Alumni Building, the Quanzhou Alumni Building, the Philippine Alumni Building, as well as provide numerous scholarships. During the 75th anniversary, alumni established the 20 million Yuan "Quanzhou #7 Scholarship" (泉州七中助学奖学基金)—Fujian's largest scholarship of its kind.

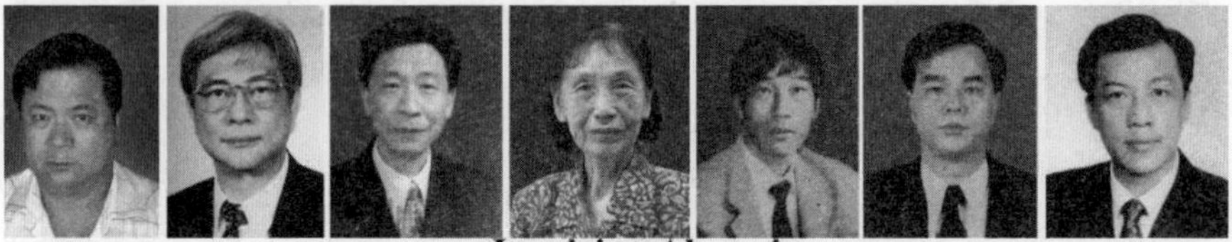

Inspiring Alumni

A large diorama near the front gate displays numerous endangered animals, all stuffed and in natural poses amongst trees and shrubs. I again joked with Vice Principal Chen and asked, "Are any good to eat?" He said, "Of course! That's why we've built this—to encourage students to protect them, not eat them!"

This diorama, the first and last thing I saw at #7, well exemplifies #7's holistic values—its emphasis upon innovation and progress balanced with stewardship of resources. I've no doubt that #7 will indeed produce not only "Modern Chinese" but also global citizens capable of leading China into the new century. So after you've toured historic Quanzhou, explore the Quanzhou of the future—at #7 School.

Address: Quanzhou Licheng District, #40 Tianhou Rd.
Postcode: 362000
http://www.qz.qz.cn
Tel：0595－22204308
FAX：0595－22207825

Giving to their Alma Mater

拳拳校友　七中的快速发展也激励了她的校友，他们给母校投入大量的资金；校友捐资建起了当时福建省中学最好的体育馆，还有图书馆、香港校友楼、泉州校友楼、菲律宾校友楼及设立巨额奖学金。在该校75周年校庆时，校友捐资成立了 2000万元的“泉州七中助学奖学基金”，是福建省中学同类奖学金中最大的。

靠近前门有一个展示许多动物标本的生态园，所有的动物都以自然的姿态摆放在海洋、森林、沙漠等模拟环境中。我又和陈副校长开玩笑，问他这些是否好吃，他说当然人们会这么想，这就是我们建这个的目的，教育学生去保护它们，而不是吃掉它们！

这个立体模型展示，是我在七中最早和最后看到的东西，却很好地展示了七中的整体价值——既鼓励创新和进步又很好地与资源保护结合。我坚信 七中将真正培养的不单是“现代中国人”，而且是能带领中国进入新世纪的国际公民。因此，参观完泉州这个历史名城，别忘了到泉州七中一游——它展示着泉州的未来。

地址：泉州市鲤城区天后路 40 号。邮编：362000　网址：http://www.qz.qz.cn

电话：0595-22204308　传真：0595-22207825

Rev. Anderson
London Presbyterian Mission

Peiyuan High School Just West of Kaiyuan Temple (we're headed there soon!), Peiyuan was started in 1904 by Mr. Anderson (安礼逊牧师), of the London Presbyterian Mission, and received the patronage of no other than Dr. Sun Yat-sen!

Rev. Anderson's father was one of the men who had helped free Dr. Sun when he was kidnapped by the Qing in London. To express his appreciation, Dr. Sun encouraged Chinese to contribute towards building Anderson's school, and in 1920 he wrote an inscription for the school. In 1980, his wife, Soong Ching Ling (Honorary President of China) wrote another inscription to the left of her husband's.

Dr. Sun's inscription reads, right to left, 共进大同. Tong Da Jin Gong: "All Enter Future Heaven." Madame Soong's inscription, read left to right, is 为国树人. Wei Guo Shu Ren: "Bring Up People for the Country."

Anderson Library, built in 1927, was Quanzhou's tallest building (aside from the East and West Pagodas). It resembles a church inside, perhaps because until the 1950s it was also used for church services.

The Philippine extension was established in the 1920s, and Taiwan's 1st of 3 branches was begun in the 1950s. The schools recent expansion and renovation has been possible in part because of generous gifts from alumni and overseas Chinese, and the school has recently bought a factory site to the south for campus expansion.

培元中学　位于开元寺西边(我们很快就赶到那里看看!)的培元中学于1904年由伦敦长老会教区的安礼逊牧师创办,并得到了孙中山博士的资助!

Peiyuan High School

当孙博士在伦敦被清朝政府绑架的时候,安礼逊牧师的父亲参与解救孙先生。为表达他的感激之情，孙博士鼓励中国人捐资兴办安礼逊学校，1920年，他为该学校题词。1980年，他的夫人宋庆龄女士(中国名誉主席)也在丈夫题词的左边题了词。

孙博士的题词,从右至左为“共进大同”。宋庆龄夫人的题字,从左至右为“为国树人”。

Peiyuan High School—100 Years of Excellence

安礼逊图书馆　建于1927年，是当时泉州最高的建筑（除了东西塔外）。馆内就像是一个教堂，或许是因为在20世纪50年代之前，它还用于教会活动的缘故吧。

菲律宾分校建于20世纪20年代，在台湾有三所分校，其中第一所分校成立于20世纪50年代。培元中学近来之所以能进行扩建与翻新，一部分原因是校友和华侨的慷慨捐助。最近，学校买下了位于校园南端的一个工厂进行校园的扩建。

Vice Premier Li Lanqing (李岚清) visited Peiyuan in 1994 and wrote the large inscription that is now beside the 300 year old tree. In 2004, the school celebrates 100 years of producing graduates who have gone on to distinctive careers in business, academics and government, and the school has branches overseas. Many exemplify the school motto on the wall beside Li Langqing's inscription:

真理自由服务 (Trust, Freedom, Service).

Community Service Peiyuan's motto seems to have also been adopted by Quanzhou Christians. Since Fujian's church services were begun again in 1979, the province has opened over 1500 churches, including over 170 churches in Quanzhou alone—and community service is a big part of Quanzhou Christians' lives. In 1998, Fujian churches donated over 800,000 RMB and over 100,000 articles of clothing to flood victims along the Yangzi, Songhua and Nen Rivers. The Quanzhou church donated 10,000 Yuan to Anxi's Bailai County for renovating primary school classrooms, and giving free medical care to Yongchun minorities. Contributions to medicine and education are also being made by individual Christians like cardiologist Dr. Lin Yinwang.

Volunteer Medical Work

Dr. Lin is former director of Internal Medicine in Quanzhou's #1 Hospital, as well as Vice Director of the 10th Standing Committee of the Quanzhou Municipal People's Congress and representative of the 6th, 7th, and 8th PPC Dr. Lin established a cardiovascular clinic in Jinjiang #1 Hospital, and has published dozens of papers in medical journals. Other Christian doctors also volunteer their services in clinics around the city.

Vice Premier Li Lanqing's Inscription

李岚清副总理 于1994年参观了培元中学并为学校题词，词碑现位于一株有 300年历史的古树旁。

2004 年,培元中学举办建校 100 周年庆典,庆祝学校培养出的毕业生在商界、学术界和政界都有着非凡的建树,学校在海外设有分校。许多校友实践了位于李岚清题词旁的校训：真理、自由、服务。

教区活动 泉州的基督教徒似乎也采用了培元中学的校训。自从1979年福建教会活动重新兴起的时候，省内就已经开设了1500多个教会，其中仅在泉州就有170多个。社团服务是泉州基督教徒生活的一大部分。1998年，福建教会捐献了80多万元人民币和10多万件衣服给生活在长江、松花江和嫩江沿岸一带的灾民。泉州教会为安溪白濑镇捐献了1万元用于翻修小学教室，并且还为永春少数民族提供免费的医疗服务。基督教徒个人也一直在医药和教育方面做贡献，比如心脏学家林应望医生。

林医生是泉州市第一医院原内科主任，也是第十届泉州市人大常务委员会副主任，第六届、第七届、第八届政协委员。林医生在晋江市第一医院设立了心血管门诊部，并且在医学学术期刊上发表了许多论文。其他信仰基督教的医生也在市区周边诊所志愿为人民服务。

Chapter 6

Quanzhou Outskirts

600 meters = 1.1 kilometers?

Quanzhou Shaolin Temple 泉州少林寺 It seems every Fujian village lays claim to: 1) tastiest food, 2) prettiest girls, and 3) deadliest Kungfu (not always in that order).

Each village has its own martial arts traditions, passed down only to those of the same surname. Many claim that all Southern Shaolin Kungfu originated right here in Quanzhou's Shaolin Temple (Fujian's Putian and Fuqing make the same claim, but 1,000 years ago Putian was part of Quanzhou anyway).

Wingin' It The Shaolin Temple, is behind the Sports Stadium at the top of Zayton St. (刺桐路，on Dongyue Hill (东岳山). It is exactly 1.1 km past the sign that says you only have 600 meters to go. I asked the abbot about the discrepancy and he said, "It's 1.1 km if you drive, but Kung Fu monks fly straight up!"

Quanzhou Southern Shaolin temple was built in the early Tang Dynasty by Zhikong, a monk from the Songshan Shaolin Temple up north. After the temple was destroyed in 1763 A.D., the Shaolin tradition continued to be taught in Congfu Temple (see below), but now that so many folks around the world are getting their kicks out of Kungfu, the Shaolin temple was recently rebuilt. Each year, thousands of Kungfu enthusiasts make pilgrimages to this Mecca for martial arts enthusiasts (and also visit the two local martial arts schools).

Kungfu Architecture Notice the trimmings and carvings under the temple eaves. Unlike other temples, they all depict Southern Shaolin monks in different fighting postures.

第六章

泉州市郊

Quanzhou S. Shaolin Temple
(Photo courtesy of Abbot Shi)

泉州少林寺　似乎福建的每个村落都声称有三绝：（1）绝佳的美食；（2）绝色的美女；（3）绝命的武功（并不总是这个顺序）。每个村落都有自己的功夫传统，由同姓传承。然而据称所有的南少林武术都起源于泉州少林寺！（福建的莆田和福清都如此宣称，但一千年前，莆田怎么说都是泉州的一部分。）

泉州少林寺位于刺桐路尽头的体育场后面的东岳山上。路标提示前方 600 米处为少林寺，实际上却是 1.1 公里。我曾向住持提及此事，问他“是不是 1.1 公里是开车上去的距离，而 600 米是和尚们直接向上爬的路程？”

泉州南少林寺于初唐由自北方嵩山少林寺云游至此的智空和尚所建。该寺历尽沧桑，于公元 763 年被完全毁坏。少林传统在崇福寺得到延续。然而，由于世界各地有如此多的人对武功的拳脚兴趣正浓，因而最近少林寺得以重建。每年，成百上千的功夫爱好者来到这个武术圣地朝拜，参观当地的两所武术学校。

功夫建筑　看！寺庙屋檐下的雕刻和其他寺庙不同，刻画着南少林和尚的各种武术招式。

Abbot Shi Changding

Abbot Shi Changding I'd have never imagined a 30-year-old like Master Shi Changding (释常定) could be abbot of S. Shaolin Temple! Since he began kung fu at age 13, Master Shi has made a name for himself, and helped put Quanzhou's S. Shaolin Temple back on the map. The young abbot is also a Wushu Colonel, assistant secretary-general of Quanzhou Wushu association, adviser to the France-Fujian martial arts association, and people's conference representative. He has also helped initiate many international exchange programs with martial arts groups and organizations throughout Asia, Europe and the Americas. Now Master Shi has set his sites on expanding the Southern Shaolin Complex.

Contact Master Shi at: Shaolin Temple, Dong Yue Mountain, Quanzhou City, Fujian, P.R. of China, 362000
Chinese Address: 中国福建泉州市东岳山少林寺 362000

Getting to S. Shaolin Temple: Bus #7, #10, #11, #13, #19
Hours: 6:00 - 22:00 **Phone**: 2279-5119

An American Delegation

Southern Shaolin Kungfu Museum
You'll get lots of kicks out of the Wushu (martial arts) hall of Quanzhou Sports Center. The four key exhibits are:

1. "Shaolin Wushu Handed on from Ancient Times and Developed in Quanzhou."
2. "Heyday of Shaolin Giving Birth to a Multitude of Heroes."
3. "Carry Forth the Good Tradition and Let 100 Flowers Blossom." (I suggested adding a "Let 100 Lawnmowers Follow" annex).
4. "Make Friends with Wushu and Let the Seeds of Friendship Spread All Over the World."

释常定住持　我从未想到年仅30的释常定大师能出任南少林寺住持！释住持13岁习武，现今已小有名气，并且促成了泉州南少林寺的重建。这位年轻的住持同时也是一个武术团长，泉州武术协会秘书长助理，法国·福建武术协会顾问和人大代表。他促成了与亚洲、欧洲、美洲的武术团体和组织间的许多国际交流项目。如今，释大师致力于扩大南少林的建设。

S. Shaolin Museum

联系方式：中国福建泉州市东岳山少林寺释常定（大师）收　邮编：362000　联系电话：（0595）22795119

乘车路线：乘 7 路、10 路、11 路、13 路、19 路公车，均可到达。

开放时间：6：00—22：00

电话：22795119

泉州南少林武术博物馆　泉州体育中心的武术馆很有吸引力。该馆主要由四部分内容组成：

1．少林传灯，衍播泉南；　　2．武风鼎盛，英雄辈出；
3．继承传统，百花齐放；　　4．以武会友，情满四海。

(Photo courtesy of Abbot Shi)

Stone Bamboo 石笋 Just outside the city's western wall, sometime before 1011 A.D., someone erected the 4.18 meter high "stone bamboo shoot." But given the totem was the object of fertility worship (生殖崇拜, shengzhi chongbai), I suspect that "bamboo shoot" is just a euphemism for the biological appendage that it closely resembles (though a bit big, granted). To make sure I did not miss the allusion, my companion exclaimed, "The shoot is aligned with those two hills. See? They're the breasts! Can you tell?" I wasn't ready to make a clean breast of things so I kept quiet (yes, it does happen).

Stone Bamboo Shoot

Fertility totems are still used in Thailand, where new brides rub against them to insure they have a baby boy. I don't know if it works or not, but given China's 1.3 billion population, I think they should erect a barricade around this shoot.

> After some personal problem, the prefectural magistrate, Gao Huilian, had the Stone Bamboo split in two; it was reassembled in the 15th century. Since this is the only fertility totem in the region, scholars assume it was erected by Indian traders (probably Shivaites).

Qingyuan Mountain 清源山 After the Maritime Museum, Kaiyuan Temple, and puppets, next on my list is Qingyuan Mountain. Just 2.5 km north of the city, this is not only a beautiful place (called "Fujian's Fairy Land") but also a holy site for many religions, including Buddhism, Taoism, Tibetan Buddhism (and, in addition, is said to be the burial site of the founder of the Cao An Manichaean Temple).

Qingyuan (Clear Water) Mountain is the perfect destination when someone tells you to go take a hike. Secluded and silent, save for the sound of waterfalls and gurgling brooks, the densely wooded trails wind past pagodas, temples, and 36 caves. Pilgrims used to worship the hundreds of statues in the caves until the Red Guard destroyed the relics. Now visitors worship empty holes, perhaps because they are holey.

石笋 在泉州西城墙外，公元1011年的某个时候，有人建造了这根4.18米高的“石笋”。以“生殖崇拜”一说，我想，“石笋”不过是对极其相似的男性生殖器的婉转说法而已（尽管有点大）。为了确认我领悟到了这种暗示，我的同伴大喊道：“这石笋和那两座山是并列着的，看到了么？它们看起来像乳房呢！你看出来了吗？”我不打算和盘托出，所以保持沉默。

Ye Olde Breasts

生殖崇拜在泰国依然存在，那里的新娘们都要去摩擦图腾，希望能生儿子。我不知道是否灵验。考虑到中国有 13 亿人口，我想他们肯定得在这特别的“石笋”围上栅栏。

> 由于某种个人原因，地方行政官高慧廉命令将石笋一分为二。石笋于15世纪被重合为一。这也是此地区唯一的一座生殖图腾，学者们认为应该是由印度高人建立的。

清源山 在介绍了海外交通史博物馆、开元寺和木偶之后，接下来我要介绍的是清源山。清源山位于泉州市北郊 2.5 公里处，它不仅是美景胜地（有“闽海蓬莱第一山”之美誉），而且还是许多宗教，包括佛教、道教和藏传佛教的圣地（除此之外，据说这还是草庵摩尼寺的建立者的埋葬地）。

清源（清澈的水源）山是徒步旅行者们的理想去处。幽深、寂静，有瀑布的声响和汩汩的溪流声，绿树掩映的小径自宝塔、寺庙和三十六洞蜿蜒而过。过去，香客们朝拜洞中的上百尊雕像，但后来雕像遭到红军摧毁。或许这些洞是神圣的，现在，游客们仍对着空洞朝拜。

Before (Buddhas) *and* After (Tibetan Lamas!)

Qingyuan's vast collection of relics ranges from "Old Stone Saint," 老君岩，China's largest Taoist statue, to the statues of 3 Tibetan Buddhist Lamas 三世佛 in Bixiao Cave (long thought to be Buddhas until the outer layer of concrete was removed to reveal Tibetan lamas). The Manichaean who founded Cao'an Monastery, the planet's last Manichaean temple, is buried on Qingyuan, though no one knows where.

Ancient Escalator?

Other popular Qingyuan Mtn. sites include the statue of a seated Avalokitesvara, beside the Thousand Hand Rocks, a statue of Sakyamuni inside Niche Cavern (on the left peak), and the tomb of Hong Yi. One of the best views of Quanzhou City is from "South Platform Rock." And you can reach all of these sites easily and safely, thanks to endless trails laid out by centuries of nature lovers and devotees of various religions who have laid out paths and steps—lots of steps!

Steps On his last trip to Quanzhou, Alan Smith, founder of LivCom (p. xvi), mopped his perspiring brow and said, "Chinese steps only go up--never down!"

Over the past 5,019 years, Chinese have built steps up every hillside and mountain in China. No doubt, even Mount Everest has steps on the Chinese side, and Tibetans at the top sell mineral water, roasted water melon seeds, and peanuts.

Many is the time I've imagined myself to be the first to hike some remote hill, only to stumble across granite steps worn smooth by time and tourists. But on the bright side—it's not likely that hikers in China can ever get lost.

Old Stone Saint 老君岩 The Song Dynasty Old Stone Saint ("#1 Laozi Under Heaven!") is China's oldest Taoist sculpture, and the largest (5.1 m. high by 7.3 m. wide). Legend claims that if you rub his nose you'll live 120 years; rub his eye and you'll reach 160. Folks used to say you'd die early if you rubbed his mouth, but such down in the mouth talk didn't exactly bolster tourism, so now locals brightly mouth off, "Rub mouth, get good luck!" Alas, 1,000 years of rubbing Lao Tzu the wrong way was rubbing his nose away, so a few years back they fenced him off and hired a guard so no else can take Lao Zi for granite.

Getting There: Bus#3, # 5, #20, or Special Tourist Bus #601

Hours: 5:30 - 16:00 **Phone:** 2278-3474

清源山宗教文物的收藏令人惊奇，从中国最大的道教雕像老君岩（见下图）到碧霄岩的三世佛雕像（要不是凿开混凝土外层，人们一直以为是如来佛像）。建造世上最后一座教寺院——草庵摩尼寺的那位摩尼教徒就安葬在清源山上，但没有人知道其具体位置。

清源山的热门景点还包括在千手岩旁的观音的坐像、瑞像岩（在左峰）的释迦牟尼的雕像和弘一法师的舍利塔。站在南台岩上眺望泉州，美景尽收眼底。您可以轻松、安全地到达这些景点，这多亏数百年来无数的爱好自然的人士和各种宗教信徒们，他们开出了路，铺上了台阶——数不尽的台阶！

台阶　“国际花园城市”发起者——阿兰·史密斯(详见第 xvii 页)，在上次泉州之行时，擦拭着满是汗水的额头说：“中国的台阶只有向上，没有向下。”

在过去的5019年里，中国人在国内的每座山都建了台阶。难怪，连珠穆朗玛峰的中国一侧也有台阶，而且，西藏人在最高处卖矿泉水、炒西瓜子和花生。

有多少次，我以为自己是某遥远山处的第一个远足者，结果发现自己蹒跚于被时间和游客磨得光滑的花岗岩台阶。但从另一方面看，远足者们在中国是不可能迷路的。

老君岩　宋朝老君岩（“老子天下第一！”）是中国道教石刻中最古老也是最大的（高 5.1 米，宽 7.3 米）。据传说，谁能摸到老君岩的鼻子，可以活上一百二，摸到眼睛呢，可以活上一百六。过去人们常说，如果摸到老君的嘴巴就会死得早。但是摸嘴巴一说不利于旅游业，所以现在当地人就干脆改口说：“摸嘴巴，有好运！”唉，近千年来摸老子像不妥的地方就是把他的鼻子摸坏了。所以，一些年以后人们给老君岩围上栅栏并雇佣一名守卫，这么一来，人们就不会把老君当花岗岩看待了。

乘车路线：3路、5路、20路，或者旅游公车601路
开放时间：5：30—16：00　　**联系电话：**22783474

Muslim Zaytun

Ibn Battuta

"The Muslims live in a town apart from the others.

"On the day that I reached Zaytun I saw there the amir who had come to India as an envoy with the present [to the sultan], and who afterwards traveled with our party and was shipwrecked on the junk. He greeted me, and introduced me to the controller of the douane and saw that I was given good apartments [there]. I received visits from the qadi of the Muslims, the shaykh al-Islam, and the principal merchants. Amongst the latter was Sharaf ad-Din of Tabriz, one of the merchants from whom I had borrowed at the time of my arrival in India, and the one who had treated me most fairly. He knew the Koran by heart and used to recite it constantly. These merchants, living as they do in a land of infidels, are overjoyed when a Muslim comes to them. They say "He has come from the land of Islam," and they make him the recipient of the tithes on their properties, so that he becomes as rich as themselves. There was living at Zaytun, amongst other eminent shaykhs, Burhan ad-Din of Kazarun, who has a hermitage outside the town, and it is to him that the merchants pay the sums they vow to Shaykh Abu Ishaq of Kazarun."

"Holy Tombs" 灵山伊斯兰教圣墓

A Ming Dynasty Stele in the Fuzhou Mosque's courtyard (behind two rusty bicycles) claims Mohammed sent 4 disciples to China between 618 A.D. - 626 A.D..[1] One went to Guangzhou, one to Yangzhou, and two settled in Quanzhou. Sashye (Sa-ke-zu--the 3rd Saint) and Gaoshi (Wu-ko-su--the 4th Saint) were buried on the hill on the east edge of town, past the Maritime Museum, on "Holy Hill." This very grave site was called "Holy Hill" because after the disciples were buried, villagers encountered supernatural signs on the hill (the hillside glowed at night, for instance).

① Muslims say there are no reputable records of this

穆斯林刺桐城

“穆斯林聚居在一个远离他人的镇上。”

Entrance to "Holy Hill"

“我到达刺桐城的那天，看到一名穆斯林埃米尔，他曾出使印度向苏丹献礼。后来他跟我们一同前行，并在海上遭遇沉船。这位埃米尔接待了我，并把我介绍给海关的负责人，把我安顿好。穆斯林的卡吉、萨伊赫·伊思朗以及一些主要的商人都来拜访我。商人中就有来自大不里士的沙拉夫·阿德丁。我抵达印度时曾求助过一些商人，而他是其中对我最好的一个。他对《古兰经》记得很牢，常常诵读。这些商人住在异教的国土上，每当看到穆斯林时都兴奋不已。他们说“他来自伊斯兰的国土”，并让他领受他们自己财产的什一税，这样，他就可以和他们一样富有了。在刺桐城住着一位来自卡泽伦的伯罕·阿德丁，他也是其他杰出萨伊赫家族中的一贵。他在城外有一隐居处。那些商人们向来自卡泽伦的萨伊赫·阿布·伊萨德许愿的钱就是支付给他的。”

——伊本·贝图塔

灵山伊斯兰圣墓 福州清真寺的庭院里有一块明朝的石碑(放在两辆生锈的自行车后面)。这块石碑称，在公元 618—626 年间穆罕默德曾派出四位门徒来到中国。[①]一位去了广州，一位去了扬州，还有两位则到了泉州。沙什濕(即三贤 Sa-ke-zu)和高仕(即四贤我高仕)葬于城东的灵山上，过了海上交通史博物馆。

这块坟墓所在之处被称为“灵山”，因为在两位门徒下葬之后，村民们在山上发现了一些超自然现象(如夜晚山坡会发光)。

① 穆斯林称此种说法无从考证。

Some say China's first Muslims were not in Quanzhou but Chang'an, the ancient capital, in 650 A.D.. But the tombs' spindle-shaped granite columns are Tang Dynasty-at least 1,000 years old, so they're ancient, regardless of who rests there, and they have been revered for a millennium. Furthermore, Mohammed is reputed to have said, "Seek knowledge, as far as China," so when his persecuted followers fled to Africa, it is likely some came to China as well (along with the Manicheans and Nestorians).

1322 Renovation. An Arabic inscription on a granite stele records the tombs' restoration in 1322. Part of it says, in effect, that Quanzhou Moslems

> "…renovated this blessed Tomb, with the purpose of pleasing the most noble and majestic Allah and obtaining rich rewards from him… the two saints came to China in the time of Faghfur. They were reported to be men of high virtue. After their deaths, they passed from this incorruptible world into everlasting eternity. People believe in them in the hope of obtaining their benediction. Once in trouble or caught between two fires, they approach the Tomb begging for enlightenment by offering sacrifice. In so doing, they always obtain what they come for and return home in peace."[①]

Arabic recounting renovation in 1322 A.D.

Admiral Zheng He's Pilgrimage Another slab records the visit of the great Muslim Chinese mariner Zheng He, who visited the tombs in 1417 before his 5th voyage, in which he also visited Mecca. After Zheng He departed, the local magistrate erected a monument to the event. It read,

> "The imperial envoy, commander-in-chief and eunuch Zheng He, is going to the country Hormuz and other countries across the sea, and made a pilgrimage to this Holy Tomb to crave the blessings and protection of the saints on the 16th of the 5th month in the 15th year of Yongle (May 30th, 1417 A.D.)."

---

① *The Islamic Historic Relics in Quanzhou*, Fujian People's Publishing House.

有人说，中国最早的穆斯林不在泉州，而在公元650年的古都长安。但坟墓纺锤状的花岗石柱子显示它是唐朝时建的，至少有一千年的历史了。因此，不管谁在这里安息，他们都已年代久远并在这里接受了一千年的顶礼膜拜。而且，穆罕默德有句名言，“你们去寻找知识吧！即使远在中国”。因此，他的门徒遭受迫害时逃往非洲，有的可能就来到了中国(与摩尼教徒和基督教教派一道)。

very
Muslim Grave Site

1322 年的修复　一块花岗石碑上的阿拉伯铭文记录了 1322 年对这座坟墓的修复。 其中一段碑文清楚地记述着泉州穆斯林“修复了这座圣墓，以让最尊贵崇高的真主阿拉得到欣慰，并获得丰厚的回报……两位圣徒在法厄福尔时代（据学者考证，法厄福尔系古代阿拉伯对唐朝皇帝的称呼——译者注）来到了中国。据说他们都是得道高僧。他们死后离开了这块圣洁之地，去往那永恒之地。人们信奉他们，以期望得到他们的赐福。当身处困境或进退两难之际，人们便来到这座墓祭祀以求得到神谕。通过这种方式，他们得到了来此所求之物，回家后逢凶化吉”。①

郑和将军的朝圣之旅　另有一块墓碑记录了伟大的中国穆斯林航海家郑和在 1412 年第五次远航之前来此朝圣的事迹。这次远航中他还访问了麦加城。郑和走后，当地的官吏立碑纪念此事。碑文写道：“钦差总兵太监郑和前往西洋忽鲁漠斯等国公干，永乐十五年五月十六日（1417 年 5 月 30 日）于此行香，望圣灵庇佑。”

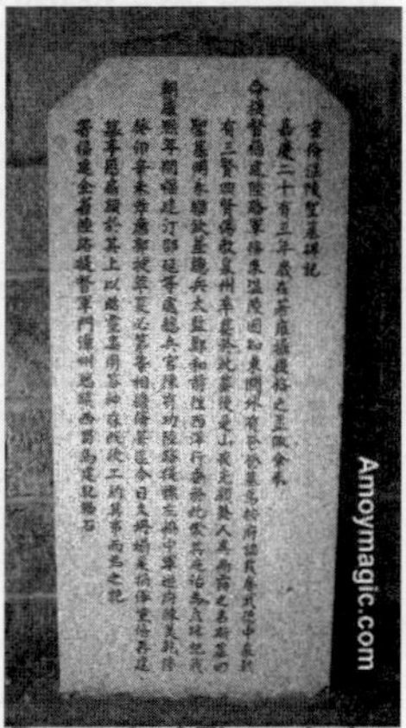

Record of Zhenghe's visit in 1417 A.D.

① 《泉州伊斯兰历史遗迹》，福建人民出版社出版。

Zheng He offered sacrifices and prayed for safety (a common practice even with Muslims then). Whether prayers helped or not, Zheng He sailed most of the known world--and, incidentally, helped spread Islam throughout Southeast Asia.

Muslims don't monopolize Holy Hill, which also has Buddhist tombs scattered about, but the Muslims are taking back the territory. An army of stone masons, directed by architects armed with intricate sketches, is building dozens of new Muslim tombs (most for the "Ding" clan—the primary clan in Chendai Village).

Windrocking Stone (风动石) As your guide leads you down the garden path to the tombs, on the right is the famous "windrocking stone," inscribed with large Chinese characters meaning "Wonder of Nature." Zhou Daoguang, a Ming Dynasty official, visited the stone, dubbed it Jaspar Ball, and carved an inscription on the rock. Considered one of Quanzhou's "Top Eight Spectacular Sights," its claim to fame is that it "sways gently with the wind and moves with a mere touch of the hand." My hosts said it was a "gift of Allah," rivaling the "Swaying Tower of Esfahan."①

Chinese have even written poems about the great wonder of nature:

> "The ball of a stone sways and sways above the lake,
> and was christened the Purple Platform by Prefect the late.
> The wintry moon from celestial palace gate emerges,
> Shooting stars shower like beads on the bronze plate of earth.
> A flowing stream swift as an arrow turns the sakya wheel,
> Which looks the look of a mirror round from the Far Ball Hill.
> Oft-time hear the shrill cries of cranes pass the sky;
> Leisurely the fairies dawdle away their time and tide."

"It's good luck to move this stone!" a Moslem said. "It moves easily for the pure of heart." Well, that's me! So I placed a fingertip on it, and then a palm, an arm, my entire body—it did not budge. We finally wedged a stick under it, balanced a cell phone on the stick, and in unison three of us shoved—and the cell phone shook a little. "See! See!"

Blessed are the pure in heart.

There is also supposed to be a sweet spring trickling from beneath the stone, but it must have dried up at my approach. This infidel didn't even see mud.
Getting There: Buses 7,10,11,13,19,23,25
Hours: 8:00-17:30 **Phone**: 2210-1631

① In Esfahan, Iran, if either of the minarets flanking the tomb of Amu Abdollah (died 1316 A.D.) is shaken, the other minaret shakes as well.

郑和贡奉了祭品祈求平安(这是当时的惯例，就连穆斯林也是如此)。不管这次祈福有没有显灵，郑和游遍了大多数当时知名的世界各国——而且无形中也促进了伊斯兰教在东南亚的传播。

穆斯林并非独占灵山，这里也散落着佛教墓地，但穆斯林正在夺回其领地。一队由泥瓦匠组成的大军，在揣着复杂图纸的建筑师的指导下，正在建造几十座新的穆斯林坟墓(其中大多数是丁氏家族——陈埭镇的主要家族)。

风动石　在导游的带领下，沿着公园小径拾级而下便来到了墓区，在右侧你会看这块著名的“风动石”，上面用巨大的汉字刻着“自然奇观”。明朝官员周道光游览了这块石头，取名为“碧玉石”，并刻在了石头上面。作为泉州“八大观光景点”之一，风动石的引人之处在于它“随风微斜，手推可动”。主人说它是一件“安拉的赠礼”，可与伊斯法罕的斜塔相媲美。

甚至有国人写诗赞叹这伟大的自然奇观：

湖边球石碧琅玕，太守题名拥紫坛。
涌月塞开云母殿，流星秋泻赤瑛盘。
动时锦水将轮转，圆处巴山作镜看。
几度鹤笙天外过，仙姝闲驻弄珊珊。

有一位穆斯林曾对我说：“移动这块石头会带来好运的！”“只有心灵纯洁的人才能移动它。”啊，我就是个心灵纯洁的人嘛！于是我放了根手指在上面，又用整只手试了试，最后用尽全身力气推它——它仍旧纹丝不动。最后我们找了木棍插在石头下面，然后把手机平放在木棍上。我们三个人合力推了一下——手机终于动了一下。“看呀！快看呀！”纯洁的心灵会得到赐福的。

还有一条甘泉从石头的下面滴沥流淌，但很显然在我来的时候已经干枯了。我连泥巴也没看到。

乘车路线：乘 7、10、11、13、19、23、25 路公交车到“圣墓站”

开放时间：8:30—17:30　**电话：**22101631

Water God Temple (Zhenwu Temple at Fashi, 法石镇武寺) Since the Song Dynasty, locals have worshipped Xianwu, the Water God, as well as offered sacrifices to the sea god, in this Shitou Street Temple. Even with rivers on both sides of the city, water has not always been easy to come by, as evident from the local legend (see page 162, "Sichuan or Xichuan").

Getting There: Buses #1, 5, 21 **Hours**: 6:00-17:30

Supplement

Traveling Out of Town

After the next chapter (on Quanzhou Parks), we head for Quanzhou's rural counties. Fortunately, roads are better than Beaton's "new roads" in 1945. They're even better than 1995, when it took me over 30 hours to drive from Xiamen to Wuyi Mtn. (now it is nine hours). Rev. Pitcher wrote in 1912:

> "Traveling in the Amoy district is a slow process, more often wearisome than otherwise,—a peculiar wearisomeness of its own."
>
> "So far as South China is concerned there are no roads. The nearest approach to a road, generally speaking, is a narrow footpath, something like the cow paths that lead to our meadows, winding and twisting like some serpent among the paddy (rice fields). These paths are raised about a foot above the fields, and were originally made so as to mark the divisional lines between the property of different owners.
>
> "The only commissioner of these highways is the tramp of ceaseless thousands bearing their heavy burdens over them, from one generation to another. One never expects them to be kept in good order. No fences mark their boundary, no sign-posts point their direction. The stranger easily becomes confused and lost among boundless fields covered with a network of paths that seem to run in every direction but the right one."

水神庙（法石镇武寺）　从宋朝开始，当地人便在这座石头街庙拜祭水神玄武了。城市两边各有河流，但人们并不能轻易得到水源，当地传说见第163页“四川或西川”。

乘车路线：乘 1、5、21 路公交车即可到达　**开放时间：** 6:00—17:30

附录　城外风光

在下一章“泉州公园”讲完后，我们将前往泉州的乡村地区。幸运的是，现在的路况比 1945 年 Beaton 的“新公路”要好多了。实际上，它们比 1995 年时的公路也要好很多。当时从厦门驱车 30 个小时才到达武夷山(现在只需 9 个小时)。皮彻牧师在他的《厦门内外》中写道：

“在厦门地区旅行进程相当缓慢，往往要比其他地方令人疲倦——这种疲倦程度是绝无仅有的。”

“说起中国南方，公路是没有的。一般来说，最接近公路的就是那些羊肠小道了，它们像牛道一样通往草甸，犹如蛇一般在稻田间蜿蜒盘绕。这些小道比稻田高出一英尺，最初是作为划定不同所有者田地的分界线。”

“这些‘公路’唯一的管理者便是背负重担的沉重脚步声，一代又一代，繁衍不息。没人去想这些路要不要维护一下。路边没有围栏，也没有路标。陌生人很容易就会迷失方向，一望无际的稻田阡陌交通，似乎可以通向任何地方，但没人知道走哪条路才是正确的。”

——皮彻（《厦门内外》，1912 年，第 265 页）

Chapter 7

Quanzhou Gardens & Parks

Ibn Battuta remarked upon Quanzhou people's love of gardens and nature, and judging from the number of parks and natural preserves, gardens are still their first love.

Micro to Macro Gardening Quanzhou is like a four-tiered miniature landscape, from prize-winning miniature gardens in residents' courtyards or on balconies to residential gardens, community parks and squares, city gardens, and parks and forests, including the nearby mountains and rivers.

Community parks, squares and forests reflect the harmony, creativity and care invested in potted landscapes, but on a much larger scale. Between 1992 and 2002, Quanzhou spent 40 million USD establishing 358.3 ectares of unique gardens. With land at a premium, they've had to be pretty innovative—building car parks below kid parks, or using "vertical" landscaping (rooftop gardens, hanging planters).

The parks are very diverse. Quanzhou Water Park attracts vacationers. Kaiyuan Temple offers serenity. Fuxin Garden Square has a musical fountain. Qingyuan Mountain, the ancient "Fairyland," appeals to both athletes and meditative types, who enjoy the Taoist setting. Some parks have entrance charges to cover maintenance costs, but where possible parks are inexpensive or free to maximize use by low-income families

Bridging the Gap With the growing generation gap, Quanzhou is seeking innovative ways to meet the needs of both young and old by emphasizing both passive and active leisure and cultural activities, educational activities for retirees, and increased opportunities for elderly volunteers. City parks offer the older generation plenty of opportunities to teach the youth Chinese shadow boxing, calligraphy, Chinese painting, or how to perform the simple but elegant Minnan tea ceremony.

第七章

泉州花园与公园

伊本·贝图塔曾经盛赞泉州人对花园和自然的热爱，从现有的公园和自然保护区的数量看，他们对花园的喜爱仍是情有独钟。

园艺：从微观到宏观　泉州就像一幅立体的盆景：小到普通百姓在自家庭院或阳台种植的获过奖的盆景，大到小区花园、社区广场、城市花园以至包括周围山河的森林公园。

社区的花园、广场和树林折射出和谐、创作力以及在浓缩景观方面注入的心血——只是规模大多了。从 1992 年到 2002 年的 10 年间，泉州市投资 4000 万美元建设总面积达 358.3 公顷，独具特色的各类花园，从最早建设的东湖公园到新近的泉州森林公园。由于土地资源奇缺，泉州人更是把创新意识发挥极致，如在儿童公园地下修建停车场，居民区的屋顶花园及阳台窗台上摆放的花盆形成一幅立体的景观。

Zhongshan Park

每个公园都各具特色。乘坐西湖公园的品茗游船，可以饱览位于湖中岛屿的鸟类保护区的景色。泉州水上乐园吸引来自四方的度假游客。开元寺呈现出一片宁静安详。福新花园广场还有音乐喷泉。古代仙境清源山吸引了许许多多的登山爱好者及善于思考的道教徒。有些公园收取门票用于支付保养费用，但只要可能，很多公园都是低收费甚至免费，为低收入家庭的进出提供方便。

消除代沟　随着代沟的增大，泉州正努力寻找新的方法，加强各种休闲文化活动和面向退休职工的培训，增加老年志愿者的活动机会，目的是满足青年人和老年人的不同需要。在公园里，经常可以看到老一代向年轻人传授打太极拳、书法、画画以及简朴优雅的闽南功夫茶。

West Lake Park Every decent sized city in China has a West Lake Park (the most famous being that in Hangzhou). But Quanzhou's newly renovated West Lake is a beauty.

Called "Northwest Ocean" by locals, this park lies in the northwest of the city, and was a swamp until the city dredged it out. Dykes and bridges connect the islands, which have once again become home to wild creatures and birds. Ornately painted wooden pleasure boats serve tea as you tour the lake. Take a camera to photograph the wild pigeons and egrets, which sometimes almost cover the trees. Also visit the many memorial forests planted by local volunteers.

Buses: #3, 15 ,17, 21, 27 **Hours**: 8:00-17:30 **Phone:** 2289-5875

Not Tom Cruise, but Tea Cruise!

East Lake Park The nicely wooded and landscaped East Lake Park, right in the middle of town, was one of Quanzhou's original "Eight Famous Sites." Scenes surrounding the "Lotus Fragrance on the Stars" lake include, Fragrance of Lotus, Pavilion of Praying for Plain Wind, and Children's Playground.

Buses: 1, 2, 7, 11, 13, 17, 20, 22 **Hours**: 8:00-17:30 **Phone**: 22280147

Zayton Park Zayton Park (Citong Park), on Zayton Road, was opened in 1997. Official sites include "Citong Sunken Flowerbed,"and "Listening to Rain in Banana Groves."

Buses: 22A or 23 **Hours**: 8:00-17:30 **Phone**: 22578935

Fragrant Grass Garden This delightful midtown garden on Xinmen Street was built by General Shilang, and was the site of the original Chongzheng Academy.

Buses: 4, 6, 25, 26 **Hours**: 8:00-17:30 **Phone**: 2238-2838

西湖公园　中国每一个中等城市都有西湖公园，以杭州西湖最为出名。但泉州新近修复的西湖公园不愧为一大美景。

西湖公园位于泉州市西北部，在政府投资疏浚之前是一片低洼地带，俗称“西北洋”。现在由堤坝和桥梁连接的湖中岛又成了野生动物和鸟类的天堂。当你乘坐装饰华丽的木船游览西湖时，还可以品茶。记得带上相机，你可以拍摄野生鸽子和白鹭，它们有时遍布岛上的树林。这里还可以参观泉州志愿者种下的纪念树。

乘车：乘 3、15、17、21、27 路公交车即可到达

开放时间：8：00—17：30　**电话**：22895875

东湖公园　树木葱茏，风景如画的东湖公园位于市中心，是泉州原来的八大景之一。七星湖周围的景点包括：东湖荷香、祈风阁、儿童游乐园。

乘车：乘 1、2、7、11、13、17、20、22 路公交车即可到达

开放时间：8：00—17：30　**电话**：22280147

刺桐公园　位于刺桐路的刺桐公园开放于 1997 年，公园里有墨潭映月、涧连清音、竹径通幽等景点。

乘车：乘 22、23 路公交车即可到达

开放时间：8：00—17：30　**电话**：22578935

芳草园　令人赏心悦目的芳草园位于新门街，是一个城中花园，由清朝施琅将军修建，是原崇正书院遗址。

乘车：乘 4、6、25、26 路公交车即可到达

开放时间：8：00—17：30　**电话**：22382823

Sub Battles on the Lake

Water World ("Aquatic Elysium") This park is a real hit with our family because it's big (47,357 m^2), fun, and inexpensive—such a bargain that during summers we load up Toy Ota with a dozen kids, make the drive from Xiamen, and return late the same evening. We like the water slides, paddle boats, and tidal pool (though I've had bigger waves in our bathtub).

Water World's sole drawback is that, like stores and shopping centers, there is no respite from nonstop 200 decibel Chinese pop music blasting from speakers strung up every 10 feet. Wax ear plugs, maybe?

After a nice wet day, order a pizza and build a towering salad in one of Quanzhou's Pizza Huts, then head home on the Quanzhou-Xiamen Freeway (which is anything but free) to recover from your sunburn. Or else head north to Luoyang Bridge (see the Fujian Bridge chapter).
Buses: 3, 15, 17, and 27 **Hours**: 8:00-22:00 **Phone**: 2277-6005

Quanzhou Amusement Park is in Quanzhou Exhibition Town, across the river to the south. The English brochure boasts it covers more than 250 mu. Moo. The 30+ amusements include the ferris wheel, roller coaster, playground, and go-karts. To quote the brochure, "It is a large modern playground integrating amusement, shopping and bodybuild." I'm sold!
Buses: 9, 18, 23, 25, 601 **Hours**: 8:00-20:00 **Phone**: 2248-1835

Parks in Rural Quanzhou

Anxi Zhimin Field Sport and Ecological Recreation Center Wow--now that's a mouthful! This outdoors center in Anxi's Longmen Township offers a good day or two of exciting outdoor activities, including white water rafting (supposedly the best in Fujian), rock-climbing, hunting, hiking, field survival, and tea making (which can be as arduous as the rest).
Getting There: Bus to Anxi, change buses to Longmen Town
Hours: All Day **Phone**: 23318787

Dehua Peach Fairy Creek Ecological Tourist Area Peach Fairy Creek (Taoxian Xi) offers bamboo rafting, rubber rafting, hiking, and traditional performances of Nanyin (Southern Music), Folk songs, and Santong Drum (三通鼓).
Getting There: Bus to Dehua, changes buses to Nancheng Town.
Hours: 8:00-17:30 **Phone:** 23618888

水上乐园　水上乐园规模宏大（面积47357平方米），无穷乐趣和低廉收费真正地满足我们一家人。夏天我们经常开着本田车，载着一群孩子从厦门来到水上乐园，深夜再返回厦门。我们喜欢七彩滑道、戏水池和造浪池（尽管我家的浴缸激起的波浪比它还大）。

水上乐园的唯一不足之处是，就像商场和购物中心一样，每隔10英尺就安装一个扩音器播放流行音乐，并以200分贝的音量播出，让人实在无暇喘息。或许该带副橡皮耳塞？

经过一天令人愉悦的水上运动，在泉州必胜客，点一份比萨饼，堆一碗塔型沙拉。之后从新建的泉厦高速公路（现在收费一点也不低！）返回厦门，好好休息，从一天的阳光曝晒中恢复过来。或者可以继续往北到洛阳桥（有关福建的著名桥梁另章介绍）。

乘车：乘3、15、17、27路公交车即可到达

开放时间：8：00—22：00（夏季）　**电话**：22776005

泉州游乐园　泉州游乐园位于桥南的泉州展览城。英文宣传小册子介绍它占地250亩。园内的30多种娱乐项目包括摩天转轮、滑行铁道和微型赛车。小册子描述"游乐园是一座大型现代化游乐场所，集娱乐、购物和健身为一体"。我是非去不可啦！

乘车：乘9、18、23、25公交车或601路专线车即可到达

开放时间：8：00—20：00　**电话**：22481835

泉州郊外的公园

安溪志闽野外运动生态游乐中心　哇，读这个名称还真需要点肺活量！该中心位于安溪县龙门镇，这里提供一至两天的刺激的户外活动项目，包括号称全省最好的乘竹筏、攀岩、狩猎、徒步旅行、战地求生和茶叶制作（茶叶制作与其他项目一样艰难）。

乘车：乘车到安溪，改乘开往龙门镇的中巴

开放时间：全天　**电话**：23318787

德化桃仙生态旅游区　桃仙溪有竹筏、橡皮筏、徒步旅游、传统南音表演、民歌、三通鼓等游乐项目。

乘车：乘车到德化，改乘开往南城镇的中巴

开放时间：8：00—17：30　**电话**：23618888

Supplement – Ancient Garden City

Every Home a Garden? About 700 years ago, the Arab traveler Ibn Battuta remarked upon Quanzhou people's love of gardening, and that love of nature is evident even today, ranging from the intimate care given miniature landscapes and balcony plants to neighborhood gardens, community parks, and city parks and forests. Gardening is a grassroots affair, from the bottom up as well as top down. And Quanzhou folks' aesthetics have transferred to architecture as well.

Garden Architecture Most Chinese cities approach to rapid modernization seem to be to raze everything old and replace it with tile- and glass-covered concrete cubicles. (Of course, who are we Americans to talk? We don't have ancient culture to preserve, but we do have a natural heritage, which we're decimating. New housing developments invariably begin with bulldozing down the ancient trees, which are then replaced with saplings bought on sale at a local nursery).

"Kid Park above, Car Park below!"

Quanzhou's marriage of old and new architecture accommodates not only the natural heritage but the cultural and historical heritage as well. The new housing areas are a delightful blend of old and new, retaining the ancient Chinese or foreign flavor, while incorporating modern technology and innovations such as solar water heating. And while the first new apartment buildings had little in the way of green space, Quanzhou leaders have a motto, "Do more, learn more," and each successive project has had more, and better, greenery (thanks in part to innovations like car parks below gardens.

Today, as in Marco Polo's day, Quanzhou's true wealth lies not in products but the place, and the people.

附录 古老的花园城市

家家都是个小花园 大约700年前，阿拉伯旅行家伊本·贝图塔盛赞泉州人对园林情有独钟，今天他们对大自然的热爱，从对盆景和阳台花卉的谙熟照料至社区花园、城市森林公园的建设中仍可见一斑。园林跟草根有关，可以从上往下，也可以从下往上。泉州人的美学观也在建筑上得以体现。

花园建筑 许多中国城市的高速现代化进程似乎就是铲平摧毁一切旧建筑，代之以瓷砖、玻璃覆盖的钢筋混凝楼房。（当然，我们美国人有什么资格加以评论？虽然我们没有古代文化需要保护，但是我们却有自然遗产，却正遭受我们的破坏。新的楼市的开发总是从推倒年代久远的树木开始，最后代之从苗圃廉价买来的小树苗。）

泉州新旧建筑的融合不但使自然遗产而且使文化遗产和历史遗产得以和谐统一。新的住宅区处处呈现令人赏心悦目的新旧建筑的交融，既保留古代建筑的风格，又具有外国建筑的风格，同时大量吸收了现代技术和创新，比如太阳能热水器的安装和应用。虽然首批小区建设预留的绿化空间少之又少，但泉州市领导有一句座右铭：“多做、多学”，之后的每个建设项目已有更多更好的绿化地。这有一部分应归功于各种创新，如在花园下面建设停车场。

就像在马可·波罗时代一样，今天泉州的真正财富不在于它的产品，而在于它的位置，它的人民。

Chapter 8

Quanzhou Bridges

"Central Fujian bridges are second to none under heaven"
Chinese saying

"The bridges of China are wonders! On some of them people build their temples and houses and shops--where they live and carry on their business. There are at least two bridges of this kind in the Amoy district, each having a population of from fifty to one hundred inhabitants--perhaps more. These bridges are generally of wonderful construction. How the largest of them were built must always remain a matter of pure conjecture.

"Twenty-five miles west of Amoy there is a famous bridge...There are natives who will tell you that man could not have lifted, by any imaginable machinery, to their present position those immense stones of which it is made. The only conclusion they can come to is, the gods must have done the work.

"The bridge is called 'The Po-lam Bridge'—a place much frequented by foreigners residing in Amoy. It is 200 yards or more long, built upon solid stone piers each about twelve feet high. Some of the stones laid on these piers are of great length and weight. One of them is seventy feet long, five feet thick and four feet wide, weighing something like 107 tons. It always has been a question: How were they put in place?"
Rev. Philip Pitcher, *In and About Amoy*, 1912, p.297-8

Land of Bridges Quanzhou is a land of bridges, both literally and metaphorically. Zaytun was not only the bridge between China and the rest of the planet (assuming they were on the same planet), but it also gave us some of the world's most unique bridges, spanning rivers, gorges, and bays. Given our vertical province's tortuous topography, it is no wonder that Quanzhou folk excelled in bridge-making. By the Song Dynasty, Minnan alone had at least 313 bridges.

My favorite bridges include the magnificent 700-year-old wooden covered bridge in Pingnan, Putian's Ninggai Bridge (protected by a modern bridge built right over top), and Quanzhou's magnificent Anping Bridge (longest stone bridge on earth) and Luoyang Bridge.

第八章

泉州的桥梁

“闽中桥梁甲天下。”

——中国谚语

“中国的桥梁尽是奇观，人们在桥上建寺庙，建房子，建商店，并在上面居住和经营生意。在厦门地区至少有两座这类的桥梁，每座桥上的居民有50～100人，或许更多。这些桥的建设通常奇特非凡。对于这些大桥是如何修建而成的各种说法都只是一些纯粹的猜测而已。

“在厦门往西25英里的地方，有一座闻名遐迩的大桥……当地人告诉游客，即使是利 到的机械，古人也无法把建造大桥的巨大石板吊装到合 置。他们得出唯一的结论：一定是法力无边的神仙完成了这些不可思议的工作。

“这座桥名字叫虎渡桥（现称江东桥），是居住在厦门的老外们经常光顾的地方。桥长200多码，建在12英尺高的坚固的石墩上。横跨石墩的石板又长又重，其中一条石板长70英尺，厚5英尺，宽4英尺，重约107吨。这给世人留下一个不解之谜：这些石板是怎么安装上去的？”

——皮彻（《厦门内外》，1912年，第297～298页）

众桥之地　泉州是桥乡，这既是比喻的说法，实际情况也如此。刺桐不仅是联结中国与世界的桥梁（如果“中国”和“世界”这两个地方位于同一星球的话），它还保存着世界上最奇异的横跨江河、峡谷和海湾的大桥。考虑到属于南北走向丘陵山脉地形，难怪泉州人是桥梁建设方面出类拔萃的行家里手。至宋朝，单闽南地区就至少修建有各种桥梁313座。

我最喜欢的桥包括屏南县有着700年历史的宏伟木盖梁桥；莆田市的宁盖桥，现在它上方建了一座现代化桥梁以保护这座古桥；宏伟壮丽的泉州安平桥——世界上最长的石桥；以及泉州洛阳桥。

Before visiting Quanzhou's mythic bridges, view them through the eyes of Ms. Averil Mackenzie-Grieve, a resident of South Fujian in the 1920s:

"Galeote Pereira, when he was captured by the Chinese as a smuggler in 1549, was taken through Ch'uan-chou [Quanzhou] on his way to Foochow, and was greatly impressed with the populous countryside, the 'gallantly paved streets' and, above all, 'the very noble and very well-wrought bridges of stone…for service over the rivers'. Ch'uan-chou's bridge was even more splendid than Foochow's bridge of Ten Thousand Ages, surpassed only by the one spanning the Loyang River ten miles to the north. For me, the great granite bridges of Fukien had an indescribable fascination. It lay, not in their uniqueness (there are believed to be none like them in the world), but, I think, in the grand, brave way in which they spanned the rivers, set their broad buttresses against the currents. Their grey bulk had personality and inspired respect; they reminded me of elephants. No one knows exactly how the stones were put into place. The buttresses supported solid granite slabs twenty-two feet long, two feet thick, laid, in the bridge over the Loyang estuary, five abreast for over a thousand feet. At the roofed gateway sat a massive stone figure, the twelfth-century builder himself. When we saw them, their function had not altered in any way since they had been built.

"For me, the Roman coliseum rises yawning like an empty wasps' nest; life has gone from it. Even in Lucca, whose coliseum is a teeming hive of cell-slums, built with the help of Lombardic bricks and Romanesque hewn stones, builders and users are buried in history—remembered it is true, but as a legend. But across the great stone Fukienese bridges the people swarmed, thinking, acting, writing, talking, exactly as their forebears had done for more than seven hundred years. The stream of pole-carriers, litter-bearers, pedestrians, flowed unbroken throughout the centuries, the strong tide of life undiminished, undiluted; an endurance so close-textured, so ubiquitous that, living in China, one accepted it and only afterwards was amazed."

(Excerpt from, ***A Race of Green Ginger***, p.112, 113)

在参观泉州这些神奇的桥梁之前，我们透过20世纪20年代居住在闽南的埃夫里尔·麦肯兹·格瑞芙女士的描述，来看看这些桥梁。

“格莱奥塔·佩雷拉，由于走私，1549年被中国人抓捕，在押往福州的途中，泉州人口众多的乡村，铺设气派的街道，特别是那些横跨江河,造型壮观，制作精良的石桥给他留下深刻的印象。泉州的桥梁比福州的万寿桥更宏伟壮观。单是横跨洛阳江长达10英里的洛阳桥就无与伦比。对我来说，福建的这些大石桥有着难以言表的魅力。洛阳桥的魅力并不在其举世无双（它们被认为是世界上独一无二的），我想，在其成功地在急流中建造宽大的桥墩，架设横跨江河大桥的那种英雄气概。这些大桥很有个性，令人肃然起敬，也让我联想到大象。谁也说不清这些石头是如何安装上去的。在宽达1000多英尺的洛阳江入海口建造五个并排的桥墩，支撑着22英尺长，2英尺厚的石板条。在桥头有一巨大的石刻人物，12世纪的建桥者自己。几百年来他一直守护着大桥。”

“在我看来，矗立的罗马大剧场像一个空蜂巢一样敞开，用伦巴第式砖头和罗马式石块建成的卢卡大剧场像一个熙熙攘攘的蜂巢，虽然其建设者和使用者早已消失在历史长河，但传说中它的确存在。然而，福建人民穿行在这些宏伟的福建石桥上。他们思索，表演，写作，交谈，跟他们700多年前的祖先一模一样。数百年来，挑担的，抬轿的，步行的，川流不息。生活的大潮并没有衰减，冲淡；一种致密组织的耐力，无处不在。居住在中国，人们接受它，然后为之感到惊奇。”

——《绿姜根》（第112～113页）

Quanzhou's three most famous bridges are Luoyang Bridge, Anping Bridge, and Dongguan Bridge. Dongguan, in Yongchun, is a bit off the beaten path, so we'll visit it after we've seen two marvelous bridges just off the 324 national highway.

Anping Bridge 安平桥 World's Longest Stone Bridge This recently renovated 2,251m bridge was the longest bridge on earth during the Middle Ages, and is still the planet's longest stone bridge. It was built in 1138 in Anhai by the monk Zupai as a replacement for the ferry, and wasn't completed until 1151. He used massive granite slabs, most of which are said to have been shipped from nearby Jinmen Island (Quemoy). It was originally called the Five Mile Bridge because it was Five Li (Chinese Miles) long--but I'm not sure if they were the long li, short li, mandarin li or common country li. Whichever li, the bridge is a long walk on a hot summer day, so take it slowli.

Luoyang Bridge 洛阳桥 To the north of Quanzhou city lies China's first seaport bridge, the Luoyang Bridge. Though shorter than Anping, it is older, and is my favorite bridge by far, in part because of the amazing story behind its builder, Mr. Cai Xiang…

Before Mr. Cai Xiang (1012-1067) was able to overcome incredible difficulties to erect the Luoyang Bridge, traversing the Luoyang river required travelers to spend an entire day going inland, or to chance crossing on small craft that were often sunk by squalls sent by evil spirits. In 1053, Quanzhou prefect Cai Xiang, who was born in Xianyou and became a Jinshi at the tender age of 19, decided to remedy the situation by building a stone bridge at the mouth of the Luoyang River.

Mr. Cai Xiang used many innovative engineering techniques, including what may be one of the planet's first attempts at biological engineering. The piers were ingeniously shaped like a ship's bow to divert the raging tides. Chinese, always poetic, call them "10,000 ships launching." (They miscounted by 9,900 but that's "liway", remember).

From MacGowan (1908)

泉州三座最著名的桥是洛阳桥、安平桥和东关桥。东关桥位于永春县，离大路稍远，所以我们先一起游览位于国道324线边上的两座令人惊叹的桥梁。

安平桥　世界上最长的石桥　最近修缮一新长达 2251 米的安平桥，从中世纪至今一直是世界上最长的石桥。安平桥由僧人祖派建造于 1138 年，用来替代渡船，历时 13 年终于在 1151 年建成。他用了大量的石板条，据说大部分是从金门岛船运而来。因为它长达五里，原先又叫五里桥，我不清楚五里是指长里、短里、官里还是乡里。但不管是哪一种长度单位，在炎热的夏日下，走上一趟，行程的确不算短，所以要放慢脚步。

Mr. Caixiang

洛阳桥　洛阳桥位于泉州以北，是中国第一座跨海大桥。虽然它长度不及安平桥，但建造的年代更久远，是我目前最喜欢的桥梁，部分是因为与建造者蔡襄的传奇故事有关。

在蔡襄（1012—1067）克服各种难以想象的困难建造洛阳桥之前，人们要跨越洛阳江，得花一整天时间绕陆地或冒险乘渡船过渡，又因鬼怪作恶，常连人带船沉入江中。1053 年，出生于仙游县，19 岁便中进士的泉州郡守蔡襄决定在洛阳江口建造一座石桥，改变这种局面。

在建造洛阳桥的过程中，蔡襄应用了许多富有创意的工程技术，包括可能是世界上最早的生物工程技术，创造性地发明了筏型基础的桥墩上以利于分水。中国人总是很有诗意地形容这些桥墩为“万帆竞发”。（记住：他们多算了9900艘，原理跟“里”一样。）

Ancient Bio--Engineering The pillars' massive granite blocks were held together with butterfly-shaped iron wedges (hence the origin of "Iron Butterfly"—almost 400 years after Kaiyuan Temple's "Purple Haze"). The pillars were further reinforced with live oysters, whose natural secretions cemented the blocks together. (I asked my guides how they trained the oysters to cooperate but they clammed up on me).

Ancient Biological Engineering

The granite slabs were up to 10 meters long and one meter wide, and weighed ten tons. Each time I traverse the bridge, I marvel that the ancients could have even hewn the mammoth blocks, much less transported them to the Luoyang River, where they battled its legendarily ferocious currents to set them in place.

Historical records relate that the completed bridge was 834 meters long by 7 meters wide, and had 500 stone sculptures to serve as railings, all supported upon 46 piers (talk about pier pressure!). Over 700 pine trees were planted on both ends of the bridge, and as further protection from typhoons, the bridge was armed with 28 stone lions, 7 pavilions, 9 towers, and numerous stone warriors.

A Border Stone in the middle bears the characters Jin-Hui JiaoJiang because the center of the bridge lay on the border between Hui'an and Jinjiang.

The bridge stood largely unchanged for centuries. Even during the 8.0 earthquake almost 400 years ago (which toppled Ashab Mosque's dome), the bridge suffered only minor damage. But Japanese invaders accomplished what nature could not. In the center of the bridge is a Pusa that used to have a moonstone in her forehead. It supposedly glowed at night, guiding seamen to safety--until the Japanese stole it.

Moonstoneless Pusa

1 Million Yuan Renovation! Luoyang bridge was renovated several times after 1949. A renovation in the early 90s cost over 1 million Yuan. When I asked why so much, an official said, "Because nowadays we have to dig away half a mountain to find a ten meter slab of granite!" Maybe they could try shorter pieces and lots more oysters?

Origin of "Iron Butterfly"

古代生物工程 修建桥基的大量石块与蝴蝶型的钢楔紧紧相连（这就是“铸铁蝴蝶” 的由来，几乎比开元寺的紫云殿早400年）。桥下种植海蛎，以固桥基，因为海蛎的自然分泌物把桥基石和桥墩石胶合凝结成牢固的整体。（我笑问导游，当时的人们是怎样训练这些牡蛎与他们进行合作，导游无言以对。）

铺架桥梁的石板条长达 10 米，宽达 1 米，重达 10 吨。每次横跨洛阳桥，我对古代人如何开凿这些巨石感到费解；更不用说他们是如何把这些石板运抵洛阳江，如何战胜汹涌的潮水而安装上位。

史载表明，当初建成的洛阳桥长 834 米，宽 7 米，桥上有 500 个石雕扶栏，所有这些均支撑在 46 座桥墩上。（想想桥墩承受的压力！）桥的南北两侧种植松树 700 多棵，为了更好保护桥梁免受台风侵袭，桥上安装 28 尊石狮，兼有 7 亭 9 塔点缀其间，武士石像分立两端。

界石 洛阳桥的中间刻有一方石碑“晋惠交江”，因为桥的中间刚好是惠安和晋江的交界线。

几个世纪以来，洛阳桥日经风雨沧桑，经久不变。即使是 400 年前的八级地震（清真寺的圆屋顶就是在这一次地震中倒塌），洛阳桥也只是受到轻微的损坏。抗日战争期间，日本侵略者对洛阳桥大肆破坏。桥的中间竖立的一尊菩萨，原来她的前额上有一颗月长石。据说它夜间会发光，为过往的水手安全导航，这一枚月长石后来被日本侵略者掠夺。

100 万元的修复 1949 年以后，洛阳桥经历过几次修缮。90 年代初期的这次修复花了 100 多万元。当我问为什么花费这么大，当地的一名官员说，“因为现在要开凿一条 10 米长的石板条，几乎要挖掉半座山”。也许他们可以采用更短的石板，养殖更多的牡蛎，这未尝不是一个好办法。

Cai Xiang Memorial Temple, (蔡襄祠, Cai Xiang Ci), is south of Luoyang Bridge. Within is a stone tablet, "The Records of Building Wan'An Bridge," inscribed by the great bridge builder himself. "Wan 'An" (10,000 Peace) was another popular name for Luoyang bridge.

Buddha's buttocks?

Making Waves One large sun-baked stone has a natural formation resembling a snake and a turtle head. It is said that before the bridge was built, a snake and turtle lived here and caused the waves. On the other side of the stone, four characters say "God (Shangdi, 上帝) sat here." Obliging locals will point out the impression left by Buddha's buttocks when he sat there trying to dissuade the snake and turtle from wreaking such havoc with the tides and waves.

Sichuan or Xichuan The "Xichuan" pavilion has a fascinating legend behind it. During the Ming Dynasty, when Quanzhou was suffering from a prolonged drought, the Mayor of Quanzhou, Fang Ke, asked people to pray for rain. Evidently, their god wasn't up on geography because he sent an angel to give Sichuan (the west of China) a good wetting down.

As the angel passed through Quanzhou he took pity upon the parched landscape, but he dared not release the rain anywhere but the god's designated target. But Mayor Fang Ke was a savvy politician. He renamed the area Xichuan, evidently figuring that god could not read (because the characters are different even if they sound similar). The angel must have agreed about his lord's literacy, because he released his rain upon Quanzhou (and Sichuan had to make do with bottle water). Hence the stone pavilion's inscription, "Xichuan Ganyu" (西川甘雨), which I was told meant, "Water is precious, one drop is invaluable."

Arm and a Leg A village temple north of the bridge used to be the bridge construction office, and is dedicated to the god who safeguarded its construction. The last Zhuangyuan of the Qing Dynasty, from Jinjiang, wrote the inscription above the temple door.

The temple has a red faced idol of an ancient monk, whom locals revere because, according to legend, when the people lacked fuel for cooking he used his own leg as firewood. "The monk really existed!" I was told, "Though we can't prove the leg story."

蔡襄祠　蔡襄祠位于洛阳桥南岸。祠内有蔡襄亲自撰写书碑的《万安桥记》，洛阳桥又名万安桥。

兴风作浪　在一块久经日晒的石头上，留下天然的形状，极像一条蛇和一只海龟的头。据说在建造洛阳桥之前，一条蛇和一只海龟居住在此，经常兴风作浪。在石头的背面有四个大字“上帝坐此”。热心的当地人介绍说是佛祖坐在这里，劝说蛇和海龟别在此发泄不满，兴风作浪而留下的臀部的印痕。

Xi Chuan

四川或西川？　有关刻有“西川甘雨”石碑的亭子，有一个迷人的传说。明朝时期，泉州经历长时间的干旱，泉州知府方克，组织民众祈雨。明显地，天上的雨神并不精通人间地理，因为他派一个天使到中国西部的四川大降暴雨。

当天使飞过泉州时，他怜悯地看了看那干裂的地表，可除了雨神指定的目标外，天使不敢私自做主随地降雨。聪明的知府重新给这一地区起名西川。很明显，他猜想雨神不懂汉字（即使“西川”和“四川”发音相近，字体还是不同）。天使肯定也认为雨神的识字水平不高，于是在泉州大地上大降甘雨（而四川人只能用瓶装矿泉水凑合啦）。因此，石碑刻上了“西川甘雨”，意思是“水是很珍贵的，是无价之宝”。

胳膊和大腿　洛阳桥北的一个村庙，原来是大桥建设的衙门，现供奉一尊佛像守护大桥。清代的最后一位状元是晋江人，他在寺庙的大门上撰写碑文。

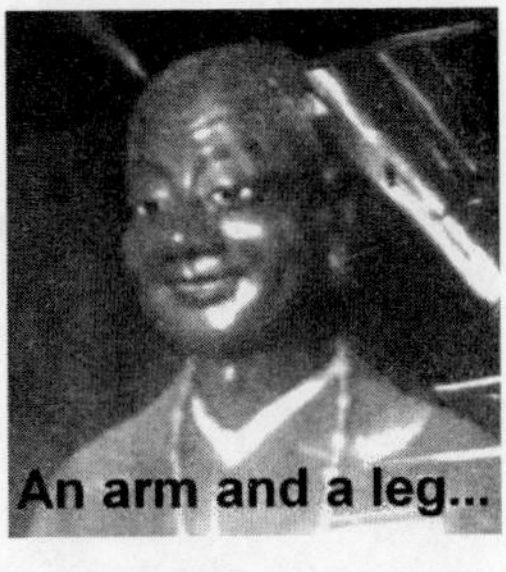
An arm and a leg...

寺庙里有一尊以古代和尚为原型的红脸佛像，很受当地人崇敬，因为传说当人们无材煮饭时，他用自己的大腿当木柴烧，“这和尚是真有其人，虽然有关大腿当柴烧的故事无从考证。”人们说。

Heavenly Luoyang Oysters

Personally, I thought they were just pulling my leg. But I said, "American restaurants are worse. They charge an arm and a leg."

Getting to Luoyang Bridge: Buses, 10, 13, and 19

Hours: 8:00 – 17:30 **Phone**: 2265-1816

Luoyang Cuisine Speaking of food... Luoyang has some legendary seafood—and it doesn't cost an arm or a leg. Awesome oysters, the size of small eggs; steamed fish soup, washed down by oolong tea that is all the better because of the excellent local spring water; and crabs that are supposedly better than Xiamen's because they are wild, not cultivated, and served in a thick sauce much like a Western gravy, but redolent of Chinese medicinal herbs. Heavenly.

Dongguan Bridge 东关桥 a wooden covered bridge between Dehua and Putian, is remote, but this provincial level protected relic is a beauty—especially since an Overseas Chinese donated 1 million Yuan to renovate it. Built in 1145 A.D. (15th year of Shaoxing in South Song Dynasty, in case you're dying to know), in Dongmei Village, Dongping Township, this magnificent 85m by 5m wooden beam bridge spans the scenic Humei Brook.

Like other ancient wooden bridges, it has a shrine in the middle, and religious paintings on the beams above. The wooden bridge is supported by stone block columns, with the upstream side shaped like a ship's bow to deflect heavy currents (they learned this from Luoyang and Anping bridges).

Getting There: Special bus from Quanzhou to Yongchun

Hours: 8:00-17:30 **Phone**: 2388-4202

Xiamen Bridge Museum Though in Xiamen, not Quanzhou, this is right next door, and the best way to appreciate China's contributions to bridge building. The museum has models and photos of bridges all over China, as well as the rest of the world, and is the best location to take photos of Xiamen's beautiful Haicang Suspension Bridge. (I'd tell you what world records it has set, but I want to keep you in suspense).

我个人认为他们在开玩笑。但是我承认，“美国餐馆更可怕，吃饭需要花掉一条胳膊和一条腿”（要花掉“一只胳膊一只腿”，英语中“an arm and a leg”有“极其昂贵”之意——译者注）。

乘车：乘 10、13、19 路公交车即可到达

开放时间：8：00—17：30　**电话：**22651816

洛阳美食　讲到美食，洛阳有名扬四海的海味，价格合理，用不了一条胳膊或一只腿：牡蛎大如小鸡蛋，实在是酷；清蒸鱼汤，最好跟乌龙茶一起喝，因为当地的水质极好；大螃蟹，据说比厦门的螃蟹好，因为是野生而非养殖的；用来调味的酱汁就像西餐的肉汁，但散发出一股中药的香味。味道棒极了。

New Covered Bridge (Yongchun, Quanzhou)

(Photo courtesy Overseas Chinese Museum)

东关桥　东关桥是一座长廊屋盖式桥梁，位于德化和莆田之间，尽管有点远，这座省级文物保护单位的古桥的确漂亮，尤其是在一位华侨捐献 100 万元修缮以后。东关桥建于南宋绍兴十五年（公元 1145 年），位于东平镇东美村，桥长 85 米，宽 5 米，飞架景色优美的湖洋溪。

像其他的古代木桥一样，桥的中间辟有一壁龛，屋梁上画着带宗教色彩的图画，桥墩上用巨石叠成支架大梁，两头俱作船型以分水势（就像安平桥和洛阳桥一样）。

乘车：乘泉州至永春专线车即可到达

开放时间：8：00—17：30　**电话：**23884202

厦门桥梁博物馆　虽然博物馆在厦门而不在泉州，这应该是下一站，那里可以欣赏中国对世界桥梁建设的贡献。博物馆保存全国及世界各地桥梁的模型和图片，还有取景角度非常好的海沧悬挂桥的相片。（后面我将告诉你该桥创下的世界纪录，不过现在要吊吊你的胃口）。

Supplement

The Legend of Luoyang Bridge

Neptune's Advice There are many legends about Cai Xiang. One says he tried ten times to lay Luoyang Bridge's foundation, but each time it was swept away by the powerful tides. In frustration, he sent an officer to find the Sea God and ask advice. The officer returned from who knows where with a one word suggestion, "Vinegar." Cai Xiang interpreted this cryptic word, and laid the bridge successfully.

Rev. Pitcher (*In and About Amoy*, 1912) has my favorite account:

> "It was during one of these squalls that a very remarkable thing happened, which led to the building of the bridge. At this particular time, while a large boat load of passengers was being ferried across, a storm came down upon them in wildest fury. Just when all hope was about to be abandoned of ever reaching the shore a voice rang out above the storm commanding one named Cai （蔡）to build a bridge across this dangerous point of the sea. They were soon after all safely landed. It was discovered later that there was but one person by the name of Cai living in that neighborhood. It was also learned that he had only just married, and that it had been revealed to his wife in some mysterious manner that she would be the mother of the man who was to build the bridge.
>
> "In due time the child was born who was named Cai Xiang and grew up a precocious youth. In his young manhood he became a mandarin. His mother took pains to tell him what had occurred in the storm, of what had been revealed to her years before, and what his mission therefore in life might be expected to be. Young Cai became deeply impressed and took steps at once to secure an appointment as mandarin in his native prefecture that he might undertake his appointed task. He knew it was against all custom and law for one to be appointed to office in his own district, he was therefore not a little puzzled to know how this desire of his was to be brought about. But fortune often favors those who are in earnest and in course of time circumstances brought out friend Cai to the palace of the Emperor, where he hit upon a novel as well as bold idea to accomplish his wish.
>
> "One day while walking in the Imperial grounds he took a pot of honey and wrote on a tree this sentence—'Cai Xiang the learned, be magistrate in your native prefectural city.' Sometime after the Emperor came walking along, and what his surprise was can only be imagined when he saw this sentence now emblazoned on a tree in living characters of armies of black ants that were feeding on the honey.

洛阳桥的传说

海神的启示　民间流传太多有关蔡襄的传说。其中一个说，蔡襄先后10次尝试为洛阳桥打桥基，但每次均被强大的海潮卷走。多次受挫之后，他派一个衙吏向海龙王求助，也不知衙吏从哪里带回一个字"醋"。蔡襄解读了龙王神秘的启示，桥基终于顺利砌成。

我最喜欢皮彻牧师在《厦门内外》一书中的描述。

"在一次狂风暴雨中发生了一件不可思议的事情，并最终促成洛阳桥的修建。有一艘载满乘客的大船横渡洛阳江，当行至江中，突然狂风大作，浪涛汹涌。乘客都以为这次要葬身大海，突然，从天空传来高声的指令，要姓蔡的人在此建造一座大桥。船上的人很快安全到达对岸。后来发现在附近的村庄只有一户姓蔡人家，并且他刚结婚不久，他的妻子得到某种神秘的启示，说她儿子将来要修建大桥。

"小孩准时出生，起名叫蔡襄，他长大成一个成熟老练的小青年。他年轻时成了朝廷的官员，母亲告诉他那次暴风雨所经历的一切，冥冥之中得到的启示以及他一生可能要完成的修桥任务。蔡襄被深深打动，并开始想办法获得回家乡为官的任命，这样才能完成建造洛阳桥的任务。当时朝廷明文规定，不准文武官员回原籍做官，因此，他也非常困惑，自己的愿望如何才能得以实现。但命运总是及时帮助渴求的人，后来他入朝为官，他无意中读到一篇故事，并萌生了完成愿望的好主意。

"有一天，他用一壶蜂蜜在御花园里的芭蕉叶上写下八个字——'蔡端蔡端，本府做官'。过了一会儿，皇帝漫步至此，当看到在芭蕉叶上由成千上万黑蚂蚁组成的这行活汉字时，感到无比惊讶。

"His surprise found expression as he read out in a loud tone of voice, 'Cai Xiang the learned, be magistrate in your native prefectural city.' Mr. Cai was conveniently near at hand, and at the same time innocently enough took the words of the Emperor as an appointment to the office he so much desired, and proceeded without delay to thank his sovereign for the great honor he had conferred on him. Though the Emperor protested that that was not at all his meaning—that he was merely reading the sentence which the ants had written (which by the way Cai had taken good pains to bring about, having carefully selected a tree with an ant nest at the base)—he held his majesty to the words as his intention to appoint him to this office. Finally the Emperor yielded...

"He began at once making preparation for building the bridge. His greatest task was in laying the foundations for the central piers as in that particular spot the rushing current never ceases its flow and ebb. How to sink the foundations there puzzled Cai Xiang for many a day, when it occurred to him to write to Neptune on the subject, asking him to be kind enough to keep the waters back from the place for one brief day, and to be so accommodating as to mention the date when that would occur. Then the question arose who was to take this letter to old Neptune.

"In answer it was discovered that there was a man living near by whose name was 'Able to Descend into the Sea.' This man was pressed into service and like a bold knight he set out to fulfill his mission, by laying himself down in a comfortable and dry spot where he proposed to stay until the incoming tides covered him, when he could communicate with the god of the waters. While he was waiting he fell asleep. How long he slept will never be known, but when he awoke he found the letter gone, and another addressed to Cai Xiang, though he was in the same spot that he was when he went to sleep.

"The letter was delivered to Cai Xiang. It contained but a single character 醋 (vinegar). It was indeed as gall and vinegar to receive such a message, for whatever could it mean! Struggle as he might with it, search his brain hard and long, he could make no sense out of it. Finally he began to break up the character into its different compound parts, and thereby he solved the problem and received his answer from old Neptune. The reply was that at evening on the 21st of the month the waters would be stayed. Thus: 二十一日酉. These directions were followed, the foundations successfully sunk and in due time the building of the wonderful bridge completed."

“他顺口大声念道：‘蔡端蔡端，本府做官。’蔡襄听罢，赶紧跪地领旨，感激皇帝对他的任命。虽然皇帝解释说，他不过是念出叶子上的字，并非当真（实际上蔡襄事先细心挑选了这颗芭蕉树，因为其根部有一个蚁巢），蔡襄争辩君无戏言，不能失信于臣。最后皇帝谕批他任泉州太守。

“蔡襄开始筹划建桥事宜，当时遇到的最大困难是无法在潮狂水急的海面上打桥基。苦想了好几天，蔡襄想到给海龙王写封信，请求他退潮一天，并告知具体是在哪一天。可由谁去给龙王送信呢？

“蔡襄问‘谁人下得海’，一个衙吏随即答道：‘小人夏得海！’此人误以为老爷叫他，随口应答。于是派他前往龙宫送信。夏得海躺在海滩上，想让潮水卷走，以便能向海龙王求助。不想他睡着了，没人知道他睡了多久，但醒来时发现信已不见，手上却有一封写给蔡襄的回信，尽管他原地不动。

“衙吏连忙把信交给蔡襄，打开一看，只见上面写着‘醋’字。蔡襄终于恍然大悟，把醋字拆开不就是廿一日酉时吗？这天果然风平浪静，潮水大退，桥基终于顺利砌成。”

Anhai Bridge (China's Longest)--in "City of Springs"

Chapter 9

Hui'an

Walled City, Stonemasons and Hui'an Maidens

Walled City of Chongwu

"…an out of the way village, in the county of Hui'an, or Gracious Peace. The situation of this village is a most picturesque and beautiful one. Just outside of it, Toa-bu, or the "Great Mother" rises abruptly from the plain, and towers up amidst the peaks and mountain-tops that range themselves around it… In front of it there flows a stream that comes out of the heart of the mountain, its waters pure and sparkling, and as yet undefiled by their touch with the outer world. It never dries up, for its fountains repose deep in the bosom of those everlasting hills; and no summer's drought, nor fiery-faced sun can penetrate to where they lie. Its music, too, never dies out, for jutting rocks, and stones worn smooth, and curves and winding passages, and miniature falls make it sing an endless song."

Reverend John Macgowan, *The Story of the Amoy Mission*, 1889.[1]

Hui'an's many claims to fame include the walled city of Chongwu (the best preserved Ming Dynasty wall in China, and one of only 3 or 4 walled cities left in the country), the uniquely costumed Hui'an maidens (Fujian's most unusual people group), and miles of beautiful beaches that are, supposedly, unlike any other on earth! Locals said of Chongwu's 13 kilometer beach, "American scientists say the sand is unlike any other sand on earth. Each grain is six-sided, and therefore very healthful for the body!"

Well, I've always thought this was another planet in the first place. But Hui'an's biggest drawing card is not its extraterrestrial sand but its stone, which locals have been carving for 1700 years.

① Macgowan, Rev. John, *The Story of the Amoy Mission*, reprinted by Ch'eng Wen Publishing Company, Taipei, 1971. Originally by Butler & Tanner, The Selwood Printing Works, Frome, and London, August, 1889, p.127

第九章

惠 安

古城墙、石匠、惠安女

“在惠安县，坐落着一个偏远的村庄，景色如诗如画。村庄的外部，突现一块平地，环山萦绕，高楼林立。村庄的正前方，一条小溪从山涧奔腾而出，虽与外界紧密相连，溪水却依然清澈见底，一尘不染；其源头深藏在崇山峻岭中，既不会有炽热阳光的照射，也不会出现夏季的干涸。叮当而过的泉水，伴随着兀突的岩石、光滑的石丸、蜿蜒的曲径、小巧的水瀑，一年四季，歌声不断。”

——约翰·麦高文在其《厦门传教纪事》一书中这样描述道[①]

惠安有许多遐迩闻名的东西，如崇武古城墙（目前国内仅存的三至四座古城墙之一，也是保存最完好的明城墙），着装独特的惠安女（据说是福建最奇特的人群）以及绵延不断、与众不同的迷人沙滩。当地人一提起 13 公里长的沙滩，总会说：“美国科学家称之为地球上无与伦比的，沙粒圆滑，对人体健康极有裨益。”

一开始，本人总认为这是在另一行星上。然而，惠安最吸引人之处在于其有 1700 多年历史的石雕工艺，而非其世外沙滩。

Extraterrestrial Beaches?

① 约翰·麦高文著：《厦门传教纪事》，1971 年由台北成文出版有限公司重印。该书最早由 Butler & Tanner 公司于 1889 年 8 月在伦敦出版，第 127 页。

Hui'an Stonemasons Over 120,000 of Hui'an's 920,000 folks work with stone. When Beijing needed stonemasons to build the People's Hall and Tiananmen Square in the 1950s, they shipped in workers from Hui'an, because with over 1700 years of stonemasonry under their belt, they are China's best.

Getting a head in life

Hui'an stone products –everything from furniture, and tomb stones to carvings of deities, demons, Mickey Mouse, and American presidents—attract tourists and buyers from all over China and Southeast Asia. (Take a statue home in your carry-on!)

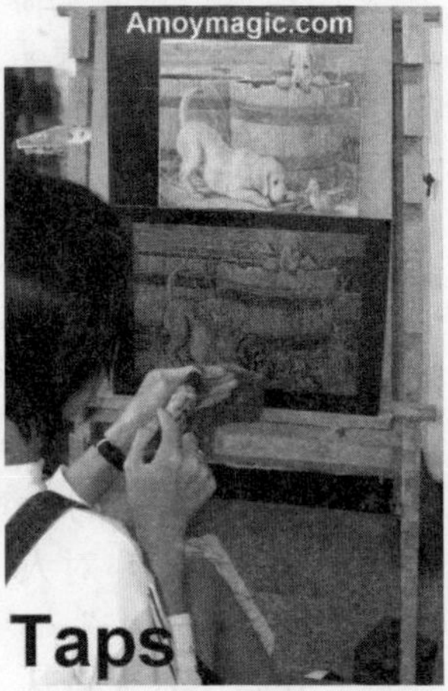

Taps

Shadow Carving Hui'an stonemasons may be the best but they aren't resting on their laurels. They continue to develop new materials, products, and techniques, including innovative shadow carving that would have Fred Flintstone clamoring for a family portrait.

Shadow carvers reproduce virtually any painting or photograph by tracing it onto a polished slab of marble, tapping out the design, dot by painstaking dot, and coloring it in. The figures are so realistic they look ready to jump off the stone.

Give the artists a good, high resolution family photo and they'll copy it for you, and mail it to your home. An 8 x 10 runs from 300 to 600 Yuan, depending upon the level of artistry desired (with some, dots are visible, whereas others really do resemble photos).

Purple Jade Shop (紫玉阁, Zi Yu Ge**)** Mr. Wang Hong (汪洪) offers great prices and service on customized shadow carvings by Chongwu's top artists, as well as stone carvings, jade jewelry, natural stones and crystals, and painted resin Hui'an Maiden figurines (small, light, easy to lug home for friends).

Phone: 0595-87686918 Cell: 13505075687.

Address: Inside Chongwu Tourism Gate, on the left (崇武旅游区 大门内)

惠安石匠 在惠安，92万人口中有12万人从事石雕工艺。20世纪50年代当北京要建造人民大会堂和天安门广场时，就是从惠安调去大批的石雕工人，他们技艺高超，堪称中华一绝。

惠安石雕产品包罗万象，既有家具、墓碑，又有神明、妖怪、米老鼠甚至还有历任美国总统，它们形态各异，神态逼真，深受国内及东南亚国家游客的欢迎（去惠安旅游，不妨随身带个石雕回去。如您有疝气，就不要带回去了！）。

Shadow Carving Magic

影雕 尽管惠安石雕工人技艺高超，但却没有停滞不前，而是不断地开拓新材料、开发新产品和新技术，影雕就是其中新拓展的雕艺，难怪乎弗雷德·弗里斯顿一直吵着要一张家庭合影的影雕。

对于影雕工人，他们可以复制出任何油画或照片。首先，在抛光的大理石上画出轮廓，尔后轻敲出图案，接着再小心地轻点，最后上色彩。图像形态逼真、栩栩如生。

你只要提供一张高度清晰的家庭照，影雕工人就可以帮你复制，甚至帮你邮寄到家。一般来说 8×10 寸的照片需花费 300~600 元人民币不等，这要取决于雕艺水准（有些影雕还可见打点，而有一些则简直是一张真实的照片）。

紫玉阁 老板叫汪洪，在那可以定做影雕，他同时还经营翡翠珠宝和精美的惠安女树脂雕像，小巧玲珑，很适宜携带或邮寄回家，作为礼物赠送亲朋好友。

电话：0595-87686918
手机：13505075687
地址：崇武旅游区大门内

Purple Jade Shop (Chongwu)

General Lin Lu – Father of Fujian Lins

Holy Land of Lin Clan

We know that Hui'an folk have been stone masons for at least 1700 years because the carved granite tomb of General Lin Lu, ancestor of all Fujian Lins, is over 1700 years old. You can visit this "Holy Land of Lins" at Tuling village, north of Hui'an about 20 minutes on the 324 highway (by the #144 km marker). There's not really that much historical about the place, since the tomb was completely made over now with new granite sculptures and concrete. But it's something to think that all of Fujian's Lins descended from this man, who in turn was the descendant of a man hiding out in the woods.

The Story of the Lins
By Miss Qu Weiwei

Bigan (比干) was a famous prime minister during the Shang Dynasty, and uncle of the stupid emperor Zhou (纣). An honest man, Bigan was forever pointing out his stupid nephew's mistakes. Eventually the heartless emperor had had enough, and cut open Bigan's heart (which did him little good because he was still heartless). The furious emperor wanted to kill Bigan's pregnant wife too, but she ran off and hid in a stone house in a forest (林, Lin), where she gave birth to a son whom she named Jian (坚, meaning hard, solid, strong).

Some years later, another tribe toppled the Shang Dynasty and set up the Zhou Dynasty (周朝). The new emperor respected Bigan's honesty, so he found his son Jian and gave him the surname of Lin because the forest had protected him from death.

So Bigan's descendant was General Lin Lu, ancestor of all Fujian Lins, including the great hero Lin Zexu, the famed writer Lin Yutang, and the sea goddess Mazu (whose real name was Lin Moliang).

Walled City of Chongwu This may be China's best preserved Ming Dynasty Walled city (one of only 3 left, I was told). This delightful town, with its uniquely clad Hui'an Maidens (considered Fujian's most exotic people group) is just up the coast from Quanzhou city and perched upon the horn-shaped Chongwu Peninsula. Originally an easily defended sentry post prized by famous heroes like Koxinga, the first Ming emperor, Zhu Yuanzhang, changed the name from Dousai to Chongwu, which means "advocating of arms," (maybe the Emperor was a Republican?). The walled city is well worth a visit—and fortunately you no longer have to endure Abortion Road to get there.

Father to son...

林禄将军——福建林氏之父 作为福建林氏宗亲的开山始祖，林禄将军的陵墓已有1700多年的历史了。据此，我们可以考证出惠安石雕工艺也至少有1700年的历史。林禄将军陵墓位于惠安北部涂岭村的林氏圣地，沿324国道（144公里处）北行大约20分钟的车程。由于陵墓已被崭新的花岗岩雕刻和混凝土所替代，因此确实无法找到那些具有历史价值的东西，但总会让人想起——所有福建林氏都是此人的后裔，而此人同样也是躲进深山丛林里一个人的后裔。

关于林家的故事

曲微微讲述

商朝有一位著名的内阁大臣，名叫比干。此人为人正直，总是不分场合数落纣王的不是。终于有一天，无情无义的皇帝受够了，残酷地剖开比干的心脏（这对纣王并无益处，因为纣王本人就是无心肠的人）。狂怒的皇帝想要把矛头再指向比干的妻子（怀有身孕），然而，比干的妻子一听说皇帝要杀她，赶紧逃之夭夭，躲进林中的一座石房里，尔后生下一个儿子，取名坚（意为结实、强健）。

几年后，另一部落推翻了商朝，建立了周朝。周朝皇帝敬佩比干的正直，找到他的儿子坚，册封他姓为林，以此纪念由于树林的保护而免于一死。

据此，比干的后裔名叫林禄将军，他是所有众多福建林氏的祖先，包括伟大的民族英雄林则徐、著名的作家林语堂以及海神妈祖（原名为林默娘）等。

崇武古城 崇武拥有中国保存最完好的明城墙（据说为目前国内仅存的三座古城墙之一）。这座迷人的小镇，位于泉州海岸线北部的呈牛角形状的崇武半岛上，居住着着装独特的惠安女（据说是福建最奇特的人群）。原先这里是一处被著名民族英雄郑成功和明朝开国皇帝朱元璋看重的极易防御的军事哨所，因此，后来把名字“兜塞”改为崇武，意为“崇尚武备”。这座古石城很值得一游。很幸运的是，你再也用不着走“流产路”到达那里了。

Abortion Road In the early '90s, the road to Chongwu was so bad that locals called it "Abortion Road" because no pregnant lady could take the pot holes and bumps without losing her child. My first trip from Xiamen to Chongwu took 8 hours, and we bounced so hard that I hit my head several times on the bus roof—which was 18 inches above my head. Fortunately, today it is smooth sailing all the way—but a century ago even an 8 hour trip would have seemed miraculous. In the 19th century, Mr. G. Philips wrote that the trip from Fuzhou to Quanzhou,

> "...which also takes five days to travel over, is bleak and barren, lying chiefly along the sea-coast, and in winter a most uncomfortable journey..." (Nowadays, it's only a 2 hour drive)

Chongwu's 2.4 km wall is easily the best preserved Ming Dynasty wall in existence, and constructed entirely of Hui'an's greatest natural resource: granite. By day and night all throughout Hui' An, young and old alike chip away with stone and chisel to create everything from intricate temple dogs and garden lanterns to Mickey Mouses (or Mickey Mice?). They also build granite homes—and I know for a fact they're cold in the winter! Worse yet, the poor men have no one to snuggle up too, as you're about to learn...

Hui'an Maidens (*Adapted from Amoy Magic*). Chongwu's isolation on its peninsula prevented the ancient Baiyue people from assimilating into the Han culture, so much of their unique culture and dress still survives today. Considered Fujian's most unique people group (though they are Han Chinese), they lure both tourists and social scientists with their unique fashions and strange marriage customs.

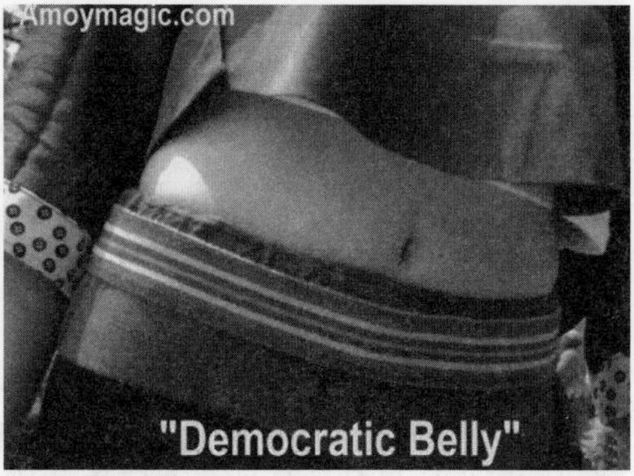

Unique Costumes Chinese say Hui'an girls have democratic bellies and feudal heads because their tight, short jackets and skintight black hip huggers that flare out baggily at the legs leave their bellies bare, but they fastidiously cover their heads with scarves. A Chongwu girl told me they emphasize the belly because in the Minnan dialect, belly "bazai" sounds like the Mandarin "facai" (to prosper). She also said the blouses were probably short to keep them out of the sea when they bent over the nets.

“流产路” 早在20世纪90年代，前往崇武的路相当糟糕。一般孕妇都因无法承受那凹凸不平的颠簸之旅而流产，因此，当地人称之为“流产路”。我第一次从厦门去崇武花了整整8个小时，一路上下颠簸，以至于我好几次头碰撞到车顶——要知道我的头离车顶还足足有18英寸！幸运的是，现在这条路像平滑的水面，任你驰骋。然而，在20世纪，八小时的路程看起来也算是不可思议的！早在19世纪，菲利普先生在其游记中写道：“从福州到泉州的行程，需要5天才能走完。这条路紧临海边，荒凉萧瑟，一毛不拔，冬天的时候更是苦不堪言……”（现在，只需2个小时的车程！）

2.4公里长的崇武古城墙是现存保护最完好的明城墙，它全部采用惠安当地的花岗岩石砌成。在惠安，不管白天黑夜，到处都有男女老少用凿子和石头雕琢出各种各样错综复杂的石雕工艺品，从寺庙里的狗到花园里的灯笼以及米老鼠等等。他们居住的房子也是用花岗岩石搭建的——我确切地知道，这种房子冬天很冷！然而，不争的事实是，穷人无依无靠，下文我们便会提到……

惠安女（节选自《魅力厦门》） 由于崇武半岛相对来说比较孤立，这使得古越人很难被汉族文化所同化，他们至今还保留着绝大部分独特文化与着装。作为福建省最具特色的人群（他们同样也是汉族人），惠安女正以其独特的习俗与婚俗吸引着越来越多的旅游者和社会学者。

独特的习俗 人们说，惠安女有“封建头、民主肚”，因为她们穿着又短又紧的上衣和宽广的长裤，头上又裹着头巾，却把肚脐暴露在外面。一个崇武女孩告诉我，她们看重肚脐是因为闽南话称肚脐为“bazai”和普通话的“发财”（恰当地说）发音相近。她接着说，惠安女的上衣又短又紧，是为了在海里弯腰拉网时不让衣服浸湿。

Hui'an Costumes (all blondes?)

Scarves Hui'an women have more scarves than Imelda Marcos has shoes. Miss Huang said they average 120 or so scarves, and some accumulate over 300. "The scarf makes my round face look longer and prettier," she explained. "And older ladies think scarves help them recover their youth."

Derriere Dowry Unmarried Hui'an girls wear a wide, colorfully embroidered belt, but Miss Huang was evidently married because she sported the heavy silver belt (from 1 ½ to 6 ½ pounds) that is not only a girl's dowry but also her marital insurance. "My husband doesn't dare leave me," she said, "because I have all his wealth around my waist." (Imagine so much silver going to waist.)

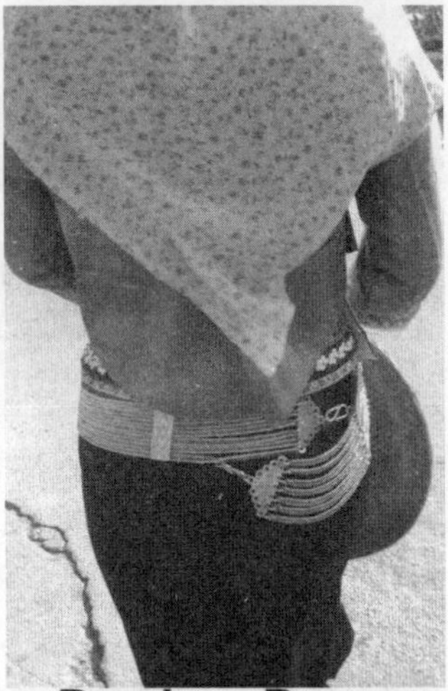

Derriere Dowry

Photophobia Hui'an women are notorious for photophobia. Miss Huang said many share a superstition common around the world—that being photographed shortens one's life. One wonders how they *develop* this *negative* outlook on photography.

Tying the Knot I like Hui'an costumes; I even have a small statue of one on my desk in the MBA Center. But I doubt they leave their bellies bare simply to keep the blouses dry. I think the uncovered tummy is simply a tantalizing 'revenge' for an ancient insult by a member of the lesser male species.

Legend has it that long ago, a young girl refused to marry a wealthy man. The man was determined to tie the knot though, so he bound her up, carried her off, and married her in spite of her protests. Even today, the designs around shirts' sleeves and waists are said to remind Hui'an girls of their tragic ancestor's bonds. I also suspect the marriage customs are a form of eternal revenge upon all men.

头巾 惠安女拥有头巾的数量比伊梅尔达·马科斯拥有的鞋子还多。黄小姐说，惠安女一般有 120 条左右的头巾，有的人甚至有 300 多条。“包上头巾使我圆胖的脸看起来细长又美丽”，她接着解释道，“许多年老的惠安女认为头巾会使她们看起来年轻。”

嫁妆 一般来说，未婚的惠安女会系着一条宽阔、色彩斑斓的有绣花图案的腰带。很显然，黄小姐已经结婚了，她系着一条很沉的银腰带（重量在 1.5~6.5 磅之间！）。那不仅是一个女孩子的嫁妆，同时也是维持婚姻的保障。“我丈夫不敢离开我，”她说道，“因为他所有的财富都在我的腰上。”（想象一下，她腰上有如此多的银子！）

忌照相 惠安女不喜欢照相是远近出名的。据黄小姐说，许多惠安女都很迷信——拍照会让人折寿。人们肯定琢磨着她们怎么会对照相一事如此消极？

结婚 我喜欢惠安女服饰。其实，在 MBA 中心我的办公桌上就有一尊小型惠安女塑像。但我并不认为她们的肚子暴露在外面只是为了不让上衣弄湿。相传，很久以前，一个年轻的女孩拒绝嫁给一个富家子弟，而这个富家子弟已经决定非她不娶。他首先把这位女孩捆绑起来，强行带走，然后不顾女孩的苦苦哀求和反抗，与她成婚。直至今天，惠安女衣袖和腰身上的花纹图案总会让她们回想起她们先辈所遭受过的悲惨的束缚。我甚至想，惠安女的婚姻习俗也许永远是对所有男人的一种报复吧。

Not This Year Dear... Ancient custom forbids bride and groom staying together on their wedding night, so the groom stays in a friend's house. On day two, the bride pays respects to the groom's family and gives gifts to the elders. On day three, the groom's sister leads the bride to the communal well to draw two buckets of water. After five days of obeying various customs, she returns to her parents' home. Bride and groom are not allowed to live together until she bears a child. But here I conceive a problem: when does she conceive?

Until a child is born, a woman cannot stay with her husband or even talk to him. If she meets him on the street she must treat him as if he were a stranger. If her husband visits her home, she must wait in back until he leaves. The newlyweds are allowed to stay together only 3 times a year: Spring Festival, Grave Sweeping Day, and Mid-Autumn Festival.

Don't take these women for granite!

Hui'an lassies may be bothersome brides, but they are also indefatigable laborers. They clean house by night and spend all day lugging ponderous loads of rock or grain on baskets slung over their deceptively petite shoulders. Meanwhile, the men fish, or chisel stone in quarries, or hawk victims for their motorcycle taxis, or hang out in tea shops moaning because their bride just told them, "Not this year, dear. I have a headache."

Chongwu Religion Religion is a big part of Chongwu life, and with wives like theirs, I can see why. On festivals, Chongwu people light candles and incense and offer sacrifices in the Temple of the 12th Lord, but nowadays, many also attend the newly renovated and expanded Protestant church, which was first built in the 1880s. As late as 1995, members sat on pews made of tree trunks split in half, but now the church has been rebuilt and expanded, and equipped with genuine pews, much to my derriere's delight. Chongwu's Catholic church attendance has also grown a lot recently. But Chongwu's most unique temple, by far, is dedicated to 27 PLA (People's Liberation Army) soldiers.

"Not this year, dear. I have a headache."

亲爱的，今年不行…… 古代习俗是不允许新郎和新娘在新婚之夜住在一起的，新郎只能借宿在朋友家。第二天，新娘才能到夫家去相互认识，同时送些礼物给年长者。到了第三天，新郎的姐姐就会领着新娘到村里的井打来两水桶的水。经过五天的各种各样习俗的洗礼，新娘子就可以回娘家了。只有当新娘子怀上第一个孩子后，夫妇才可以生活在一起。我感到好奇的是，她何时才会怀胎呢？

孩子出生前，新娘是不能和新郎住在一起的，即使谈话也是不允许的。假如他们在街上擦肩而过，也必须当成外人。如果新郎到新娘家去，新娘务必躲在里头直至新郎离开。他们一年只能有三次机会住在一起，即春节、清明节和中秋节。

也许惠安女是不讨人喜欢的，然而却是相当勤劳的。她们白天用娇细的肩膀承受那挑石挑谷的重活，晚上回家还得忙着家务活。而她们的丈夫，或者出海捕鱼，或者在采石场雕凿，或者骑摩的去载客，或者在茶馆唉声叹气，因为他们的新娘刚告知："亲爱的，今年不行，我头痛。"

崇武的宗教信仰 宗教信仰是崇武人生活的重要组成部分，尤其是家庭主妇。遇上节日，她们都会到第十二主教堂去献祭、烧香、点烛。近年来，很多当地人也会去刚修复扩建的始建于1880年的基督教堂。就在1995年基督教徒还坐在用树干劈成对半做成的简陋的长凳子上做礼拜，而如今，值得欣慰的是，都换成了有靠背的。崇武当地人去教堂做礼拜的也越来越多。在崇武，最奇特的庙宇当数供奉27尊解放军雕像的解放军庙。

A Chongwu Church

PLA Temple Imagine a temple that plays not Buddhist chants but revolutionary songs. Chongwu has one, thanks to Ms. Zhenghen, who grinned and hugged me like I was the prodigal son returned, then gave me the red carpet tour of her red army temple, and told me the tale behind it.

Zhenghen's family moved from Singapore to Chongwu when she was twelve. The following year, September 17th, 1949, the thirteen year old girl was strolling the beach when Taiwanese bombers began strafing the shore. Gallant PLA soldiers rushed out to her rescue; 24 died in the attempt. Miss Zhenghen tried to show her thanks and respect by offering sacrifices and incense to the deceased soldiers.

In 1991, with two million Yuan in donations, she built the PLA temple. Initially, the army objected, fearful she was creating another religion, but in the end they saw it as a great opportunity for folks to show respect for the PLA, and over the years not a few army officers have visited the unique temple.

Behind the altar loaded down with offerings of fruit, incense, crackers, soda cans, mineral water, wine and roasted watermelon seeds are the 27 little hand painted PLA soldiers. (Three other local PLA martyrs were added for good measure). The figurines are fully uniformed and supplied with rifles and pistols, mobile phones, whistles, first aid kits (a bit late for those?) and everything else a soldier needs. The 27 inhabitants are surrounded by toy tanks, airplanes, police cars, battleships, toy phones, and a pink plastic grand piano with a clown at the keyboard.

Miss Zhenghen has come a long way from the 13-year-old girl paying her respects with incense and fruit. I daresay that in a few centuries, folks will repeat the tale of how the 27 heavenly warriors descended upon a cloud to save Zhenghen from the evil minions across the Dire Straits.

解放军庙 你可能很难想象，一座庙里传出的不是佛经念诵，而是雄壮的革命歌曲。这座庙就在崇武。郑恨女士一见到我，笑得很开心，走过来拥抱我，好像见到失散多年的浪子回家。她一边带我走进庙里，一边讲述着有关庙的故事。

郑恨12岁时跟随父母从新加坡返回到崇武。第二年，即1949年9月17日，她正在海滩上闲逛，忽然，台湾军队的炮弹向海滩上轰炸过来，英勇的解放军战士急速跑过去，把她救回来，然而，却有24位战士为此献出了年轻的生命。从那以后，郑恨开始烧香、上供品，以表达对那些牺牲战士的感激和崇敬之情。

1991年，她用获得的200万元捐款修建解放军庙。起初，部队一直反对，主要是担心她会无中生出一种宗教来。但后来，庙宇修建好以后，部队觉得此举极大地方便了老百姓表达对解放军战士的崇敬之情。几年来，不少部队首长也纷纷来此瞻仰这一天下奇庙。

Well supplied-forever!

这座庙的供坛上插着香，供着水果、饼干、罐头、矿泉水、酒和瓜子。上面供拜的27尊手工描绘的解放军战士小雕像（其中，24位是救她的战士，另外3位是牺牲的当地部队烈士），个个全副武装，身上配有步枪、手枪、对讲机、哨子和急救箱（这对战士来说备得太迟了），以及战士的其他必需品，四周放有塑料的坦克、飞机、警车、战船、电话机和一台粉红色的塑料钢琴，键盘上还有一个小丑。

从少女时代开始，长期以来，郑恨都在为这些战士烧香和奉果，以表达对他们的崇敬之情。我敢断言，再过几个世纪，民间一定会流传着这么一个传说——27个天兵天将是如何降落在一朵云彩上，飘过海峡，把郑恨从恶魔中拯救出来。

Forest of Statues I think the Walled City's greatest attraction is… the Walled City! But even though this is the best preserved Ming Dynasty wall in China, many Chinese tourists give it but a cursory glance and head to the seaside to view Chongwu's biggest tourist attraction—the forest of 500 new statues. Why bother? You can see thousands, for free, in the stores and factories lining former Abortion Highway. But one walk through the Forest of Statues and I changed my tune.

Over 500 statues in this stone forest

Over 500 statues portray fascinating people and events in history and literature (like "Dream of Red Mansions" 红楼梦). The 108 famous generals are also a big hit (Chinese are really into generals; I doubt I could name a dozen American generals if my life depended upon it).

Hire a good guide to explain the stories behind the statues. For example, I'd have never known the polished black bull was stone, and that gave you good luck if you smacked it. Sounded like a lot of bull to me, but I smacked it, and the stone bull rang like a bell. I especially liked the chubby Maitreya Buddha, which I told my host looked like a Disney dwarf. "No way!" he said. "This beats Disney!" But I must have worried them because when I visited again a few months later, a granite Mickey Mouse stood behind Maitreya—for good measure, perhaps. Pretty mickey mouse, I thought.

Filial Piety A set of 24 statues represent the model sons in 24 tales epitomizing Confucius' ideal of filial piety. Eight-year-old Wu Meng bared his body so mosquitoes would feast upon him first and spare his aged parents. Wang Xiang was so pious that when his wicked stepmother wanted fish in the winter, he lay upon the ice to melt the river with his body heat. Heaven took pity upon him and gave him the fish. A pious daughter breastfeeds her ailing mom. A pious emperor obeyed doctor's orders and tasted his father's excrement to help diagnose his father's disease. Hindsight helped.

Deng deng (or, better yet, dung dung).

Deng deng, and Dung dung

石雕园 崇武古城最吸引人之处在于它至今仍是国内保存最完好的明城墙。然而，许多国内游客对此只是匆匆一瞥，便走向那雕有500尊石像的石雕园里游览。何必呢？你在惠崇公路（以前称为“流产路”）两侧的商店或厂房里可以很容易地看到成千上万个石雕产品。可是，当走进石雕园时，我的想法改变了。

石雕园里的500多尊石像都是有关历史上或文学书本上的那些令人着迷的人物或事件（如《红楼梦》）。《水浒传》里的一百零八将石雕像也是相当吸引人的（中国人对将军确实很感兴趣，换成我的话，我不知道能否举出几个美国将军的名字来）。

A Mickey Mouse Exhibit

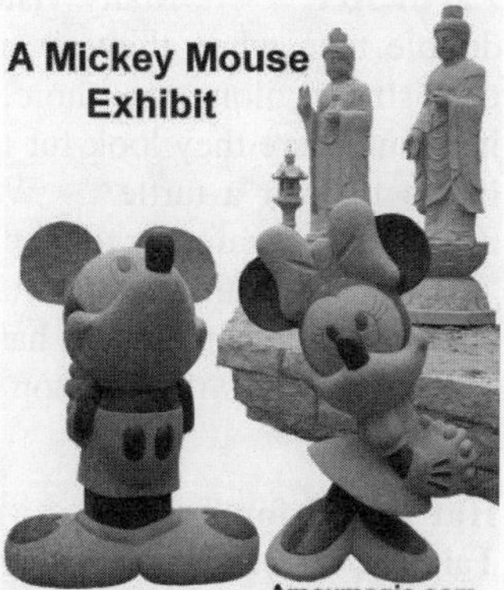

请个导游来讲解一下石雕背后的故事吧。就拿我来说吧，我从来都不会想到那头光滑的黑牛是石头雕成的，而且你击拍它的话，它还会给你带来好运。听起来很可笑，然而我一击拍，它就发出像钟声一样的声音。我还特别喜欢那尊胖乎乎的弥勒佛，看起来就像是迪斯尼的小矮人。“不，它可比迪斯尼的小矮人强多了。”我的同行说。几个月后，当我再次来到这里，发现弥勒佛后面立着一尊花岗石雕成的米老鼠，只为装饰而已吧。好可爱的米老鼠！

Breastfeeding Mom

孝道 这24尊石雕像充分体现了二十四孝的民间故事。如八岁大的吴蒙如此裸露身体，就是为了吸引蚊子咬他，而使他年老的双亲免遭蚊子叮咬。王祥那恶毒的后妈冬天里叫嚷着要吃鱼，他毫无怨言，平躺在结冰的河流上，以他炽热的身体融化冰块。苍天有眼，他终于破冰得鱼。心地善良的女儿给年老的母亲喂乳汁，以治疗她的病痛。……

Black and White Cats My favorite statues are the two colossal cats representing Deng Xiaoping's famous saying, "It does not matter if the cat is black or white as long as it catches rats." The black cat has not only the mouse but also ancient Chinese coins under its paw and on its tail. Noting the lesson here, I thought it appropriate to photograph Hui'an native Prof. Wu Shinong in front because he can sure "catch mice" (his story is at the end of this chapter).

Fishy example of "Earth Art"

Earth Art Many visitors do a double take when they see the boulders strewn along the shore, because here and there they look for the world like a fish, or a turtle. We have a Zhejiang art professor to thank for this "earth art." With a few deft taps of the chisel here and there, he has transformed rocks and boulders into various sea creatures. I was right on top of a giant fish before I saw it. Good thing I wasn't Jonah.

Hot Bread for Taiwan Many of the white ships anchored offshore are from Taiwan. Closer to Taizhong harbor (94 miles) than Xiamen, Chongwu was the mainland's first harbor to accept Taiwan ships. Chongwu and Taiwan folk jest that fresh baked Chongwu bread is still hot after making the two hour crossing to Taiwan. With so many delays implementing the long-awaited "San Tong" (Three Links), its nice to see that Chongwu already has her own "Mini San Tong" (小三通).

Enter here, exit...where?

Amazing Walled City Maze The walled city is amazing. It's also quite a maze. Of course, it's no problem getting out because all you have to do is head in one direction long enough until you reach the wall, which you can ascend to get your bearings before you descend and lose them again. I've considered tying a piece of string around my waist and reeling myself in afterwards, but some enterprising Hui'an peasant would probably cut the string and sell it. But after much trial and error (mostly error), I've figured out a surefire way of getting in and out.

黑猫和白猫　我最喜爱的是石雕园里的两尊巨大的石猫，体现了邓小平的经典名言：“不管黑猫白猫，只要能抓到老鼠就是好猫。”那只黑猫抓着只老鼠，尾巴上还有一枚中国古代的钱币。看到这，我突然想起，在石猫的前面拍一张惠安知名的企业家的相片是非常吻合的，因为他肯定会抓“老鼠”。（这个人就是厦门大学副校长吴世农教授，有关他的故事在本章末尾会阐述）

Prof. Wu Shinong and Black Cat
Two of a kind!

大地艺术　海岸边的岩石，有的看起来像鱼，有的像乌龟，使得许多游客看到了的是双重的景色。“大地艺术”出自于浙江的一个艺术教授之手，他用娴熟的双手略施雕琢，一块块岩石就成了各种各样的海生动植物。我站在一块巨石上面，还不知道它就是一条巨鱼。还好，我不是约拿。

送给台湾热乎乎的面包　离岸不远处停泊的白色船只是台湾渔船！崇武港比起厦门港来说，离台湾的台中港更近。它是祖国大陆第一个台轮停泊点。崇武和台湾的老百姓开玩笑说，在崇武刚刚烤出来的面包，经过2 个小时的横渡，到达台湾时还是热的。人们期盼已久的“三通”由于种种原因至今无法实行，然而，可喜的是崇武已有了自己的“小三通”。

叹为观止的古城迷宫　崇武古城很神奇，简直就是一个迷宫，很容易让人迷路。当然啰，走出来也并非难事，你只要朝着某个方向一直往前走，到达城墙后，爬上去好好看一看，辨明方向，然后爬下来，随即又迷路了。我也考虑过拿来一条绳子沿着自己的腰部卷轮状捆绕起来，可是一些胆子大的惠安农民也许会剪断绳子并将其卖掉。经过反反复复的尝试（大多情况是失败），我终于理出了一条清晰的进出路线。

The walled city has several large gates, and a few small ones. Enter the gate at the top of the narrow road that begins at the Protestant church and step back in time 300 years—except for the kamikaze motorcyclists who careen around corners, hands glued to their horns. Just down the path on the left is the Chen family's ancestral home.

Chen's Ancestral Home

Chen Family Ancestral Home The first time I peeked through the courtyard door of the Chen home, a granny grinned, spouted off something in the dialect, grabbed my arm, and led me inside for tea. They gave me a tour of their home, and showed me the ancestral paintings and photos.

They've been in this home for hundreds of years, and much hasn't changed—but Mrs. Chen *does* have a topnotch kitchen. Of course, this came as no surprise. Chinese are not only the planet's best cooks but also the best eaters, spending much of their waking lives cooking and eating delightful (most of the time) foods.

"What's cooking, Granny Chen?"

Their son was bent over a giant basin of dough making some of Chongwu's famous fish rolls. This family has sold them for several generations, and I bought about ten pounds to give to friends back home. Sliced and fried, they are heavenly.

At the T My landmark is the "T" intersection's temple (Sue misses it, every time). Turn right at the "T" and follow South Gate Street (Nanmen Lu 南门路) all the way to the seaside gate. Note the architecture—the rounded Minnan roofs, and the "flying sparrow" eaves. Also note the tailor, Mr. Chen. He uses a 100 year old Min River sewing machine—much the same as those used a century ago. Newly minted machines are made much the same, but no point in reinventing the wheel. They work, and they don't require electricity.

Chen family's fine fish rolls!

古城有好几个大大小小的城门。沿着狭窄的道路往前走，尽头就是城门，进入城门，里边有一座新教教堂，把你带回到300年前的时光（只是路上那些疯狂的摩托车手沿着城墙左右摇晃地飞驰，喇叭响个不停）。沿着小路走下去，左边就是陈家古宅了。

陈家古宅 我一走进陈家古宅的院子，一位老奶奶看见我在东张西望，她脸上带着微笑，不停地嘟囔着方言，然后，走过来拉住我的手，领我进屋喝茶。陈家人带我详细地参观了他们的古宅，还给我欣赏了他们保存的古画相片等。

据说，他们祖祖辈辈已在这古宅生活了几百年，大部分保留原貌。真没想到，陈大妈还有一间一流的厨房，当然啰，也不足为怪。因为中国人不仅精于烹饪，而且善于享受美食，他们总是把大把大把的时间花在烹调和饮食上。

他们的儿子正蹲在一个大盆子边制作崇武有名的鱼卷。陈家做鱼卷已有好几代了，我向他们买了约10磅重的鱼卷，回家后送给朋友。切片煎着吃，味道好极了。

在T形交叉路口 我在崇武古城内的认路标记是T形交叉路口的寺庙。（我的妻子苏珊每次路过都会忘掉）在T形交叉处向右拐，然后沿着南门路一直往前走，就到达靠海边的城门。

一路上遍览闽南建筑的圆屋顶、飞雀脊。裁缝陈师傅使用的“闽江”牌缝纫机已有100年历史了，确实跟那些100年前的缝纫机一模一样。现在的缝纫机构造大致相同，不同之处在于机轮重新改造过了，旧的缝纫机绿色环保，工作时根本不需要用电。

Lighthouse Ascend the wall opposite the temple and walk north to the lighthouse, which offers a nice view of the walled city, and of the large crescent of a beach, with its fine white extraterrestrial sand (Hui'an has miles of beautiful beaches). Then either return the way you came, or walk along the top of the wall (which helps you avoid the funerals, which can back you up a *dead* end).

Along the wall to the lighthouse

Funerals It seems that every time we visit Chongwu we encounter a long funeral procession of paid professional mourners, musicians – and plastic babies? The tail end of the procession often has several men bearing a litter containing naked plastic baby dolls. I asked what they symbolized but they said they didn't know. Rebirth, perhaps?

After seeing the third funeral in one day, I told an MBA student who was with me, "China has more dying people than any place on the planet."

"That's not true!" he protested. "We have great medical care here."

"It's mathematics, not medicine," I said. "Biggest population, remember?" His feathers slowly unruffled.

The walled city's streets are so narrow there is no way to escape funeral processions, so you just press your back to the wall and cover your ears to shut out the cacophony of cymbals, drums, trumpets, and suona. Suona is the horn commonly played at funerals, but I'd think the shrill thing would wake the dead, not comfort them.

The professional mourners were so surprised to see us Laowai, backs to the wall, that they forgot to wail and stared as us as if we were demons from hell itself, instead of just standard issue foreign devils from afar. I waved, they grinned and waved back—and then got down to business again, wailing piteously as if in apology to the extinguished object of this parade.

The Mourning After

灯塔 从寺庙对面的城墙爬上去，往北一直走，到了灯塔，环绕四周，古城全貌尽收眼底。那绵延的半月湾沙滩以及晶莹剔透的沙质确实让人心醉（惠安有好几海里长的美丽沙滩）。尔后你可以原路返回或继续沿着城墙走（这样可以避免碰上送葬队伍）。

葬礼 其实，每次去崇武观光，都会碰到一支排成长队的送葬队伍，队伍中有的是花钱雇来的职业送丧者和表演人员，还有塑料婴儿？通常在队伍的最后，会有几个男子抬着个轿子，里面装着几个裸体塑料玩具婴儿。我也问过他们，这些塑料婴儿做什么。他们也不清楚。也许是一种再生吧？

一天当中看了三支送葬队伍，我忍不住对随行的一个 MBA 学生说："中国每天去世的人比任何国家都多。""不对，"他抗议道，"我们国家有良好的医疗服务。""是数字，不是医药。你们有全球最多的人口，知道吗？"这时他才慢慢平静下来。

崇武古城里的街道很狭窄，碰到送葬队伍你就无处可躲，只得背紧贴着墙壁，双手捂着耳朵，以避免那些震耳欲聋的铜钹声、击鼓声、喇叭声和唢呐声（唢呐是送葬中经常使用的一种吹号）。这些刺耳的声音与其说是在慰藉死者，不如说是在试图弄醒他们。

送葬队伍看见我们这些老外背紧贴着墙壁，感到不可思议，他们止住了哭声，盯着我们，好像我们不像远道而来的外国魔鬼，而更像是来自地狱的恶魔。我向他们挥挥手，他们都微笑着回应，尔后又继续忙着手中的正事，哭得很伤心，好像是在为刚才的突然中断而愧疚吧！

Funeral Babies

The Chinese Stare One thing that has changed little over the past century is the Chinese Stare. Everywhere, people gather around the Laowai and stare. It's unsettling at times, but understandable if you realize that we also stare at unusual sites, or people. If I recognize a movie star in Los Angeles, I do a double take. If I see an Arab in robes and headdress, I stare. And let's face it—as we Laowai tourists roam the narrow winding streets of Chongwu, we stare at them! Worse, we take photos as they go about their lives, as if they were exhibits. So if we, the very unusual foreigner, are stared at, or surrounded by crowds, or have parents with little children point at us and say, "See, Little Plum Blossom, that's a foreigner!" (to which I often respond, "I can't help it!"), it's understandable. But fortunately, the crowds are friendly—and were even back in 1889.

THE STARE

Sue stops, crowd gathers in seconds

3 Minutes Later

7 minutes later, Sue vanishes.
Ann abandons her to her fate

When McGowan wrote *The Story of the Amoy Mission* in 1889, the Chinese were still smarting from the humiliation of defeat in two Opium Wars, and foreigners were not always the most welcome site. Yet even then, McGowan wrote that, once the Chinese got to know you,

> "The crowd becomes sympathetic. The sneer dies out of their faces. There is nothing that touches the Chinese heart so mightily as practical benevolence. It is a virtue they highly appreciate. Their stolid, emotionless features begin to light up with genuine feeling, and the eyes of some are twinkling and flashing as their hearts are moved…[what] has just happened has been a mighty revelation. It has brought you closer to the Chinese heart than you were before, and it has revealed to you the wondrous possibilities of the future…"

See no evil, hear no evil, do no evil

中国人的“盯视” 有种东西长期以来几乎一成不变，那就是中国人的“盯视”。在每个地方你都可以看到，人们围着老外，盯视着他们。偶尔会让人感到不自在。其实，如果你意识到我们老外对某些不寻常的人或事也会盯着看时，你就能理解了。比如我在洛杉矶碰见一位电影明星，我一定会多盯几眼；看见一个穿着长袍、包着头巾的阿拉伯人，也同样会盯着他看。因此，对于“盯视”，再说，我们这些老外游客在崇武曲折狭窄的街道上闲逛时，不也一直盯着当地人吗？而且更糟糕的是，还把他们在劳动、生活的情景当作是展览品进行拍摄。所以说，当人们围着我们这些奇异的老外盯视时，抑或有父母领着孩子手指着我们说，“瞧，小乖乖，那就是外国人”（对此，我通常的反应是：“我也没办法啊！”），我想那是能让人理解的。况且，围观群众也是很友好的。其实，这种友好早在1889年就有了。

1889年，麦高文撰写《厦门传教纪事》时，中国人正因两次鸦片战争失败的屈辱而深感痛心，老外也是不大受欢迎的。即使在那种情况下，麦高文在书中写道，中国人一旦跟你混熟——

> “围观的人群越来越富有同情心了，讥诮的表情也逐渐消失了。我想没有什么比实实在在的善行更能让中国人的心灵如此触动，他们极其看重品行。随着心灵上的震动，那种冷淡无情的表情逐渐被发亮的眼神、真挚的情感所代替，这真是巨大的变化，它让你能更贴近中国人的心，也预示着将来更多奇迹的发生……”

Talking Turkey

So as you stare at the places and peoples, accept their good natured stares in return! And given that they *are* going to stare, give them their money's worth, as I do when I talk to the village pigs, goats, chickens, and turkeys (both two and four legged varieties).

Huiquan Beer Quanzhou is famed not only for Anxi tea but also, more recently, Huiquan Beer. Though I'm not one to root for beer (root beer is more my speed), bona fide beer aficionados claim Huiquan beer is one of China's best—and ***the*** best with seafood.

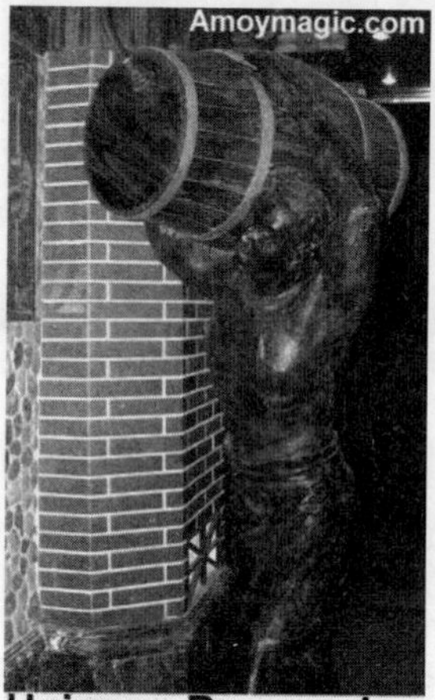

Huiquan Beergarden

Huiquan has invested hundreds of millions to give Qingdao Beer (produced in the former German colony) and the imports a good run for their money. After Professor Wu Shinong showed me around the sprawling, modern Huiquan factory, we visited the biergarten downtown (just outside the old factory), where my companions tasted various brews while I stared at the sculpture on the back wall that looked suspiciously like a giant marijuana leaf.

I can't really judge Huiquan beer, so I checked with the pros at **www.beeradvocate.com** and found this review by "Stoutman":

> "A Chinese surprise!!!! Very light and easy to drink with a hint of fruitiness in the aroma. The yeast culture provides the perfect refreshing spicy and fruity character that is expected of a wheat beer. Even stranger, this beer has an almost pale green color. It also has considerable more hop flavor than any of the traditional wheat styles of beer I have sampled. I generally dislike wheat beers, but this one is good."

Address: #157 Jianshe Street, Huian, Luocheng Township, 362100, PRC
Phone: 0595 8738-2369
Chinese website: **http://www.huiquan-beer.com/index.shtml**

因此，当你在盯着某人或某地看时，同时也接受他们回过头来友好地盯着你吧。而且既然他们确实是会盯着你看的，就好好给他们表演一回吧，就像我在崇武同村里的猪、羊、小鸡以及火鸡交谈（各种各样两条腿或四条腿的都有）。

Huiquan Beers

惠泉啤酒 泉州的安溪茶闻名海内外，近几年来，惠泉啤酒也很出名。我并不十分热衷于喝啤酒。但坦诚地说，惠泉啤酒是中国最好喝的啤酒，尤其配以海鲜为佐餐，味道绝对一流。

几年来，惠泉公司在青岛啤酒投入了大量的资金，也取得了丰厚的回报。吴世农教授带我们参观了惠泉啤酒公司和惠泉啤酒新厂区后，我们就到闹市区的啤酒吧（在旧惠泉啤酒厂门口）去参观，在那里同行的朋友品尝了各种各样的啤酒，而我却盯着后墙上的一幅雕塑作品发呆，这幅作品很像是一片巨大的大麻叶。

我确实不懂得品尝惠泉啤酒。因此，我就上 www.beeradvocate.com 网站浏览，发现以下的评论：

> “一个中国奇迹！淡而爽，略带水果味，因发酵而使得香料和水果味更让人心旷神怡，这就是人们所期望的小麦啤酒。更奇的是，这种啤酒呈淡绿色，它比我曾经品尝过的其他任何一种传统小麦啤酒更显得有苦味。平心而论，我并不喜欢小麦啤酒，但这却是例外，确实不错。”

地址：福建惠安螺城建设大街 157 号 邮编：362100

电话：0595-87382369

网址：www.huiquan-beer.com/index.shtml

Wood Carving While Hui'an's biggest drawing card is stone carving, the city also has quite a few factories producing quality wood statues. I waltzed in unannounced at the Hui'an Jusheng Crafts Company , and even though they knew I wasn't going to buy, the general manager, Mr. Lu Peiyang (卢培养) and his 16-year-old son Lu Dongqiang (卢东强) , served up the tea and gave me a tour of the four story factory.

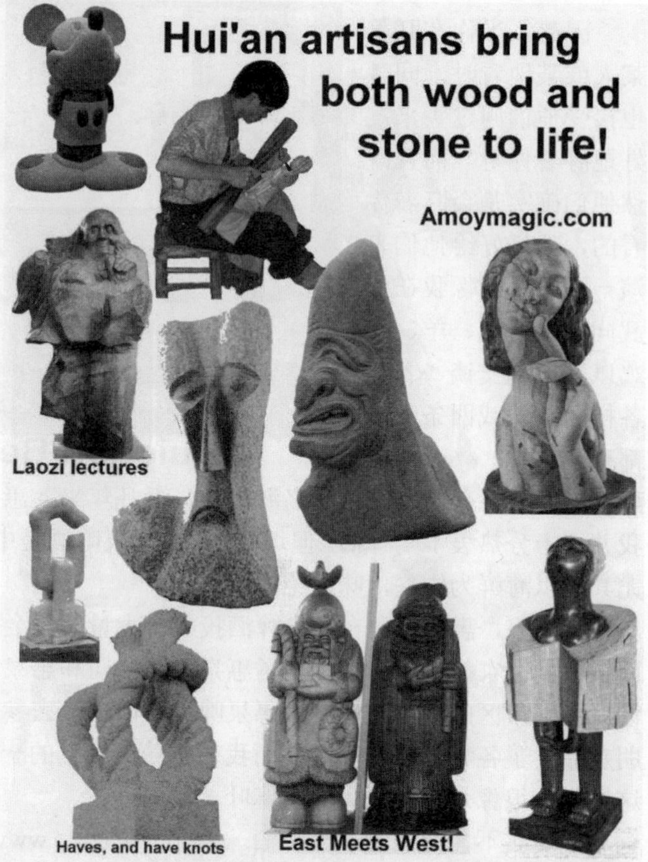

Mr. Lu said most of Hui'an's wooden statues are religious objects for export, and suggested I look for secular carvings in Putian or Xianyou, up the coast towards Fuzhou. I was surprised that, given the high quality of the wood and the artistry, the statues were painted, gilded and smothered in wigs and costumes. I asked what the point was of using expensive wood when mass produced plastic of ceramic would look the same. "Tradition," manager Lu said. "Temples want wood."

Jusheng Crafts Address: west side of 324 highway, just north of Luoyang Bridge.

Tel: (0595)8733-1199 E-mail: lupeiyang@21cn.net

木雕 尽管惠安最吸引人的是它的石雕艺术，然而在惠安，也有相当多的工厂在制作精美的木雕。在毫不知情的情况下，我心情愉快地踏进了惠安聚盛雕艺公司。该公司卢培养总经理和他 16 岁的儿子卢东强尽管得知我没有购买欲，他们还是很盛情地招呼我，献上茶水，带我详细地参观了他们四层高的厂房。

卢先生介绍说，大部分惠安木雕都是供出口的宗教用品（他建议我挑选一些靠近福州的莆田或仙游制作的非宗教木雕）。令人称奇的是，优质的木料配以高超的技艺，生产出了各种各样头戴假发、身穿盛装、上过油漆或镀金的木雕产品。当我问起为何不用塑料或陶瓷替代昂贵的木料（其实效果看起来是一样的），卢经理解释说：“这是传统工艺，寺庙也更喜欢木质的。”

聚盛雕艺公司地址：惠安县洛阳桥北，324 国道西侧

电话：0595—87331199

电子邮箱:lupeiyang@21cn.net

Malaysia's Nadu Gong
a down-to-earth fellow

Idol Talk The endless array of wooden idols brought to mind the old Chinese saying, "He who carves the Buddha does not worship them." And I wondered what kind of deities they were, and who on earth (or China) worshipped them. For example, the nattily attired idol wearing a fez and clasping a pile of gold coins in his lap looked Muslim—which wasn't too farfetched. Muslim traders, after all, were the best businessmen in the ancient Orient. But Muslims don't worship idols, and Miss Qu Weiwei checked it out and found he is Nadu Gong (拿督公), a local earth god (土地公, Tudi Gong) for overseas Chinese in Malaysia. When they first moved to Malaysia they discovered the natives worshipped the local earth in the hopes of a good harvest. The Chinese adapted the idea by piling some gold in the down-to-earth deity's lap so he would know just what kind of harvest the enterprising Chinese wanted.

For your edification, Overseas Chinese University's Miss Qu Weiwei gives us the stories behind three of the most common idols.

The Chinese Zorro! **Jigong Living Buddha** (济公活佛, or Geekung) is a favorite subject for sculptures and paintings, and one of China's most colorful characters. Also called "Crazy Mong" (Jidian Monk, 济颠), this wine swilling meat munching monk was loved by the common people because he cared for the poor and put the rich in their place—kind of like a Chinese Robin Hood（罗宾汉）or Zorro.

Jigong was born to the Li family during the South Song Dynasty in Zhejiang province. By age 12, he was already a Xiucai (秀才 skilled writer), but he was obsessed with the sutras and became a monk, changing his name from Li Xiuyuan (李修远) to "Daoji" (道济). Jigong loved meat, especially dog meat, and getting drunk, and in general acted like a mad man. This unorthodox behavior earned him the nickname Crazy Monk. Today, a cave by Linyin Temple's (灵隐寺) Flying Stone（飞来峰）has beds and tables named after Jigong because it is said that he went here to roast dogs and guzzle wine.

神像　眼前这些无数的木雕神像让人想起中国的一句古语："雕佛者，不拜也。"我不知道它们是属于哪种神，在地球上（或者在中国）谁来祭拜它们。例如，那尊着装华丽的神像，戴着红盖帽，膝部紧扣着一叠金币，看起来像回教徒（一点也不夸张）。毕竟，穆斯林商人是古代东方最杰出的商人，可是穆斯林并不崇拜神像，曲微微小姐仔细看了看，发现它是拿督公（即马来西亚华侨供奉的本地土地公）。当回教徒移居到马来西亚后，发现当地人崇拜土地公是为了祈求好收成。中国人沿袭了这种习俗，把金币叠放在所祭拜的神像膝部，神明就会知道富有创业精神的中国人需要的是哪种收获。

为了使我们有所启迪，华侨大学的曲微微小姐给我们讲述了三种最常见的神像背后的故事。

济公活佛　常见于雕塑和油画中的神像，是中国最具传奇色彩的人物之一。济公活佛也称济颠和尚或疯和尚，他是一个既大吃大喝却又受人尊敬的和尚，因为他一心想着贫苦人，对付有钱人就像是个中国式的罗宾汉。

Jigong, the Mad Monk

济公于南宋年间出生在浙江省的一个李氏家庭。十二岁时，他就中了秀才，但是对佛经着迷的他做了和尚，也将他的名字李修远改为道济。他的叛逆行为（喜好食肉，尤其是狗肉，而且经常喝得酩酊大醉，简直就像个疯子）使他得了一个绰号叫"疯和尚"。如今，在杭州灵隐寺的飞来峰上有一个洞，里面有许多床和桌子是以济公命名的，据说是因为济公曾到那里烤狗肉和畅饮酒。

Jigong used a ratty old folding fan for a weapon, which in his magical hands was deadlier than the sharpest sword. Armed with this magical fan, he fought injustice and punished stupid or bad officials. The Chinese saying for his behavior is, "When encountering injustice, aid the oppressed" (路见不平拔刀相助, lu jian bu ping bo dao xiang zhu). Like Zorro, Jigong fought injustice with style, usually causing the villain to look ridiculous, which earned him the affection of the downtrodden.

Ji Gong prepares to wok his dog

The Story of Jigong 《济公传》) was written about the mad monk, and some people believe he was one of the 500 arhats, but because Buddah did not approve of his behavior (especially his wine guzzling and penchant for roasted puppy legs), his statue is always in the temple aisles and not with the other more holy arhats (who still manage some mighty bellies for being vegetarians; I suspect they had a few hot dogs too).

Nazha（哪吒), the fat little boy with the funny haircut, is another frequent subject of paintings, sculptures, and folk tales. The story actually come from India. The boy Nalakuvara was said to be the third son of General Li Jing (李靖) in heaven. His father disliked the boy and treated him like a monster because he was in his mother's womb for three years and emerged round like a ball.

Nazha's powerful teacher gave him a magic ring 乾坤圈—a great gift, but one that led him to his doom when he practiced with it upon the seashore. The ring was so powerful that it stirred up the dragon king's underwater home. Nazha wasn't really trying to make waves, but the infuriated lizard sent his son to fight Nazha. After Nazha killed the dragon's son, the dragon king determined to kill the entire family of General Li Jing (who was much lower rank than the dragon). To save his family, Nazha committed suicide by cutting his body and bones to pieces. His powerful teacher then saved him by using a lotus for his body, after which he became the original flower child. Over the years, the legends multiplied. In "Journey to the West" (西游记) Nazha even battled the monkey king (but was defeated by the superior simian).

济公以一把破旧的折扇作武器，凭借着魔力般的双手，舞起扇来比起锋利的剑更具杀伤力。他用这把魔力般的扇来对付不公的行为和惩治愚蠢、邪恶的官员。中国有句古语，“路见不平拔刀相助”。济公以自己的方式对付不公的行为，往往使恶人看起来荒谬可笑，因此，也赢得了广大受压迫者的爱戴。

《济公传》就是有关这位疯和尚的故事。有些人把济公当成五百罗汉之一，但因为佛教教义不允许他的异常举止（尤其是饮酒和吃狗肉），他的塑像总是置放在寺庙的通道上，而没有跟其他罗汉排放在一起（这些食素的罗汉也搞得肚子大大的，我想，恐怕他们也多少吃些热狗吧）。

哪吒　一个留着滑稽发型的胖小孩，也是经常被作为油画、雕像和民间传说的题材。故事真正来源于印度，这个男孩名叫哪拉库娃拉，据说是天国李靖将军的第三个儿子。由于他母亲怀胎三载，他出生时像是一个圆球，他父亲对他很是厌恶，把他当成怪兽看待。

哪吒的师傅送给他一个神奇的礼物——乾坤圈，正是这礼物导致他的毁灭。当他在海边舞弄练习时，乾坤圈威力如此之大，以至于搅乱了龙王的地下宫殿。哪吒本意并非要惹是生非，然而，愤怒的龙王还是派他的儿子与哪吒决斗。结果，当哪吒杀掉了龙王的儿子后，龙王决定株杀李靖将军整个家族（其家族地位远远低于龙王家族）。为拯救家族，哪吒把自己的身体及骨剁成一块一块的。可是哪吒那个威力无比的师父使用一朵莲花救活了他——这就是原先最早的莲花小孩。几年过后，各种各样的传说也在民间应运而生了。在《西游记》里，哪吒甚至还与孙猴王决斗过（但最终还是被猴王击败了）。

Black and White Wuchangs These two demons stick out above the crowd because their long red tongues are always sticking out, lolling down past their fat chins. Mr. White Wuchang has a white face, white clothes, and a tall white hat upon which are the four characters Tianxia Taiping (天下太平), meaning "All under heaven is peaceful. Mr. Black Wuchang has a black face, black clothes, and a black hat with the characters Yijian Facai (一见发财), meaning, "You prosper as soon as you see him." Both phrases are nice (peace, and prosperity), but Chinese fear seeing them because what is the point of either peace or prosperity if you're dead?

White Wuchang

Mr. White and Mr. Black have different personalities but the same job description: kill folks and escort their souls to hell, where they are judged by the king of hell after they have undergone various procedures and ordeals such as crossing the Naihe bridge (奈何桥), where they must drink the Mengpo Soup (孟婆汤) so that they forget everything that happened during their life.

It seems a bit unfair to be judged for a life you've totally forgotten, but Mengpo soup or not, in Chinese mythology, once you die there is hell to pay.

Supplement

Professor Wu Shinong —Hui'an Entrepreneur

It's easier to understand Hui'an's rapid economic growth when you've spent a few years in the shadow of a Hui'an entrepreneur like Professor Wu Shinong, of Xiamen University's MBA Center (now the University's Vice President). He epitomizes the local talent and drive that made ancient Zayton a City of Light, and that is rekindling that light today.

Prof. Wu Shinong

Dynamic Duo
(a little tongue in cheek there!)

黑白无常　由于这两个魔鬼又长又红的舌头垂伸而过下巴，因此，他们看起来总是很显眼、与众不同。白无常惨白的脸，一身素白，头上戴着一顶高高的白帽，上面写着“天下太平”四个字；黑无常漆黑的脸，身着黑装，戴着一顶黑帽，上面写着“一见发财”四个字。这两个短语都很吉祥（和平、富贵），然而，人死了，再拥有这两样东西有何用呢？因此，中国人都很惧怕看见黑白无常。

尽管白无常和黑无常个性不同，他们做事却异曲同工：杀人后，把人们的灵魂带入地狱。在地狱里，人们要经受各种各样的酷刑，如过奈何桥、喝孟婆汤，以此忘掉世间诸事，所有这些过后，阎王就会给他们一个准确的评价。

其实，对彻底忘掉的人生作一个评价看起来似乎有点儿不公，然而，孟婆汤喝也罢，不喝也罢，就像中国人迷信所言：人死后就要去见阎王。

附录　吴世农教授——惠安籍企业家

当你用几年的时间与惠安籍的企业家如厦门大学 MBA 中心的吴世农教授（现为厦门大学副校长）相处在一起时，你就不难理解为何惠安经济发展如此之快。他身上体现了古代光明之城——泉州当地人的聪明才智和进取精神，如今这座城市仍然散发着光芒。

Wu Shinong was born in Hui'An county, and after graduating from high school in 1974, he spent four years as a factory worker during the Cultural Revolution. His parents owned a small grocery store before 1949, and after Liberation escaped being labeled capitalists because of their stores' small scale—but since then the Wu family has proven to be entrepreneurs to the bone.

After 1949, they became sales people in a State store. Today, they have two houses and several stores. Wu Shinong has three older sisters and one older brother. The brother runs a small watch store, the older sister is retired, the middle sister runs a small transportation company with three trucks, and the youngest sister works at Huiquan Beer (her policeman husband was my guide on one of few dozen Chongwu trips).

Wu Shinong, like the rest of his family, is an entrepreneur. In fact, I joke that his name should be Wushi buneng (无事不能) because I suspect there's not much he can't do when he puts his mind to it. But fortunately for me, he has focused his talents on China's future: MBA business education.

In 1978, Wu Shinong entered Xiamen University, majoring in economics, and in '86 received an MBA from Dalhousie in Canada. From 1987 he worked on a joint Ph.d. program between Xiamen University and Dalhousie; spending two years in Xiamen and one year in Dalhousie, was a Fulbright scholar in Stanford in 1994, and returned to Xiamen in 1995. Today, he is one of the three vice chairmen of China's MBA Education Supervision Commission.

Though young (my age!), Professor Wu Shinong has been integrally involved in every step of China's development of management education, beginning with the initial feasibility study in 1987 to 1989, and the test group for MBA education in China (18 professors from 9 universities organized this).

In 1999, Prof. Wu was selected as one of the ten Chinese professors who have had the most influence on empirical research in economics and management. The prolific professor has written 4 books, co-authored three, and published 60 pieces in leading journals. He also helped translate Steven Ross' bestseller, "Corporate Finance." Prof. Wu was the first person in China to study security market efficiency, and the effect of financial information on capital markets.

Early on, Prof. Wu upset the apple cart when he published a paper on China's accounting in *General Accounting Research*. In part because Professor Wu is not an accountant, traditional economists heatedly argued his points, but younger scholars recognized the validity of his arguments and approach. During his studies, Professor Wu saw that the holistic viewpoint was crucial—"seeing the interrelationships between capital markets, accounting information, and how they affect one another and investors."

Professor Wu, who studied economics and statistics, said,

吴世农教授出生于惠安县，1974年高中毕业后，恰逢"文化大革命"，就进厂当了四年的工人。解放前，其父母开了一家小杂货店，解放后，怕被列为资本家而外出逃生了。然而，从那时起，吴氏家族就显示出了经商的天赋。

1949年以后，其父母在国营商店当营业员。如今，他们拥有两幢楼房和好几个店面。吴世农上有三个姐姐和一个哥哥，哥哥经营着一家小型手表店，大姐已退休在家，二姐拥有一家三部货车的运输公司，三姐在惠泉啤酒厂工作（其丈夫是个警察，在我崇武之行曾当过我的向导）。

正如家庭其他成员，吴世农也是一位企业家。其实，我曾开玩笑说，他的名字应改为"无事不能"。只要他用心去做，没有什么难事可言。对我来说幸运的是，他对中国的未来——MBA教育倾注心血和才智。

1978年，吴世农考入厦门大学经济系，1986年在加拿大达尔霍斯大学取得工商管理硕士学位，1987年起从事厦门大学与达尔霍斯大学联办的哲学博士课程研究，其中两年在厦大，一年在达尔霍斯。1994年在斯坦福大学做福布莱特学者，一年后回到厦门。如今，他是中国MBA教育管理委员会的三位副主席之一。

尽管年轻（跟我一样年纪！），吴世农教授长期以来全身心投入到中国经济管理教育的发展上，从1987年至1989年的初始的可行性研究，到中国MBA教育的测试小组（来自9所大学的18名教授组成该小组）。

1999年，吴教授被推选为从事中国经济与管理的基础性研究领域最具影响力的10个教授之一。这位著作颇丰的教授自撰4本书，合著3本，在权威的杂志上发表论文60篇。同时他还协助翻译史蒂文·罗斯的畅销书《公司金融》，他还是中国第一个研究证券市场效率和金融信息对资本市场的影响的人。

早些时候，吴教授在中国会计专业杂志《综合会计研究》上发表的一篇论文引起了不小的轰动。可能是因为他不是一个会计师，传统经济学家严厉抨击他的观点，而年轻一代的学者却认同他的论点和方法。在学术研究中，吴教授发现全局的视角很关键——"资本市场与财会信息之间相互关联、相互影响，并影响到投资者的决策"。

在研究经济学和统计学时，吴教授提到：

"In 1991, because the Chinese capital market was just established, there was no precedence, very short history, and no promotion of empirical studies. In 1995 I started thinking about this problem, and we had a better information base at that time, and I was able to show that the capital market did react to financial information, and corporations' announcements. So I started thinking about this. In 1993 I wrote the first paper about capital market efficiency, but I only had 16 firms from Shanghai and Shenzhen security exchange to study. It was a small number, but it was only the first attempt. Nowadays we have larger samples--sometimes more than 1000 firms. And now you can find that there is relatively stable behavior, or patterns to examine, and you can compare or use western capital market theory to apply to China's situation, and you can see differences, and explore the reasons for the differences. There are so many questions of interest."

Regarding Xiamen University MBA, Professor Wu said,

"Only a handful of Universities can offer comprehensive Ph.D.s in management (in all specialties). Xiada is one of them. In July 1990, Xiada was the first Chinese university allowed to offer a Chinese MBA; Nankai followed one week later. MBA degrees weren't official then, so the graduation certificates said, "Economics (Business Administration M.A.)." Students were upset, so we called it the "Masters of Economics (Business Administration).

"Nankai, like Xiada, began as a joint project with Canada. They had the first graduates one week after Xiamen University MBA—they were told by Beijing to follow the procedures already worked out with Xiamen University."

In his copious free time, Professor Wu is a husband and father--and judging from his daughter, doing pretty well at that too. His daughter is a math wiz, as well as good at English and Chinese, in the top 15 of her school, and wants to study journalism, law, or management—first at Beijing University, and then on to Harvard, Stanford, or Cambridge.

“在 1991 年，中国的资本市场刚刚建立时，没先例可借鉴，没有实证研究。因此，在 1995 年，我开始着手思考这个问题，那时，由于有较好的信息基础，我很快能够证明——资本市场的确对金融信息和公司通告产生影响，我随即琢磨、研究。1993 年我首次写了一篇关于资本市场效率的论文，当时从上海到深圳的证券交易市场里只有 16 家公司可研究，确实少得可怜，但毕竟只是尝试而已。如今，已有更大样本，有时甚至有 1000 多家公司。你可以发现，当中有相对稳定的模式值得去探索、检验，你也可以把西方资本市场理论应用到中国的现实进行比较、分析，从中可以看出不同之处进而研究此种不同的成因，的确很有趣。”

谈到厦门大学 MBA 教育，吴教授说：

“国内只有少数几所大学能授予管理方面（所有专业）的综合性的哲学博士学位，厦大是其中的一所。1990 年 7 月，厦大是中国第一所能授予 MBA 学位的高校，一周以后，南开大学紧跟其后。当时，MBA 学位并非正式的，毕业证书上注明的是“经济学”（企业管理），学生们也颇有微词。因此，我们也就称之为“经济学硕士”（企业管理）。

像厦大一样，南开大学也开始与加拿大合作办学，有了自己首届毕业生，但这只是厦大 MBA 授予一周以后的事了。同时，南开大学也被告知要按照厦门大学 MBA 的程序进行授予。”

从他女儿那里了解到，空闲时间，吴教授扮演着一个好丈夫、好父亲的角色。其女儿是个数学迷，在学校里她的英语和中文总是名列前 15 位。将来她打算在北京大学而后到哈佛大学、斯坦福大学或剑桥大学学习新闻、法律和管理专业。

Chapter 10

Nan An—Home of Koxinga

Jiuri Mountain (九日山) The official starting point of the Silk Road of the Sea was not Quanzhou city proper but Jiuri (9th Day) Mtn in Nan 'An, about 7 km from Quanzhou City's west gate. The Han Chinese had a big (or actually, a very small) reason for not settling down on the coast—mosquitoes.

The coast teemed with malarial mosquitoes, and tens of thousands died before they moved inland. Only after a massive land reclamation effort, which drained the malarial marshes, were Chinese able to move to the coast itself. But Jiuri was an auspicious place to begin because of its perfect "fengshui" ("wind and water" – the Chinese geomancy that dictates much of Chinese life).

A Chinese guide in N.E. Fujian told me that a NASA photo showed glowing spots all over China, and on inspection they all turned out to be ancient tombs—thus proving, scientifically, the validity of fengshui (either that, or China has a few dozen Chernobyls).

The mountain is called Jiuri (9th day) because from the Jin to the Song Dynasties, disposed nobles in Quanzhou climbed the mountain each year on the ninth day of the ninth month, and gaze with longing towards their former home in the north. And here they performed the Safe Passage Ceremony, for both Chinese and foreign ships, to the "God of Transportation" (precursor of California Highway Maintenance).

Yanfu Temple. Fujian's oldest temple (or second oldest, some argue), was built in 288 A.D. at the base of Jiuri Mountain, facing the river to the south, with hills on the west, east and north, like an armchair. Jiuri offers ideal 'fengshui'—and a picturesque pallet for centuries of calligraphers.

第十章

郑成功的故乡——南安市

九日山 官方认定的海上丝绸之路的起点并不在泉州，而是在泉州西门外约7公里的南安九日山。汉族人不在海边居住有一个巨大的理由（实际上，只个很“小”的理由）——蚊子。

由于海岸充满传播疟疾的蚊子，造成成千上万人死亡。经过大规模的土地改造，排干疟疾衍生的湿地，人们终于能够移居海岸边，但九日山因为是个风水宝地（“风水”是能预示生活方方面面的中国式占卜），一直是海上丝绸之路的吉祥起点。

> 一位闽东北的中国导游告诉我，美国宇航局提供的一张宇航照片显示，中国大地有许多闪光的点，经过认真考察，证实这些全是古墓。于是，从现代科学技术方面证实了风水的有效性（或者，中国拥有许许多多切尔诺贝利式的核电站）。

从晋代到宋朝，被流放泉州的衣冠士族每年九月九日登上此山，登高远眺，寄托乡思，久而成习，故称此山为九日山。在这里，人们为中国和外国船舶举行仪式，向“交通神”（即加州养路工的前身）祈求航程平安。

延福寺 福建最古老（又有人说第二古老）的寺庙延福寺修建于公元288年。它位于九日山下，南面临河，东、西、北面均为山脉，形状就像一张太师椅。九日山是一处风水宝地，几百年来也是书法名家一处别致的砚墨台。

Yanfu Temple (288 A.D.).

Chinese Scholar (Smith, 1908)

> At Dr. Lim's we met a calligrapher of note. Persuaded to write an inscription for us, his brush almost miraculously brought life and movement to the paper. With a superbly graceful precision, his hand seemed to be evoking beauty that was already there, rather than making a dogmatic statement. But the Chinese have, it seems, always known that truth and beauty cannot be taken by storm.
>
> Averil Mackenzie-Grieve

Calligraphy While Yanfu Temple is one of Jiuri Mountain's 36 official sites, the real drawing card is calligraphy. My Chinese guide boasted, "Every meter of these cliffs is covered in ancient calligraphy!" Rather like American subways, I thought.

UNESCO Calligraphy Jiuri even has English calligraphy! The 1991 UNESCO Maritime Silk Road Expedition visited Jiuri Mountain and left an English inscription, with signatures in many Western languages. The English UNESCO inscription reads,

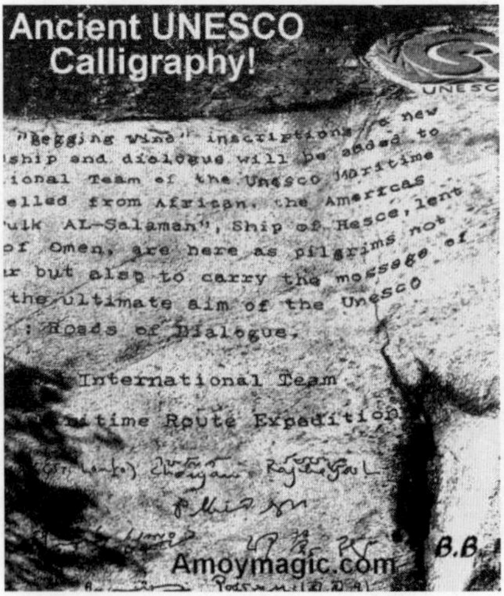

"Seven centuries after the 'begging wind' inscription a new inscription illustrating friendship and dialogue will be added to Jiuri Hill. We, the international team of the UNESCO maritime route expedition, who have traveled from Africa, the Americas, Asia, and Europe on board the "Fulk al Falan" ship of Hefoe lent for the occasion by the Sultan of Oman, are here as pilgrims not only to renew that age old prayer but also to carry the message of peace between peoples which is the ultimate aim of the UNESCO integral study of the silk road. Roads of dialogue. 15th February 1991, International Team Maritime Route Expedition."

> 在林博士家，我们遇到了一位著名的书法家。大家请他给我们写幅字，只见他手中的毛笔神奇般地把生命和韵律带到纸上。他下笔优美、精准到位，好像双手是在唤起已经存在的美，而不是在做机械的工作。看来，中国人已经知道，真理和美是不能被剥夺的。
>
> ——埃夫里尔·麦肯齐·格里夫

书法　虽然延福寺是九日山的三十六景之一，但真正吸引人的是九日山石壁上的书法，中国导游夸口说九日山有“山中无石不刻字”之美誉。我想，这与美国的地铁极有相似之处。

联合国教科文组织的考察记事石刻　九日山上竟然还有英文碑文！1991 年联合国教科文组织海上丝绸之路考察团参观九日山，留下一方英语碑文，还有许多种西方文字的签名。英语的碑文翻译如下：

“在九日山最后一次祈风仪典之后 700 余年，我们，来自非洲、美洲、亚洲和欧洲的联合国教科文组织海上丝绸之路国际考察队员，乘坐阿曼苏丹提供的‘和平号’考察船来到这里。作为朝圣者，我们既重温这古老的祈祷，也带来各国人民和平的信息，这也正是联合国教科文组织丝绸之路——对话之路综合研究项目的最终目标。为此，特留下这块象征友谊与对话的石刻。海上丝绸之路国际考察团，1991 年 2 月 15 日。”

The most important inscriptions are the records of the sacrificial rites held by South Song Dynasty Quanzhou officials when they prayed for smooth sailing (what UNESCO called “begging winds”, I suppose). Other key inscriptions include those by famous philosopher Zhu Xi, and the unique inscription by Luoyang Bridge’s builder Cai Xiang. Where other calligraphers wrote on paper and had it transferred to stone, Cai Xiang wrote directly on the stone—but what would one expect from a man who could get bridge building advice from King Neptune himself (see page 166).

Chenxu Pavilion

A concrete pavilion near the peak, crafted to resemble wood, honors the esteemed poet Chenxu, who lived there 23 years. A round, flat stone is inscribed with 翻经石(Translating Sutras Stone), in memory of the Indian monk (拘那罗陀, Indian name, or 真谛三藏, Chinese name), who lived here about 300 A.D. while translating Buddhist scriptures into Chinese. He must have had company because he scratched a Chinese chess board into a stone.

One of the most unusual inhabitants was a monk who lived in a tiny cave for 44 years. Some say he was Chinese, others say Indian. Regardless, its hard to believe he could have spent his entire life in that hole-in-the-wall.

Stone Buddha 石佛 is 300 years older than the Old Stone Saint in Quanzhou. After he lost his head during the Cultural Revolution, Hui’an artisans crafted a cement head, which probably helps give Stone Buddha a more concrete philosophy on life.

Getting to Jiuri: Bus: # 6, or tourist bus line # 602 **Hours**: 8:00-17:30

这里最重要的碑文是那些记载南宋泉州地方官吏为求得行船顺风，举行祭海祈风仪式的文献。（我猜就是联合国教科文组织所说的“祈风石刻”。）其他留下碑文的名人还包括著名哲学家朱熹、洛阳桥的修建者蔡襄。奇异的是，其他书法家都是把碑文写在宣纸上，再印刻到石壁上，而蔡襄却是直接在石壁上书写的。对一个能从海龙王那里得到造桥秘诀的人，还有什么事做不成呢？

在山顶建有一个水泥亭（精心制作，外观像木亭）以纪念令人尊敬的在此生活 23 年的古代诗人陈煦。在一块正面平坦的巨石上刻着“翻经石”，纪念公元 300 年在此居住的印度和尚（其印度名叫拘那罗陀，中文名叫真谛三藏），他把印度佛经翻译成汉语。从他在石头上刻画中国象棋棋盘这一点判断，当时他应该还有同伴。

This Stone Buddha offers concrete advice

这里最奇特的居住者应是一位在小山洞居住了 44 年的和尚。有人说他是中国人，也有人说他是印度人。不管怎样，他毕生生活在那狭小黑暗的山洞里，实在令人难以置信。

石佛　石佛比泉州的石圣徒早 300 年，“文化大革命”期间，石佛的头丢失，之后惠安的石匠精心制作了一个水泥的佛头。

乘车：乘 6 路公交车或 602 路旅游专线即可到达九日山

开放时间：8：00—17：30

Mr. Cai serves tea

Minnan Village Cultural Landmark 蔡资深古民居 For a delightful look at 19th century life, visit Nan'an's sprawling Minnan village just south of Guanqiao, and 2 km west of the 324 highway. The 16 house complex, which now has 200 residents, was built between 1865 and 1911 by Mr. Cai Qian （Cai Zishen), a Nan An native with three brothers and ten sons. At age 16 he emigrated to the Philippines, where he prospered, and after carving a name for himself in the Philippine history books, he returned to Nan An to carve (literally) a home for himself and his descendants.

None Like Mr. Cai's What makes Mr. Cai's home really stand out is the profusion of intricate stone, wood and tile carvings, from granite foundations to intricate ceramic eaves. The endless carvings gave rise to a local saying, "You can have millions, but not have a house like Mr. Cai."

The caretaker, a 4th generation descendant of Mr. Cai, gave us tea, and then a tour. The village has stone sidewalks covering the drainage, firewalls between each row of buildings, and large courtyards to dry grain. As I entered the home, I was told that Minnan homes always had 3 steps to represent Tian (天,heaven), Di (地, earth), and Ren (仁, benevolence). There are also four doors, and a Minnan tradition reminds one to "respect parents when entering the right door," and "respect others like brothers" when exiting the left door. Of course, one should never, ever, enter through the two center doors!

Mr. Cai's Minnan Village

蔡资深古民居　想痛痛快快地了解19世纪闽南人的生活，可以参观位于官桥镇南部、324国道以西2公里的蔡氏古民居。这片有16座汉式古厝的建筑群，是由蔡资深于1865—1911年间修建的，现仍有200多人居住其间。蔡资深是南安人，有3个兄弟10个儿子。他16岁随父漂洋远渡菲律宾，历经十余年苦心经营和积攒，成为当时菲律宾的巨富，在菲律宾的历史书留下英名后，他功成名退回到南安，为自己和子孙后代雕琢（毫不夸张地说）这一民居群。

Mr. Cai

无与伦比的蔡氏古民居　蔡氏古民居真正引人注目的是那些复杂精细的石雕、木雕和泥雕，从花岗岩墙根到精细的陶瓷屋檐。因不计其数的雕刻，闽南一带流传着一句谚语“有百万富，无蔡氏厝”。

古民居的馆长，蔡资深的五世孙，用好茶招待我们，并引领我们游览古民居。古民居有石板材铺成的人行道，下面是下水道；每排建筑之间有隔火墙；古厝前有宽敞的庭院用来晒谷子。老蔡介绍说闽南房屋的台阶都有3级，分别代表天、地、仁。每座房子的大门均有4扇，闽南的传统习俗，从右门进记得“尊重父母”，左门进“兄弟般尊重他人”，但是，任何人不能从中间双扇门进出房屋。

Doors Traditional houses had four front doors, but the two center doors, with their brightly painted celestial guardians, were always kept barred, and opened only for the Emperor. Everyone else, including the master of the house (and her husband) used the side doors.

Last year, a man in West Fujian threw open his center doors with a flourish and said, "Only for the emperor—and today, for you!" It was a nice gesture, but with everyone watching, I could not bring myself to step over the lintel, so I said, "Not even us American devils are that fat!" And as my host laughed, I slipped in through the right door.

Ming Dynasty Styrofoam The chipped corner of an old, richly carved "beauties bench" (美人靠, upon which footbound beauties spent their days on display) revealed not wood but some white material. I looked closer and discovered it was Styrofoam! But I wasn't overly surprised. Chinese invented everything else, so why not Styrofoam? But it turned out that a 20 part TV series about Koxinga's descendants had been filmed here and this was just a leftover prop.

Mr. Cai's Unusual Well Chinese love wells, the older the better—like the 1,000 year-old-well at Ashab Mosque, or the 2,000-year-old well at Wuyi Mountain's Minyue King Palace. And of course, they swear that the water in each well is as clear as the day it was dug (regardless of decades of tourists losing within its depths their eyeglasses, cameras, handkerchiefs). Mr. Cai's well was not old, but it was allegedly very unusual. The water is supposedly warm in winter and cool in summer. Professor Wu Shinong drew some water from the well to prove the point, but it seemed neither hot nor cold. Near the well was the Cai clan stone tub in which girls bathed in water to which had been added aromatic herbs.

门 传统的房屋的大门有4扇，中间两扇画上色彩鲜艳的守门神像，平时总是上闩，只有皇帝进出才开。其他任何人，包括房屋主人（以及她的丈夫）只能从边门进出。

去年，一个闽西人用炫耀的手势打开他家的正门，对我说："正门只为皇帝开，但今天，为你开！"他很礼貌地迎宾，但众目睽睽之下，我不敢轻易跨过门槛。于是，我说："即使是我们美国鬼子也没有那么胖！"主人听完大笑，我急忙从右门溜进去。

明代的泡沫塑料 一张有破损缺口的"美人靠"（顾名思义，乃裹脚美人展示自己，消磨时光的地方）露了马脚。它并不是木头而是某种白色的材料。我靠近一看，发现它居然是聚苯乙烯泡沫塑料！对此，我并没有过于惊讶。中国人什么东西都可以发明创造，为什么泡沫塑料就不可能呢？最后查实，有一部有关郑成功后代的20集电视连续剧曾在这里拍摄。这只是剧组遗留下的一个道具。

Ancient styrofoam?

奇特的水井 中国人都喜欢水井，年代越久越好，比如清真寺有1000年历史的古井，武夷山闽越宫有2000年历史的古井。人们都一致肯定地说，井水如同开挖时一样地清澈（无视水井深处数十年来游客丢落的眼镜、相机和手帕）。蔡氏古民居内的水井年代并不久，但据说很奇特：冬天温和，夏天凉爽。为了证实这种说法，吴世农教授特地从井中打了一桶水。蔡氏家族的石浴缸就在井边，当放进一些芳草后，家庭中的女孩子们就可以在水中洗澡。

Well done!

Virgin Mazu?

Virgin Mazu? The ancestral shelf's various gods included a local god with a flowing white beard, and a small Pusa that evoked quite a debate. One man claimed it was the Virgin Mary, because Mr. Cai had spend most of his life in the predominately Catholic Philippines. Another argued she was a Buddhist goddess, perhaps Guanyin (the Hindu god who had a sex change to become the Chinese goddess of mercy). Yet another said it was Mazu, who like Mary was also a virgin, and therefore perhaps the same person. I stayed out of the conversation.

Eclectic Architecture Given the architecture, who knows what religion they worshipped! One wall's base has a Hindu lotus motif, while a nearby roof has Muslim style eaves (the roof dragons, by the way, were allowed on the homes of 7th level government officials or higher).

Tom ate Jerry?

Tom & Jerry Many carvings illustrate historical stories or fables. One wall's base has a granite mouse stealing a gourd, but his days are numbered because a granite cat is eyeing him. A wooden wall carving depicts the 24 models of Confucian filial piety that we saw represented in Chongwu's Field of Statues—the son baring his arm for mosquitoes to keep them off his parents, the youth melting ice with his bare back to get a fish for his ailing wicked stepmother, the maid breastfeeding her ailing mother, the pious Emperor tasting his father's excrement to help diagnose his disease, deng deng and dung dung. We could also learn a lesson or two from the headless horseman…

Headless Horseman During the Cultural Revolution, Red Guards destroyed cultural treasures in even the most remote places, so Mr. Cai's home, so close to a highway, was not neglected. They destroyed or defaced carvings, and chiseled off so many heads and faces that that Mr. Cai's house has more headless horsemen than Sleepy Hollow. Like the carvings of Confucius' tales, these headless statues also teach a lesson to those of us who want to get a head—or keep our head.

贞女妈祖？ 祖传下来的佛龛供奉的众多神佛中，有一尊飘着松垂白胡子的本土佛像，这尊小菩萨的来历存在争论，有人认为它是贞女玛丽，因为蔡资深毕生大部分时间生活在天主教占主导地位的菲律宾。也有人说它应是佛教中的观音菩萨（改变性别的印度神佛，之后成了中国的慈悲大佛）。还有人说它应该是妈祖，像玛丽一样，她也是贞女，或者她们甚至是同一个人。我不介入这些争论。

兼收并蓄的建筑风格 谈到这里的建筑，真搞不懂他们究竟信仰什么宗教！在一面墙根上有一幅印度荷花图案，而在附近的屋顶上却有穆斯林风格的屋檐（而只有朝廷七品或七品以上官员的住宅才允许在屋脊上雕龙）。

猫和老鼠 很多雕刻讲述的是历史故事和传说，在一面墙根上，一只石雕耗子在偷窃油葫芦，可它的时日不长了，因为一只石猫正对它"猫"视眈眈。一堵木墙上雕刻着儒家二十四孝，在崇武的石雕工艺博览园也可以看到，如卧冰求鲤、乳姑不怠、亲尝汤药等等。我们也可以从石刻无头骑马人身上得到一些教训……

Headless horseman

无头的骑马人 "文化大革命"期间，红卫兵横扫许多文化宝藏，位于偏僻山村的文物也不能幸免于难，更何况离公路很近的蔡氏古民居。红卫兵摧毁或涂掉各种人物和动物雕刻上的头和脸。于是，蔡氏古民居的无头骑马人比"断头谷"还多。就像儒家传说二十四孝故事的雕刻一样，这些无头的塑像也给我们深刻的教训（我不知这教训是什么，但必定是一种教训）。

Elegant old furniture. Rooms were rather bare by American standards, but what little furniture they had was exquisite. One room was empty but for a round mahogany table with inlaid marble top, and benches. The canopied beds now fetch thousands of dollars in antique stores, though Xianyou has excellent reproductions. (Imagine my dismay when an Anxi peasant friend told me they had just burned a beautiful 200-year-old carved canopy bed because a grandmother had died in it!)

Renovations Endless carvings and calligraphy are nice, but for me it was a bit overkill. What I most appreciated was the sheer functionality of the place, right down to small details like the sliding slatted wooden windows. But if Mr. Cai's mansion cost a pretty penny to build, it is now costing the government a small fortunate to keep it up as well. Nan An's former Mayor Chen said the government has spent over one million Yuan in restoration and installation of fire alarms, and hires security guards to protect their investment. Unfortunately, these guards are about 30 years too late to stop the Red Guards' from beheading horsemen.

Mayor of Nan 'An Enjoys Local Music

Music to my Ears At the Cai mansion guard gate we came across elderly gents playing traditional instruments. They gave us a rousing performance of Southern Music and Mayor Chen unabashedly belted out the accompaniment for some ancient Minnan folk songs. But high pitched folks songs in the nasally Minnan dialect aren't exactly my cup of tea (or coffee either), and it must have showed. The man playing the two-stringed Chinese fiddle (二胡, erhu) apologetically explained that Minnan singers are limited because they have only the five notes of the ancient pentatonic scale. It sounded to me like they had dozens of notes, and none in a key that I'd ever heard of. But I smiled, and said, "No problem. I know all eight notes and I can't sing either."

Getting There: Bus #9 **Hours**: 8:00 – 17:30 **Phone:** 86892290

典雅的古家具　按照美国人的标准，这里房间摆放太简单了，但他们所有的家具都很精致。房间的空间很大，只有一张嵌有大理石花纹的圆形红木桌和几张板凳。现在那些带有排楼的古式床在古董商店里要价数千美元（虽然你可以在仙游县的工艺城买到漂亮的仿制品）。一位安溪的农民朋友告诉我，他们刚把一张十分精致的，具有200年历史的镂花排楼床烧掉，就因为他祖母在床上去世，我听呆了！

Sliding windows

古宅修缮　无数的雕刻和绘画虽好，但在我看来实在是太多了。我更欣赏的是其十分实用的整体空间布置，以及房屋的一些细部如可以两边滑动的百叶木窗。如果说当时蔡氏古建筑群是花巨资修建的，今天政府花在房屋维护的支出也不菲。原南安市长陈先生介绍，政府已投入100万元修复房屋和安装消防警报系统，还雇请了保安人员保护古民居。可惜的是，这些保安不是30年前雇请的，要不他们也许可以阻止红卫兵敲掉浮雕上骑马人的头。

天籁之音　在蔡氏古民居的大门前，我们遇到一些正在演奏传统乐器的老年人。他们弹奏着动人的南音，陈市长也劲头十足地随着乐曲吟唱起南音。但说实话，带着很重鼻音的闽南话吟唱音调极高的南音，我不太喜欢，我一定把这种不喜欢暴露出来了。其中的二胡弹奏者略带歉意地解释说，演唱南音者不多，因为在古代五音阶体系中，只有5个音符。而在我听来似乎有数十个音符轮换跳跃，只是没一个是我熟悉的。我还是微笑告诉他："没关系，就像我虽然8个音符都懂，却一句也不会唱。"

乘车：乘9路公交车可达蔡氏古民居

开放时间：8：00—17：30　**电话：**0595－86892290

Nan'an Cuisine After visiting the Cai Mansion, we had a delightful lunch of Nan'an Cuisine (Minnan cuisine, but with some delightful twists I'd not seen elsewhere). I especially enjoyed the lamb rib (羊排, yangpai) with peanut sauce, the taro and black mushrooms, and the Minnan rice with dried oysters and taro (芋头饭). I thought it would be hard to stomach the local specialty, "Twice boiled fish stomach in pork broth" (鱼鳔煲), but it was actually quite tasty. We also enjoyed bitter melon and pine nuts (苦瓜和松子) and Nan'an's most expensive fish, Eastern star fish (东星鱼), which costs 175 Yuan a jin (1.1 lbs) even here in the outback. I think they misnamed it. It should be named Eastern 5-star fish! After a dish of hot succulent crab (which Chinese call a "cool" food), we were served piquant ginger tea, which is "hot." This balanced the body's "heat" and also cleared the palate for the next course.

As we ate, Mayor Chen explained that the son-in-law of Tan Kah Kee (Chen Jiageng) was born in Nan An, and after the Japanese war most of Xiamen University's money came from the son-in-law, not Tan Kah Kee—hence Xiamen University and Nan An's close relationship. But Nan'an's favorite son is, of course, the Japanese/Chinese pirate-cum-hero liberator of Taiwan, Koxinga! So we trudged off to his ancestral home's Koxinga memorial hall.

Koxinga Memorial Hall (郑成功纪念馆, Zheng Chenggong Jinian Guan**).** Koxinga, who liberated Taiwan from the Dutch, is as much a hero to the Japanese as the Chinese. For one thing, Koxinga was partly "made in Japan"—born in Japan of a Japanese mother and Chinese father from Nan'an. Japanese also admire his bravery and loyalty, and during the 19th century, plays about Koxinga were as popular in Japan as Shakespearean plays in England. Koxinga died in Taiwan and was buried in Tainan until his grandson brought his body back to his ancestral home in 1699, but today Taiwan has over 100 temples dedicated to Koxinga.

南安美食 参观完蔡氏古民居，午餐我们享用南安美食（属闽南菜系，但有一些新花样以前从来没见过）。我特别喜欢带花生酱的炸羊排、芋头、黑木耳、海蛎干芋头饭。我想要吃下那道特色的鱼鳔煲可能受不了，可是它味道实在好，还有苦瓜松子、东星鱼（南安最贵的鱼，即使在沿海一斤也高达 175 元）。要我说，这鱼的名字起错了，应叫东“五星”鱼才对！享用了一盘美味的蒸蟹（中国人叫它冷菜）后，

Koxinga

上了开胃的热姜茶。据说这样可以平衡人体的“冷热”，也为更好地品尝下一道菜清清味觉。

我们边吃菜，陈市长边解释陈嘉庚先生的女婿是南安人，抗日战争爆发以后，厦门大学资金主要由其女婿提供，因此厦门大学与南安有很密切的关系。当然，南安人最喜欢的儿子还应算上抗击荷兰侵略者收复台湾的郑成功。于是，我们又跋涉前往郑成功纪念馆。

Koxinga
Forest of steles

郑成功纪念馆 郑成功从荷兰侵略者手中收复台湾，在中国人和日本人眼中一样是个英雄。首先，郑成功一半是“日本制造”，出生于日本，母亲是日本人，父亲是中国南安人。日本人对他的勇敢、忠诚也十分钦佩，19 世纪有关郑成功的戏剧在日本有如莎士比亚戏剧在英国一样流行。郑成功死于台湾，安葬于台湾，直至 1699 年他的孙子才将其迁柩归葬在故乡。但今天，台湾仍有 100 多座用于纪念郑成功的寺庙。

Calligraphy or charicature?

Man of Steles The Koxinga memorial has photographs, paintings and artifacts, and to the right of the memorial is a "stele forest" with a large collection of stone steles graced with the calligraphy of famous folks. When I asked how they got important personages to laboriously carve Chinese characters onto stone, my guide looked at me as if I were from outer space and not just another country (though Chinese does strike me as another planet at times), and said, "They didn't carve the stone. They wrote it on paper, and workers traced it onto polished granite or marble and carved it out."

I had no idea what they said, but I appreciated their innovativeness. In fact, they were so innovative that my Chinese friends could not read some of them either. Maybe they were doctor's prescriptions?

The characters on one stele were stylized roses. Another used the beautiful ancient characters that resembled what they represented (sun, moon, mountains) until centuries of scholars so stylized them that they became unrecognizable. One calligrapher drew his characters in such a way that they resembled a scholar (for the life of me I could not figure out what it said).

The exhibit also has some of Koxinga's calligraphy, in which he warned, "Study is most important." Maybe so, but good marksmanship didn't hurt either—especially after the scholar Koxinga burned his Confucian robes and went to war. While Edward Bulwer-Lytton claimed "The pen is mightier than the sword," I suspect that usually only holds true when the pen is 22 caliber.

After the memorial and forest of steles, check out Koxinga's ancestral home at the bottom of the hill, and then visit the Koxinga Mausoleum.

Getting There: Quanzhou Bus to Shuitou (水头)

Hours: 8:00 – 17:30 **Phone**: 8698-7138

Koxinga Mausoleum(郑成功陵墓, Zheng Chenggong Lingmu)

Getting There: Special Quanzhou Bus to Shuitou (水头)

Hours: 8:00 – 17:30 **Phone:** 8690-8271

Koxinga's Ancestral Home

郑成功碑林 郑成功纪念馆陈列相片、绘画和手迹，在纪念馆右侧有一片碑林，雕刻着历代名家的书法作品。当我问他们如何让这些名人成功地把这些文字刻到石碑上时，导游用奇怪的眼光看着我，似乎我不是来自另一个国度，而是来自另一个星球（尽管有时中国对我来说确实像另外一个星球）。他介绍说："这些名人并不是直接把字刻到石碑上，而是写在宣纸上，由石匠把它描摹在抛光的花岗岩或大理石上面，然后雕刻而成。"

我听不大懂，但我十分欣赏他们这种富有创新的精神，实际上有些名人太有创意了，结果连中国朋友也看不懂其中的某些字（或许这些是医生的处方？）。

在一方石碑上，所有的文字组成一朵玫瑰。另一方石碑上，书法家用优美的古汉字非常逼真地表现出其所代表的物体（如日、月、山）。数百年来，书法家就是这样追求风格，结果汉字也就变得无法辨认了。有一位书法家运笔独特，结果整幅字就像一位古代文人（我无论如何也搞不明白上面说了什么）。

展馆还保存着郑成功的墨宝，他警示世人"至乐无如读书"，这或许是对的，可好枪法同样是有百利而无一弊，尤其是在郑成功烧毁儒巾儒服从军以后。尽管爱德华说过"笔比剑更锋利"，我猜想，当笔是手枪时，才是这句名言唯一正确的时候。

参观了纪念馆和碑林，来到位于小山坡下方的郑成功故居，最后参观郑成功陵墓。

乘车：乘泉州至水头专线车即可到达郑成功纪念馆和碑林。

开放时间：8：00—17：30 **电话：**0595－86987138

郑成功陵墓

乘车：乘泉州至水头专线车即可到达郑成功陵墓

开放时间：8：00—17：30 **电话：**0595－86908271

Supplement 1 Legend of the "Made in Japan" Chinese Hero Koxinga

Zheng Chenggong (1624-1662), called Koxinga by the Dutch, learned his trade from his father Zheng Zhilong.

Zheng Zhilong was from Shijing 石井 (stone well), at the mouth of Anhai creek (location of the famous Anping Bridge). In his youth he studied foreign trade in Macao, then sailed to Japan and applied Portuguese trade principals to piracy. By the 1620s, Zhilong's enormous fleet literally ruled the Fujian coast. In 1626 and 1627 he attacked and took possession of Amoy (Xiamen) Island, which became the base for his piracy and smuggling operations. In 1628, Zhilong surrendered to the Ming authorities so he could enjoy official status, and as a reward he was promoted to major and then provincial military governor, thus making the transition from pirate to politician (which was not much of a transition). By now, Zhilong's family were practically the overlords of Fujian province, and with his tremendous wealth, he built a walled town south of Quanzhou in Anping (Anhai), which became a prosperous trading center.

Zheng Zhilong supplemented his enormous fortune by selling protection to traders—which they dared not refuse, because Zhilong had over 1,000 ships and a private navy under his control. But Zheng Zhilong sealed his fate when he surrendered to the Manchus after they invaded Fujian, because he was opposed by no less than his son, Koxinga.

Somewhere in Zhilong's busy pirating schedule he had found time to marry a Japanese maid, Miss Tagawa, who bore a son: Fu Song, aka Zheng Chenggong, aka Koxinga. Legends claim that stars fell and the heavens sang on the night of his birth.

When Koxinga was seven, his father shipped him back to the ancestral home of Nan An for school. Like all fathers before and since, Zhilong wanted his son to have what he did not have as a youth—namely, lots of homework.

Koxinga was an excellent scholar and survived both school and homework, and at age 21 headed off to Nanjing State College, never dreaming that his future lay not in scholastics but in piracy and politics—thanks to the militant Manchus.

After a peasant army overthrew the Ming dynasty, the Manchus waltzed into the power vacuum and created the Qing Dynasty. After a fight in Fuzhou in 1646, Tagawa (Koxinga's mother) was raped by Manchus on Amoy and committed suicide. When Koxinga's father surrendered, Confucian filial piety dictated that Koxinga also throw in the towel (remember the 24 parables of Confucian piety?), but for some reason (perhaps his mother's suicide?), Koxinga parted ways with his father.

附录 1 驱逐荷寇的爱国者——郑成功传奇

郑成功（1624—1662 年），荷兰人叫他 Koxinga（国姓爷），是一位驱逐荷寇的爱国者。他早年跟随父亲郑芝龙学做生意。郑芝龙是安平桥附近安海港入海口的石井镇人。早年郑芝龙在澳门学做生意，之后东渡日本，做起了葡萄牙人的海盗生意。至 17 世纪 20 年代，毫不夸张地说，郑芝龙的庞大船队已经统治了福建沿海。1626—1627 年，他攻占厦门岛，从此这里成了他从事海盗和走私的基地。1628 年郑芝龙降清，作为回报，被授予朝廷官职，还被提拔为福建总兵（实际上他的地位跟以前比，并没有多大改变）。至此，郑氏家族成了福建省实际上的最高统治者。他花巨资在安平（安海）修建了带城墙的城镇，这里也成了繁荣兴旺的贸易中心。

郑芝龙积累巨额财富的另一条途径是向从事贸易者收取保护费，这些人并不敢拒绝，因为郑芝龙当时拥有 1000 多艘船只，并且有一支由他控制的私人水师。满清攻占福建后，郑芝龙拱手投降，这也注定了自己的命运，因为反对他的不是别人，正是他自己的儿子郑成功。

在郑芝龙从事海盗生涯期间，他娶了一位日本姑娘田川氏，生下儿子取名郑成功。传说郑成功出生当晚，天上星星坠落，天神合唱。

当郑成功 7 岁时，父亲把他送回南安老家读书。每个父亲从来如此，想要给孩子自己小时候没有的东西，比如家庭作业。

郑成功是个很优秀的学生，从学校和家庭作业中逃生出来，在 21 岁那年，从家乡来到南京，进入国子监太学。此前他做梦都没想到，自己的未来不是读书做学问，当然，这与满清铁骑入关有关。

在李自成的农民军推翻了崇祯皇帝后，明朝灭亡，满族人轻而易举地填补了中国的权力真空，建立了清朝。在 1646 年，在清军攻占福州后，郑成功母亲不堪被辱自缢身亡。郑芝龙降清后，儒家孝道促使郑成功也不得不顺从（记得前面提过儒家二十四孝吗？），但是其他的原因（或许是母亲的死），促使郑成功最后与父亲分道扬镳。

In 1647, at the tender age of 23, Koxinga and 90+ followers began his Gulangyu-islet based anti-Ming rebellion.

Koxinga changed Xiamen's name to Siming (思明, "Remember the Ming"), which is the name of one of Xiamen's two main streets even today. Gulangyu Islet's Sunlight Rock was command center, and training ground for Koxinga's legendary fighters. He chose as his body guards ("Tiger Guards") only those who could pick up a 600 pound iron lion and walk off with it.

Koxinga's legendary fighters wore iron masks and iron aprons, wielded bows and arrows painted green, and used long handled swords for killing horses—a brilliant strategy he learned in school days while studying about the Great Wall. (The Great Wall was built to keep out not the barbarians but their horses, for while the Tartars were well nigh invincible on horseback, on foot the Chinese easily made Tartar sauce out of them).

On April 21, 1661, Koxinga set sail with 25,000 men and hundreds of war junks to drive the Dutch from Taiwan and return the island to the motherland. This mission cost him his life, but forever endeared him to Chinese on both sides of the straits. On January 27, 1662, the Dutch surrendered, and Koxinga's men kicked back and played the "Mooncake Gambling Game" (you will too if you're in South Fujian or Taiwan during Mid-Autumn Festival). But patriotism had taken a greater toll on Koxinga's health than piracy had. He died five months later on June 23. One Chinese historian noted somberly that Koxinga "died of overwork." May it be a lesson to us all.

Koxinga's son took over his father's work, but in the end Koxinga's descendants were done in by the descendants of a young soldier that Koxinga wronged and vastly underestimated…

Supplement 2 General Shilang 施琅

The great hero General Shilang was but one of Koxinga's tens of thousands of nameless soldiers when Koxinga ordered him put to death because of some petty infraction or mistake. Shilang escaped, so Koxinga had his entire family put to death instead, but Shilang had revenge (of a sorts) on Koxinga's descendants.

Years later, when the Qing Emperor wanted to oust Koxinga's descendants from power in Taiwan, he asked Premier Li Guangdi (李光地) which general to send. Li Guangdi was from Hutou (湖头) town in Quanzhou's Anxi County (安溪县). You can visit his former home (李光地故居, Li Guangdi Guju) in Hutou (see Anxi chapter).

1647年，23岁的郑成功带着大约90多名追随者，开始以鼓浪屿为基地，进行反清复明的斗争。

郑成功把厦门改为思明（反清复明，意即纪念已经灭亡的明朝）。思明路至今仍然是厦门两条最主要的街道之一。鼓浪屿上的日光岩是他的指挥中心和操练水师的基地。只有那些能够提起600磅重的铁狮并走上一段的士兵才能入选郑成功的左右虎卫。

郑成功的士兵身穿铁盔铁甲，手持绿色弓箭，用长剑砍杀敌人坐骑。这个策略是郑成功在学校时研究长城得到的灵感。据说古人修建长城，并不是害怕入侵之敌，而是他们的铁骑。因为对汉人来说，要战胜马背上的游牧民族很难，可是一旦游牧民族下马，问题就好解决了。

1661年4月，郑成功率领战舰一百多艘，将士25000名穿越台湾海峡，驱逐荷兰侵略者，收复台湾。这一战几乎要了郑成功的命，但也为他赢得海峡两岸人民永远的尊重。1662年1月27日，荷兰人投降，郑成功的士兵兴高采烈地玩起了“博饼”（如果你在闽南或台湾过中秋节，你也可以参加博饼活动）。但是郑成功的身体却每况愈下，1662年6月，郑成功不幸在台湾病逝。

一个中国史学家沉痛地说，郑成功是“死于操劳过度”。也许大家应该从中吸取经验教训。

郑成功的儿子郑经继承了父亲的事业，但最终郑成功的后代被施琅残杀，因为当年郑成功对施琅不公并大大低估了他。

附录2　施琅将军

施琅将军是郑成功成千上万个无名战士中的一个，因为轻微违规或细小错误，郑成功命令将其处死。在施琅侥幸逃脱之后，郑成功下令处死其全家。

数年后，清朝皇帝准备罢黜郑成功后代在台湾的掌权，皇帝征求丞相李光地派哪位将领合适。李光地是泉州安溪县湖头镇人，人们可以参观位于湖头的李光地故居（请参阅安溪章节）。

Premier Li knew of Shilang's hatred for the Zheng clan, so he urged the Emperor not to appoint a northerner, who had no feelings about the matter, but to appoint a local who had vested interests in the matter—Shilang. Shilang was of course delighted to cross swords with the descendants of the man who had murdered his family, but upon his victory, instead of seeking revenge, Shilang allowed Koxinga's descendants to return to Quanzhou, and to bring back the body of Koxinga to be buried in Nan An. This rare combination of military prowess and benevolence earned Shilong wide-spread respect and admiration (though once in power, the Shi family turned out to be fairly rascally as well).

General Shilang is also remembered for rebuilding and expanding Nanputuo Temple in 1684, during the reign of Emperor Kangxi. Shilang added the "Great Mercy Hall" for the worship of Guanyin, and changed the temple's name from "Pu Zhao" to "Nanputuo" The large bronze bell was cast during his reconstruction project. On the emperor's orders, Shilang also expanded the Mazu Temple on Meizhou Island because he attributed his success on Taiwan to the sea goddess's intervention. If you'd like to meet the great man, drop by his tomb—not in Nan'an but to the north of Quanzhou, but while we're on this grave subject, I'll throw in a few words about tombs.

Supplement 3 Tomb Raiders

China's historic tombs are a grave site for anyone expecting to encounter something really historic. Most tombs resemble Lin Lu's resting place, where the emphasis is more on the extinguished gentleman's comfort than on preserving historic relics. Not only have significant tombs undergone complete face lifts, with new stone and concrete embellishments, but ancient carvings have vanished. Of course, some are in museums, where they are protected from the elements, vandalism, and theft. But at least the folks in charge should put up a sign (and photos) explaining what used to be on the site, and where it has gone to.

Seeking (futilely) ancient relics at Wangchao's Tomb

Wangchao Tomb

李光地知道施琅对郑氏家族的仇恨，于是力劝皇帝不要指派北方籍将领，因为他们对这件事不带个人情感，而极力推荐有杀父之仇的当地将领施琅。施琅当然乐于与残杀其全家的郑成功的后代进行搏斗。在取得胜利以后，施琅没有采取报复手段，还允许郑成功的后代回到泉州，把郑成功的遗体迁柩归葬于南安。军事上的威力和处事上的仁慈难能可贵地结合起来，使施琅获得了广泛的尊重和钦佩（尽管一旦掌权，施氏家族最终也一样卑劣）。

施琅将军受后人缅怀的另一功绩是，他在康熙年间大约 1684 年重修和扩建了南普陀寺，施琅增建“大悲殿”，用于拜观音菩萨，把寺庙的名字由“普照寺”改为“南普陀寺”。寺庙里的巨大铜钟就是重建南普陀寺时铸造的。遵从皇帝圣旨，施琅还扩建了位于湄州湾的妈祖庙，因为施琅成功收复台湾，妈祖神灵处处扶佑。如果你想瞻仰这位英雄，可以参观其陵墓，不在南安，而是位于泉州北部。既然我们谈到这个话题，我想插几句说说中国的坟墓。

All that's left of the Wangchao tomb carvings

附录 3　盗墓贼

人们都期望能在中国古墓里发现一些真正有历史意义的东西，大多数就像林禄的坟墓一样，更多的是强调让这些显赫的宦官贵族住得舒适，而不在于保护历史遗迹。一些重要的坟墓遭受盗掘，经过新石方和混凝土修复，年代古老的那些雕刻早已消失得无踪影了。当然，有些放置于博物馆的，避免遭破坏和盗窃。其实，负责管理的当地人至少应张贴一块公示牌或一张图片，说明墓地原来有哪些雕刻，以及现在安放何处。

Wangchao's Tomb A Chinese book described the marvelous old stone animals around Wangcao's tomb so I headed Toy Ota down a narrow winding rutted road, through a village and across fields, until I finally found—a new construction site!

The grand arch is impressive, but I climbed all over the site and found nothing but a little chunk of stone sheep that was cowering in the grass. Disappointing. But Shilang's Tomb turned out to be a site for sore eyes!

General Shilang's Tomb Just above the Luoyang river, on the 324 highway, a sign for General Shilang's tomb points west. I figured it would be just off the road, but it took half an hour to get there. It turned out to be 15 km away, and I stopped every few minutes to make sure I had not missed it. It's not that easy to find, but it is one tomb that is well worth the trip. And judging from the size of the parking lot, the locals are expecting a lot of tourists to visit the final resting place of the benevolent general.

The entire site has obviously been recently renovated, but with style. The stone path leading to the tomb crosses a river and winds underneath shrubs that have been pruned to form shady arches. The general still rests in his old tomb in the back, up against the hillside, his top two wives on either side. Rows of newly hewn granite officials guard the general's grave, and before them are two rows of original carved animals.

It's a great tomb—and worth the ride to get there.

Shilang's Tomb

王潮墓　有一本书上描写王潮墓周围雄伟的古代石刻动物。于是，我开着丰田车前往，经过一段狭窄弯曲、坑坑洼洼的小路，穿过一个小村庄和一片田地，最终呈现眼前的却是一方建筑用地。

墓地前大型的拱门令人难忘，但我爬遍了墓地，什么古迹也没找着，唯一留下的是蜷缩在草丛中的一头石羊的残片，真令人失望。但施琅墓却是一个极受欢迎的景点。

施琅墓　在 324 国道洛阳江北岸，有一块标示牌告诉游人，施琅墓朝西方向走。我猜想或许就在路边不远处，后来发现施琅墓离 324 国道有 15 公里远，驱车足足要半个小时。害我一路不时停车问路，以确信没有错过目标。尽管不大好找，这还是值得旅游者一游的古墓。从停车场的规模上判断，当地人期望有许多游客来参观施琅将军的安息地。

很明显，整个墓地近年修缮一新，但保留着原来的风格。连接墓地的石板条小路横跨一条小溪，迂回在被修剪成拱形的灌木间。施琅将军安葬在山坡上的古墓里，他的两位夫人分别安葬在两侧，新近雕刻的花岗石官员护卫着将军墓，前面还有两排保存完整的石雕动物。

这是一片规模宏大的古墓，也值得驱车前去一游。

Chapter 11

Jinjiang and Shishi

My apologies for lumping the two fine cities of Shishi **(石狮, Stone Lion City)** and Jinjiang **(晋江)** together in one chapter, but I am less familiar with these areas, even though they do have quite a few interesting historical sites. In fact, I have an entire book on Jinjiang sites (which was settled earlier than Quanzhou city proper, and is the home of many famous Overseas Chinese), but I am personally familiar with only three: Cao'an Manichaean Temple (草俺摩尼教寺), Chendai Village's Ding Clan Ancestral Temple (陈埭丁民回族祠堂), and the Ancient Kiln in Cizao 磁灶古窑址 (we'll look at kilns and porcelain more closely in Dehua). But for the record, here are some key sites:

Cao'An (草庵) Planet's Last Temple to the Religion of Light Manichaean Temple, not far from the Sisters-in-Law Tower, is the planet's last bastions of the Persian religion Manichaeism, "The Religion of Light" (an esoteric combination of Gnosticism, Zoroastrianism, Christianity, and any other religion that was handy). Mani's followers arrived in China in the late seventh century—just about the same time as their arch rivals, the Moslems and Nestorian Christians.

Planet's last Manichaean Temple

The Persian founder Mani (216-276 A.D.) taught that existence is nothing but an eternal battle between good and evil, light and dark. He adopted elements of many religions, reasoning that each contained at least a grain of truth. Mani's malleable metaphysics appealed to St. Augustine, who followed the religion for a decade until his conversion to Christianity.

第十一章

晋江和石狮

本人对晋江和石狮这两座城市知之甚少，尽管它们有许多有趣的史迹，实在抱歉我只好把它们融为一章介绍。其实，我手头上很早就有一本详细介绍晋江（其人类居住活动比泉州市区更早，是许多著名华侨的故乡）景点的书籍。我本人只对三处景点熟悉：草庵摩尼教寺、陈埭丁民回族祠堂和磁灶古窑址（在德化章节将会更详细地接触到古窑址和瓷器）。以下列举的是一些主要的景点。

草庵——世界上明教的最后一个寺庙 距离姑嫂塔不远的安海摩尼教寺，可以说是地球上仅存的一座波斯摩尼教寺。明教融合了身边所有的宗教：拜火教、诺斯替教、基督教等。摩尼信徒于公元7世纪来到中国，几乎与回教徒和基督教徒同时到达。

Mani

来自波斯的明教创始人摩尼认为，世界的存在永远都是善与恶、明与暗之间无休止的较量。他吸取了许多宗教的东西，据理推断每一种宗教都蕴藏着真理的成分。摩尼的玄学使得圣•奥古斯丁感兴趣，他追随摩尼教十多年，直至后来转为信仰基督教。

St. Augustine. The famous Catholic saint and scholar knew too well the eternal battle between good and evil—at least during his hormone driven youth. The intellectual genius partied by night and prayed by day, "God, grant me chastity—but not yet!" After his illegitimate teen-age son died, he entered the Catholic clergy, denounced Mani, wrote a bestselling series of anti-Mani literature, and became a bishop and a saint. The jury is still out on where he ever achieved chastity, but from the expression on paintings of the man, I doubt it.

St. Augustine

Tang Dynasty Chinese called the increasingly popular religion Moni, Momonifa (Law of Moni), Xiao Moni (Little Moni), Da Moni (Great Moni), etc., and after the Tang it was called Ming Jiao (Religion of Light). For 600 years, this "Religion of Light" found increasing acceptance throughout China, especially around Quanzhou. In 1954, workers outside Quanzhou's Tonghuai Gate unearthed the tombstone of a high-level Yuan Dynasty clergymen responsible for governing foreign religions, including Manichaeism and Christianity.

Mani's influence in Fujian was so extensive that there is even a small Mani shrine on the peak of Ningde's remote Taimu Mountain, though today it is used by worshippers of the Taimu goddess.

The growing popularity of the white-robed Manicheans, led by priests wearing violet headpieces, worried Buddhist competitors. The Buddhist history "Fozu Tongji," compiled between 1258-1269, denounced Mani worshippers as vegetarian" devil worshippers. (Odd they should note the vegetarian aspect, since Buddhists too, in theory, avoided meat).

Mani's minions worried the government—with good reason, it turned out. The politically-inclined Mani worshippers helped overthrow the government and enthrone Taizu, who named his new dynasty "Ming," and then rewarded the Ming Religion by banning it. Supposedly, one reason was that he objected to the Ming Religion having the same name as his new Ming dynasty (which just proves China's early concern for intellectual property rights).

Mani

圣·奥古斯丁　作为一位出名的天主教圣人和追随者，奥古斯丁深明善与恶之间永恒的较量——至少在他充满活力的青年时代。这位天才的圣人晚上放荡不羁，到了白天却祈祷“给我圣洁和节欲吧！”在年幼的私生子死后，他加入了天主教会，写了一系列广为流传的反对摩尼的书籍，抨击摩尼教，最终成为主教，尔后成为圣人。很多人都在考究他是否已得到圣洁，然而，从画像的表情上看，这是值得怀疑的。

这种不断发展、影响日深的摩尼教在唐朝先后被称为摩尼法、小摩尼和大摩尼等。唐朝以后，就改为明教。六百多年来，明教在中国（特别是在泉州）得到了广泛流传。1954年，在泉州通淮门外挖掘出了一块元代牧师的墓盖石，此人专管外来宗教，包括摩尼教和基督教。

摩尼教在福建传播影响深远，在宁德太姥山峰上至今仍有一座规模不大的摩尼教圣堂（目前已被挪作供奉太姥娘娘）。

身着白长袍的摩尼教徒不断发展壮大，由于受那些头戴蓝紫色头盔的牧师影响，他们对佛教徒一直怀有戒意。1258—1269年编纂的《佛祖通记》把摩尼教徒贬为素食者的魔鬼崇拜者。（奇怪的是，他们本应吃素，就像佛教徒一样是不吃荤的）

摩尼信徒长期以来让政府担惊受怕，的确如此。那些有政治倾向的摩尼教徒最终推翻了当朝政府，推崇太祖就位，立号“明”。但是“明教”最终被禁止，据说它的“明”与明朝的“明”是同一个字（这证明中国很早就开始关注知识产权）。

Despite persecution, Mani's religion kept a toehold in Quanzhou, which today boasts the planet's last Mani temple— the "Thatched Nunnery." It was built in 1339, after villagers had spent 26 years carving statues of Mani all over the cliffs of Huabiao Mountain. The artists must not have had a good photo to go by because Mani bears a striking resemblance to standard issue Chinese deities—except that he sports four braided dreadlocks, and has rays of light emanating from behind.

In spite of its uniqueness, some worshippers still think Mani is in fact Guanyin, the popular Goddess of Mercy. I asked a nun the if they worshiped Mani or Buddha and she said, "Mani, of course!"
"What's the difference between Mani and Buddha"" I asked her.

She pondered this, then said, "You'll have to ask someone in charge, but there's no in charge at the moment."
Getting There: Special bus to Anhai, get off at Luoshan.
Hours: 8:00-18:00 **Phone**: 8568-1046

Chendai Mosque

Chendai Village & Ding Clan Ancestral Hall Chendai Village has so many Hui minority folks surnamed Ding that I had to drive at a snail's pace lest I get a Ding in my bumper. Some of the Dings, with their big noses, curly hair and beards, looked like they were ready to burst out in Arabic, not Chinese. Many are not practicing Muslims, but they are fiercely proud of their ancestry, and their Arab forebears' achievements. And modern Ding are quite the entrepreneurs as well!

Mr. Ding Jinhua 丁进华, gave me a tour of the Ding Clan Ancestral Hall (Hui Nationality Exhibition Hall) 陈埭丁民回族祠堂 This unusual ancestral hall is built in southern Fujian architectural style, but the decorations are Islamic, and it has been carefully designed to resemble the Chinese character Hui 回, with a square hall in the center of a larger square courtyard.

尽管摩尼教被禁，在泉州还是渐渐流传开来，至今还保存有世界上唯一的摩尼寺庙——草庵。草庵始建于 1339 年，之后，当地村民花了整整 26 年时间在华表山的悬崖峭壁上雕琢了许许多多的摩尼雕像。这些雕琢艺术家们当时一定没有一张像模像样的摩尼相片可模仿，结果，除了它胸前飘有四条发辫以及背雕有毫光四射外，摩尼雕像更像那些标准的中国诸神像。

虽然摩尼是独一无二的，有的人却认为摩尼就是慈悲女神观音。我问一位尼姑是信奉摩尼还是佛祖。“当然是摩尼！”她回答道。但是，当我问及如何区分这两种宗教时，她略一沉思：“你要去问管事的，不过今天没人上班。”

乘车：乘往安海的专线车，然后在罗山下车。

开放时间：8:00—18:00

电话：0595－85681046

陈埭丁氏回族祠堂　在陈埭，生活着许许多多丁姓回民，我们一路上开车小心翼翼，唯恐撞上。有些丁姓回民，高鼻子、留着卷发、蓄着胡须，与其说是中国人，不如说更像阿拉伯人。许多丁姓回民如今已不再遵循回教教规了，但是，他们对于祖先特别是阿拉伯先辈所取得的成就还是备感自豪。现在的丁姓回民更多的是企业家了！

丁进华带我参观了丁氏回族祠堂，这座祠堂是典型的闽南建筑规格，其装饰是伊斯兰风格的。整个祠堂设计成汉字的“回”字，外围是方形庭院，而中部是方形厅堂。

Amoymagic.com

"Arabic Chinese!"

Pools The Ancestral Hall is quite a museum, with three walls of photographs and displays behind glass. They have also prepared a nice little pamphlet on the history and contributions of the Ding clan (but no English version).

I tried everything to get a good photo of the "Hui" shaped hall, including climbing to the tip top of the Mosque. Mr. Ding solved the problem by leading me to the market across the street and borrowing a rickety 30 foot bamboo ladder. While two Muslims held the swaying ladder from below, I climbed it, praying silently that they held no historical grievances against Christians But I made it to the roof, and snapped some good photos of both the hall and the pool in front. Buddhist temples have similar pools, which are used for gaining merit by freeing captive fish, but Muslims have no qualms eating fish. Perhaps it's the "Pool for freeing captive pigs?" (After that crack, I won't let Chendai Muslims hold any more ladders for me).

Getting There: Special Chendai Bus **Hours**: 8:00-17:30

On Ancestral Worship

"But the foundations of ancestral worship are not laid on shadowy, visionary soil of myths and legends, but on substantial, solid, historical ground. Ancestral worship has its origin both in the family and nation and is both a family and a national custom. It is as old as the empire itself. Contemporary with the birth of the nation, it has become so interwoven in the warp and woof of its history, that to attempt to disengage the strings would be to destroy the whole fabric... No other one thing in its entire history has tended more to bind this people together or to perpetuate the nation than this universal respect (whether sincere or a sham) for the living and devotion for the dead; and no other one thing has so bound them to the dead past or so diverted their attention from the living future.

Pitcher, *In and About Amoy*, 1912.

Ding Jinhua

池塘　丁氏祠堂更像是一座博物馆，三面墙上挂满了各种各样的图片和展示品。祠堂里有一本有关丁氏家族历史和所作所为的精美的小册子（可惜没有英文版本）。

我想方设法拍一张“回”字形祠堂的照片，甚至爬到清净寺的屋顶上。最终还是丁先生帮了大忙，他带我到街道对面的市场上，借来一架并不十分牢固的 30 码高的竹梯子。两位回民在底下扶住摇摆不定的竹梯子，我爬了上去，心里默默祈祷，但愿它们没有对基督徒的历史怨恨！我顺着竹梯爬上了屋顶，抓拍了好几张图片，既拍到了祠堂，又拍到了祠堂前面的池塘。佛教寺庙一般都有类似的池塘，这种池塘是用于放鱼归塘以求积德。（自从那次爬竹梯后，我想我再也不会让他们帮我扶梯子了，实在太可怕了）

交通　乘往陈埭的专线车　**开放时间**：8:00—17:30

关于祭拜祖先

“祭拜祖先并非基于那些模糊空幻的神话或传说上，而是基于真实可靠的史料记载上。祭拜祖先源于家庭和国家，它既是一个家庭也是一个民族的习俗，就像一个帝国一样历史悠久。从一个国家的成立开始，祭拜祖先就像是民族历史的经纬线一样交叉纵横，你一旦想脱离丝线，就会破坏整块织物。不管这种祭拜（尊重活着的人，祭祀死去的人）是虔诚抑或虚假的。我想在一个国家的历史长河中，没有任何东西比这种祭拜祖先更能把人们的心系在一起，使一个民族永垂不朽；也没有任何事像这样——把人们的心捆在一起祭拜先人，直面未来生活。

——皮彻，《厦门内外》，1912 年

If the Shoe Fits[①] Mainland China produces 80% of the world's sports shoes; 80% of these come from Fujian; most of these are from China's "Shoe Town," Chendai Village!

Not even Imelda Marcos could have dreamed that this sleepy village would end up with over 1,000 shoe enterprises doing over 2 billion Yuan business annually, and have a 22.3 million USD 150,000m^2 shoe market. Nearby Anhai town is China's largest leather tanning base, and Baiqi is the center for rubber sole production.

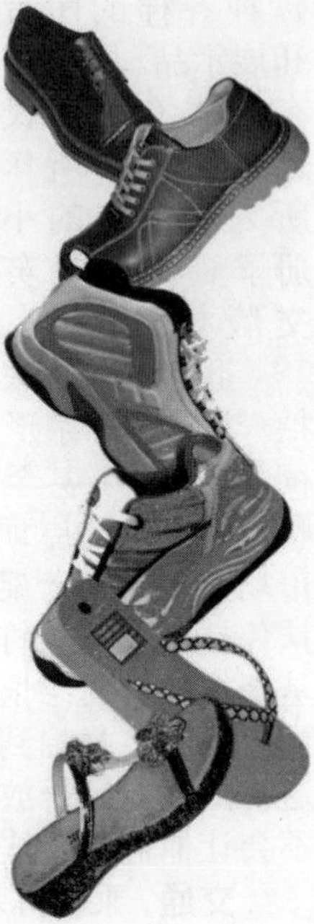

Quanzhou as a whole now has over 300,000 people employed in 4,000+ industries producing every make of foreign and domestic shoe possible (excluding, possibly, horseshoes). In fact, Quanzhou produces fully 20% of the world's sports and casual shoes. But no wonder. Quanzhou has 100,000 shoe salesmen, and 30 subsidiaries and agencies abroad.

Jinjiang, which produces over 500 million pair of shoes annually, hosted the 1st Jinjiang International Shoe Fair in March, 1999. The four day fair displayed over 5000 kinds of shoes, shoe machines and shoe materials. Over 100,000 people took part in the show, 21 agreements were signed, and sales reached 1.3 billion Yuan. In addition, two Hong Kong specialists gave lectures to 400 business and government leaders.

The latest in computerized design and production technology enables Quanzhou firms to not only keep quality high and costs low but also to go green. Many firms are substituting rubber for azo, and PU for PVC, using benzene-free glue, and replacing white glue laminators with thermosol versions of shoe parts.

For more on the Quanzhou shoe industry, please turn to the supplement at the end of this chapter.

① Before criticizing someone, walk a mile in their shoes; that way you're a mile away and you've still got their shoes.

这鞋合适吗[①] 全世界80%的运动鞋产自于中国大陆，而其中80%来自于福建，更绝的是，绝大多数来自于“鞋都”——陈埭镇。

即使是伊梅尔达·马科斯也绝不会想到这座毫不起眼的城镇会有1000多家鞋厂，年产值超20亿元人民币，同时还投资2230万美元兴建了一个 15 万平方米的鞋业市场。临近的安海镇是中国最大的皮革制造基地，而百崎乡是鞋底制造中心。

目前，在泉州，4000多家制鞋厂里有30多万从业工人，他们生产出国内外各种款式的鞋（当然不可能包括马蹄形的）。事实上，泉州的运动鞋和休闲鞋产量占了世界的20%。这一点实在不足为奇，因为泉州有10万人的鞋业营销大军和30多家海外办事处。

仅在晋江市，每年就产鞋5亿双。1999年3月成功地举办了首届晋江国际鞋博会。为期四天的鞋博会，展示了 5000 多种鞋样、制鞋机械和鞋材，接待了10多万个参展商，签订了21项协议，协议金额13亿元人民币。与此同时，来自香港的两位专家还给400多位企业界和政界人士作了精彩的演讲。

先进工艺和设计不仅提高了质量、降低了成本，而且还绿色环保。许多企业用偶氮代替橡胶，用聚氯乙烯代替聚氨酯橡胶，用无苯粘胶代替用于粘鞋用的热溶胶制成的压层材料。

想了解更多有关泉州制鞋业信息，请参阅本章末附录。

---

① 在批评一个人的时候，先设身处地替他们想想（即“穿上他们的鞋子走一段路”体验一下），这样你就可以穿着他们的鞋子跑掉啦！

Rizal Int'l Shrine (Jinjiang)

Rizal International Shrine in Jinjiang In 2002, Jinjiang invested 10 million Yuan to create the 5-hectare Rizal Memorial Park, with its 18.61 meter high statue of Rizal (much higher than the 12-meter statue of Rizal in Manila). Filipino business leaders invested an additional 2 million Yuan. Filipino House Speaker Jose de Venecia said that China's park was a "great symbol of the 1,000-year-old friendship between our two nations," and, "This Rizal Park in China helps elevate the status of our Philippine national hero Dr. Jose Rizal as a hero for the whole Asian region."

Rizal's Humble Ancestral Home The Rizal park will become a must-see for Filipino-Chinese, 80% of whom, like Rizal himself, trace their roots to Southern Fujian. But more impressive than the sprawling (and expensive) park is his tiny ancestral hovel in the little village right beside the park. It is amazingly small and in poor repair for a man of his stature, but refreshing. It shows where the man came from. In a few years it will probably have been replaced by some concrete monstrosity of an ancestral temple, with magnificent arches, Rizal idols, and calligraphy explaining how he descended from the heavens to save the Philippines.

晋江黎刹国际公园　2002年，晋江市（在泉州市郊）投入1000万元建造了一个占地5公顷的黎刹纪念公园，公园内有尊18.61米高的黎刹雕像（比马尼拉那尊 12 米高的黎刹雕像高得多）。菲律宾企业界也为此捐赠了200万元。据菲律宾议会发言人扶西·得·维尼西亚说，“中国（晋江的）这座黎刹公园是 1000 多年来中菲两国之间友谊的象征，它对于提升菲律宾民族英雄扶西·黎刹博士作为全亚洲人的英雄地位发挥了积极的作用”。

简陋的黎刹祖屋　黎刹公园已逐步成为菲律宾华人的必看景点。在菲律宾，80%的华人和黎刹一样，其“根”可寻至闽南。但比起这座恢弘的公园（耗资也大）更令人印象深刻的是公园附近小村庄的那座小祖屋。这座祖屋对于黎刹这样地位的人来说的确太小，而且破落不堪，但看了以后却令人振奋。它（祖屋）让人知道黎刹这个人的出身。也许几年后，一座宏大 的古庙将取而代之，内设有拱形门廊、黎刹神像以及一些有关黎刹如何由天上下凡、拯救菲律宾民族的书法作品等等。

Rizal's Ancestral Home

Rizal

Jose Rizal
The Filipina Hero from Quanzhou

Jose Rizal was born June 19th in Calamba, Philippines, and died December 30th, 1896, in Manila. This patriot, physician and intellectual was an inspiration to many generations of Filipinos.

Rizal was the son of a wealthy landowner on the island of Luzon, and his mother was one of the most educated Filipino women at that time. Rizal studied medicine in the University of Madrid and became leader of the Filipino students in Spain. He pursued reform of Spanish rule in the Philippines, though he stopped short of demanding Filipino independence of Spain. In Rizal's eyes, the Philippine's primary enemy was not Spain, which was undergoing dramatic reform, but the Catholic faction that clung to power in Spain's impoverished colony.

Rizal continued his medical studies in Paris and Heidelberg, and in 1886 he published his first novel, in Spanish. "*Noli e Tanger*e" exposed the evils "of the Catholic friars'" rule much as *Uncle Tom's Cabin* brought to light the evils of America's slavery.

Rizal returned to the Philippines in 1892 to found a nonviolent reform society, La Liga Filipina, in Manila, but was exiled for four years to Mindanao, in the northwest, where he continued his scientific research and founded a school and hospital.

A nationalist secret society, the Katipunan, launched a revolt against Spain in 1896. Though Rizal had absolutely no connections with Katipunan, he was arrested, found guilty of sedition, and executed before a firing squad in Manila. The evening before he was executed, he wrote the Spanish masterpiece, "Mi Ultimo Adios" ("My Last Farewell"), which helped Filipinos realize that there was no alternative to independence from Spain.

扶西·黎刹——来自泉州的菲律宾英雄

扶西·黎刹6月19日出生于菲律宾卡郎巴，1896年12月30日在马尼拉去世。这位伟大的爱国者、医生、学者激励着一代又一代的菲律宾人。

黎刹是吕宋岛一位富裕地主的儿子，其母亲是当时菲律宾妇女中受教育程度最高的妇女之一。在马德里大学学医后，黎刹成了在西班牙的菲律宾学生领袖。尽管致力于将菲律宾从西班牙独立出来，他还是坚持用西班牙的方式来进行菲律宾改革。在黎刹看来，菲律宾的主要敌人并非处于巨大改革中的西班牙，而是在西班牙贫穷殖民地上统治的天主教派系。

在巴黎和海德堡，黎刹继续坚持医学研究。1886年，他出版了第一本西班牙文小说 *Nolie Tangene*，揭露了天主教修道士的罪恶统治，就像小说《汤姆叔叔的小木屋》揭露了美国奴隶制度的罪恶一样。

1892年，黎刹回到了菲律宾，在马尼拉成立了一个非暴力改革协会“拉尼咖”。后来，他被驱逐到西北部的民答那峨岛。在民答那峨岛度过了四年的流放生涯，他一直坚持科学研究，并创办了一所学校和一家医院。

1896年，一个独立运动秘密组织“卡堤普南”发起了反抗西班牙的暴动。尽管黎刹与该组织没有任何关系，他还是被逮捕了，罪名为“煽动叛乱”，并在马尼拉被行刑组处死。在临死的前一个晚上，他用西班牙文写了一篇杰作《最后的告别》，唤醒了菲律宾人——只能从西班牙独立出来，别无其他选择。

Other Jinjiang Sites

Anping Bridge The longest bridge on earth during the Middle Ages, and still the longest stone bridge today (see the "Bridges" chapter). But it's a long bridge, so avoid the midday heat). And while you're in Anhai…

Anhai Starry Pagoda

Anhai Starry Pagoda (安海星塔, *Anhai Xingta*) Pagodas don't excite me, usually, but the Starry Pagoda is very distinct. This beautiful red and white four-sided five level pagoda was built in 1629, and is elegant in its simplicity of design.

Dragon Mountain Temple's 1,000 Handed Guanyin, Goddess of Mercy (Longshan Si Qianshou Guanyin). Taiwan's famous Longshan Temple is an offshoot of this sprawling Buddhist complex, which was first built during the Sui Dynasty (581-618 A.D.). A millennium later, this was one of the temples that Koxinga's nemesis, General Shilang, helped to renovate. The Guanyin's 1,000 hands, with an eye upon each palm, represent her omnipotence and omniscience, but a Buddhist abbot confided to me, "That's just symbolic. If she really had 1,000 hands and eyes she'd be quite a monster!"

Buddha and Relief Cliff Carvings of Nantian Temple (Nantian Si Shifo Moya Shike). Three cliffside carved stone Buddhas are said to be the crown jewel of Southern Fujian stone carving. Nantian's calligraphy is also popular, particularly the 泉南佛国, Quannan Foguo—"Buddhist Kingdom of Quannan") written by Wang Shipeng (王十朋).

Stone Lion City (Shishi) In just over a decade, the 1300-year-old city of Shishi has metamorphosed from a backwater town into a modern center of commerce and industry. Shishi is now the garment capital of Fujian, and perhaps the largest garment center in Asia, and hosts the Cross-Straits Garment and Textile Expo.

Shishi's 5,000+ factories in the clothing industry did over 7.6 billion Yuan in business in 2001, and the way things are going, businesses like the 5,000 square meter Xinhu Bra and Underwear Factory aren't going bust anytime soon.

晋江其他景点

Dragon Mtn. Temple

安平桥　中世纪时是“天下无桥长此桥”，而今也是最长的古石桥。去游览之前先好好浏览一下有关“桥”的文章（这座桥太长了，要注意避免中午的太阳照射）。在安海，你还可以看到……

安海星塔　对于塔，我并非十分感兴趣，然而，安海星塔却与众不同。这座红白相间呈四边形的五层塔始建于 1629 年，它的美在于其设计简朴、高雅。

龙山寺千手观音　龙山寺始建于隋朝（公元 581—617 年），台湾最著名的龙山寺也是从这里分炉出去的。1000 多年后，郑成功、施琅将军先后予以修缮。千手观音的每个手掌上都有一只眼睛，代表着她无所不知、无所不能，然而一个方丈悄悄告诉我：“那只是象征性的，如果她真有千只手千只眼，那不成了怪物吗？”

南天寺石佛摩崖石刻　南天寺的三尊摩崖石佛雕像据说是闽南石雕的精品杰作。里面的书法也相当出名，特别是王十朋所书的“泉南佛国”四个字。

石狮市　仅仅十年时间，有着 1300 年历史的石狮就从一个贫穷落后的小镇发展成为现代工贸中心。如今，石狮被誉为中国服装名城，有的人甚至认为它是亚洲最大的服装中心。石狮成功地举办了海峡两岸服装与纺织品博览会。

2001 年，5000 多家服装厂家产值超过 76 亿元，而且发展态势良好，再也不会出现像拥有 5000 平方米厂房的新湖胸罩内衣厂破产的事情了。

Shishi Tour Sites

Sisters-in-law (Gusao) Pagoda If you get high on pagodas, head east to Shishi's 22.86m tall Sisters-in-law Pagoda (Gusao Ta), which was built on Baogai Hill (宝盖山) in 1146. Women used to wait upon this hill for the return of husbands and sons from sea voyages.

The Legend A Song Dynasty man sailed to Southeast Asia to seek his fortune and promised to return in 3 years. His wife and sister missed him so badly that they piled up stones by the river and watched for him, year after year, but he never returned. The two girls died of grief, and the sympathetic villagers called the rock pile "Sisters-in-Law Tower." And somewhere along the line (1146, actually), the rock pile metamorphosed into a 4-story pagoda that is one of Quanzhou's navigational landmarks even today.
Getting There: Bus to Shishi **Hours**: 8:00 - 17:30 **Phone:** 8870-7902

Six Victory Pagoda (六胜塔) is located on the very northernmost tip of a Shishi peninsula. Description: tall.

Gold Coast Villas, Beach, Aquarium

Shishi's Gold Coast Holiday Village (Shishi Huangjin Hai'an) The "South Fujian Golden Seashore Holiday Village" is quite a massive undertaking. The first phase includes the Golden Beach Paradise, Yacht Club, Food Plaza, Seaside Resort, and China's largest ocean theme park, the South Fujian Ocean World, which includes an Aquarium, Dolphin Performance Hall, Diving, Underwater Performances, etc.

Shishi has miles of beautiful beaches. Yakou (衙口), just a few km south of Shishi, has one of the finest stretches of sand in China. While you're in Yakou, you might want to visit Shi Clan's Ancestral Temple (衙口施氏宗祠).

Getting There: Special Bus from Quanzhou to Golden Seashore
Hours: 8:00-22:00 **Phone**: 8860-5588, 8860-5188

石狮旅游景点

姑嫂塔 姑嫂塔位于宝盖山上，建于1146年，高22.86米。以前，当地妇女总是登高望远，翘首盼望丈夫与儿子远航平安归来。

姑嫂传说 宋朝时，有个男人远航到南洋去谋生，临别前许诺三年内回来。他的妻子和妹妹日夜思念，她们不断地在河边叠起石块，翘望他的归航，日复一日，年复一年，他始终没有回来。姑嫂两人备感伤心，抑郁而终。当地村民非常同情她们，把这些垒石称为姑嫂塔。最终这些垒石演变成一座四层高的塔，即使在今天，这座塔仍然是泉州的航海标志。

乘车：泉州至石狮的专线车

开放时间：8:00—17:30　　**电话：**0595－88707902

六胜塔 高耸在石狮半岛的最北端。特征：高。

石狮黄金海岸度假村 闽南黄金海岸度假村的确是一个巨大的工程。首期项目包括金沙乐园、游艇俱乐部、美食广场、海滨浴场以及中国目前最具规模的海洋主题乐园——闽南海洋世界（包括海洋馆、海豚表演馆、潜水、水下表演等等）。

石狮拥有绵延数里的美丽沙滩。离石狮不远的衙口，是中国最好的沙滩之一。到了衙口，你不妨去衙口施氏宗祠参观一下。

乘车：泉州至黄金海岸专线车　**开放时间：**8:00—22:00

电话：0595－88605588，88605188

Bumper Cars with Cannon!

Inway Ni—a young Quanzhou entrepreneur. Inway, from Anhai, was one of the most driven MBA students I've ever had. Even before graduating he had started several businesses. But he also knows balance. When his wife had a daughter, he exclaimed to me happily, "Before, I was a full time businessman. Now I'm a full-time father—and part-time everything else!"

Supplement 1

Getting Your Foot in the Door with

AIDER, Ltd. 厦门艾德鞋业有限公司

Opportunities are endless in Quanzhou's shoe business, but you can save a lot of time and money with a good go-between to arrange contacts with the more reputable and dependable firms. A good place to start is Fujian's largest footwear exporter, Aider Co., which exports over 300 40' containers annually to customers all over the globe.

Over the past 8 years, Aider has developed a reputation for forging a global network of shoe contacts and building win-win relationships and friendships. And as Aider reps trot around the globe each year to attend shoe fairs, they also give out material to help foreigners better understand Xiamen, Fujian and China. To this end, they bought 2,000 copies of my "*Amoy Magic*" to give away at foreign trade fairs. (Hopefully they're giving away quality literature too; we want to attract foreign investment, not frighten it off!)

Add: Aider Ltd., 9/F., Xinghu Commercial Bldg. #46 Huli Da Dao
Xiamen, China 361006
Tel: +86(592)5699288 Fax: 86(592)5699299
Email: aider@public.xm.fj.cn john@aider-xm.com
Website: www.aider-xm.com

倪英伟——一位年轻的泉州企业家

来自安海的英伟，是我所教的 MBA 学生中最刻苦的学生之一，毕业之前他就已经展开了好几项工作，但是他却懂得如何保持平衡。当他的妻子生了女儿后，他兴高采烈地告诉我："以前，我是一个专职商人，如今我是一个全职父亲，其他都是副业啦！"

刻苦，但要保持平衡，这才是我们社会所需要的企业家的品质。

附录 1　走进艾德鞋业有限公司

泉州的制鞋业相当发达，与制鞋有关的业务随处可找。为了节省大量时间和金钱，你完全可以找一家中介公司安排一些信誉好、可靠的厂商接洽。作为福建省最大的鞋类出口商，艾德公司每年有300多个40英尺的标准集装箱出口到世界各地，是你理想的选择。

在过去的 8 年里，艾德公司已逐渐构建起全球性的鞋类贸易网络，彼此间互惠互利、友好合作。一年一度的鞋业展销会使艾德公司的业务网络急速扩张，他们也趁机分发资料，让外国人更好地了解厦门、了解福建、了解中国。为此，他们购买了2000本我编著的《魅力厦门》一书，在海外展销会上免费赠送给参展商。（很高兴他们同时也赠送高质量的资料。我想，我们需要的是吸引外商来投资，而不是吓唬他们！）

地址：厦门湖里区湖里大道46号兴湖商务大厦9楼 邮编：361006

电话：86（592）5699288　传真：86（592）5699299

电子信箱：John @aider-xm.com，或者登录网站查询。

Supplement 2

The Quanzhou Tiger

"Asian Tigers" usually brings to mind countries, but Quanzhou City is a tiger in its own right.

During Marco Polo's day, when Zaytun was the start of the Maritime Silk Road and a global commercial and cultural crossroads, the city traded in everything imaginable. Today, the new Quanzhou seems to actually produce about everything imaginable, and has been making great contributions to Fujian and all of China. Over the past two decades, Quanzhou's economy has accounted for ¼ that of Fujian province, and 1.3% that of the entire nation! Private enterprise is playing a pivotal role, accounting for 80% of Quanzhou's GDP in 2000, and thanks to the first Cyber Expo, the entire planet can take advantage of Quanzhou's innovation and production skills.

Cyber Expo—the E-Silk Road Quanzhou has so many thousands of enterprises that it can overwhelm the potential buyer or investor. Fortunately, the city has embraced the latest internet technology and practices to create a "Cyber Expo" that is open to the world 24 hours a day, year round. A mere click of the mouse at http://www.qzfair.com or http://www.21marketing.com/qzfair/en/companies.htm opens endless opportunities for partnerships and business deals between thousands of Chinese and foreign firms the world over.

Early on the Quanzhou government recognized the growing role of e-commerce and net marketing, and in Sep. 1999 initiated the first on-line product expo (the "Never Closing Expo"). The Cyber Expo offers each participant a standard cyber-booth, which includes a home page, sub-domain name, e-mail box, pages for 10 products with text and photos, order-and-pay system, information release system, and net management system. The expo website also offers cyber-booths for companies outside of Quanzhou.

The Cyber Expo's 1st session included 1145 enterprises and over 12,000 projects. The 2nd session, opened Dec. 8, 2000, had 1,500 companies and 20,000 products. The first two sessions resulted in over 1000 orders with a value of USD 17 million. The 3rd session, which opened Nov.03, 2001, doubled the previous session, with 2,580 companies and over 30,000 products.

附录2 泉州虎

“亚洲虎”通常会让人想起某些国家，而泉州作为一只老虎却名副其实。

马可·波罗时代，刺桐（泉州别称）作为海上丝绸之路的起点和全球经济文化交流中心，对外贸易无所不及。如今，泉州制造的产品品种繁多，无所不包，为福建乃至中国经济的发展做出了巨大的贡献。过去的20年，泉州经济总量一直占全省的四分之一、占全国的1.3%。泉州民营经济发挥着举足轻重的作用。2000年民营经济约占泉州GDP的80%。自举办第一届网上博览会以来，全球都可以充分利用泉州的创新和制造技术了。

网上博览会——电子丝绸之路　成千上万个泉州企业吸引了众多买家和投资商。泉州充分利用先进的英特网技术，举办了一个24小时对外服务的网上博览会。你只要进入主页 http://www.qzfair.com 或 http://www.21marketing.com/qzfair/en/companies.htm，成千上万个中外企业之间的合作与业务往来的机会将展现在你面前。

早些时候，泉州市政府认识到电子商务与网络市场的重要性，于1999年9月首次举行了网上产品博览会（永不闭幕的博览会）。网博会给每家参展商提供一个标准的网上交易平台，这个平台包括主页、次域名、电子信箱、10种产品的文字与图片介绍、定购与付款系统、信息发布系统、网上管理系统。网博会也同时为泉州市以外的企业提供网上交易平台。

首届网博会有1145家企业的12000多种产品参展，第二届网博会于2000年12月8日开幕，吸引了1500家企业的20000种产品参展。前两届网博会总共达成了1000多份订单，价值1700万美元。而2001年11月3日开幕的第三届网博会的参展企业成倍增加，有2580家企业的30000多种产品参展。

The 4th session of "China Enterprises & Products On-Line Expo," (Nov.02, 2002—Nov.01, 2003) includes over 3,000 companies from many industries, including textile, shoes & clothing; construction & building materials; arts & crafts; food & beverage; hardware & machinery, petrochemical; electronics & information; tourism & service, and such new ventures as biology & medicine, new materials, environmental protection, and deep processing of farm and side-line products.

The 4th session also held concurrently the 2nd session of China Enterprise Cyber-Marketing Cooperation Conference, and was attended by global business and government representatives, and cyber-marketing experts.

"China Enterprises & Products On-Line Expo" is sponsored by Quanzhou Municipal Government, Fujian Economy & Trade Commission, Fujian Township Enterprise Bureau, and organized by the Quanzhou Township Enterprise Bureau, insuring participants of a top quality program. Contact:

Mail Add.: P.O. Box 98 Quanzhou, Fujian 362000, China
Hot Line: 0595-22105731
Fax: 0595-22106712, 22989071
Web: http://www.21marketing.net
E-mail: info@qze.gov.cn

第四届“中国企业与产品网上博览会”（2002年11月2日—2003年11月1日）总共吸引了各行各业3000多家企业参展，包括纺织、服装鞋业、建筑材料、工艺美术、食品饮料、五金、机械、石油化工、电子信息、旅游服务以及新兴产业如生物医学、新材料、环境保护、农副产品的深加工等。

与第四届网博会同时举行的是第二届中国企业网上市场合作论坛，全球企业界、政界与网络市场营销的专家学者参加了论坛。

中国企业与产品网上博览会由泉州市人民政府、福建省经贸厅、福建省乡镇企业局联合主办，泉州市乡镇企业局承办，以此确保参展企业的质量与水平。请按以下方式联络：

邮寄地址：中国福建泉州98号邮箱　邮编：362000

热线电话：0595—22105731

传真：0595—22106712，22989071

网址：http://www.21marketing.net

电子信箱：info@qze.gov.cn

Supplement 3

Strike Gold at CIFIT (China Int'l Fair for Investment & Trade)

The best place to scout out business opportunities, whether in Xiàmén or elsewhere, is our annual **CIFIT** (Zhōngguó Guójì Tóuzī Màoyì Qiàtán Huì, 中国国际投资贸易洽谈会).

Every September 8th, CIFIT hosts pavilions with investment opportunities in every province in China, from coastal Fujian to the Himalayan heights of Tibet.

CIFIT has been responsible for ***over half*** of foreign investment to small and medium enterprises, and for much of large businesses as well, with over 100,000 visitors and exhibitors from over 144 countries and over 2000 international and governmental institutions, business associations and enterprises. CIFIT's 1800+ forum and seminar speakers have included top Chinese leaders, Nobel Prize winners, U.N. officials and vice premiers of various countries. As of 2005, CIFIT had witnessed the signing of some 11,362 investment projects worth over 60 billion USD.

Want to know more? Municipal government officers are glad to provide information and materials on investment opportunities, and other Laowai and Laonei businessmen should also have a good handle on how to go about setting up shop, and home, in Xiamen.

CIFIT Contact:

Address: 2/F, Foreign Trade Bldg. Hubin Road N., Xiamen, China 361012.
Phone: 0086-592-5079898-631, or 5068459
Fax: 0086-592-5129898, or 5146205
Website: www.chinafair.org.cn E-mail: 98xiamen@public.xm.fj.cn

Past Quanzhou Attendees of CIFIT have included:

福建惠泉啤酒集团股份有限公司 Fujian Huiquan Beer Inc. Ltd.

恒安国际集团有限公司 Heng'an Int'l Group Co. Ltd.

泉州金山石材工具科技有限公司 Quanzhou Jinshan Stone Tools Technology Co. Ltd.

泉州市奔达纺织有限公司 Quanzhou Bunpat Textiles Co. Ltd.

泉州市四方数控技术有限公司 SFA Numerical Control Technology Co. Ltd.

泉州三盛橡塑发泡鞋材有限公司 Quanzhou Sansheng Rubber Plastic Foamed Shoes Materials Co., Ltd.

泉州东科食品有限公司 Quanzhou Dongke Foodstuff Co., Ltd.

附录3　中国国际投资贸易洽谈会

中国国际投资贸易洽谈会（以下简称“投洽会”——译者注）给你提供了了解泉州企业的极好机会（当然也包括中国其他地方的企业）。中国的投资促进活动主要集中在吸引外商投资上，在过去的5年时间里，投洽会不但吸引了全球顶端的 MNC，而且它负责将二分之一以上的外资（总投资额在500亿美元以上）投入到中国的中小企业。

2002年，第六届投洽会吸引了5万多名参展商和来自近100个国家和地区的10107位客商，签订合同663份，投资总额70.3亿美元。出席开幕盛会的有中国高层领导人、诺贝尔奖获得者、联合国官员以及多个国家的副总理。

到投洽会去淘金吧！不管你是否与泉州企业或中国其他地方企业有业务上的拓展关系，为了你自己的发展，赶快联系：

中国（厦门）国际投资促进中心

地址：中国厦门市湖滨北路外贸大厦二楼（邮编：361012）

电话：0086—0592—5079898转631或5068459

传真：0086—0592—5129898或5146205

网址：http://www.chinafair.org.cn

电子邮箱：98xiamen@public.xm.fj.cn

参加过投洽会的泉州部分企业

福建惠泉啤酒集团股份有限公司

恒安国际集团有限公司

泉州金山石材工具科技有限公司

泉州市奔达纺织有限公司

泉州市四方数控技术有限公司

泉州三盛橡塑发泡鞋材有限公司

泉州东科食品有限公司

Chapter 12

Anxi–Oolong Tea Capital of China

No Anxi, No U.S.A.?

Dec. 16, 1773, angry American colonists, disguised as Native Americans, protested against the British tea tax by throwing 342 crates of Anxi tea into Boston Harbor. Thus Anxi helped pave the way for American independence.

Fujian has long been China's tea capital, and Quanzhou's Anxi County the chief source of Oolong tea, which at one time was so precious in Europe that only royalty drank it. There are many legends about how tea drinking came about. One says that the Indian monk who introduced Zen Buddhism to China around 530 A.D. cut off his eyelids so he would not fall asleep while meditating, and where the eyelids fell, a plant with leaves shaped like eyelids sprang up. And as luck would have it, these leaves, when brewed, created a stimulating beverage that further helped both the eyelidless master and his pupils stay awake during meditation.

It's a nice story, but I don't see eye-to-eye with it because Chinese drank tea long before Bodhidharma played his eye-opening prank. Many Chinese believe tea drinking began with the "father of agriculture," the almost mythical Emperor Shen Nong (2737-2697 A.D.). The first real proof of tea drinking comes from the Three Kingdoms era (222-277 A.D.), and it gradually increased in popularity until the Tang Dynasty, when it became one of the great national pastimes of China—along with poetry, painting, calligraphy, music, martial arts, and all of those other peculiarly Chinese practices that they have perfected over the past 5,019 years.

> "Our trouble is that we drink too much tea. I see in this the slow revenge of the Orient, which has diverted the Yellow River down our throats." J. B. Priestley

第十二章

安溪——中国乌龙茶之都

没有安溪，就没有美国？

1773 年 12 月 16 日，愤怒的美洲殖民地居民伪装成美洲土著，将 342 箱安溪茶叶扔进了波士顿港，以此抗议英国殖民者开征茶叶税。因此，安溪帮助美国铺平了独立的道路。

很长一段时间以来，福建一直是中国的茶都，而泉州的安溪县则是乌龙茶的主要生产地。在过去，乌龙茶在欧洲曾经是如此昂贵，以至于只有皇室才能喝得起。有关人类喝茶的起源有多种传说。一种说法是，在公元 250 年左右将禅宗佛教引入中国的印度高僧，为了在沉思的时候不至于睡着，将自己的眼睑割了下来。而当眼睑坠地的时候，一种叶子形状像眼睑的植物出现在他的面前。还好当这些树叶发酵以后，能酿制出具有提神作用的饮料，这样的饮料能更好地帮助那位没有眼睑的大师以及他的学生在沉思的时候保持清醒的状态。

这是一个美好的传说。但是我并没有亲眼目睹，因为早在菩提达摩表演他那让人大开眼界的魔术之前，中国人就已经开始喝茶了。许多中国人相信，在“农业始祖”神农皇帝的时候，他们就已经开始喝茶了。历史上最早有关喝茶的真实记载是在三国时期(公元220—公元280年)，之后逐渐普及开来。到了唐朝，喝茶已经成了中国人最重要的业余消遣方式之一。在过去 5019 年来，喝茶跟作诗、作画、书法、音乐、武术以及其他所有中国特色的习惯一道，逐步得到完善。

“问题是我们茶喝得太多了。我看到来自东方神不知鬼不觉的报复，她们已经将黄河水倒进我们的喉咙。”

——英国作家 J.B.普里斯特利（1894—1984 年）

Chinese claim that tea not only tastes good but also cures everything from bad eyes to impotence, and was a chief ingredient in the Taoist's elixir of immortality. Tea must also be highly addictive, because we foreign devils fought two Opium Wars and forced the drug on China at gunpoint, for a century, just so we could balance our trade deficit and pay for our tea (and silk, and porcelain).

Minnan Tea Ceremony

Tea fanned the flames of American independence in Boston, when colonists threw it overboard during the Boston Tea Party. Tea made the Hatter Mad.[1] But the tea that tantalizes Laowai and Laonei alike nowadays is a far cry from the concoctions Chinese used to brew up.

While Chinese abhor foreigners' adulteration of quality tea with cream and sugar, only 1500 years ago (yesterday by Chinese' standards), the citizens of the Celestial Empire added not just sugar but also rice, ginger, salt, orange peel, spices—even onions. Fortunately, either tea tastes better nowadays or Chinese are inured to it because except for the Tibetans (who still add rancid yak butter), and groups like West Fujian Hakkas (who add pounded meat and veggies), the only thing added to tea nowadays is pure water, preferably spring water, and if not that, then running river water. And it is served up in elegant yet simple Minnan Tea Ceremony, which many consider the precursor to the elaborate Japanese Tea Ceremony. But whereas Japanese have almost made a religion of preparing, serving and sipping tea, the Chinese ceremony has retained a pragmatic simplicity. Chinese do tend to stand on ceremony about a lot of things, but when it comes to food and drink, their primary aim is to please not protocol but the palate.

So while you're in Anxi, or anywhere else in Southern Fujian, make sure you take in the Minnan Tea Ceremony. Who knows? It might just cure you of everything that ails you.

---

① Mad Hatter: character in Lewis Carroll's classic tale, *Alice in Wonderland.*

中国人宣称，茶不仅好喝，而且能够治疗从白内障到阳痿的各种疾病。在道家的长生不老药中，它是主要成分。而且茶叶一定很容易上瘾，因为我们外国鬼子在一个世纪的时间里打了两场鸦片战争，用枪口对准中国人强迫他们吸食鸦片，只有这样我们才能够实现贸易收支平衡，用这些钱为茶叶（还包括丝绸和陶瓷等等）埋单。

在波士顿倾茶事件中，殖民地居民将茶叶扔进大海，茶叶为美国的独立革命点燃了燎原之火。茶叶塑造了“疯狂制帽人”①的形象。今天，逗弄老外和老内的茶叶跟中国人曾经用来泡茶的调制品有着天壤之别！

当中国人憎恨外国人在高品质的茶叶中掺入奶油和糖的时候，也就在 1500 年前（按照中国人的历史来算，这只是昨天发生的事），天朝人（指中国人）不仅在茶叶中加入糖，而且还加入大米、生姜、食盐、橘皮和香料，甚至还有大葱！幸运的是，不是今天的茶尝起来更香，就是中国人已经养成了习惯，因为除了西藏（这里的人们仍然将变质黄油加到茶叶里）以及闽西的客家（他们将捣碎的肉和蔬菜加到茶叶里）之外，唯一加到茶叶中的东西是纯净水，如果是矿泉水会更佳，当然如果两者都没有的话，流动的河水也可以。茶在幽雅且简单的闽南茶道中泡出来，很多人认为，闽南茶道是精细的日本茶道的先驱。但是，日本人已经养成了备茶、泡茶和品茶的习惯，而中国的茶道更多的是一种简易的实用主义。我通过观察发现，中国人确实在很多事情上讲究礼节，但是当他们吃东西或者喝饮料的时候，他们的首要目的不是为了遵守礼节，而是满足人的味觉。

因此，当你在安溪或者闽南的任何一个地方，必须确保你领会了闽南茶艺的内涵。谁知道呢？没准儿它就真的可以驱除你身上的任何病魔。

① 疯狂制帽人：刘易斯·卡罗尔经典童话《爱丽丝梦游仙境》中的人物。

And while you're in Xiamen or just about anywhere else in China, drop by the award-winning Huaxiangyuan Tea shops, run by three generations of an Anxi tea family.

Tao of Tea

"Chinese tea lovers never developed an intricate tea ceremony like chanoyu in Japan—which, by the way, they tend not to like because its elaborate stylization is quite contrary to the Taoistic feeling of spontaneity and carefree informality they associate with tea drinking. Nevertheless, there is definitely a Chinese art of tea. It is known as *ch'a-shu.*

"…Tea is at its best when enjoyed in pleasant surroundings, whether indoors or out, where the atmosphere is tranquil, the setting harmonious….Nevertheless, a perfect combination of these five—setting, company, tea, water and tea-things—will fail to work its magic in the absence of the special attitude required to do them justice.

"The key to that attitude is mindfulness…

"When the mind, having freed itself from the trammels of past and future, is fully concentrated on the Here and Now, a whole range of pleasures involving ears, eyes, nose, palate and mood can be enjoyed by two or three people who have come together to make and drink fine tea. However, that enjoyment would fade in the presence of reverential silence, stiff formality or self-consciousness.

John Blofeld[①]

Anxi Tea – Elixir of Life?

"We Told You So"…1.3 billion times! Chinese are indefatigable proselytizers, especially of Chinese medicine and tea. If I so much as sniffle, every neighbor, colleague and student on campus accosts me with sure-fire Chinese herbal cures, or compel me to swallow two dozen tiny black pellets made from poisonous toad venom (I kid you not!). One fellow assured me that a patent medicine cured colds, guaranteed, in 3 days. I asked why, if this was true, his own daughter h had a cold for over a week. He looked at me as if I was proof of why some animals ate their young, and said, "It was two different colds."

① Blofeld, John, *The Chinese Art of Tea,* Shambhala, Boston, 1997, Preface.

还有，在厦门或者中国任何其他一个地方，你可以走进华祥苑茶庄。这个茶庄是由一个安溪茶叶家族三代人经营的，获过大奖。

茶　道

"中国的茶叶爱好者从来没有将茶艺发展成像日本那样的茶道。顺便说一下，中国人并不喜欢日本茶道，因为在喝茶的时候如此拘泥于精细的礼节，与道教自然随意性非常不符。然而，在中国也有一种茶艺，它被称为'茶术'。

"……如果周围的环境温馨，那么享用茶叶是最佳的，这时候不管在室内还是在室外，气氛最安宁，环境最和谐……然而，即便有环境、茶友、茶叶、水以及茶点这五个重要因素的绝妙组合，如果缺乏泡茶的特别心态，那么茶叶将无法发挥它的神奇功效。

"泡茶的关键是'用心'……

"当一个人的心境从过去和将来的束缚中解放出来之后，才能完全集中精力。这时候两三个人聚在一起，泡开一壶好茶，通过听觉、视觉、嗅觉、味觉以及感觉享受茶叶带给人的一系列乐趣。不过，如果因为恭敬而沉默，或者场面过于正式，或者太忸怩，这种乐趣将会消失。"

——约翰·布洛菲尔德[①]

安溪茶——长生不老药?

"我们早告诉你了"……有 13 亿遍了吧！中国人是不屈不挠的改变宗教信仰的人，特别是中药和茶叶。如果我鼻塞了，那么我身边的每一位邻居，每一位同事，以及校园里的每个学生都会跟我搭讪，叫我服用中草药，或者强迫我吞下两粒用蟾蜍毒液做成的小小黑色药丸（我不是在开玩笑）。有一个家伙甚至向我保证，有一种专利药品保证在三天内治愈感冒。我问他为什么，这是不是真的，因为他自己的女儿感冒一周了却还没好。他看着我，好像我在证实为什么有些动物会吃掉它们的后代似的，然后他说："这是两种不同的感冒。"

Amoymagic.com

500-year-old courtyard

① 约翰·布洛菲尔德：《中国茶艺》，香巴拉，波士顿，1997年版，序言。

Likewise, all of my Chinese friends feel compelled to recite a litany they no doubt learned in school, "Coffee's bad for you but tea is healthy." And how I hate a smug, "I told you so" – especially 1.3 billion of them. Scientists in the U.S. and Japan have discovered that when it comes to fighting cancer, green tea is twice as effective as red wine, 35 times more effective than vitamin E, and 100 times more effective than vitamin C at protecting cells and their DNA. Of course, that's just a restrained Western scientist's viewpoint. Chinese enthusiasts believe the leaf is the long sought after Taoist elixir of immortality.

500-year-old home! (Anxi, Hutou)

Anxi Tea Tackles Cancer? Anxi "Chinese Long Life Tea," which won 1st prize in the 2001 Fujian Province Tea Competition, is a popular "medicinal" tea. One website claims this supposedly 2200-year-old tea blend (Anxi wasn't even around 2200 years ago!) regenerates the body at cellular level, attacking free-radical onslaughts, delaying cellular aging and detoxifying the liver, as well as "cure nervous disorders, arteriosclerosis, cardio-vascular failures, premature aging, divers skin conditions including boils, kidney and liver insufficiencies, rheumatoid arthritis, and gout."
As if reading my mind, the author went on to say,

> "Regrettably, recalcitrant Western Medicine does not only reject any remedy that lists a too splendid array of claims, but will violently antagonize its spread, branding it as a sheer hoax. Which is the reason why Anxi Tea is still widely unknown in the Western world."

I must rank among the recalcitrant Westerners, because when they claimed that folks in Siberia and Ecuador, as well as China, live up to 120 years because they drink Anxi tea, I wondered how on earth those remote people got hold of it. Amazon.com, perhaps?

Tea Tours Anxi tea is big business nowadays, and produced in sprawling tea processing factories, but you can still run across peasant households producing fine teas using time honored methods and homemade machines. You'll need a local or a guide to help you find them, but it's worth the search, especially when they pull out their cheap little red clay tea sets and, with care and reverence, brew up some homegrown leaf.

同样，我所有的中国朋友都觉得有必要向我重复他们在学校里学到的一句话："咖啡对你不好，茶叶有益身体健康。"我讨厌沾沾自喜的人，"我早告诉过你了"——特别是他们有13亿人啊！美国和日本的科学家已经发现，在抗癌方面，绿茶的功效是红酒的两倍；在保护细胞和DNA方面，绿茶的功效是维生素C的100倍。当然，这只是西方科学观点的一个局限的说法罢了。中国的热心人相信，茶叶就是道家苦苦追寻的长生不老药。

安溪茶可以抗癌？安溪的"长生不老茶"在 2001 年举办的"福建省茶王赛"上获得第一名，是一种家喻户晓的"药效"茶。有一个网站甚至号称有 2200 年历史的茶叶（2200 年前连安溪都还不存在呢！）能够在细胞的基础上再生人的机体，对抗自由基侵害、延缓细胞衰老、为肝脏解毒，还可以"治疗神经紊乱、动脉硬化、心血管衰竭、早衰包括脓肿在内的各种皮肤病、肝肾功能不全、类风湿性关节炎以及痛风"。

好像知道我在想什么，网站继续往下说：

"令人遗憾的是，不能包治百病的西药不仅拒绝茶叶列出的一系列绝妙药方，而且还恶意阻止它的传播，说这是'绝对的谎言'。这也是安溪茶叶在西方国家还不广为人知的原因。"

我必须说说桀骜不驯的西方人，因为每当他们说到西伯利亚人和厄瓜多尔人，还有中国人能活到 120 岁，都是因为喝了安溪茶的时候，我纳闷，身在万里之外的这些人是怎么知道安溪茶的。通过亚马孙网站（Amazon.com），也许是吧？

茶乡之旅　在今天，安溪茶占领巨大的商业市场，它们基本上是在不断扩张的茶叶加工厂里生产出来的。但是你还是能够碰到农户采用传统的做法和自制的机器生产出的质量上乘的茶叶。你需要当地人或者导游的帮助才能找到他们，但这是值得探索的，特别是当他们很细心地、用崇敬的态度取出廉价的红色小茶具，泡上他们自己加工的茶叶的时候。

Your best bet to find such a family is to visit the smaller villages like Longmen (龙门, Dragon's Gate) south of Anxi City proper. And a suggestion: take a generous bag of candy for the kids and you'll have little friends for life.
Another suggestion: photos! Every family wants a good photo of the elderly to display after they pass on, but an 8 x 10 costs a small fortune for a peasant household. As you travel throughout the countryside, take photos, get their addresses, and mail them a copy. You'll have a friend for life—or maybe even longer!

Fujian China International Travel Service (CITS) provides guided Tea Tours of farms, factories, markets, and the Anxi Tea Museum.
For more info on Fujian CITS, visit **www.citsfj.com/en**
Email: fujicits@public.fz.fj.cn
Phone: (591)8337-0110, 8337-0071

Touring Anxi There's more to Anxi than tea! Every time I visit this rural county, I discover new historical, cultural and natural treasures. For instance, I've visited the remote township of Hutou (湖头) at least a dozen times because it's the hometown of Lixi, our baomu (保姆, household helper), who has been with us since 1988 and is now the 5th member of the family. But the only thing I really knew about Hutou was that it produced South Fujian's best rice noodles (米粉条, mifentiao). Then last year I learned that Lixi was born in a marvelous 500-year-old earthen building.

The deeper I delve, the more fascinating Anxi becomes—and it changes each time I visit, shifting shape with the seasons and the unique cultural and religious traditions and festivals that are celebrated monthly (probably even weekly).

Half the town turned out for this celebration, and the other half of the town joined in when the foreigner showed up in **Toy Ota!**

要找到这样的农户，你必须拜访像龙门镇（位于安溪县南部）的一些小村庄。建议你：给当地的小孩子带上一大包糖果，相信你会交到不少小朋友。

Anxi Religious Festival

另一个建议：给他们拍照！作为纪念，每个家庭在他们的长者去世后，都会在墙壁上挂上一张不错的照片。但是对于一个小农户来说，一张8×10寸的照片是一笔不小的开支。当你到乡下旅游的时候，给他们拍拍照片，把他们的地址记下来，照片洗出来后寄给他们。你会结交到一生的朋友——甚至有可能更长！

福建中国国际旅行社（CITS）有导游陪伴的茶叶之旅，参观农场、工厂、市场以及安溪茶叶博物馆等等。

想得到更多有关福建中国国际旅行社的消息，请登陆网站www.citsfj.com/en ,电子邮件：fujicits@public.fz.fj.cn
电话：(0591)83370110,83370071

走遍安溪 除了茶叶之外，关于安溪还有很多要说的。每次我来到这个农业县，我总能发现新的历史、文化和自然宝藏。比如，我去过偏远的湖头镇至少有十几次，因为那里是我家的保姆李西的故乡。自从1988年以来，李西一直跟我们生活在一起，如今她已经是我们家的五个成员之一。但是我对湖头镇的唯一认识是，它是闽南最著名的米粉的故乡。直到去年，我才知道李西是在一间具有500年辉煌历史的土木房子里出生的。

我对安溪的探索越多，安溪就变得越有魅力。每次我到安溪，都会发现那里发生了变化。安溪特有的文化和宗教传统活动每个月（很可能是每周）都会举行一次，安溪的面貌因此随着季节的改变而改变。

有半个镇的人参加庆祝活动，而当老外开着丰田车出现时，另外一半的人也会来凑热闹啦！

Prime Minister Li Guangdi's Former Residence Li Guangdi Guju) in Hutou (湖头）. I had visited Hutou, our baomu's hometown, a dozen times or more, never imagining that this little backwater was home to an illustrious Qing Dynasty Prime Minister, Li Guangdi, who recommended to the Emperor that Shilang be the man in charge of ousting Koxinga's descendants from Taiwan.

Ming Dynasty Prime Minister's Home

The 3,120m^2 home, first built in 1698 (37th year of Emperor Kangxi, in case you're dying to know) is in Hu'er Village, Hutou Township, Anxi County (安溪县湖头镇湖二村，Anxi Xian, Hutou Zhen, Hu'er Cun).
Getting There: Bus to Anxi, change for bus to Hutou Township.
Hours: 8:00 – 17:30 **Phone**: 2340-1091

"Are we there yet?"

Anxi Confusion Temple As I noted earlier, the Quanzhou English map has the location for an "Anxi Confusion Temple," (安溪文庙, Anxi Wenmiao), built in 1001 A.D and, according to the literature, "renovated in every generation since then." The present architecture is primarily Qing Dynasty.
Getting There: Bus to Anxi. **Hours**: 8:30-7:30 **Phone**: （0595）23232553

Qingshui Cliff Temple (Qingshui Yan) One of China's most picturesque temples, this rambling three-story affair was built in 1083 A.D. right up the side of Penglai Village's densely forested Pengshan Hill, clinging to the hillside rather like the Potala Palace in Lhasa, Tibet. After it burned down in 1277 A.D., monks raised money for the 12-year renovation project that was completed in 1317. When renovated in 1564 A.D. the temple was home to over 70 monks and nuns.

清朝宰相李光地故居（湖头镇）我去过我们家保姆的老家湖头镇十几次，从来没想到在这个与世隔绝的偏僻地方，竟然诞生了一名清朝杰出的宰相——李光地，他向康熙皇帝力荐施琅，由施琅统率军队将郑成功的后代从台湾驱逐出去。

李光地故居占地 3120 平方米，始建于康熙三十七年（1698 年）。故居位于安溪县湖头镇湖二村。

交通：坐汽车到安溪县城，再转乘汽车到湖头镇。

时间：8：00—17：30

电话：（0595）23401091

安溪文庙 我早先从一张泉州市英文地图上就注意到“安溪文庙”（地图上的英文误将“安溪文庙”写作“安溪糊涂庙”）这个地方，它建于公元 1001 年。根据文献记载，“自从那时起，每一代都进行修复”。目前的建筑主要是清朝修建的。

交通：坐汽车到安溪县城

时间：8：00—17：30 电话：（0595）23232553

清水岩 中国最有风姿的庙宇之一。这座布局不规整的三层庙宇建于公元 1083 年，位于蓬莱镇蓬莱村森林茂密的蓬莱山上，它依山傍水的风格跟西藏的布达拉宫非常相似。公元 1277 年，清水岩毁于一场大火，和尚们筹集资金，经过 12 年的重新修缮，清水岩在 1213 年得以完工。到了公元 1564 年再次修缮的时候，庙里的和尚和尼姑总数已经超过了 70 人。

Hillside Holy Water

Qingshui Cliff Temple is a very holy place for Buddhists, and its incense burner has been used to light incense for over 100 burners scattered about Taiwan. A brochure claimed that Qingshui attracts over 600,000 visitors annually, and I can see why. Nice temple—but for me, the biggest attraction is the incredible scenery, and the massive trees. An ancient camphor tree is so large it takes half a dozen people holding hands to reach around it. The ancient sentinel is called "Facing North" because when the tree heard that the good general Yue Fei (岳飞) had been murdered by a treacherous official, the tree held out all its branches to the north to express its sorrow.

Getting there: Bus or train to Penglai Town
Hours: 6:00 - 17:30 **Phone**: 2335-5322

Lovely Paths at Qingshuiyan

Nine Peaks Cliff is another of Penglai Town's cliffhanging sites. Built in 1415, during the time of Muslim Navigator Zheng He, it's eight official sites include "Nine Mountains," "Three Tablets," "Lions," and "Huge Rock" (catchy name, that one). The real attraction, for me, is the surrealist scenery, with fog-enshrouded peaks covered with forests of bamboo and camphor, and villages nestled in the valleys. But Chinese like the calligraphy, the number one piece probably being the poem by Ming Dynasty Premier Zhang Ruitu (张瑞图), which reads, "乔木千枝原为一本，长江万派总是同源" A thousand tree branches have but one trunk, numerous branches of the Changjiang River have but one source." It is particularly appropriate because the little town of Penglai is the source of many streams of Overseas Chinese, many of whom have returned to their ancestral homeland to help rebuild it.

对于佛教徒来说，清水岩是一个非常神圣的地方，它的香火已经被用来点燃遍布台湾各地的100多个分炉。一份旅游小册子上声称清水岩每年接待的游客达60万人次，我也知道其中的原因。对我来说，这座漂亮的庙宇最吸引人的地方是它周边令人难以置信的风景，以及茂密的树林。其中有一棵古老的樟树，它的树干很粗，要六个人手拉手才能将它抱住。这棵古老的樟树被人称为“枝枝朝北树”，因为当它听到爱国名将岳飞被奸臣所害时，它所有的树枝突然之间全部朝北，表达它的哀伤。

交通：坐汽车或者火车到安溪蓬莱镇

时间：6：00—17：30 **电话**：（0595）23355322

九峰岩　蓬莱镇另一座处于悬崖边的庙宇。九峰岩建于1415年，也就是郑和下西洋的时候。它有“九峰插汉”、“三笏摩天”、“巨石飞腾”、“狮子参前”等八景。对我来说，真正吸引人的是它超现实主义的美景：雾气笼罩的山上到处是竹林和樟树，还有那些在山谷中若隐若现的小村庄。但是中国人更喜爱书法，寺中堪称书法第一的当属明朝相国张瑞图的对联：“乔木千枝原为一本，长江万派总是同源。”这个对联特别适合蓬莱镇，因为就是这样一个小镇，却成了许多海外华侨追根溯源的地方。许多海外华侨回到祖国，帮助修缮九峰岩。

Like Qingshui Cliff Temple, (and just about every other temple in Quanzhou, as well as Christians churches and the Muslim Mosque), Nine Peaks has been renovated with the aid of generous donations from members of Penglai's 100,000+ Overseas Chinese community. They had good reasons for leaving Anxi, and fortunately, even better reasons for returning.

Anxi Fights the Poverty Amidst Plenty Anxi is the ancestral home for well over 700,000 Overseas Chinese, mainly in Singapore, Indonesia, and Malaysia. Nearly one fourth of Anxi residents have overseas relatives or have lived abroad, and 2 million Taiwanese are of Anxi ancestry. Anxi folks cut the apron strings and went abroad because Anxi, though blessed with rich natural resources, was also impoverished.

.

Anxi has long been famous not just for tea (the best coming from Changkeng, Xiping and Gande) but also for other resources like fruits, minerals, and the forests of Gande, Fengtian, Lutian and Longjuan townships. In Northern Anxi, Jiandou and Weili produce anthracite, Qingyang has manganese, and Pantian mines produce ore with over 55% iron content. The area also has some beautiful crystals.

Anxi Serves Up "Chicken Soup for the Soul!" My farmer friends in Anxi's Hutou and Jiandou know that I've collected rocks, gems and crystals since I was a child, and several times have phoned to say, "Professor, we've found another rock for you!"

When I was ill a few years back, two Hutou friends made the long (and costly) trek to Xiamen bearing gifts for both body and soul. They presented me with a live mountain chicken, which they had lugged on the bus for hours (it was for medicinal broth), and a beautiful crystal that a farmer had found in a field and saved for me.

Anxi people are rich indeed—at least in the ways that count.

和清水岩一样（几乎和泉州每一座寺庙、基督教教堂和穆斯林清真寺一样），九峰岩在蓬莱镇 10 多万海外乡亲的慷慨解囊之下，多次进行了修缮。这些海外乡亲有很好的理由离开安溪，幸运的是，他们有更好的理由返回故乡。

安溪脱贫致富 安溪是 70 多万海外华侨的祖籍地，这些华侨大多定居在新加坡、印度尼西亚和马来西亚。接近四分之一的安溪人有海外亲戚或者曾经在海外居住的亲戚，另外，有 200 万台胞的祖先在安溪。那么多的安溪人切断围裙带到海外生活，因为安溪虽然有丰富的自然资源，但仍然很贫穷。

安溪不仅因为茶叶而远近闻名（最好的茶叶来自长坑、西坪和感德），其他一些资源还包括水果和矿产，感德、福田、芦田和龙涓等地的森林也很出色。在安溪北部，剑斗和尾利村（音译名）生产无烟煤，青洋有锰矿，而潘田的铁矿含铁量超过 55%。这些地方还有一些不错的天然水晶。

Anxi style "Chicken Soup for the Soul!"

安溪“心灵鸡汤” 我在安溪湖头和剑斗的农民朋友知道我从小开始收藏玉石、珠宝和水晶，很多时候，他们会打电话告诉我说：“教授，我们又给你找到了一块玉石。”

几年前，我有一次病倒了，两个湖头朋友经过长途跋涉（还花了不少路费）来到厦门，给我带来礼物。他们为我带来了一只活的山鸡，这只山鸡跟他们一起在车上颠簸了好几个小时（山鸡和中药一起炖汤），还有一块一位农民朋友在地里发现并特意为我保留下来的漂亮水晶石。

安溪人确实是富裕的，至少从某方面来说是如此。

Though rich in resources, Anxi was until recently impoverished economically. In the mid '80s, Fujian's poorest county was Fu'an; Anxi was second. The primary cause of their poverty was the county's remote location. Even in the mid 90s, the bus from mountainous Anxi to Xiamen's markets took eight hours, but new concrete roads, many built with the aid of Overseas Chinese, have cut the journey to two hours.

Markets are now mushrooming for Anxi's mountain mushrooms and edible fungi, which are excellent income generators for forested areas because they don't require a large initial investment or long gestation period.

Anxi Anti-Poverty Strategies My little Anxi friends have a much brighter future today, thanks to Anxi's anti-poverty strategies, which have earned it honor as a model county. Anxi's strategies include measures like providing capital and expertise to impoverished villages, preferential policies for mountain-area development, and an emphasis upon trade and investment.

Anti-poverty teams have helped set up local enterprises and mushroom farms, renovate existing enterprises, improve mining operations, raise tea production, combat soil erosion, start fisheries, overcome transportation problems and find markets both in Fujian and throughout China.

After selecting Longmen (龙门, Dragon Gate) Township as a "Science and Technology Anti-Poverty Demonstration Site," The Fujian Academy of Agricultural Sciences sent in experts to improve agriculture and livestock practices. Over a four-year period, household incomes reportedly grew 160%.

The "Oolong Tea Research Institute" and "Oolong Tea Quality Control Center" has helped improve teas, gained footholds in lucrative markets like Shanghai, and exhibited the tea in national and international exhibitions.

Thanks to the concerted efforts of Anxi county, Quanzhou city, and the Provincial Government, Anxi farmers can now have their tea and drink it too! Of course, it helps a lot that Anxi people aren't just waiting for aid but taking matters into their own hands with grassroots movements—like the Longmen bridge project.

安溪虽然资源丰富，但是在经济上直到最近仍很贫穷。在20世纪80年代中期，福建最贫困的县是福安，安溪排第二。安溪县贫困的最主要原因是地处偏远山区。即使到了20世纪90年代中期，从安溪县城坐大巴绕着山路到厦门市还得花上8个小时。现在通过华侨的资助，安溪到厦门终于有了水泥路，行程也缩短到2个小时。

如今，市场对产自安溪的食用菌的需求量猛增。对地处深山老林的农民朋友来说，它们是很好的经济来源，因为它们无须大规模投资或者很长的酝酿期。

Typhoon washes bridge out

安溪致富战略 在贯彻脱贫致富战略后，如今的安溪已经赢得了“模范县城”的美称，我的那些安溪小朋友将有一个更加美好的未来。安溪的致富战略包括：采取措施为贫穷乡村提供资金和技术、为偏远山区的发展提供倾斜政策以及重视贸易和投资。

Wade... or walk for miles

脱贫致富队伍已经为当地建立企业，革新现有的产业，帮助建立蘑菇生产基地，改善矿产开发状况，增加茶叶产量，提高茶叶质量，对抗土壤腐蚀，开展渔业养殖，克服交通运输难题以及在福建省内乃至全国寻找市场。

Now that's a bridge!

在选择龙门镇作为“科技脱贫示范区”之后，福建省农科院派来专家，帮助提高农业生产和家禽的养殖。据报道，示范区实施之后的头四年里，龙门镇的家庭收入平均增长了 160%。

“乌龙茶研究机构”以及“乌龙茶质量控制中心”的成立，帮助提高了茶叶生产质量，帮助在像上海这样蕴含无限商机的市场站稳了脚跟，以及安排乌龙茶在国内外大型展览会上展出。

感谢安溪县、泉州市以及福建省出台的一系列具体措施，安溪的农民朋友们现在已经能够拥有自己的茶叶而且可以好好喝上几杯了。这些战略非常有针对性，当然，安溪人民也不只是单纯等待政府的扶持，他们已经开展了轰轰烈烈的民间运动，就比如龙门的桥梁工程。

Supplement 1 Huaxiangyuan Tea (华祥苑)

While most Chinese love tea, South Fujian people seem to live on it, and take great pains to ensure their daily fix. Xiamen's Secretary General Mr. Cáo Fàng (副秘书长曹放), said to me, "In the rest of China, people go to tea shops, but Minnan (S. Fujian) people carry their own tea with them." Of course, that is because Minnan folk, unlike most other Chinese, grow the best tea right in their own backyard.

When I was in Europe with delegations from Xiamen and Quanzhou, even while in the finest Chinese restaurants my colleagues pulled fancy foil packets of Anxi tea from their breast pockets. "This is the best!" they boasted. "Anxi tea! You can't buy this in stores!" In the same way, I've had laborers and farmers proudly produce ordinary plastic bags stuffed with very unordinary leaves and exclaim as they put the kettle on the fire, "From our family's field! You can't buy this in stores!"

Anxi teas were indeed hard to find in stores, at least until the mid 90s, because poor roads made markets inaccessible, but Anxi tea is now sold throughout China, thanks to entrepreneurs like Xiao Wenhua （肖文华）, of Longyuan Town (龙绢)., whose family has produced fine teas for almost a century. In 1994, Xiao took advantage of Anxi's new roads and Xiamen's preferential investment environment to introduce their quality high-altitude organic Tieguanyin tea to the world.

Xiao Wenhua, Caofang, Bill

附录 1　华祥苑茗茶

泉州精艺达翻译服务有限公司

大多数中国人喜欢茶，而闽南人似乎以茶为生，并花大力气维持其日常需要。厦门市副秘书长曹放对我说：“在中国的其他地方，人们到茶店去买茶，但是在闽南这边，人们随身带着自家的茶。”这很正常，因为闽南人不像其他地方的中国人，他们在自家后院里就能采摘最好的茶叶。

当我在欧洲和来自厦门和泉州的代表团一起时，即使是在最好的中国餐馆里，我的同事也会从胸前口袋里掏出一袋用箔纸包装精巧的安溪茶叶，无比炫耀地说：“这可是最好的安溪茶叶，你在商店里买不到的。”同样，我看到过一些工人和农民，他们从最普通的塑料袋子里拿出不同寻常的茶叶，一边将水壶放到火上烧水，一边喊着：“这是从我们老家带来的！你在商店里也买不到！”

20 世纪 90 年代中期以前，因为交通闭塞，安溪茶叶的确很难在商店买到，不过现在安溪茶叶在全中国都有销售，这得归功于一些企业家如龙涓镇的肖文华，他们家世代制茶，已有近百年的历史了。1994 年，肖文华利用安溪新建的公路以及厦门的有利投资环境，将他们高质量高海拔的有机铁观音推向世界。

Xiao's Earliest Tea Workshop

Harmony with Tea, Harmony with Nature, (自然天成，人茶合一) Xiao chose Xiamen as his strategic base because of its reputation as a center of tea culture. He then recruited a passionate team of tea producers committed to their motto, "Attention to detail; always seek perfection" (注重细节，不断完善).

Today, 100 hectares of organic high altitude tea plants thrive on an Anxi mountainside at over 1000m, nourished by fine soil, clean air, mountain mists and pristine mountain water. Quality is paramount at every stage, from picking to packaging. National-level senior tea appraisers in Tong'an's 2-hectare ISO9001-certified processing center scrutinize every detail, from appearance, bouquet, taste and hue (汤色) to leaf bottom (叶底). The finer grades require over 600 days of processing! Personally, I don't even know what "leaf bottom" means, but I can vouch for the taste, which lingers sweetly upon the palate long after I've drained my miniscule Minnan teacup.

Into the World! From the humble Zhongshan Rd. shop opened in 1994, Huaxiangyuan is now sold in almost 100 stores across China, as well as in numerous other countries, and has landed over 200 domestic and international awards. Huaxiangyuan was designated as the official tea for Beijing's Diaoyutai State Guesthouse (钓鱼台国宾馆), and in 2006 was chosen as the commemorative tea for the "United Nations Silk Route Investment Forum" (联合国丝绸之路投资论坛纪念茶").

Seeing Stars Huaxiangyuan comes in 3 primary grades—Sun, Moon and Star. I'm happy with the humble Star, but for a treat, shoot for the moon—or even the Sun. Though a word of warning: once you've pandered your palate with these royal leaves, you'll never again be able to brew cheap tea bags with a clear conscience.

3-Years of Tea School! Want to learn more about Anxi tea? Huaxiangyuan has teamed up with Xiamen's Little Egret Art School (小白鹭民间舞团) to provide a 3-year program in tea culture and arts. Courses cover Minnan tea ceremonies, history of tea culture, tea practices, tea-related cultural courses, South Fujian dialect, ballads, Southern opera, dance and vocal training, tea production and marketing, etc.

Haven't got 3 years? Never fear. Visit Huaxiangyuan's elegant 2/F, 300m^2 flagship store on Hexiang Rd. in Xiamen. Or check out their website: www.hxytea.com E-mail: hxy@hxytea.com Tel: (0592)505-0588

自然天成，人茶合一 肖文华选择厦门作为其战略基地，是看重了其作为茶文化中心的声望。接着，他招募了一支热情四溢的专业制茶团队，致力于其“注重细节，不断完善”的企业理念。

今天，华祥苑在安溪海拔1000多米的高山上建立了100公顷的高海拔有机茶叶培植基地，山上优良的土壤、清新的空气、缭绕的云雾、清冽的山泉滋养着茶树。从采茶到包装，质量一直是居于首位的。华祥苑在同安拥有2公顷ISO 9001认证的生产中心，在那里，国家级资深茶叶评审师从外观、香味、汤色和叶底等方面挑剔每一个细节。要制作出一泡好茶，往往需要600多天的时间！其实，我自己都不知道叶底是什么，但是我能保证口感超好，我把小小的闽南茶杯里的茶饮尽后，甘甜的茶香还在嘴里留存了好久，回味无穷。

走向世界！ 1994年华祥苑在中山路开了一家小店，现在华祥苑在全中国已有近100家专卖店，在其他许多国家也设有专卖店，已荣获200多项国际国内奖项。华祥苑被指定为北京“钓鱼台国宾馆专用茶”生产和销售企业，于2006年被选为“联合国丝绸之路投资论坛纪念茶”。

品尝星星级的茶叶 华祥苑的茶叶分为三个主要级别——太阳、月亮和星星。我喝着星星级的茶叶就很开心了，如果要犒赏一下自己的话，可以品尝一下月亮级——甚至太阳级的。不过警告你哦：一旦你用这些皇家茶叶把自己的嘴养刁了，你就绝对再也喝不下便宜的茶袋泡出来的茶了。

三年的茶艺专业学校！ 想更多地了解安溪茶叶？华祥苑已和厦门小白鹭民间舞团合作，提供为期三年的茶文化艺术培训项目。课程涵盖闽南茶艺、茶文化历史、茶艺实践、与茶有关的文化课程、闽南方言、民歌、闽南戏曲、舞蹈和发声训练、茶叶生产和销售等。

没有三年的时间？没关系。到华祥苑雅致的旗舰店看看，位于厦门禾祥路，有2层楼300平方米大呢。或访问他们的网站：www.hxytea.com E-mail: hxy@hxytea.com 电话：（0592）5050588

Supplement 2

The Book of Tea

Kakuzo Okakura's *The Book of Tea*, published in 1906, is a marvelous little treatise on the influence of tea on Asian culture, of the differences between East and West, and of why we should try to narrow the gaps. A reviewer wrote of the book, "The words linger with you long after you have finished, and tea, once an ordinary beverage, acquires a soul—a source of peace."

> "[Teaism influences] our home and habits, costume and cuisine, porcelain, lacquer, painting—our very literature…the initiated may touch the sweet reticence of Confucius, the piquancy of Laotse, and the ethereal aroma of Sakyamuni himself."
>
> "The average Westerner, in his sleek complacency, will see in the tea ceremony but another instance of the thousand and one oddities which constitute the quaintness and childishness of the East to him…. When will the West understand, or try to understand, the East? We Asiatics are often appalled by the curious web of facts and fancies which has been woven concerning us. We are pictured as living on the perfume of the lotus, if not on mice and cockroaches. It is either impotent fanaticism or else abject voluptuousness. Indian spirituality has been derided as ignorance, Chinese sobriety as stupidity, Japanese patriotism as the result of fatalism. It has been said that we are less sensible to pain and wounds on account of the callousness of our nervous organization!"
>
> "Why not amuse yourselves at our expense? Asia returns the compliment. There would be further food for merriment if you were to know all that we have imagined and written about you. All the glamour of the perspective is there, all the unconscious homage of wonder, all the silent resentment of the new and undefined. You have been loaded with virtues too refined to be envied, and accused of crimes too picturesque to be condemned. Our writers in the past—the wise men who knew—informed us that you had bushy tails somewhere hidden in your garments, and often dined off a fricassee of newborn babes! Nay, we had something worse against you: we used to think you the most impracticable people on the earth, for you were said to preach what you never practiced.

附录 2　《茶书》

由日本人冈仓古志郎（Kakuzo Okakura）撰写的《茶书》(1906 年出版)，是一本描写茶叶对亚洲文化的影响的优秀专著。该书写出了东方文化与西方文化之间的差异，以及我们必须缩小两者之间差距的原因。一位评论作家是这样评论《茶书》的，他说：“书中的每个词，在你读完很长时间之后，仍然历历在目。而茶叶，曾经的一种普通饮料，却拥有了一种灵感——一种和平的源泉。”

“（茶文化的影响）我们的家乡和习惯、服饰和烹调、瓷器、漆器和绘画——我们特有的文学……这些有可能触动孔夫子和蔼的缄默、老子的深刻以及释迦牟尼本人缥缈的韵味。

“一般的西方人用他时髦阔气的自满来看待茶道，对他来说，这是让西方人觉得东方人古怪和幼稚的一千零一个例子中的一个……什么时候西方人才会理解东方人，或者试着去理解他们呢？我们亚洲人经常被交织在我们周围的不可理解的事实和幻想的网所惊吓。我们被描绘的形象如果说不是靠老鼠和蟑螂维生的话，也是靠荷花的芳香生存的。它不是无能的狂热，就是绝望无助的纵欲。印度人的脱俗被嘲弄成漠不关心，中国人的节制被说成是愚蠢，日本人的爱国被描绘成宿命。据说，由于我们神经组织的麻木不仁，我们对伤痛的敏感度比较低下。

“为什么不尽情让自己快乐起来呢？亚洲将恭维物归原主。如果你愿意知道我们对你的想法和看法，会得到更多庆祝胜利的食物的。所有这些景观的魅力，所有这些没有意识的效忠，所有这些对新兴事物以及不明确事物的默默怨恨都在那里。你身上的品德过于高尚，以至于遭到人们的嫉妒；你遭指控的罪行过于别致，以至于遭到人们的谴责。以前那些作家——那些无所不知的智者——曾告诉我们，在我们衣服的某个地方，隐藏着毛茸茸的尾巴，而且经常在就餐时会吃下一块新生婴儿的肌肉。而且，我们对你还有一些更可怕的做法：我们曾以为你是世界上最难对付的人，因为据说你竭力宣扬你从来不付出行动的事情。

"Such misconceptions are fast vanishing amongst us. Commerce has forced the European tongues on many an Eastern port. Asiatic youths are flocking to Western colleges for the equipment of modern education. Our insight does not penetrate your culture deeply, but at least we are willing to learn. Some of my compatriots have adopted too much of your customs and too much of your etiquette, in the delusion that the acquisition of stiff collars and tall silk hats comprised the attainment of your civilization.

"Pathetic and deplorable as such affectations are, they evince our willingness to approach the West on our knees. Unfortunately the Western attitude is unfavorable to the understanding of the East.

"Perhaps I betray my own ignorance of the Tea Cult by being so outspoken. Its very spirit of politeness exacts that you say what you are expected to say, and no more. But I am not to be a polite Teaist. So much harm has been done already by the mutual misunderstanding of the New World and the Old, that one need not apologise for contributing his tithe to the furtherance of a better understanding.

"Let us stop the continents from hurling epigrams at each other…We have developed along different lines, but there is no reason why one should not supplement the other."

“像这样的误解在我们之间很快就会消除。商业往来迫使欧洲人将触角伸向东方的港口。许多亚洲的年轻人云集到西方的大学，接受现代教育。我们的洞察力并没有深深洞悉你们的文化，但至少可以这样说，我们愿意去学习。我的一些同胞们已经过多采纳了你们的习惯和礼仪，这会给人一种错觉，说穿竖领衣服以及戴高高的丝绸帽子来自于你们的文明。

“像这种做作的行为既可怜又可悲，它们唤醒我们走出国门，去接触西方世界，很不幸的是，西方了解东方的态度并不受欢迎。

“可能是因为我的坦率背叛了我自己对茶道的漠视。这种特别有礼貌的精神恰好说明，你说出了人们期待你说出的话，除此之外没有别的。但我不想成为一个礼貌的茶叶爱好者。因此，在新旧世界相互误解的过程中已经造成了很大伤害，一个人为了促进更好的相互理解而捐款，他没有必要对此进行道歉。

“让我们阻止大陆与大陆之间的相互恶言……如果不是更加聪明的话。我们踏着不同的主线，但是东西半球不互相弥补是没有理由的。”

Chapter 13

Dehua—Porcelain Paradise, and Yongchun

> "The Chinese pottery [porcelain] is manufactured only in the towns of Zaytun and Sin-kalan… The best quality of [porcelain is made from] clay that has fermented for a complete month, but no more… The price of this porcelain there is the same as, or even less than, that of ordinary pottery in our country. It is exported to India and other countries, even reaching as far as our own lands in the West, and it is the finest of all makes of pottery."
>
> Ibn Battuta, Arab Traveler

A Passion for Porcelain While it is true Westerners sold opium, for centuries Chinese trafficked in porcelain, which for Europe's royalty was more addictive than any poppy product. Thin as eggshells, translucent in sunlight, ringing like a bell when struck, porcelain captured the imagination of Westerners like nothing since Cleopatra's Chinese silk negligees, and was so seductive in its allure that Europeans used "China" as a euphemism for "sex."

A delicate Dehua teaset

Janet Gleeson, author of *The Arcanum*,① an absorbing account of the Europeans' pursuit of porcelain, notes that in Wycherley's 1675 play, *The Country Wife*, an admirer sees Mr. Horner with Lady Fiddler and begs, "…don't think to give other people china, and me none; come in with me too." After Lady Fiddler comments, "… we women of quality never think we have china enough," the exhausted Mr. Horner says, "Do not take ill, I cannot make china for you all…"

European monarchs gleefully bankrupted national treasuries to satisfy their passion for porcelain. And like monarchs who a millennia earlier were obsessed with spying out the secrets of silk, so Europe's kings were driven to fathom the secret behind porcelain, which like silk was worth more than its weight in gold. Countless potters and scientists were imprisoned until they either produced porcelain or rotted in the attempt. Most rotted. But Quanzhou had the answer.

---

① *The Arcanum—The Extraordinary True Story*, by Janet Gleeson, reads better than a mystery or thriller as Janet Gleeson recounts the incredible lengths to which Europeans went to discover the "Arcanum" (the secret of porcelain production), and the extremes they went too to preserve the Arcanum once they discovered it. The European's passion for porcelain created an entire industry for corporate espionage, and counter-espionage.

第十三章

德化——瓷器的天堂，永春

“中国陶瓷（瓷器）仅在刺桐（泉州）和新卡兰（广州）的乡镇里生产……极品瓷器是用瓷土历经整整一个月烧制而成的……在那里，这种瓷器的价格跟我国普通的陶瓷一样，甚至更低。他们的瓷器出口到印度和其他国家，甚至远销我们西土诸国，系所有陶瓷制品中的精华。”

——伊本·巴图塔（阿拉伯旅行家）

对瓷器的热爱　西方人贩卖鸦片，中国人运出瓷器。欧洲贵族爱瓷器胜过毒品。中国瓷器薄如蛋壳，放在日光下晶莹透彻，轻轻敲击则脆如铃声。自克利奥帕特拉穿上中国丝绸制成的锦绣文绮以来，再也没有比瓷器更能诱发西方人的想象力了。中国瓷器如此诱人，以至于欧洲人把“瓷器”一词当“性爱”的委婉说法。

简奈特·葛里森，《梦幻火焰》[1]的作者（英文书名“*The Arcanum*”，意为《大秘笈》或《神秘配方》），详细描述了欧洲人制造陶瓷的历史，非常耐读。葛里森称，在威彻利 1675 年撰写的戏剧——《乡村生活》中，一位崇拜者看到訇奈先生和菲德勒女士在一起，就哀求道：“……千万别把瓷送给别人，却不送给我一点；也送一点给我吧。”菲德勒女士回答说：“……我们这些有品位的女士从不以为我们的瓷够用。”精疲力竭的訇奈先生说：“千万别病倒，我无法为你们所有女士做瓷……”

欧洲权贵为了追寻瓷器不惜亏空国库。就像欧洲君主一千多年前想方设法破解丝绸的秘密那样，国王们前赴后继想要探测的则是瓷器背后的谜团，因为在当时的欧洲，跟丝绸一样，瓷器的价钱超过同等重量的黄金。无数的陶匠、专家被监禁，直到他们制成瓷器，或者就蹲在狱中。大多数就这样将牢底坐穿。但是，泉州人有办法。

① 《梦幻火焰——非凡的真实故事》，作者简奈特·葛里森，读起来更像一个神秘或惊险故事。作者讲述了欧洲人发现“神秘配方”（陶瓷生产的秘密）的漫长过程，以及他们在发现配方后为保存秘笈所采取的各种极端措施。欧洲人对陶瓷的热情催生了企业间谍与间谍行业。

Zaytun, one of ancient China's two great porcelain centers, was famed for its pure white porcelain, which is considered even today by connoisseur's to be the most sublime of porcelains. Zaytun shipped its celestial crafts, via the Silk Road of the Sea, to the four corners of the earth. Song Dynasty porcelain went for a Song and a dance at home, but it fetched a king's ransom abroad--with good reason.

While Chinese were wielding chopsticks and delicate tableware, my European forebears used fingers and wooden boards, so they descended upon China in the search for plates, bowls, spoons, and spices (medieval Europeans, lacking refrigerators, used Asian spices to doctor spoiled meat).

Wits and Half-Wits Chinese researchers have claimed, in all seriousness, that Chinese are smarter than us barbarians because chopsticks require more dexterity than knives and forks. This may be true. But knife and fork require two hands, whereas chopsticks only use one. Therefore we use both sides of our brain, whereas chopstick wielders only use one. In other words, our full wit, versus… I rest my case.

About 1,000 years ago (give or take 19), clusters of kilns were located all over Quanzhou, from Hui'an and Jinjiang to Tong 'An (Tong 'An and Xiamen were part of Quanzhou back then). 11th century comb-decorated bowls from Tong 'An have been found in Japan and Southeast Asian countries.

During the Song and Yuan Dynasties, production expanded and gradually moved from the coast to the inland regions of Anxi and Dehua, where output grew fivefold during the Ming and Qing dynasties. Alas, much of the ancient porcelain trade went to pot after the Ming shut China's doors.

Qudougong Ancient Kiln 屈斗宫古窑址 Since 1949, archeologists have found over 180 ancient porcelain kilns, dating from the ancient Song Dynasty to the recent Qing. These kilns have fired the imagination of guidebook authors, who have written of the 17 chamber Qudougong Kiln, "Such a large-scale kiln of ancient times looks like a dragon crouching on a hill, magnificently." Archaeologists recovered over 6,700 Song and Yuan Dynasty relics from the kiln's 17 chambers.

刺桐，中国古代两大瓷器生产中心之一，以制作白玉瓷闻名。至今，行家仍然认为泉州的瓷器是瓷中极品。泉州人通过海上丝绸之路把瓷器工艺品运往世界各地。在国内，宋代的泉州瓷器受到赞赏；在国外，简直要了国王的命——理由很简单。

在中国人挥舞筷子和精致的餐具之时，我的欧洲祖辈们用的却是手指和木盘。因此，我的欧洲祖先屈尊前往中国寻找盘子、碗筷、汤匙和香料。（在中世纪的欧洲，没有电冰箱，欧洲人用亚洲的香料来保存肉食，以防变质。）

全智与半智 中国学者非常严肃地称，中国人比我们这些蛮子聪明，因为用筷子比用刀叉更需要技巧。这也许是对的。不过，刀叉需要用双手，而筷子只要用单手。因此，我们双脑并用，而用筷子的只用了大脑的一半。也就是说，我们智力正常，而……陈述结束。

Qudougong Ancient Kiln

大约 1000 年前（加上或者减去 19 年），无数的瓷窑散布在泉州各地，从惠安、晋江到同安（同安和厦门当时还是泉州的一部分）。11 世纪时日本和东南亚各国相继发现了来自同安近 1000 年前的珠光青瓷碗。

宋元时期，泉州的瓷器生产逐步地从沿海扩展到安溪和德化等内陆地区。到了明清时代，安溪和德化的陶瓷产量增长了五倍。可惜的是，自从明朝关起国门之后，中国古代的陶瓷贸易就每况愈下了。

屈斗宫古窑址 1949 年以来，考古学家在泉州发现了 180 多处古瓷窑，时间从宋朝到清代不等。这些瓷窑激发了旅行指南作者的想象力。他们在描述屈斗宫的 17 间窑室时写道："规模如此宏大的古瓷窑就像一条蛟龙，盘踞在山间，蔚为壮观。" 从屈斗宫古窑址的 17 个窑室，考古学家发掘了 6700 多件宋、元陶瓷器物。

Dragon kiln

This well preserved ancient kiln, discovered in 1976, is located on the southwest hillside of Mount Pozai, in Baomei Village, Xunzhong Township, Dehua County. Whether you're an expert or a layman, this fascinating site gives insights into Song and Yuan Dynasty ceramic technology and technique.

Getting there: Bus to Dehua
Hours: 8:00-17:30
Phone: (0595)2358-6130

Modern Porcelain Modern Dehua kilns produce every porcelain product imaginable, provided you've a limited imagination: fine dishes, statues of deities and demons, and gigantic vases big enough to hide in (see "Porcelain Street below). I loved the trolls, perhaps because I've got Norwegian blood in me (bitten by a Scandinavian mosquito). I could see a faint resemblance.

Jinhua Porcelain's Manager, Mr. Yan Dongsheng (颜东升), kindly showed us his kilns, workshops and display rooms. Fascinating! Give them a visit. Better yet--give them an order for export!
Fujian Dehua Jinhua Porcelain Co. Ltd, 福建德化锦华陶瓷有限公司
Add.: Huancheng Rd. Dehua 环城路. Ph: (0595) 2351 8890
E-mail: jinhua@800.com.cn

Porcelain Street The large arch near the river, with the characters 陶瓷街, marks the beginning of Porcelain Street and probably the end of your budget. Get great bargains on everything from tableware and statuary to porcelain lamps and waterfalls.

Endless roses – petal by petal

屈斗宫古窑址位于德化县浔中镇宝美村破寨山西南坡，发现于1976年，至今保持完好。无论你是专家还是外行，这个迷人的景点都可以让您深入了解宋元时代泉州的陶瓷技术和工艺。

交通：泉州——德化专线巴士

开放时间：8：30—17：30 **电话**：0595－23586130

现代陶瓷 现代德化瓷厂生产各种各样你想象得到的陶瓷产品，如精美的器皿、神仙雕像和大可藏人的花瓶（详见下页的“德化陶瓷街”）。

Mr. Yan Dongsheng

我喜欢瓷器小精灵，可能是因为我的身上有挪威的血统（被斯堪的纳维亚半岛的蚊子咬过）。我觉得自己跟这些小精灵有些许相似……

德化锦华陶瓷公司经理颜东升友好地带我们参观他的瓷窑、工厂和陈列室。实在令人陶醉！不妨去看看，最好是给他们下个出口订单。

公司地址：德化县城关环城路 电话：0595—23518890

电子邮箱：jinhua@800.com.cn或 jinhua@pub1.qz.fj.cn

陶瓷街 河滨大拱门，上面写着“陶瓷街”三个大字，就是德化陶瓷街的起点（可能也是你腰包的终点）。从餐具、小瓷雕到瓷器灯具、流水玄关，陶瓷街上应有尽有，物美价廉。

Porcelain Street
Where budgets go to pot

I bought some plates made for export at Mr. Lin Shuangyang's small shop on Porcelain St. No one in his immediate family was in the porcelain business, so Mr. Lin's cousin attended the technical school by the ancient Dehua kiln, and opened his own factory in 1973. It wasn't until 1999 that they finally achieved their dream of opening this shop.

Bone Up on blanc de Chine! Learn more about Dehua's exotic porcelain in the fascinating book, *Blanc de Chine—the Great Porcelain of Dehua*. Written by Robert H. Blumenfield, an American collector of Dehua's blanc de Chine, the 240 page book is available on Amazon.com for only $52.50 (a bargain, compared with the $75 retail price). Or try *Blanc de Chine: the porcelain of Tehua in Fukien*. Amazon.com has two used copies—a steal at only $495 USD.

Dehua Pottery Museum — being rebuilt

Dehua Cuisine! Dehua has fine food, and even finer prices. Try the Yiyuan Restaurant 益源大酒家 (on Xingnan St.兴南, the same street as "Porcelain Street", but downtown, past the river). We fed a crowd in a private room for less than 100 Yuan. They offer most Laowai favorites, but also try mountain delicacies like red mushroom soup. Because they're red, Chinese say they cure anemia and replenish women's blood after childbirth. I doubted that I suffered from either anemia or childbirth, even though my love for Chinese food may cause me to appear like I'm in the second trimester. Still, red mushroom soup is excellent, especially if you have the good fortune to eat it fresh, right after they're picked (only during two weeks at the end of August).

Yiyuan Restaurant 益源大酒家 Address: 德化兴南街商业综合大楼 B 瞳 2 层 Phones: 0595-2352-25999 or 2352-25998

Dishes galore on "Porcelain St."

在陶瓷街林双阳先生的小店，我买了几个出口盘子。尽管林的直系亲属都没有做过陶瓷生意，林的表亲还是进入德化古瓷窑附近的技工学校学习，并于1973年创办了自己的工厂。直到1999年，他们才最终实现了开店的梦想。

注意，中国白！ 要想知道奇特的德化陶瓷，请参阅《中国白——德化好瓷》。这是一部引人入胜的好书，由美国中国白收藏家罗伯特·H.布卢姆撰写，总共240页，在亚马孙网上书店可以买到，标价52.5美元（相对于75美元的零售价来讲可是便宜货）。如果你还再想淘便宜货，亚马孙还有两本旧书，是《中国白：福建德化的陶瓷》，极便宜，要是能偷来只用495美元。

德化陶瓷博物馆 （正在装修）

德化美食！ 德化美食不错，价位更合理。到兴南街益源大酒家试试，陶瓷街也在这条街上，过河，在城区里。在包间里，我们一大群花不到100块。这里供应老外最喜欢的大部分中国菜。不过，你也可以尝一下诸如红菇汤这样的山珍。中国人说，红菇汤能治贫血，也能帮助孕妇产后补血，因为红菇是红的。尽管对中餐的喜爱让我看上去像是孕妇，但我还是不相信自己贫血。不过，红菇汤还是不错的，特别是如果你运气够好，能够在采菇期后不久吃到（红菇仅在一年当中的几周内生长，一般是接近八月底的时候）。

益源大酒家地址： 德化兴南街商业综合大楼B幢2层
电话：(0595)23525999或(0595) 23525998

For Whom the Road Tolls After photographing the bridge I was on Cloud 9 – until I hit the tollbooth. Every 2-ox town is building tollbooths and charging going and coming. Fortunately, a few years ago the Provincial government cracked down on the illegal tollbooths, so at least the remaining highway robbery is legal.

Jesting aside, I'm thankful for tolls. A decade ago, roads were so bad that on one trip Toy Ota's shock absorber flew right off and somersaulted down the road. The motto back then was, "Fix cars, not roads." But nowadays, thanks in part to tolls, the new motto is, "Fix roads, not cars," and our beautiful new roads are easier on cars and passengers both. So I don't mind the tolls—but I still have a couple of axes to grind.

One, Toy Ota is charged double on freeways because she is a van, so the 2 ½ hour drive from Xiamen to Fuzhou sets us back over $60 USD in tolls! But even that I can deal with. What really gets me is the towns that build beautiful glass and tile tollgates with 6 or 8 lanes, but invariably close off all but two. This is so one person can collect the money and the other 15 can drink tea and watch the growing line of cars. It almost seems as if the toll takers aren't going anywhere so they see no reason why anyone else should either.

But… it's getting better. And frustrations aside, Fujian roads are now some of the best in the country, making travel faster, fun and safe. So I won't complain. Much.

过路费为谁而收？拍完伏口桥，我心中狂喜——直到收费站。每个小镇都建了收费站，向过往车辆收费。幸运的是，几年前，省政府制止了非法收费。因此，现有的收费站“抢劫”是合法的。

事实上，不是开玩笑，我应该感谢收费站！十几年前，（福建的）道路很差。有一次，我的丰田车避震器被震掉了，车子翻出了路面！当时的至理名言是“修车，而非修路”。现在则是“修路，而非修车”，其中部分原因应为收费。上好的新公路对车辆和行人来说都是舒适的。因此，我不在乎收费——只是有些话不吐不快。

因属有篷货车，我们的丰田车在高速路上加倍收费。福厦高速两个半小时的车程，收费60多美元！这个我能接受。让我恼火的是，乡镇收费站建起了 6~8 个收费车道，用玻璃和琉璃瓦装饰。但是，只开通两个车道，其他全部关闭。如此一来，一人收费，其他 15 人就可以在那里一边喝茶，一边看着车辆排长龙。看上去好像是，收费员无处可去，然后认为别人也应如此。

不过……现在情况好多了。困惑归困惑，福建的道路如今属中国最好的道路之一。行车快多了，也安全、有趣。因此，我不再抱怨那么多。

Daiyun Mountain 戴云山 "The Ridge of Min" (Fujian Province), this 1856m high provincial-level natural preserve is a delightful place to stroll on sizzling summer days. Attractions include rare animals and plants, which you won't likely see since they're rare, and Daiyun Temple, which was built in the 2nd year of Taiping in the Liang Dynasty (557 A.D.).

Nine Immortals Mountain, in the Daiyuan range, gets its name from the legend that it was the meeting place for Zhang Guolao (张果老) and seven other immortals. The site has 99 caves, twelve scenic areas, and over 40 calligraphic inscriptions with so many stories behind them that you'd need to be an immortal yourself to hear them all.

Getting there: Bus from Dehua to Daiyun Village.

Hours: 8:00 - 19:00 **Phone**: (0595) 2364-8858

Shiniu (Stone Ox) Mountain 石牛山 The 1781m Stone Ox Mount, in eastern Dehua County, is a circular volcanic basin famous for "graceful and marvelous stone caves," though apparently not all are natural. I read that the Stone-Pot Cave of the Lion Cliff was "built" in the South Song Dynasty.

Popular attractions include the Ming Dynasty Stone-Pot Temple, and Daixian Waterfall, which descends into a picturesque, winding creek 30 km long. Bamboo raft rides are the best way to emjoy the tranquil scenery.

Getting there: Bus from Dehua to Stone Ox.

Hours: 8:00-17:00 **Phone: (**0595) 2362-8118

Lingjiu Rock Temple 灵鹫岩寺 This temple's drawing card is the view. Situated on the northwest of Jiuxian Mountain, the misty scenery changes constantly, but you can always find the 12 official sites of "strange rocks and queer caves" with names like Vulture Rock.

Getting there: Bus to Dehua bus, and then to Chishui.

Hours: 6:00-17:30 **Phone**: (0595)2358-6896

Dongguan Bridge 东关桥. See "Bridge Chapter."

戴云山　有“闽中屋脊”之称，这个海拔1856米的省级自然保护区是夏日避暑的好去处。景点包括许多珍稀动植物（因为珍稀，所以不太可能看到）和戴云寺（建于梁太平二年，即公元557年）。

九仙山　位于戴云山脉，相传是张果老与其他七位神仙聚会的地方，因此得名。山上有 99 洞、12 景和 40 多处题刻。每个景点背后都有一个故事。要听完所有的故事，估计你自己也得成为神仙。

从德化县城到戴云村有定期班车

开放**时间**：8:00—19:00

电话：0595－23648858

石牛山　位于德化东部、海拔 1781 米的石牛山是一个放射状的火山塌陷盆地。尽管不全是自然天成，此地却以“丰富多姿、奇妙无穷的岩石山洞”而闻名。我了解到，狮子峰上的石壶洞始于南宋时期。

受欢迎的景点包括明朝石壶殿和岱仙瀑布。瀑布下游有一条 30 公里长的蜿蜒小溪，风景如画。欣赏两岸宁静景色，最好要乘竹筏。

从德化县城到石牛山有定期班车。

运营时间：8:00—17:00，**电话**：0595－2362-8118

灵鹫岩寺　这个寺庙最吸引人的地方是景色。位于九仙山的西北部，这里的云雾景观变幻莫测。不过，你还是能够找到官方推荐的 12 处类似灵鹫岩这种美名的“奇岩怪洞”。

从德化县城到赤水镇有定期班车。

开放时间：6:00—17:30，**联系电话**：0595－23586896

东关桥　想了解东关桥的更多资讯，请参阅第八章“泉州桥梁”。

This business is in the red!

Incensed in Yongchun In China, the drive is always at least as interesting as the destination, and the trip to Dehua is no exception. The nicely paved concrete road snakes through valleys and past unique villages Hankou (汉口村), which was dusted in crimson as if the Red Tide had become a red snowfall. Even the ducks were red. It turned out that red-dusted Hankou was a village of incense makers (and gave a whole new twist to my notion of "Red China")—a tradition they have inherited from their Muslim trader forebears of 800 years ago.

The salvaged Song Dynasty ship on display near Kaiyuan temple is mute testimony to the perils of sea travel even during Zayton's heyday. The ship was returning to China with many Southeast Asian products. It also had over 2,400 Km of the coveted incense that Muslims were famous for making (I'd have been incensed if my ship of incense sunk). Eventually Muslims began making the incense right in Quanzhou, and a few centuries later moved to the hinterlands of Yongchun. Today, the Hui minority Pu family still makes incense in a Hankou factory run by Mr. Pu Chongqing (蒲重庆).

Mr. Pu said his Muslim ancestors came to Quanzhou about 1200 A.D.. One of his illustrious extinguished ancestors was Mr. Pu Shougen (蒲寿更), the Chief of Customs whose wheeling and dealing accounted for so much of the foreign trade at that time. The extent of Muslim influence is seen in that yet another of his ancestors was governor of Chongqing, in Sichuan.

The Pu family's award-winning Pu Qinglan incense is now as popular overseas as in China, with annual domestic and foreign sales each equaling about 6-7 million USD. Visit their factory at 永春县达浦镇汉口村。

Mr. Pu Chongqing "nose" his stuff

永春神香　在中国，驱车上路总是和抵达目的地一样有趣。前往德化的旅程也不例外。整洁的水泥路穿过许多奇特的村庄，在山谷里蜿蜒。汉口村沐浴在一片绛红中，好像赤潮已经变成了红雪，连白鸭也被染成了红色。原来，红尘下的汉口村是神香专业村（彻底改变了我对“红色中国”的看法）。制香的传统是 800 年前村民从他们信奉伊斯兰的祖宗那里继承下来的。

Very Red China

开元寺旁边的博物馆陈列着打捞上来的宋代古船。它无声地证明：即使在刺桐港最鼎盛的时期，海上旅行也是危险的。这艘船返回中国时，满载着东南亚的货物。其中包括 2400 千克令人垂涎的神香，是回族同胞擅长制作的（要是我的运香船沉了，我会发火的）。无奈之下，穆斯林只好在泉州就地制作神香。数百年后，他们移居永春山区。直到今天，汉口村的回族蒲氏家族还在蒲重庆经营的一家工厂里制作神香。

蒲先生说，他的祖先大约在公元 13 世纪来到泉州。在他家族众多的先人中，蒲寿更最为杰出，曾经领导过泉州的市舶司，想方设法对海上贸易进行管理。穆斯林的影响范围之大还体现在蒲重庆另外一位祖先身上。他当过重庆的地方长官。

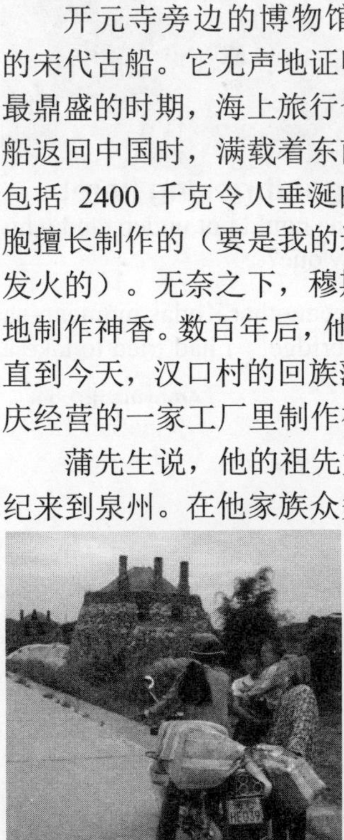
Kilns

蒲氏家族蒲庆兰制作的神香得过奖，在海外跟国内一样受欢迎，国内外两个市场年销售额各有六七百万美元。可在永春县达浦镇汉口村参观他们的神香厂。

Yongchun Brickmakers Not far from Hankou are fields of domed kilns on both sides of the highway. I was fascinated at how quickly they could fashion bricks by hand with wooden forms. Not near as exotic, I suppose, as the fashionable porcelain up the road in Dehua, but much more practical.

No goldbricking here!

Hankou Bridge and Farmhouse! A beautiful old wooden farmhouse with an enclosed courtyard snuggled up against a hillside, and shaded by massive trees. To get a halfway decent photo I stood in the middle of the highway, one eye on the viewfinder and one on the kamikaze truckers who seemed bent on redressing opium era grievances upon my person. Finally, I asked a fellow who owned a three store place across the road if I could take the photo from his rooftop. He happily agreed, though he could not understand why I'd want to photograph an old house. Why not a new one?

I clamored onto his rooftop and was rewarded with yet another Kodak moment—a panoramic view of the brand new Hankou covered bridge! I had tried to take a photo of it the previous year and couldn't get the right angle. This bridge isn't in any guidebooks, but it should be, because it proves that bridge building is not a lost art in South Fujian!

Hankou's new bridge is a beauty!

永春制砖工人　离汉口村不远的田间有几座半球形的砖窑，矗立在公路边。用手工和木模，工人们飞快地把泥土制成砖块，让我看得神魂颠倒。我想，制砖虽然不像德化制瓷那样时尚流行，但是却更加实用。

汉口桥和农舍！　一座漂亮的木制结构旧农舍依偎在山坡上，四周树木茂盛。为了在半路上拍摄一张像样的照片，我站在公路中间，一眼对着取景器，一眼盯着神风队员般的卡车司机。他们似乎想把鸦片战争的怨恨发泄到我身上。最后，我到马路对面问一栋三层楼房的主人是否可以上他家的屋顶拍照。尽管无法理解我拍摄旧房子的意图，这位屋主还是愉快地答应了我的请求。为何不拍新楼房？

上了他家屋顶，我得到了另外一个柯达精彩瞬间的奖赏——全新汉口廊桥的全景！前一年我就想拍，但一直未能找到合适的角度。这座廊桥未收入任何旅行指南。我想应该收入，因为这证明造桥工艺在闽南并没有失传！

Amoymagic.com

A classic farmhouse

Chapter 14

Quanzhou Cuisine①

"One should eat to live, not live to eat!"
Moliere (1622-1673)
"Moliere never had Chinese food!"
Bill Brown (1956-?)

The earnest Beijing reporter who asked why I moved to China and obtained permanent residence expected a weighty answer on the lines of "To serve the masses," and so I gazed at her solemnly and said, "Because Chinese food is too expensive in America."

There was some truth to that. Let's face it, eating is a big part of life, so we might as well enjoy it, and Chinese are masters of both cooking ***and*** eating! But Chinese food in China is a far cry from the sweet 'n sour and lemon chicken we get back in America. Chinese delight in eating anything that doesn't eat them first, and they are proof positive that Adam and Eve were not Chinese. Had Eve been Chinese, she'd have tossed the apple and eaten the snake.

Quanzhou cuisine is essentially Minnan (South Fujian) Cuisine, but each area, be it Nan An, Anxi or Hui'An, has its own specialties. The area around Luoyang Bridge, for example, serves succulent oysters so large I could make a sandwich with them. Nan An dishes up excellent leg of lamb with peanut sauce. Anxi's remote hamlet of Hutou is famed for its rice noodles. Quanzhou City itself, located between two rivers and facing the sea, prides itself on rich seafood.

You'd have to travel far and wide to sample them all, but fortunately, Quanzhou City is almost wall-to-wall restaurants. Better yet, the Wenling Delicacy Street packs just about every kind of local food and snack there is into one 613 meter lane!

---

① Part of this chapter has been adopted from my book *Amoy Magic—Guide to Xiamen*, Xiamen University Press.

第十四章

泉州美食①

"人吃饭是为了活着，而不是活着为了吃饭！"

——莫里哀（法国剧作家，1622—1673）

"莫里哀肯定没吃过中餐！"

——潘维廉（1956— ）

热心的北京记者曾经问我为什么移居中国并申请永久居住。她期望我顺着"为人民服务"的思路给一个有分量的答案。我严肃地看着她，回答道："因为在美国，中餐太贵。"

我这么回答是有依据的。这么说吧，吃饭是生活中的一个大问题。我们要懂得享受，而中国人就是烹饪和美食方面的大师。中国的中餐与我们在美国能吃到的酸甜柠檬鸡大不相同。中国人乐于品尝任何不会先吃掉他们的东西。他们可以生动地证明，亚当和夏娃不是中国人。要是夏娃是中国人，她肯定会扔掉苹果，吃掉老蛇。

泉州美食基本上属于闽南菜系。不过，每个地方，无论是南安、安溪，还是惠安，都有自己的地方特色。例如，洛阳桥附近的牡蛎个大、多汁，我完全可以拿来做三明治；南安有极美味的花生酱羊腿；安溪偏僻的湖头山村出产的米粉很有名气。泉州市区本身位于福建两大河流之间，面向大海，海产品非常丰富。

要遍尝泉州美食，你非得四处奔走。幸运的是，泉州市区的餐馆几乎是一家紧挨着一家。更棒的是，温陵路613米长的美食街包罗了当地几乎所有的美食和风味小吃！

Wenling Delicacy Street

① 此章部分摘自我的另外一本书《魅力厦门》，由厦门大学出版社出版。

Wenling Delicacy Street(温陵美食街), which runs north and south between Jinhuai St. and Fengze St., has "more than 130" (which probably 131) quaint snack shops and restaurants built with traditional architecture, and offering a wide variety of local Quanzhou snacks and fine cuisine.

Both ends of the streets have memorial gates with inscriptions. The couplet on the Northern gate reads, "Enjoy here the gentle wind and soft moonlight of hometown; raising your glass for a toast, you are intoxicated with love and affection for your townsmen."

Pig blood soup for breakfast

One morning, as I happily set forth to enjoy a simple barbarian's breakfast, I was accosted by my kind host and taken to Wenling to feast upon gelatinous sweet potato powder cakes and…

Barbarians and Breakfast Americans say the way to a man's heart is through his stomach, and Chinese have certainly won my heart—except with breakfast.

While by noon I can stomach salted minnows, pork fat, deep fried fish lips and sea worms in jellyfish mold, first thing out of bed in the morning my heart and stomach cry out for the familiarity and simplicity of an American breakfast: coffee, eggs, and toast.

The breakfast buffet at Quanzhou's Zaytun Hotel, my Quanzhou home away from home, offers over 60 hot and cold items (yes, I counted!), as well as dimsum, and a chef who will fry up eggs (and then douse them in soy sauce). But I consistently forego these delicacies and ask for eggs, toast, and coffee. This totally bewilders Chinese, for whom any meal must include at least ten courses, half of which are critters seen only on National Geographic channel, and the half being strange veggies harvested from mountains or scavenged from cracks between sidewalks.

After a long day in which I'd had little for lunch and missed supper altogether, I went to bed hungry but happy in the knowledge that next morning the Zaytun Hotel would, albeit begrudgingly, serve me eggs, toast and coffee.

Next morning, just as I was headed to the dining room, my hosts burst upon the scene, exclaimed, "None of that buffet stuff today. We've something special," and led me straight to Wenling Delicacy Street and a big bowl of steaming congealed pig blood soup. Yum.

温陵美食街南至津淮街，北临丰泽路，按传统建筑风格建成，共有 130 多家（可能是 131 家）精致的风味小吃店和餐馆，提供各式各样的泉州风味美食小吃。

美食街南北两个大门的牌楼都雕上了对联。北门牌楼的对联是："此处有家乡风月，举杯是故土乡情。"

一天清晨，当我兴高采烈地准备去简单地吃一下野蛮人的早餐时，热情的主人招呼我并把我带到温陵路去享用粘糊糊的地瓜饼。结果……

蛮子与早餐　美国人常说，要赢得男人的心，必先抓住他的胃。中国人显然已经赢得了我的心——早餐除外。

到中午的时候，我的胃装得下咸鱼干、肥猪肉、油炸鱼唇和土笋冻。但是，每天早上起床，我的心、我的胃呼唤的是自己熟悉且简单的美式早点：咖啡、鸡蛋和土司。

泉州刺桐饭店的自助早餐提供 60 多种热菜和冷盘（没错，我数过！），还有各种小点包括煎蛋（煎蛋师傅把煎好的鸡蛋沾酱油）。不过，我始终不看这些美食，直接要蛋、土司和咖啡。这完全让中国人迷惑不解。对他们来说，任何一餐都必须要上至少十道菜。其中有一半是只能在国家地理频道才能看到的山珍海味，另外一半是从山里采摘，或从人行道的石缝里拔出来的珍奇野草。

一整天下来，我没什么胃口吃午饭，就连晚餐也一起免掉了。我饿着肚子上床休息，但内心很快乐，因为我知道，尽管不情愿，刺桐饭店第二天早上会为我提供鸡蛋、土司和咖啡。

第二天早上，正当我准备去餐厅的时候，主人突然出现了，嚷着："今天我们不吃自助餐了，去吃点别的。"他们把我直接带到温陵路上的美食街，给我上了一大碗热气腾腾的猪血汤。味道好极了！

Local delicacies include vermicelli paste, white sugar rice cake, Anhai frozen seaworms, fried oysters, rouzong (rice, pork and other ingredients wrapped in reed leaves), Shenhu fish balls, orange rice dumplings, deng deng. And given Quanzhou's location on the sea, between two rivers, seafood takes up a large part on fishy menus. So eat up—and ***eat slowly…***

Seize or Savor? Chinese are not only the best cooks but also the best eaters, and their language shows it. A typical greeting is "Have you eaten?" And a common phrase at the table is "Eat slowly!" Where we Americans are always urging the waitress to hurry so we can gobble, guzzle, and get out the door, Chinese are forever admonishing the waitress as she serves up plate after plate, "Slow down! Let us enjoy our food!"

For an American who lives by the motto Carpe Diem! (Latin for "Seize the Day!") it is hard to handle Chinese who would rather savor a morsel or a moment than seize a day or anything else. Whether walking their birds and dogs or wokking them, Chinese do it slowly. After 20 years in China, I too am slowing down, though I think it is not a philosophical breakthrough but simply the unwinding that accompanies age. Nevertheless, I well relate to the insights shown by Ms. Averil Mackenzie-Grieve, who wrote of her experiences in South Fujian in the 1920s in *A Race of Green Ginger* (next page).

Zhong Mingxuan（钟明选） The Master of Quanzhou Cuisine

I was very fortunate to enjoy a meal prepared by Quanzhou's most celebrated chef, Mr. Zhong Mingxuan. Mr. Zhong is the host of Quanzhou TV's popular Minnan Cuisine program, and has been filmed by TV crews from Hong Kong, Macao, Taiwan and Zhejiang Province.

All of the guests clamored for Chef Zhong to make an appearance in their private dining rooms, so he would chat a few minutes, race out, race back in, race back out again—but I gradually managed to pin down a picture of the man's career, which is being carried on by his 31 and 27 year old sons, Zhong Yichuan (钟驿川) and Zhong Yidong (钟驿东).

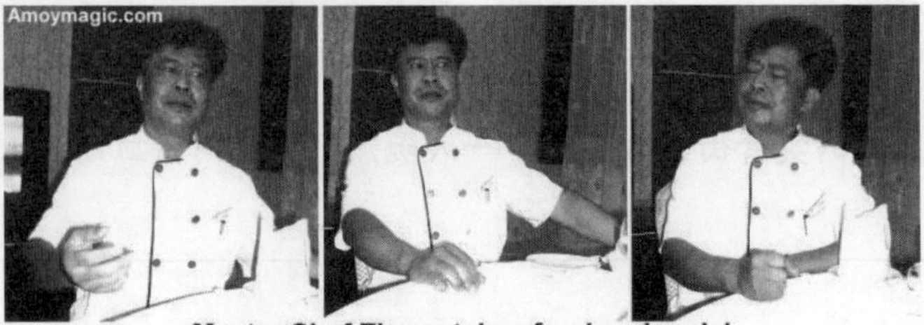

Master Chef Zhong takes food seriously!

当地的风味小吃包括线面糊、白糖米糕、安海土笋冻、海蛎煎、肉粽（糯米、猪肉和其他配料包在粽叶里）、深沪鱼丸、桔红糕等等。由于泉州所处的地理位置靠海，位于两条大河之间，因此海鲜占了很大的比例，连菜单都有鱼腥味。坐下来，慢慢吃，吃干净……

狼吞虎咽，还是尽情享受？ 中国人不仅是最好的厨师，而且还是最好的吃客。他们的语言证明了这一点。他们常用的问候语是“你吃了吗？”餐桌上常用的话是“慢慢吃！”我们美国人经常催促女招待上菜，这样一来，我们就可以狼吞虎咽、暴饮暴食，然后逃出店家。看到女招待一盘接着一盘地上菜，中国人则会警告她：“慢点上菜！让我们慢慢吃！”

对一个以“及时行乐”为座右铭的美国人来说，很难理解中国人为什么宁可尽情享受一小口的食物或者一瞬间，而不愿意抓住一整天或者别的什么的。就像上面提及的那些伙伴，无论是遛鸟和遛狗，还是烹鸟，他们总是慢慢来。在中国生活 20 年，我也减速了。我想这不是思想上的突破，而只是伴随着年龄增长所带来的松弛。尽管如此，我还是很欣赏埃夫里尔·麦肯齐·格里夫的观点。在《绿姜根》一书中，格里夫描述了她 20 世纪 20 年代在闽南地区的各种经历（见下页）。

钟明选 泉州烹饪大师 我很荣幸能够享用到泉州最著名的厨师钟明选先生制作的美食。钟先生是泉州电视台颇受欢迎的一档闽南菜烹饪节目的主持人。香港、澳门、台湾和浙江省等地的电视节目摄制组拍摄、采访过他。所有的食客强烈要求钟师傅到包厢里露个脸。因此，钟师傅只好进来聊了几分钟，然后跑出去，再跑进来，再跑出去——不过，我还是抢拍到了一代名厨的照片。眼下，钟师傅 31 岁的儿子钟驿川和 27 岁的儿子钟驿东正在努力继承他的衣钵。

Excerpt from *A Race of Green Ginger*

(Ms. Averil Mackenzie-Grieve, Fujian resident in the 20s)

"We could not help contrasting their slow and contemplative savoring of each object of sensuous pleasure with the Western habit of grasping, and discarding half-assessed, a multiplicity of objects or experiences. The Chinese cult of beauty in all forms never lacked elaboration, but it was an elaboration in depth. A spreading downwards of understanding which, like the roots of a tree, nourished and increased pleasure. The foreign traders set themselves to create this Western multiplicity of needs. They had successes chiefly because the Chinese are a practical people and by the end of the nineteenth century, too hidebound by traditions to develop, too arrogant to learn, they had fallen far behind the West, but were shrewd enough, nevertheless, to appreciate the products and inventions of Western science. The foreigners, too, were successful in selling to men and women incapable of making a bad or ugly thing, cheap, mass-produced goods, ugly and badly made, which seemed to us an anomaly until we realize that a Chinese buyer rarely bought foreign goods for aesthetic reasons. The Chinese admired neither the appearance of the Westerners nor that of their goods. They were, however, fascinated by the mechanical ingenuity of the West. The Western merchants found a market, too, among the poor and unlettered, to whom the opening of the Treaty Ports brought, if not an increase in prosperity, at least a raising of subsistence level. Inland, however, the Chinese were still extremely conservative.

"'If you want to make money out here, you've got to make the Chinese want things, and want 'm so badly that they get so's they bloody well can't do without 'em'; Mr. Tulser poured more brandy into his beer. 'That's the secret.' ..

"I surveyed the long and, to me, still bewilderingly complex civilization of the Chinese, and said, 'I should have thought the Chinese wanted enough things.'

"'Ah, but,' Mr. Tulser pointed a knowing, nicotine-stained finger, 'you've got to make 'em want the things you want 'em to want. Why, many's the time as a young ''un—believe it or not—I've stood on a soap box in a village up-country teaching the Chinese how to smoke cigarettes. Never seen 'em before—and look at 'em now; smoke like lime-kilns…. And are they grateful?... ''Nough to drive you to drink, isn't it?'"

节选自《绿姜根》

（埃夫里尔·麦肯齐·格里夫，20世纪20年代居住于福建）

“对某一事物的感官享受，他们（中国人）总是细嚼慢咽，深入思索。我们西方人一次总想紧抓多个事物、多种经验，然后一知半解地放弃。我们忍不住将两者进行对比。中国人对各种形式的美的膜拜从来不乏详尽的细节，但这种详尽是有深度的。向下传播知识就像树的根须，滋养了树体，增加了快乐。外国商人致力于创造这种西式的多样需求。他们获得了成功，主要是因为中国人是一个务实的民族。到了19世纪末，拘于传统而故步自封，太过于傲慢自大而不重学习，他们（中国人）远远落后于西方。尽管如此，他们还是非常精明，能够欣赏西方科技发明和产品。品质低劣、外观丑陋的东西都是一些便宜、批量生产的产品。外国人成功地向不会生产这些东西的男男女女兜销了自己的产品，这对我们来说是不可思议的。后来，我们发现中国顾客很少为审美的因素购买洋货。中国人既不欣赏西方人的外表，也不喜欢他们的货物。然而，他们却对西方灵巧的机械十分着迷。西方商人在贫穷、未受过教育的中国人身上找到了市场。对这些人来说，五口通商带来的如果不是繁荣程度的提升，至少也是生活水平的提高。在内地，中国人还是极端保守的。

“‘如果你想在这里赚到钱，你就得想方设法让中国人想要某些东西。很想要，然后就一天都不能没。’塔尔萨先生一边把更多的白兰地倒进啤酒，一边说，‘这就是秘密。’

“复杂且又令我困惑的中国古文明，我考察了很久。我说：‘我应该想到，中国人需要足够的东西’。

“‘是呀，不过，’塔尔萨先生非常世故地指着他沾满烟碱的一个手指头说，‘你得想方设法让他们要你想让他们要的东西。你信不信？一个年轻人，我经常到乡下去，站在肥皂箱上，教中国人怎么抽烟。以前没有见过，现在看到了。他们抽烟抽得像石灰窑在冒烟……他们感谢我吗？’够让你想喝酒，不是吗？”

Chef Zhong, now aged 55, has been whipping up prize-winning Quanzhou cuisine since 1965, but he doesn't stay at one place long. "I don't go to the best places but to the places that need help," he said. "I need a challenge." So either I was eating at a less than best place or this man was a miracle worker because he'd only been at this restaurant for two months.

"I don't like to just rely on tradition," Chef Zhong said. "I'm bold. I like to experiment. Xiamen was first to use foreign flavors, like garlic. Quanzhou leads in Minnan cuisine, but Xiamen is second, and Zhangzhou third."

A crabby dish
Osmanthus crab is heavenly!
Through Dante's Inferno...
...to 7th Heaven!

I don't know if his dishes were classics or just experiments to pawn off on foreigners, but each one was so tasty I was hard put to photograph them before devouring them. I especially enjoyed Minnan spring rolls (闽南薄饼, Minnan Bobing), chicken rolls (鸡卷, jijuan), silk gourd gum soup (丝瓜蛏根汤, sigua chengen tang), sesame sweet potato cakes （芝麻地瓜并,zhima digua bing—which differ everywhere）, and Baoshao Tofu (包烧豆腐, baoshao doufu). But I thought I had died and gone to heaven when it got a taste of Osmanthus Crab (桂花蟹, Guihua Xie), which looked like scrambled eggs and crab, but tasted like nothing in this world.

Minnan spring rolls are quite unlike any others in China. Diners are often given the various veggies, meats, sauces and peanut powder on saucers, and they assemble their own mix and wrap it in paper thin soft white wrappers. Now that I'm used to this, I prefer them to the more common deep-fried spring rolls because they aren't drenched in oil.

Baoshao Tofu (excellent!)

Fish 'n crispy rice

钟师傅今年 55 岁，1965 年起开始从事烹饪工作，多次获奖。不过，他并没有在一个地方呆太久。“我去需要帮助的地方，不去条件最好的地方，”他说，“我需要挑战。”所以，要么是我的用餐地点不够好，要么这个人本身就是一个奇迹的创造者，因为他刚到这个餐馆工作两个月。

“我不喜欢依赖传统，”钟大厨说，“我很大胆。我喜欢试验。厦门最早引进像咖喱之类的外国调味品。泉州的烹饪闽南第一，第二位是厦门，漳州排第三。”

我不知道钟大厨做的菜是不是一流的美食，或者只是把老外当人质的试验。不过，每道菜都很好吃，很快就被一扫而光，弄得我没有办法拍照。我特别喜欢闽南薄饼、鸡卷、丝瓜蛏干汤、芝麻地瓜饼（每个地方风味都不一样）、包烧豆腐。吃到桂花蟹的时候，我想我已经死亡并升天了。这道菜看上去像鸡蛋炒蟹，吃起来却非人间风味。闽南的春卷跟中国其他地方的大不一样。食客可从盘子里挑选蔬菜、瘦肉、调味品和粉末花生等配料，混在一起，然后用薄如纸、又白又软的面皮包起来。比起常见的油炸春卷，我现在很习惯吃这种东西，而且更喜欢，因为这种春卷不是用油炸透的。

Shark lips!

Quanzhou Favorites

Fish in Rice Krispies (麦香银卷鱼, Maixiang Yinjuan Yu) –Absolutely my favorite! (They said it was crisped wheat, but I think it was rice).

Tofu (一品豆腐, Yiping Doufu). There are few things healthier or more versatile than doufu, and this is one of the best dishes I've had. Also try the incredible baoshao tofu.

Pickled red veggies with preserved egg (苋菜, Xiancai). It tastes a lot better than it looks!

Beef and Oyster Sauce (蚝油牛肉, Haoyou Niurou). Pork is king in China, so beef is sometimes not up to snuff. I've suspected some beef as being sole food (recycled shoe soles). But Zaytun's beef melts in your mouth.

Shark Lips (鱼唇煲, Yuchun Bao). I told them not to give me any lip but they did anyway—shark lips! It wasn't that bad, actually. Not lip smacking, but tasty. They're sort of chewy, like rubbery fish jello.

Pickled Beans (豇豆, Jiangdou) – a tasty little appetizer.

Fried Veggie buns (煎饱, Jianbao). Excellent!

Lamb ribs in foil （手撕羊排). Delightful; reminds me of Mongolian lamb, but without the baked sheep's head staring me in the face.

Quanzhou Noodles (卤面). Nice way to end a meal! (Long noodles symbolize long life).

泉州部分美食

麦香银卷鱼　绝对是我的最爱！（他们说麦香银卷鱼，我想应该是米香银卷鱼）

一品豆腐　没有比豆腐更健康、功能更多的东西了。一品豆腐是我吃过的最棒的一道菜。也可以尝尝极棒的包烧豆腐。

皮蛋苋菜　吃起来比看上去好多了！

蚝油牛肉　在中国，猪肉是老大，牛肉有时就不那么地道。我觉得有些牛肉吃起来更像鞋底，而且是再生的鞋底。但是，泉州的牛肉入口即化。

鱼唇煲　我告诉他们不要把嘴唇靠过来，但是他们还是靠过来了，而且是鲨鱼唇！实际上，吃起来还好。没有咂嘴，但味道不错。有点耐嚼，像橡胶鱼胶似的。

豇豆　可口的开胃小菜。

煎包　极好吃！

手撕羊排　好玩，让我想起内蒙古的羔羊，但不像烤全羊的头那样直逼我的脸。

卤面　结束正餐的好办法！长长的线面象征长寿。

Home Cooked Quanzhou Style Minnan Cuisine Recipes

(adapted from *Amoy Magic*)

Swimming Crab Dish—the #1 dish (in my eyes, and stomach too). Steam live crabs, shell them, remove inedible parts (I was surprised to learn that Chinese deemed anything inedible!). Cut the pork, water chestnuts, scallion stalks and bamboo shoots into 1 inch strips and mix with beaten eggs and salt. Thoroughly mix in the shelled crabs, stir-fry in hot oil with oil and shredded ginger, add Shaoxing wine.

Coral Prawn: I'm not sure how they corral coral prawns, but they're heavenly. Clean live prawns, deep-fry quickly, and season with diced ginger, garlic, sugar, thick Minnan chili sauce, scallions, Shaoxing wine, and clear broth. Sprinkle with pepper powder and sesame oil. Devour—slowly, if possible. If not, at least take a photo so while they're digesting you can remember what they looked like.

River Eel: I was glad my hosts bore me no eel（ill） will then they served this excellent dish. Clean Jinjiang River eel and cut into two inch slices. Marinate eels for one hour in a blend of salt, crushed ginger, and wine. Deep fry the eel slices and add oil, sugar, soup-stock, small pieces of pork, soy sauce, and Shaoxing wine. Steam in a steamer (duh!), then spray with sesame oil.

Steamed Perch: I was perched on the edge of my chair waiting for this one! Select a two pound or larger perch and then scale and clean it. Place on a large bamboo steamer with small chunks of pork, slices of winter bamboo and ginger, shoots, winter mushrooms, scallion stalks, and some salt and water. Steam on high flame for 20 minutes, and then remove scallion stalks and ginger slices (personally, I like to eat these).

Fried Red Crabs: The crabbiest diner mellows after feasting on red crabs, which are harvest in the winter in Shihu of Hanjiang (Quanzhou Bay) produces the best red crabs. Pickle large red crabs (at least one pound) in sorghum liquor and then wrap in fatback. Place the lard-wrapped red crabs upside down in a pot with ginger slices and sorghum liquor and allow them to steam for ten minutes. When done, remove the fatback, clean the crabs, and cut each crab into eight slices.

Spicy Fried Rolls Wrap these ingredients in a round sheet of dried tofu: cubed pork, fish meat, onions, water chestnuts, soy sauce, five spices, sweet potato starch. Deep fry, cut in slices, serve.

闽南家庭菜谱（泉州风味）自己动手做菜！

——选自《魅力厦门》

炒活蟹 最好的菜肴（至少在我眼里——还有肚子里），将活蟹蒸熟，去壳，去掉不能吃的部位（我很惊奇地了解到，中国人居然还相信有不能吃的部位）。切好猪肉、荸荠、葱头，把笋尖切成一英寸大小的细条，与鸡蛋和食盐搅拌混合。把去壳的蟹放进去并搅匀，用油和酱丝在热油锅里煸炒。炒熟后，加入绍兴酒。

盐焗大虾 我不知道他们是怎么捉大虾的，但味道好极了。将大虾洗净，快火油炸，然后用姜块、蒜头、闽南沙茶酱、大葱、绍兴酒和清肉汤调味。撒上胡椒粉，滴上芝麻油。细嚼慢咽——如果可能的话。如果做不到，至少拍张照片。这样的话，吃完后你还记得住它们的容貌。

河鳗 很高兴主人上这道好菜的时候，没有任何恶意。把河鳗洗净，切成两英寸的小段。把盐、姜末放进米酒，将鳗段放入浸泡一小时。将鳗段热炒，加入油、食糖、高汤、肉片、酱油和绍兴酒。放入蒸笼蒸熟（咄！），然后撒上芝麻油。

清蒸鲈鱼 为了这道菜，我特意坐在椅子的边沿（可以更靠近餐桌）！选一条两磅或者更大的鲈鱼，宰好，洗净。加入一些小瘦肉块、冬笋片、生姜、芦笋、冬菇、葱秆、量的盐和水，放进大蒸笼，旺火蒸20分钟，然后去掉葱秆和姜片（我个人倒是喜欢吃这些东西）。

蒸红蟳 吃过红膏蟳，再差劲的饭菜也可以令人接受。红膏蟳以泉州湾蚶江石湖冬季出产的最佳。用高粱酒浸泡大红膏蟳（至少一磅），然后用肥猪肉包起来，再将包好的红膏蟳放进蒸罐，加入姜片、高粱酒，蒸十分钟。蒸熟，去肥猪肉，清理红膏蟳，并切成八块。

五香条 把肉丁、鱼肉、洋葱、荸荠、酱油、五香粉、地瓜粉等配料裹进圆形豆腐干。炸透，切片食用。

Minnan Spring Rolls These delightful delicacies are a Minnan version of Mexican burrito. Buy spring roll wrappers at markets; for the filling, mix shredded carrots and bamboo shoots, green peas, shredded meats and shrimp, tofu, and anything else that strikes your fancy or wanders in off the street. Cook well, add salt and soy sauce, and wrap in spring roll wrappers, along with a little mustard, chili sauce, plum sauce, scrambled eggs, leeks, and Chinese parsley (coriander). Enjoy.

Oil-Scallion Cake Add fish meat to diced pork and water chestnuts, then add a little sweet potato starch, some scallions, a dash of Five Spice, and some sugar and salt. Form into balls and coat with rice starch in bowls and steam. Let cool, and sprinkle with your favorite Chinese condiments (chili paste, pickled radish, deng deng).

Tosun (Jelly Fish and Sea Worm) Xiamen's #1 specialty—and my least favorite! But you haven't lived until you've tried it.

These culinary delights are dug from the mud on the beach. Enough said. Wash the Tosun (jelly fish) clean and stew over a slow fire until the gelatine dissolves. Pour soup into cups and let cool into a jello-like substance (somewhere along the line adding seaworms).

Force down with Chinese chili sauce, mustard sauce, vinegar.

Fried Squid Our favorite! Clean squid thoroughly and soak in clear water for a couple of hours, then cut it into thin slices and score with intersecting diagonal cuts. Fry the squid with bamboo shoots, scallions, tomato, sugar and vinegar until they roll up into a tube shape. (Don't overcook or they'll have the texture of rubber grapes).

Fried Oysters (sort of an oyster-egg pancake) Dip oysters in sweet potato starch, add soy sauce, and fry. Pour beaten eggs on the mixture and continue to fry until done. Add Chinese parsley (coriander); eat with mustard or chili sauce.

Stir-Fried Rice Noodles Deep fry rice vermicelli until golden, rinse in boiled water to remove grease. Stir-fry shredded pork, fish, mushrooms and bamboo shoots in peanut oil and add chicken bouillon, Shaoxing wine, and salt. Add noodles, serve hot. Awesome.

Zongzi My wife's favorite: pyramidal dumplings of glutinous rice and other ingredients, wrapped in bamboo leaves. Originally served at Dragon Boat Festival, they are now eaten year round. First, stir fry glutinous rice, pork, chestnuts, mushrooms and shrimp (or some use red beans), and wrap them with bamboo leaves into a pyramid shape, and tie them, then braise them in a soup until well done. Dip the zongzis in a mixture of soy sauce and garlic.

春卷 像春卷这样的精美食品其实就是闽南版的墨西哥卷饼。到市场购买春卷皮，用胡萝卜丝、竹笋、豌豆、肉丝、虾仁、豆腐等做馅料，只要是你喜欢的或在街上偶遇的都可派上用场。加盐、酱油，将馅料炒熟，裹入春卷皮，加少许芥末、辣椒酱、果酱、炒鸡蛋、韭菜和香菜（芫荽），便可尽情享用。

葱油饼 将鱼肉、肉丁、荸荠搅匀，加适量地瓜粉，些许小葱（或韭菜），撒入五香粉，加食糖和食盐。冷却，配上你喜欢的中国佐料（如辣椒酱，萝卜干等等）。

土笋冻（海蜇和沙虫） 厦门的头号特色菜，也是我一直做不来的东西——可是如果不试一试，你就白活了。这些美味佳肴是从海边的淤泥里挖出的。点到为止。把土笋（沙虫）洗净，用低火炖至胶质溶解。将熬出的汁倒入杯中，冷却成冻胶（我想，在这期间你应该把沙虫加进去）。然后，沾上中式辣酱、酱油和姜末，吞服。

鱿鱼卷 这是我们最爱吃的！将鱿鱼洗净，放入清水浸泡两三个小时，切成薄片，再切成花瓣状。加竹笋、葱、西红柿、糖、醋翻炒，鱿鱼卷成试管形状时，即刻起锅。切记：别炒得太久，否则吃起来就跟橡胶一样硬。

海蛎煎 海蛎—鸡蛋煎饼，将海蛎蘸地瓜粉，加酱油，煎炒。把鸡蛋打匀后倒入锅中，煎透为止。加香菜（芫荽），蘸芥末或辣椒酱一起食用。

炒米粉 把米粉（面线）炸至金黄色，放入开水洗去油脂。用花生油翻炒肉丝、鱼肉、蘑菇和竹笋，加入鸡精、绍兴酒和食盐。装盘，趁热吃。味道好极了。

粽子 我妻子的最爱！粽子呈金字塔形，用竹叶裹上糯米和其他配料而成。粽子原先是端午节特有的菜肴。但现在全年都可以买到。自己动手做一做。翻动煮透的糯米、猪肉、板栗、蘑菇和虾仁（有些人用红豆沙），用竹叶将料子包成金字塔形，用线将其裹紧，放入水中焖煮至熟透为止。

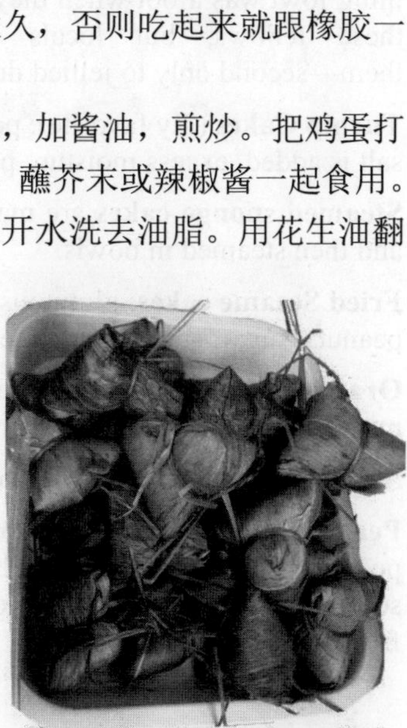
Zongzis (Sue's favorite)

Quanzhou Snacks

Oyster Chowder: a hearty porridge made of glutinous rice, fish, pork, oysters, soy sauce, and pepper, often accompanied with youtiao (twisted deep-fried dough sticks) or turnip cakes.

A local favorite: Quanzhou beef

Quanzhou Beef is served in shops around town, two of the best just around the corner from the 4-star Quanzhou hotel.

Stuffed Fishballs (another of my favorites, some say the best come from the walled city of Chongwu). Finely diced pork, dried shrimp and water chestnuts are mixed, wrapped in a coating made from fresh fish and starch, and boiled until done. Serve with mashed garlic and pepper in soy sauce.

Somethin' fowl's afoot.

Pickled Chicken Feet. I was sure something fowl was afoot when they served up these fellows, but locals sure love them—second only to jellied duck webs.

Turnip Cakes (my favorite): powdered turnip, rice and flour are mixed, a dash of salt is added, excess moisture pressed out, cut into slices, and deep fried.

Steamed sponge cakes are made from rice flour and sugar, which is fermented and then steamed in bowls.

Fried Sesame cakes: glutinous rice paste is stuffed with a blend of sesame seeds, peanuts, sugar, and diced winter squash, then deep fried.

Orange Cakes: powdered glutinous rice is steamed, sugar is added, and the mixture is molded into different shapes.

Sesame Cakes: sesame cakes are steamed, and sprinkled with sesame seeds.

Peanut Soup: a favorite in Southern Fujian, where folks have long worked for peanuts, this is simplicity itself to make. Simply boil peanuts to form a milky soup, and serve up at the end of the meal—either with, or in place of, the fresh fruit platter.

泉州风味小吃

海蛎粥 用糯米、鱼肉、瘦肉、海蛎、酱油和胡椒粉做成的咸稀饭，营养丰富，配油条或萝卜糕吃。

泉州牛肉 在市区的许多餐馆里都有供应。最好的两家在四星级泉州宾馆附近的一个角落里。

泉州鱼丸（我最喜欢的另外一种鱼丸。有人说，泉州最好的鱼丸来自崇武古城） 将瘦肉、虾米和荸荠捣烂、拌匀，放入鲜鱼肉和淀粉做的粉团里。煮熟，在酱油里放入蒜泥和胡椒粉，蘸着吃。

盐渍凤爪 上这道菜的时候，我想他们肯定知道凤爪下踩的是什么，但当地人还是很喜欢吃——仅次于卤鸭掌。

萝卜糕（我特别喜欢） 将萝卜捣烂，与米饭和面粉拌匀，加入少量食盐，挤干水分，切成片，用油炸熟。

发糕 将面粉和食糖拌匀，放入小碗，蒸熟。

油炸芝麻糕 将芝麻、花生、糖和冬笋块拌匀，塞入糯米粉团，然后油炸。

桔红糕 将糯米粉蒸熟，加入食糖，然后做成各种形状的糕点。

麻糕 蒸桔红糕，再撒上芝麻。

花生汤 长期以来，闽南人收入甚低。花生汤在闽南很受欢迎，做法简单：只要把花生煮成乳白色，和水果一道，或者替代水果，作为饭后的甜点。

Western Food in Quanzhou (泉州的西餐)

Mandarin Garden Cafeteria & Lounge Excellent Chinese & Western
Mandarin Hotel 泉州悦华酒店 Add: W. Citong Rd. S. Section 刺桐西路南段
Phone: (595)2801-9999 Website: www.yeohwaqz.com

Blenz Coffee (Baiyi Kafei, 百怡咖啡) Starbucks-clone; free Wifi
Add: -27 Nan Junxiang (南俊巷 #25-27) Phone: 2219-3533

Café de Paris, Quanzhou Hotel （泉州酒店） English Menu; good breakfast buffet.
Add: 22 Zhuangfu Xiang 庄府巷22号 Phone: 22289958

Pizza Huts (Bishengke 必胜客)
#1 Add:: Dong Jie (Street), Yu Ping Bldg. 1/F (泉州市东街玉屏大厦一楼)
Phone: 22762301
#2 Add: Fengze Square, S. Tian'an Rd. 田安南路丰泽广场1－2层
Phone: 22181810

Chapter 15

Chinese-English Menu

(adapted from *Amoy Magic—Guide to Xiamen*)

"It is a sad truth, but we have lost the faculty of giving lovely names to things. Names are everything. The man who could call a spade a spade should be compelled to use one. It is the only thing he is fit for." Oscar Wilde

Getting a Handle on Chinese Food

Chinese prefer strange and exotic foods, but failing that, they give common foods strange and exotic names. They pass off plain chicken as "Phoenix Breast," or duck eggs as "Lotus Eggs." And the famous "Monk Climbing the Wall" soup has neither monk nor wall. I hope.

The playwright who quarreled with words would have appreciated these offerings from Chinese menus:

Silver Fish Wrapped in Snow, from Beijing, is neither winter precipitation nor the ornery bugs that ate holes in my wool Scottish tie. It is simply cooked macaroni fried in whipped egg white.

Chicken in a Lantern, also from Beijing, is cooked chicken and vegetables wrapped in clear cellophane and tied with a ribbon.

Phoenix Breast, from Sichuan, is not the legendary Egyptian fowl but plain old cheap chicken breast.

Lotus Eggs are not the lotus' source; they're just chicken eggs.

Dragon and Phoenix Ham, from Sichuan, is naught but duck, pork, water chestnuts, chicken wing bones, ham and white bread – mixed and fried. (So who was the dragon?).

Steamed Dragon's Eye rolls, from Sichuan, are strips of pork rolled around red bean paste, topped with a cherry, and served on glutinous rice.

By the time I've worked my way to a menu's soup section and come across, "Bright Moon in a River" and "Buddha Leaps the Wall," I'm ready to climb the wall myself. But it's worth the climb. China's elegantly named dishes are invariably just as elegantly prepared and served, and well worth the wait.

To make life easier, I've compiled this handy dandy Amoy Magic Menu in English, Chinese, and Pinyin—and this version I've added tone marks. If you still can't say it—**just point!**

Note: Some folks have told me this menu is so helpful they've photocopied it and carry it everywhere. Go for it!

But please buy the book before you photocopy it. ☺

第十五章

中英对照菜谱

（节选自《魅力厦门》）

我们失去了给事物取个有趣名称的能力。这是一件很悲哀的事情，因为名称代表着一切。那些没法有话直说的人，应该强制他们使用词典。

——奥斯卡·王尔德

了解中餐

中国人喜欢稀奇古怪的食物。找不到稀奇古怪的食物，他们就会给普通的食物起些稀奇古怪的名称。比如说，普通的鸡肉他们叫做“凤胸”，鸭蛋叫“莲卵”。著名的“佛跳墙”既没有佛，也没有墙给和尚跳——我希望如此。

看到这些中餐食谱的叫法，对字句非常挑剔的剧作家肯定会大加赞赏的。

雪裹银鱼：北京菜，既没有冬天的雪花，也找不着专吃我苏格兰羊毛领带的“银鱼”（蠹鱼，西洋衣鱼）。这道菜只不过是用搅匀的蛋白炸煮熟的通心粉。

灯笼小鸡：也是一道北京菜。用透明的玻璃纸把煮熟的鸡肉和蔬菜裹在一起，然后打上红缎带。

凤胸：四川菜，用的也不是什么传说中的埃及凤禽，而是你在美国大型连锁超市西弗威用 69 美分就可以买上一英磅的普通鸡肉。

莲卵：跟莲没什么关系，只是普通的鸡鸭蛋。

龙凤火腿：四川菜，不过是把鸭肉、猪肉、荸荠、鸡翅、火腿和白面搅在一起炒炸。真搞不清楚龙在哪里！

蒸龙眼卷：四川菜，肉丝包上红豆酱，顶部放个樱桃，跟糯米饭一起食用。

当我写到菜单的汤水部分，又遇上“河中明月”和“佛跳墙”这些菜时，我自己都快跳墙了。不过，很值得跳。中国菜不仅名字起得雅致，做工精致，上菜也很讲究。等多久都值。

编写老外实用中国烹饪词典，目的是让你在厦门的生活更加方便。万一碰上某些中国菜你读不清楚，就用手指！

注释：有人告诉我，本菜谱很实用。于是就复印一份，随身携带。试试看吧！

不过，复印之前，先买一册。嘿嘿！

Amoy Magic Menu

Over 200 Choices!

(For tips on mangling Chinese tones, please turn to the "Mad About Mandarin" chapter of *Amoy Magic—Guide to Xiamen*)

CHICKEN 鸡类 jī

* Stir Fried Diced Chicken and Peanuts 果仁鸡丁 guǒrén jīdīng
* Chicken & Peanuts (spicy) 宫爆鸡丁 gōngbǎo jīdīng
* Cashew Chicken 腰果鸡丁 yāoguǒ jīdīng
* Lemon Chicken 柠檬鸡片 níngméng jīpiàn
* Sizzling Chicken (iron skillet) 铁板鸡肉 tiébǎn jīròu
Stir Fried Chicken & Green Peppers 青椒鸡丁 qīngjiāo jīdīng
Chicken in Ginger Sauce 姜汁热味鸡 jiāngzhī rèwèijī
Fried Breaded Chicken Nuggets 软炸鸡片 ruǎnzhà jīpiàn
Fried Chicken Slices 炒鸡片 chǎo jīpiàn
Stir Fried Chicken & Bamboo Shoots 冬笋鸡片 dōngsǔn jīpiàn
Sweet 'n Sour Chicken Strips 糖醋鸡条 tángcù jītiáo
Chicken with Mushrooms & Bamboo Shoots 双冬鸡条 shuāngdōngjītiáo
Stewed Chicken and Chestnuts 栗子鸡 lìzi jī
Stewed Chicken with Tofu 油豆腐鸡 yóu dòufu jī
Crispy Fried Chicken 油酥鸡 yóusū jī
Shredded Chicken in Oyster Sauce 蚝油手撕鸡 háoyóu shǒusī jī
Fried Chicken 炸鸡 zhàjī
Paper Wrapped Fried Chicken 炸纸包鸡 zhàzhǐ bāojī
Fried Chicken Shish-ka-bob 炸鸡肉串 zhà jīròuchuàn
Roast Chicken 烤鸡 kǎo jī
Stewed Gizzards & Bamboo Shoots 冬笋门胗 dōngsǔn ménzhēn
Steamed Chicken & Straw Mushrooms 草菇蒸鸡 cǎogū zhēngjī
Lotus-wrapped Chicken & Chestnuts 荷包栗子鸡 hébāo lìzi jī
Sesame Chicken 芝麻鸡 zhīma jī
Curried Chicken 咖喱鸡 gālí jī
Braised Chicken Wings with Brown Sauce 红烧鸡翼 hóngshāo jīyì

DUCK & OTHER FOWL PLAY 鸭类, 鸡类, 等等

Spicy Sparrow & Walnuts 核桃禾花雀 hétao héhuāquè
Baked Stuffed Sparrow 烤酿禾花雀 kǎoniàng héhuāquè
Fried Minced Pigeon Meat 炒鸽松 chǎo gēsōng
Braised Swallow's Nest, Minced Chicken 鸡茸燕窝 jīróng yànwō
Beijing Duck 北京烤鸭 běijīng kǎoyā
Braised Duck with Oyster Sauce 蚝油扒鸭 háoyóu bāyā
Whole Braised Duck 'n Soy Sauce 红烧全鸭 hóngshāo quányā

EGG DISHES 蛋类 dàn

Egg & Bitter Melon Casserole 苦瓜烘蛋 kǔguā hōngdàn
Fried Pigeon Egg, Minced Meat 炸象眼鸽蛋 zhàxiàngyǎng gēdàn
Steamed Ham and Eggs 火腿蒸蛋 huǒtuǐ zhēngdàn
Minced Pork Omelette 肉末鸡蛋 ròumò jīdàn

PORK 猪肉类 zhūròu

* Sweet & Sour Pork (Boneless) 糖醋里脊 tángcù lǐjǐ
* Pineapple, Green Pepper & Pork Strips 菠萝古唠肉 bōluó gǔláoròu
Sweet & Sour Pork Rib 糖醋排骨 tángcù páigǔ
Deep Fried Sweet & Sour Pork 锅包肉 guōbāoròu
Sizzling Pork (iron skillet) 铁板里脊 tiébǎn lǐjǐ
Breaded Pork Strips 软炸里脊片 ruǎ nzhà lǐ jipiàn
* Stir Fried Pork & Veggies on Sizzling Rice 锅巴肉片 guōbā ròupiàn
* Fried Pork Balls 炸丸子 zhà wánzi
Stir Fried Pork & Green Peppers 青椒肉丁 qīngjiāo ròudīng
Chicken Fried Pork Strips 包肉丝 bāoròusī
Sesame Pork 芝麻里脊 zhīma lǐ ji
Beggar's Ribs (fried) 叫花排骨 jiàohuā páigǔ
Green Peppers Stuffed with Pork 青椒塞肉 qīngjiāo sāiròu
Stir Fried Pork Slices 炒肉片 chǎo ròupiàn
Stir Fried Pork Slices & Eggs 木须肉 mùxū ròu
Braised Pork with Brown Sauce 红烧猪肉 hóngshāo zhūròu
Braised Pork with Chestnuts 栗子红烧肉 lìzi hóngshāo ròu
Stir Fried Pork & Bamboo Shoots 冬笋肉丝 dōngsǔn ròusī

BEEF 牛肉类 niúròu

* Sizzling Beef, Onions, Peppers 铁板牛柳 tiěbǎn niúliǔ
* Beef Curry 咖喱牛肉 gālí niúròu
Garlic Beef 黑蒜子牛肉 hēisuànzi niúròu
* Beef with Broccoli 西兰花菜牛肉 xīlánhuācài niúròu
Stir-fried Sliced Beef 炒牛肉片 chǎo niúròupiàn
Beef & Potato Stew 土豆炖肉 tǔdòu dùnròu
Twice-Fried Beef 回锅牛肉 huíguōniúròu
Beef Wrapped in Rice Paper 纸包牛肉 zhǐbāoniúròu
Braised beef in Soy Sauce 红焖牛肉 hóngmèn niúròu
Braised Beef in Oyster Sauce 蚝油牛肉 háoyóu niúròu
Braised Beef Tenderloin in Soy Sauce 红烧牛腩 hóngshāo niúnǎn
Beef & Green Peppers 青椒牛肉 qīngjiāo niúròu

SEAFOOD 鱼 yú

* Steamed Mandarin Fish 清蒸桂花鱼 qīngzhēng guìhuāyú
* Sweet and Sour Fish 糖醋鱼片 tángcù yúpiàn
* Sweet 'n Sour Garoupa 糖醋石斑鱼 tángcù shíbānyú
* Deep-Fried Mandarin Fish 炸桂鱼 zhà guìyú
** Whole Fish with Apple & Tomatoes 鲜果松鼠鱼 xiānguǒ sōngshǔyú
* Steamed Fresh Fish 蒸鲜鱼 zhēng xiānyú
* Crispy Fried Garoupa Slices 酥炸鱼条 sūzhà yútiáo
Stir-Fried Fish Strips 炒鱼片 chǎo yúpiàn
Deep Fried Fish Strips 炸鱼条 zhà yútiáo
Braised Fish in Soy Sauce 红烧鱼 hóngshāoyú
Braised Eel in Soy Sauce 红烧鳗鱼 hóngshāo mányú
Braised Carp in Soy Sauce 红烧鲤鱼 hóngshāo lǐyú
Braised Turtle in Clear Broth 清炖甲鱼 qīngdùn jiǎyú
Stir-Fried Squid 炒鱿鱼 chǎo yóuyú
**Deep-Fried Squid (family favourite!) 炸鱿鱼 zhà yóuyú
Braised Fish Lips in Oyster Sauce 蚝油鱼唇 háoyóu yúchún

SHRIMP 虾 xiā 和 **CRAB** 蟹 xiè

Boiled Shrimp 盐水虾 yánshuǐ xiā
Stir-fried Shelled Shrimp 清炒虾仁 qīngchǎo xiārén
Deep-Fried Shrimp Balls 油炸虾丸 yóuzhà xiāwán
Shrimp & Cashews 腰果虾仁 yāoguǒ xiārén
Sizzling Shrimp & Onions (iron skillet) 铁板虾仁 tiěbǎn xiārén
Braised Prawns in Brown Sauce 红烧大虾 hóngshāo dàxiā
Deep-fried Prawns 炸大虾 zhà dàxiā
Fried Prawn Shish-ka-bob 炸虾串 zhà xiāchuàn
Fried Prawn Cakes 炸虾饼 zhà xiābǐng
Fried King Prawns in Soy & Ginger 煎酿大明虾 jiànniàng dàmíngxiā
Crispy Fried Prawns & Bamboo Shoots 炸竹笋脆虾 zhà zhúsǔn cuìxiā
Fried Prawn Balls 炸虾球 zhà xiāqiú
Steamed Crab 蒸螃蟹 zhēng pángxiè
Stir-Fried Crab Meat 炒蟹肉 chǎo xièròu
Stir-Fried Crab Meat in Cream Sauce 奶汁蟹肉 nǎizhī xièròu

OTHER SEA CREATURES 其他海鲜 qǐtā hǎ ixiā n

Braised Sea Cucumbers in Brown Sauce 红烧海参 hóngshāo hǎishēn
Stewed Sea Cucumbers with Shrimp 虾仁海参 xiārén hǎishēn
Fried Dried Scallops with Vegetables 油爆干贝 yóubào gānbèi
Stewed Dried Scallops in White Sauce 白汁干贝 báizhī gānbèi
Stewed Abalone in Oyster Sauce 蚝油焖鲍鱼 háoyóu mèn bàoyú
Braised Abalone in Brown Sauce 红烧鲍鱼 hóngshāo bàoyú
Braised Abalone & Black Mushrooms 冬菇鲍鱼 dōnggū bàoyú
Fried Razor Clam 清炒蛏子 qīngchǎo chēngzi
Fried Oysters 面拖牡蛎 miàntuō mǔli

VEGGIES 蔬菜 shūcài

Stir Fried Mixed Vegetables 炒素菜 chǎo sùcài
Eggplant in Brown Sauce 红烧茄子 hóngshāo qiézi
Sautéed Chinese Cabbage 醋熘白菜 cùliū báicài
Fried Eggplant Stuffed with Pork 炸茄盒肉 zhà qiéhéròu
Batter Fried Eggplant in Sauce 鱼香茄子饼 yúxiāng qiézi bǐng
Stir Fried Cabbage with Meat 小白菜炒肉 xiǎobáicài chǎoròu
Sweet and Sour Cabbage 糖醋莲白 tángcù liánbái
* Stir Fried Spinach & Mashed Garlic 蒜泥菠菜 suànní bōcài
Stir Fried Spinach 炒菠菜 chǎo bōcài
Braised Bamboo Shoots 油焖笋 yóumèn sǔn
Stir Fried Bamboo Shoots 炒青笋条 chǎo qīngsǔntiáo
Stir Fried Mushrooms, Bamboo Shoots 炒香菇笋片 chǎo xiānggū sǔnpiàn
Stir Fried Vegetables & Mushrooms 菜心扒鲜菇 càixīn bā xiāngū
Stewed Fresh Mushrooms & Veggies 烩鲜菇蔬菜 huì xiāngū shūcài
Stir Fried Heart of Greens 清炒空心菜 qīngchǎo kōngxīncài
Stir Fried Onions and Carrots 元葱炒胡萝卜 yuáncōng chǎo húluóbo
Stir Fried Broccoli 清炒 西兰花菜 qīngchǎo xīlánhuācài
Stir Fried Snow Peas 清炒荷兰豆 qīngchǎo héländòu
Soybeans and Ground Pork 青豆焖肉 qīngdòu mènròu
Quick Fried Rapeseed Leaves & Stems 炝油菜苔 qiǎng yóucàitái
Romaine Lettuce in Oyster Sauce 蚝油生菜 háoyóu shēngcài
Corn with Pine Nuts 松子玉米 sōngzǐ yùmǐ
Scrambled Eggs and Tomatoes 西红柿炒鸡蛋 xīhóngshì chǎo jīdàn
Teriyaki Cauliflower & Egg 酱油炒蛋花菜 jiàngyóu chǎodànhuācài
Green Beans with Shredded Pork (Spicy) 干煸四季豆 gānbiān sìjìdòu
Stir Fried Sliced Lotus Root 炒藕片 chǎo ǒupiàn
"Tiger Skin" Cooked Whole Green Peppers 虎皮青椒 hǔpí qīngjiāo
Shoestring Potatoes 干煸土豆丝 gānbiān tǔ dòusī

French Fries 油炸土豆条 yóuzhà tǔdòutiáo
Spicy Potato Pie 土豆饼 tǔdòu bǐng
Mashed Potatoes 土豆泥 tǔdòu ní
Pickled Vegetables (cold) 泡菜 pàocài
7-Flavor Chinese Cabbage (cold) 七味白菜 qīwèi báicài

MUTTON 羊肉类 yángròu
Braised Beef with Soy Sauce 红烧羊肉 hóngshāo yángròu
Roast Mutton 烤羊肉 kǎo yángròu
Stir Fried Lamb and Onions 葱煲羊肉 cōngbāo yángròu
Roast Mutton Chops 烤羊排 kǎo yángpái
Fried Mutton with Sesame 芝麻羊肉 zhīma yángròu

MISC CARCASSES & CRITTERS
(Lassie, Bambi, Kermit, Thumper, Winnie…)

Twice—Boiled Dog's Weenie (Chinese hot dog?) & Herbs
过江龙牛七炖狗鞭 guòjiānglóng niúqī dùn gǒubiān
Stir Fried Bunny Rabbit 炒兔片 chǎo tùpiàn
Braised Bambi in Brown Sauce 红烧鹿肉 hóngshāo lùròu
Braised Bear Paw, Soy Sauce 红烧熊掌 hóngshāo xióngzhǎng
Fried Frog Legs 炸田鸡腿 zhà tiánjītuǐ
(For broader selection, visit the zoo after hours)

TOFU 豆腐 dòufǔ
* Home-style Tofu 家常豆腐 jiācháng dòufǔ
Stir-Fried Tofu 炒豆腐 chǎo dòufǔ
Deep-Fried Tofu 炸豆腐 zhà dòufǔ
* Tofu Cubes in Spicy Sauce (hot!) 麻婆豆腐 mápó dòufu
* Braised Tofu in Brown Sauce 红烧豆腐 hóngshāo dòufǔ
Japanese Tofu with Shrimp & Cashews 日本豆腐 rì běn dòufǔ
Stinky Tofu (and it really does!) 臭豆腐 chòu dòufu
Bear Paw Tofu (fried, spicy) 熊掌豆腐 xióngzhǎng dòufǔ
Braised Tofu with Mixed Vegetables 素什锦豆腐 sùshíjǐn dòufǔ
Braised Tofu, Shrimp, Meat 红烧什肉虾仁豆腐
hóngshāoshénròu xiāréndòufǔ
Soft Tofu and Beef Slices 牛柳豆腐 niúliǔ dòufǔ
Tofu Stuffed with Minced Fish 鱼脊肉酿豆腐 yújǐròu niàng dòufǔ
Tofu Stuffed with Minced Pork 猪肉酿豆腐 zhūròu niàng dòufǔ
Tofu in Oyster Sauce 蚝油豆腐 háoyóu dòufǔ

SOUPS 汤 tāng

Chicken Corn Soup 鸡茸玉米汤 jīróng yùmǐtāng
Beef Soup 牛肉汤 niúròu tāng
Duck Soup 鸭汤 yātāng
Fish, Shrimp & Pork Ball Soup 三鲜汤 sānxiāntāng
Abalone & Chicken Soup 鲍鱼鸡片汤 bàoyú jīpiàntāng
Hot & Sour Soup 酸辣汤 suānlà tāng
Bird's Nest Soup 燕窝汤 yànwō tāng
Tofu Soup 豆腐汤 dòufǔ tāng
Tofu & Egg Flower Soup 蛋豆腐汤 dàn dòufǔtāng
Egg Drop Soup 鸡蛋汤 jīdàn tāng
Mushroom & Crispy Rice Soup 锅巴口蘑汤 guōbā kǒumótāng
Dried Scallop Soup 干贝汤 gānbèi tāng

WHEAT, RICE (Dumplings, Rolls, etc.) 面，米

Steamed Bun 馒头 mántóu
Steamed Bun Stuffed with Veggies 素菜包子 sùcài bāozi
Steamed Bun Stuffed with Pork 肉包子 ròu bāozi
Boiled Chinese Dumpling 饺子 或水饺 jiǎozi 或 shuǐjiǎo
Steamed Chinese Dumpling (Jiaozi) 蒸饺 zhēngjiǎo
Steamed Seafood Jiaozi 三鲜蒸饺 sānxiān zhēngjiǎo
Lightly Fried Jiaozi 锅贴 guōtiē
Mini Dumplings in Bamboo Steamer 小笼包 xiǎolóngbāo
Deep Fried Spring Roll 春卷 chūnjuǎn
Pancake with Green Chinese Onion 葱花饼 cōnghuā bǐng
Fried Meat Pie 肉饼 ròubǐng
Baked Sesame-Seed Cake 烧饼 shāobǐng
Steamed Rice Cake 米糕 mǐgāo
Deep-Fried Dough Sticks (breakfast food) 油条 yóutiáo

NOODLES 面条 miàntiáo

Hand Pulled noodles (usually Muslim) 拉面 lāmiàn
Pulled Noodled with Beef 牛肉拉面 niúròu lāmiàn
Noodles with Pork Rib 排骨面 páigǔmiàn
Fried Noodles 炒面 chǎo miàn
Beef Fried Noodles 牛肉炒面 niúròu chǎomiàn
Shrimp Fried Noodles 虾炒面 xiāchǎomiàn
Seafood Fried Noodles 海鲜炒面 hǎixiān chǎomiàn
Fried Noodles and Vegetables 蔬菜炒面 shūcài chǎomiàn
Instant Noodles 方便面 fāngbiànmiàn
Rice-Flour Noodles 米粉条 mǐfěntiáo
Noodles with Shredded Pork 肉丝拌面 ròusī bànmiàn
Noodle Soup 汤面 tāngmiàn
Seafood Noodle Soup 三鲜汤面 sānxiān tāngmiàn

Famous Hutou Rice Noodles

FRIED RICE 炒饭 chǎofàn

White Rice 白米饭 báimǐfàn
* Yangzhou-style Fried Rice 扬州炒饭 yángzhōuchǎofàn
Egg Fried Rice 蛋炒饭 dànchǎofàn
Fried rice with shrimp, mushroom & chicken 什锦炒饭 shíjǐnchǎofàn
Pork Fried Rice 猪肉炒饭 zhūròu chǎofàn
Beef Fried Rice 牛肉炒饭 niúròu chǎofàn
Chicken Fried Rice 鸡炒饭 jī chǎofàn
Vegetable Fried Rice 蔬菜炒饭 shūcài chǎofàn
Mushroom Fried Rice 蘑菇炒饭 mógūchǎofàn

DESSERTS 饭后甜食 fànhòu tiánshí

* Apple Fritters 拔丝苹果 básī píngguǒ
* Banana Fritters 拔丝香蕉 básī xiāngjiāo
Sweet Almond Paste 核桃酪 hétao lào

DRINKS 饮料 yǐnliào

Coca Cola 可口可乐 kěkǒukělè
Pepsi 百事可乐 bǎishì kělè
Bottled Water 矿泉水 kuàngquánshuǐ
Sprite 雪碧 xuěbì
Tea 茶 chá
Coffee 咖啡 kāfēi

MISC. SURVIVAL 杂项 záxiàng

NO MSG, Please! 请不要放味精 !Qǐng búyào fàng Wèijīng!
Menu 菜单 càidān
Bill 账单 zhàngdān
I'm out of money! 我没有钱! Wǒ méiyǒu qián!
Where's the back door? 后门在哪里？Hòumén zài nǎli?
Etcetera… 等等 děngděng
Where's our Consulate? 我们的领事馆在哪里？
Lǐngshìguǎn zài nǎli?
How do I get back to planet earth? 我怎么回到世界呢？
Wǒ zěnme huí dào shì jiè ne?
这章到底有完没完……？

Chapter 16

Quanzhou Specialties

"The Chinese are of all peoples the most skilful in the arts and possessed of the greatest mastery of them. This characteristic of theirs is well known, and has frequently been described at length in the works of various writers. In regard to portraiture there is none, whether Greek or any other, who can match them in precision, for in this art they show a marvelous talent...

"...they had come to the palace while we were there and had been observing us and drawing our portraits without our noticing it. This is a custom of theirs, I mean making portraits of all who pass through their country. In fact they have brought this to such perfection that if a stranger commits any offence that obliges him to flee from China, they send his portrait far and wide. A search is then made for him and wheresoever the [person bearing a] resemblance to that portrait is found he is arrested."

Ibn Battuta, Ancient Arab Traveler

Quanzhou is famed for originating many unique Chinese crafts and traditions, such as fine silk, porcelain, stonemasonry, puppetry. Even today the streets are a nonstop variety show as wandering artisans create insects of grass, or intricate little figurines of colored flour, or in minutes whip out charcoal sketches or caricatures.

While you're in mystic Quanzhou, stock up on a few of these local treasures (and, as always, e-mail me with your own discoveries or additions). You can also browse online. Google led me to hundreds of fine Quanzhou company websites.

第十六章

泉州特产

“中华民族举世闻名，他们精于艺术、熟练掌握各种技艺。许多作家在其作品中都详细地描述过。至于人物画像，不管是希腊人抑或任何其他民族都无法与之（中国）相媲美，因为他们在这方面的确有神奇的天赋……

“当我们到达宫殿时，他们早已在那里了，一边注视着我们，一边画着我们的肖像，我们一点也没有察觉到，这就是他们的习俗。只要经过他们的国家，没有一人不被他们画过肖像的。事实上，他们做得如此完美，以至于如果一个陌生人犯罪，逃离中国后，他们就会把他的肖像散发到世界各地。而后进行查找，只要哪个人与该肖像相似，注定会被抓走的。”

——阿拉伯旅行家伊本·贝图塔

泉州独特的传统工艺闻名于世，如丝绸、瓷器、石雕、木偶艺术等。即使在今天，街道两旁随处可见街头艺人在编织草虫、制作糕人，甚至几分钟内勾画出我们的人物素描或漫画。

当你行走在泉州这座魅力城市时，不妨收集一些这方面资料（通常你可以把你自己的一些新发现发电子邮件给我）。当然，你也可以在网上浏览。通过 Google 搜索，我找到了数以百计的泉州企业网页。

Dehua Porcelain—a limitless variety of fine China, as well as the ivory white porcelain figurines.

Dehua Famous Alcohol—brewed with herbs, it is "pure, mellow, fragrant, and "curative effect is prominent." Drink enough and you won't care if you're cured or not.

Hui'an Stone Stone Carvings and Shadow Carvings. Family portrait, perhaps! Take home a granite dining room set in your carry-on.

Puppet Heads. The hand carved camphor wood heads are rapidly giving way to mass produced plastic puppets, so buy them while you can (and while you can afford them).

Old Fan Zhi Magic Lees—a concoction of corn, beans, and over 50 Chinese herbs, it is said to cure everything from stomach and spleen ailments to indigestion deng deng and perhaps dung dung.

Silk Flowers and Lanterns. Quanzhou Silk Lanterns are legendary. If possible, visit the city on Lantern Festival (15th day of the Chinese New Year). Check the internet for English websites of silk flower companies like Quanzhou Meifeng Gardening Co., Ltd.,

http://www.china-fair.com/2cpzl/fj/fjmeifeng/eindex.htm

> "Silk is very plentiful among them …For that reason it is so common to be worn by even the very poorest there. Were it not for the merchants it would have no value at all, for a single piece of cotton cloth is sold in their country for the price of many pieces of silk." Ibn Battuta, Arab Traveler

Qingyuan Tea Cake , made from herbs and tea, has for a century been reputed to be just what the doctor ordered for increasing appetite, strengthening the spleen, (Chinese seem to have a thing about spleens!), helping digestion, etc.

Anxi Oolong Tea—the tea that sparked the American Revolution—we threw it overboard during the Boston Tea Party. I can see why that would have tea'd the British off; I'd have been madder than the hatter myself.

Anxi Rattan and Bamboo—several factories produce quality baskets, shelving and furniture; you can even get it made to order. Check the internet for sites. Anxi's Xin Long Handicraft company's fine English website has photos of hundreds of products:

http://www.fjneway.com/english/about_us.htm

德化瓷器——品种繁多、雕塑精美，包括象牙白人物瓷雕。

德化名酒——用药草酿制，“纯、醇、香，疗效显著”。喝够了，也就无所谓病情了。

惠安石雕、影雕——包括家庭肖像影雕，你也可以随身携带一套花岗岩餐具回家。

木偶头雕刻——传统手工雕刻的樟木木偶头很快被铺天盖地的塑料木偶头所替代，因此，当你有机会携带并能支付得起的话要多购买些传统手工制作的木偶头。

老范志神曲——由谷类、豆类以及 50 多种中药草调配而成，据说能治百病，从胃脾疾病到消化不良等等。

料丝花灯——泉州的料丝花灯闻名海内外，有机会的话，你可以在农历正月十五日到泉州过元宵节。你也可以上网垂询英文网页的料丝花灯制作公司，如泉州梅峰园艺有限公司（网址：http://www.china-fair.com/2cpzl/fj/fjmeifeng/eindex.htm）。

“泉州盛产丝绸，即使穷人穿戴丝绸也相当普遍。一块棉布可以抵得上许多块丝织品，假如没有商人的话，丝绸也就一文不值了。”

——阿拉伯旅行家伊本·贝图塔

清源茶饼——由药草和茶叶制作而成。一百多年来，医生一直认为它是一种增进食欲、健脾和助消化的良药。

安溪乌龙茶——茶直接导致了美国独立革命——在波士顿倾茶事件中，我们把茶倒入海里。我很清楚英国人为什么会恼火。要是我的话，我会比疯帽子商更生气。

安溪竹藤器——在安溪，有好几个工厂生产各种各样的竹藤篮子、框架和家具，你甚至可以下定单订做。在网上你可以浏览到他们的网页，如安溪新隆工艺公司的英文网页附有几百张产品图片，相当精美，其网址为：http://www.fjneway.com/english/about-us.htm。

Yongchun Preserved Vinegar, a black vinegar reputed to be one of China's "Four Famous Vinegars," has been a Quanzhou staple since the Song Dynasty. But I'd be careful with vinegar. "Drink vinegar" is a Chinese euphemism for "jealousy" and infers one's spouse is unfaithful.

Shishi Sweet Rice Cakes Dating from the Ming Dynasty, these are said to be some of the best rice cakes, but I wouldn't know. I prefer German chocolate cakes myself.

Hui'an Maidens Just kidding!

The Chinese Artisan

"I came upon a man in Amoy proper who with his ancestors had for generations made with rare perfection those tiny figures taken from Chinese legend and theater that one here and there sees fashioned in the streets. Made of rice-flour, each mass of dough colored a vivid green, red, blue, and so on with German dyes, the figures, about four inches long, are each spitted on a little stick, which when twirled between thumb and forefinger makes them kick up their legs and wave their arms like whirling dervishes...He worked with his son in the little mud hovel that had served his father and grandfather before him, producing forty figures a day when he worked steadily, setting them up in holes in a board to dry. As he was the only expert, there was a ready sale for all he could make; imitators made them, too, but heir usually cracked even before they dried. He could have made more, one gathered, but being a true, even though unconscious, artist he insisted on always doing his best. The work was entirely free-hand; as the man put it, with his constant smile and an occasional gesture of his rough workman hands with a suggestion of the suppleness of the artist in the fingers, he just made what was in his heart. Real artists neither live in palaces nor wear silks in China. More than once I have seen one who outwardly was only a ragged coolie in a dirty street, sitting at a makeshift bench or table making these fantastic stage figures of colored dough on whirling sticks, or something else as intricate and full of life, while the crowd surged, children jostled and fingered, men quarreled noisily about him, and still his deft fingers plodded on, copying some artistic little thing directly from generations of memory and selling them at a copper or two each."

Franck (1925, p.198)

永春老醋——中国四大名醋之一，宋朝时就是泉州的名产了。然而我对醋却持谨慎态度，因为“吃醋”是中文“嫉妒”的委婉说法，一般用于配偶之间。
石狮甜粿——源于明朝。据说是上等的米粿，但我并不知道。其实本人更喜欢德国巧克力饼。
惠安女——开个玩笑而已！

中国艺人

“在厦门市区，我偶遇到一个人，他的祖祖辈辈身怀绝艺，在街头上制作各种各样的微小人物像（其实就是妆糕人——译者注），这些微小人物像都取材于中国传说中或舞台上的人物，相当逼真。他们用面粉做原料，在每一块生面团上染上绿色、红色、蓝色以及德国染料。这些微小人物大概有 4 英寸高，每尊插在一根小木棒上，只要你用大拇指和食指捏住转动，它们就会像苦修僧人一样手舞脚踢地旋转不停……这个艺人和他的儿子住在他们祖辈遗留下来的小泥屋里，通常他一天可以制作 40 尊小人物像，而后把它们插在木板的洞孔里风干。由于他制作技艺高超，每天做多少都能很快销售一空。周围也有人模仿他制作，但他们制作出来的小人物像总是在风干前就裂开了。有人推测，他一天应制作不止 40 尊，然而，身为一个真正的并非他能自我意识到的艺术家，他做事历来是竭尽所能。这种工作对他来说完全是随意的，他脸上总是挂着笑容，偶尔也会用他那粗糙的手扮个鬼脸，以暗示他手指上小人物的柔顺，他的制作纯粹是随心所欲。在中国，真正的艺术家并非住在宫殿里，也不会穿丝戴玉。我曾经不止一次看到这些艺人，外表上看起来与那些在肮脏不堪的街道上干苦力的衣衫褴褛的人毫无两样，他们坐在一临时替代的长板凳或小桌子上，用彩色面团在旋转的小木棒上捏作各种各样的舞台上的或其他错综复杂、活力十足的人物。围观的人越来越多，小孩子用手指推来推去，大人们则围着他品头论足，然而他不为所动，用他那灵巧的手指，不知疲倦地捏造出记忆中先辈们流传下来的艺术小作品，售价也无非一两个铜币而已。”

——弗兰克（1925 年，第 198 页）

第十七章

泉州的酒店和旅行社

5 Star（五星级）

Quanzhou Mandarin Hotel 泉州悦华酒店 Quanzhou's Best! (See next page). Nice restaurants, good gym and best pool.（泉州最好的酒店，餐厅、健身房和游泳池俱佳）

Add: W. Citong Rd. S. Section 泉州刺桐西路南段

Phone: (595)2801-9999 Website: www.yeohwa-qz.com

4 Star（四星级）

Quanzhou Hotel 泉州酒店

Great location, near historic Zhongshan Rd.; excellent cuisine, nice gym, good pool; reasonable prices.（毗邻中山路，地点很好，餐饮、健身房和游泳池俱佳）

Add. 22 Zhuangfu Lane, Downtown， 泉州市区庄府巷 22 号

Phone: (595)2218-2128 FAX: (595)2218-2128

Jinjiang Aile Holiday Hotel, 晋江爱乐度日酒店

Add. Yangguang Industrial Town， 晋江市青阳杨光工贸城

Phone: (595)8566-6666 FAX: (595)8566-6999

3 Star（三星级）

Quanzhou Zaytun Hotel, 泉州刺桐饭店

My home away from home—beautiful garden ambience.（我的家外之家——园林式的环境）

Add. North Tian'an Road, Downtown, 泉州市区田安路北段

Phone: (595)2210-2222 FAX: (595)2210-2108

Quanzhou Overseas Chinese Hotel, 泉州华侨大厦

Another favorite—perfect downtown location, EZ walk to everything.
（我最喜欢的另一酒店——地理位置极佳，走路出去办事非常方便）

Add. Baiyuan Rd. Downtown, 泉州市区百源路

Phone: (595)2228-2192 FAX: (595)2228-4612

Quanzhou Huxin Hotel, 泉州湖心大酒店

Add. Huxin Street, Downtown, 泉州市区湖心街

Phone: (595)2228-2888 FAX: (595)2219-7889

Quanzhou Taihe Hotel, 泉州泰和大酒店

Add. Tian'an Road, Downtown (by stadium), 泉州市区田安路

Phone: (595)2210-5888 FAX: (595)2210-5888

Quanzhou Qunsheng Hotel, 泉州群盛大酒店
Very reasonable rates, spacious rooms（房价非常合理，客房宽敞）
Add. Huxin Street, Downtown, 泉州市区湖心街
Phone: (595)2216-6788 FAX: (595)2216-6298

Hui'an Dapeng Hotel, 惠安大鹏酒店
Add. Dapeng Store, Downtown Hui'an City, 惠安城关大鹏商店
Phone: (595)8737-7777 FAX: (595)8738-2471

Shishi Overseas Chinese Hotel, 石狮华侨大厦
Add. Jiu'er Road, Downtown Shishi, 石狮市九二路
Phone: (595)8878-7108 FAX: (595)8878-1643

Nan'an Overseas Chinese Hotel, 南安华侨大酒店
Add.Ximei, Downtown Nan'an, 南安市溪美
Phone: (595)8638-8888 FAX：(595)8638-9999

Nan'an Gold Deer Hotel, 南安金鹿大酒店
Add. Honglai Town, Nan'an, 南安市洪濑镇
Phone: (595)8669-9999 FAX: (595)8669-6333

Nan'an (Shuitou) Mingchao Hotel, 南安明超大酒店
Near Koxinga Memorial and Cai Minnan Village
（在郑成功纪念馆和蔡氏古民居附近）
Add. Xiasheng Rd., Shuitou, Nan'an, 南安水头厦盛路

2 Star（二星级）

Anxi Overseas Chinese Hotel, 安溪华侨大酒店
Add. Lianyi Building #1, North Street, Anxi, 安溪北街 1 号联谊大厦
Phone: (595)2326-6979 FAX: (595)2326-6979

Yongchun Qiaolian Hotel, 永春侨联大厦
Add. 143 Huancheng Rd., Taocheng Township, Yongchun County
永春县桃城镇环城路 143 号
Phone: (595)2388-4202 FAX: (595)2388-4205

Yongchun Hotel, 永春酒店
Add. 61 Huancheng Rd., Downtown Yongchun, 永春县环城路 61 号
Phone: (595)2388-6990 FAX: (595)2388-2863

Dehua Cidu （Porcelain Capital) Hotel, 德化瓷都酒店
Add. Downtown Dehua, 德化县城关
Phone: (595)2358-8188 FAX: (595)2358-8988

Quanzhou Mandarin

You can't fully appreciate Quanzhou by day unless you've had a good rest by night. Fortunately, Quanzhou has one of our favorite hotels…

The Princess and the Pea My wife must be related to the princess who felt the pea beneath 50 mattresses because she has found fault with fine establishments across the planet, from the legendary Princess Hotel in Acapulco and Hyatt in Maui to the Intercontinental in Vienna and the Bilderberg in Holland (Tsar Peter the Great liked it; my wife said it did not deserve five stars). We've also stayed in numerous Quanzhou hotels and each has pros and cons—except for the Mandarin, for which even my wife has only praise.

Room But No Board I'm not in my wife's class (she says I have ***no*** class) but even I appreciate the Mandarin's laid-back luxury—a rare marriage of elegance and comfort, imposing but inviting. The 380 well-appointed rooms are perfect for relaxing, resting, or getting a bit of work done in private. I also like the small touches, such as fresh flowers, fruit platter, reading materials, and city map. And while "room and board" in most Chinese hotels means the beds are as hard as a board, even my princess appreciated the Mandarin's luxurious beds. I'd have been happy to hide out in our room—except for meals, of course, which one should not miss at the Mandarin.

Global Cuisine The Mandarin's Lotus Restaurant serves many styles of Chinese cuisine in a classical setting, and the Kansai Japanese Restaurant could have been teleported straight from Tokyo. We enjoy buffet breakfasts in the Mandarin Garden Cafeteria and Lounge, which felt more like the South Pacific than downtown China. And the icing on the cake is Jeffrey's Bakery. Fujian's top pastry chef, Jeffrey offers everything from tiramisu, tarts and Napoleons to specialty breads and rolls. Or try a DIY (do-it-yourself) pastry for a loved one! Tel: 28019999 x5166

Learn More Visit Mandarin's website for more on their comprehensive business and conference facilities, or their excellent gym, sauna and heated pool (Quanzhou's best), or their business center, or the elite Executive Floor's exclusive services and privileges.

http://www.qzmandarin.com

泉州悦华酒店

泉州有很多让人留恋的风景，当然，如果你想白天能够好好欣赏它们，晚上睡个好觉，养足精神是非常重要的。幸运的是，在泉州，有一家我们特别喜欢的酒店，为我们每一次旅行留下了很多美好的记忆……

挑剔的“豌豆公主” 我太太有点像安徒生童话里的豌豆公主。不论是在阿卡普尔科传说中的“豌豆公主”酒店，还是在维也纳的凯悦酒店，抑或是彼尔德伯格公园酒店（这个连沙皇彼得都喜欢得不得了的豪华酒店，我太太却认为它不够档次），每一次入住，我太太都能从中挑出一些毛病来。可是住在悦华酒店，我太太除了赞扬还是赞扬。

我旅途中的“家” 尽管我跟我太太的品位不同（她经常说我没品位，呵呵），但是，就喜欢悦华这一点，我们却出奇的相似。悦华的雍容华贵带给人无比的优雅与舒适，是我一直所赞叹的。这里有380间设备齐全的房间，是放松和休息的理想场所，并且也可以做一些私人的工作。我也很喜欢房间里的一些小摆设，鲜花、水果拼盘、报刊读物、市区地图等。不管你从什么角度看它，在你的视野里，它所带给你的不仅仅只是“舒适”二字可以阐释得完的。每一个细心的设计都带给你与众不同的感觉。要不是为了到餐厅吃饭，我宁愿一整天都呆在房间里。当然，悦华的美食也是让人赞叹的！

悦华的美食 酒店的荷风中餐厅提供了中国各地的传统美食；二楼石山日本料理的菜肴口味更是正宗，因为它的很多原材料都是从日本东京直接空运过来的；悦园咖啡厅非常宽敞舒适，我和我太太喜欢在悦园咖啡厅悠闲地吃着早餐，这让我感觉像是在自己的国家，而不是在中国；杰弗里大师做的提拉米苏、拿破仑酥、黑森林等很多糕点常常让我念念不忘；悦华酒店还有完善的商务和会议设施，先进的健身设备，以及服务周到的桑拿中心、商务中心，如果想了解更多更全面的信息，你可以登录悦华酒店的网站（www.yeohwa-qz.com）。

Travel Agencies（旅行社）

International（国际社）

Quanzhou China Travel Service, 泉州中国旅行社
General Manager: Li Zhangbin，李章彬
Add. #1 Baiyuan Rd., Quanzhou, 泉州市区百源路 1 号
Phone: (595)2282192 FAX: (595)2218-2901
Quanzhou China Int'l Travel Service, 泉州中国国际旅行社
General Manager: Lin Zhenxing, 林振兴
Add. Mid-Wenling Rd., Quanzhou, 泉州市区温陵路中段
Phone: (595)2228-5552 FAX: (595)2228-1089
Shishi China [Int'l] Travel Service, 石狮中国旅行社
General Manger: Deng Baolian, 邓宝廉
Add. Jiu'er Road, Shishi, 泉州石狮市九二路
Phone: (595)8878-7105 FAX: (595)8878-1643

Domestic Travel Agencies（国内社）

建议：如果你想更多地了解各县（镇或当地）丰富的文化和历史，最好请一位当地旅行社的导游。可就近联系当地的中国旅行社，聘请当地导游。

Hui'an Tianma Int'l Travel Service, 惠安天马国际旅行社
General Manager: Wang Bingkui, 王丙奎
Awarded "Best 100 Domestic Travel Agencies"
（曾荣获过中国国内旅游百强社，地址：惠安大红埔中总商住楼 1～3 号）
Add. 1-3, Zhongzong Commercial Office Bldg.
Phone: (595)8732-0008 FAX: (595)8733-2889
Yongchun China Travel Service, 永春县中国旅行社
General Manager: Dai Dejun, 戴德俊
Add. #61 Huancheng Rd., Yongchun, 永春县环城路 61 号
Phone: (595)2388-2863 FAX: (595)2388-2863
Nan'an China Travel Service, 南安市中国旅行社
General Manager: Ye Yixin, 叶贻新
Add. #139 Xinhua Rd., Nan'an, 南安市新华路 139 号
Phone: (595)8638-6213 FAX: (595)8639-7138

Hui'an China Travel Service, 惠安县中国旅行社
General Manager: Rao Zheqiang, 饶哲强
Add. #1 Keshan Rd., Downtown Hui'an, 惠安县城关科山路1号
Phone: (595)8738-7201 FAX: (595)8739-8302

Jinjiang China Travel Service, 晋江旅行社
General Manager: Chen Jianmin, 陈建民
Add. #10 Qipai St., Qingyang, Jinjiang, 晋江市青阳镇旗牌街10号
Phone: (595)8568-4176 FAX: (595)8568-0840

Dehua China Travel Service, 德化中国旅行社
General Manager: Xu Wanyan, 徐婉燕
Add. #28 N. Longjin Rd., Dehua, 德化县龙津路北段28号
Phone: (595)2352-2321 FAX: (595)2352-2321

Dehua Cidu Travel Service, 德化瓷都旅行社
General Manager: Lin Hongfu, 林鸿福
Add. 1st Floor, Nanmen Cinema, Dehua, 德化县南门电影院一楼
Phone: (595)2358-6896 FAX: 2358-9552

Anxi Aviation Holiday Travel Service Co. Ltd., 安溪航空度假旅行社有限公司
General Manager: Xie Wenjiang, 谢文江
Add. #149 Datong Rd. Fengcheng, Anxi, 安溪风城大同路149号
Phone: (595)2326-0999 FAX: (595)2326-0989

反馈

如果你想推荐一家比较好的旅行社（或者敬告其他人的），请发电子邮件给我：**amoybill@gmail.com。**

同时别忘了浏览苏珊的网页，获取更多新的资讯：

http://www.amoymagic.com (outside of China)
http://www.amoymagic.mts.cn (within China)
http://www.xiamenguide.com
http://quanzhouexpat.blogspot.com

Miscellaneous

Traveler's Checks and Credit Cards

Traveler's checks can be cashed at any Bank of China, or one of its foreign exchange offices. Credit cards are accepted in many stores, hotels and restaurants. (A big change from the early '90s, when Bank of China took five weeks to clear a money order!).

Xiuxi--China's Siesta

Working Hours

Government and bank hours are, officially, 8:00 – 11:30 AM, and 14:30 -17:30 PM (summer) or 14:00 – 17:00 PM (winter), Monday thru Friday. The noon interval includes the 3 hours lunch and xiuxi (siesta), when everything shuts down (except for post offices—which are open all day, 7 days a week!).

Our university gate guards, who zealously accost visitors morning and afternoon, leave the gates wide open and unattended during xiuxi (and when it rains). If anyone ever attacks China during xiuxi on a rainy day, we're doomed.

Currency and Exchange – Changee Money!

Foreign currency can be exchanged for China's RMB (人民币，Renminbi, or People's Money) at any Quanzhou bank, and most hotels and guest houses open to foreigners.

Tourist Transport

Special Tourist Bus Lines

Quanzhou has two special tourist bus lines on which you can travel comfortably and safely to most of the major tourist spots. Narrators use Chinese, but perhaps for an extra fee you can arrange for an interpreter.

For information, call: (0595) 2228-3842.

"One-Day Tour" Bus Lines

Quanzhou has 15 special "One-Day Tour" bus lines, guides included, covering major city tourist spots. The program is managed by Quanzhou General Automobile Transportation Company, Tourist Taxi Branch. For information, call: (0595) 2220-6220.

实用资讯

旅行支票和信用卡

旅行支票可以在任何一家中国银行或者其外币兑换点兑换成现金。信用卡在许多商场、酒店或酒楼都可以使用。（与20世纪90年代相比，变化确实很大，当时办理一张汇票需要整整5个星期）

工作时间

政府机关和银行每周工作五天，上午8:00—11:30，下午14:30—17:30（夏季）或14:00—17:00（冬季）。中午间隔3个小时，用于午餐和午睡，不营业（除了邮政一周七天营业外）。

厦门大学的门卫一天从早到晚热情地招呼着每一位来访者，中午午休的时候却敞开大门不管（下雨天也一样）。我想，如果有人在下雨天的午休时间攻击中国，我们注定会完蛋的。

货币与兑换

在泉州的任何一家银行，外币都可以兑换成人民币，绝大多数酒店和宾馆都向外国人开放。

旅游交通

旅游专线车

泉州市区目前开辟两条旅游专线，往返于市区主要景点的班车安全舒适。旅游专线车还配备中文讲解员，也许你可以花点钱请个翻译来帮忙。咨询电话：(0595) 22283842

“一日游”专线车

泉州目前推出15条“一日游”线路，覆盖全市各主要景点（区），车上还配备导游。具体工作由泉州市汽车运输总公司旅游汽车出租分公司经营。咨询电话：(0595) 22206220

City Buses

Quanzhou's comprehensive bus network is convenient and cheap, and runs from 6:00 a.m. until 10:00 p.m. The bus number, and places of departure and destination, are clearly marked above the windshield. The fare, either one or two Yuan, is paid after boarding.

Taxis

Minimum fare for Quanzhou taxis is 6 Yuan, and 1.4 to 1.6 Yuan for each additional kilometer. Pay the fee on the taximeter unless you are taking the taxi a long distance, in which case you can negotiate a set fee. In my experience, most taxi drivers are friendly and honest, but if you do have a bad encounter, report it at: 12315 (consumer complaints) or 258-8103 (taxi complaints). I've only filed one complaint, but got fast results! In the end I felt sorry for the guy. Almost.

Emergency Phone Numbers

Fire or Police: 119

Public Security: 110

Traffic Accident Reporting: 122

First Aid Center: 120

Local Directory Assistance: 114

Consumer Complaints Hotline: 12315

Tourist Complaint Hotline: 2227-4888
(Tourist Quality Supervisory Institute)

Tourist Inquiry: 160

Medical Facilities

Quanzhou #1 Hospital: 2277-3906

2nd Affiliated Hospital of Fujian
Medical College: 2277-0061 ext. 8041

Quanzhou People's Hospital: 2228-5221

Quanzhou Traditional Chinese

Medicine Hospital: 2220-7200

Quanzhou Children's Hospital: 2219-5920

公交汽车

泉州的公交服务网络既方便又实惠，服务时间从早上 6 时到晚上 10 时。在公交车挡风玻璃上都标明公交线路号和起止地名，票价 1~2 元，上车购票。

的士

在泉州乘坐的士起步费为 6 元，尔后每行走 1 公里增加收费 1.4～1.6 元。除了较远的路要同司机事先讲好价格外，其他的均使用计价器收费。我所经历过的的士司机绝大多数都很友好、诚实，当然，如果你发现有欺诈行为，可拨打电话：12315（消费者投诉）或者 22588103（出租车投诉）。我只投诉过一次，不过，很快有了处理结果。最后，我倒觉得很抱歉（几乎很抱歉）。

应急电话

火警：119
公安报警服务台：110
交通事故报警：122
急救中心：120
市内电话查询：114
消费者投诉服务台：12315
旅游投诉电话（旅游质量监督所）22274888
旅游咨询电话：160

医疗机构

泉州市第一医院：22773906
福建省医学院附属第二医院：22770061 转 8041
泉州市人民医院：22285221
泉州市中医院：22207200
泉州市儿童医院：22195920

其他资讯？请联系：

Quanzhou International Club (泉州国际俱乐部)
网址 http://www.qzintlclub.com/
E-mail: qzintlclub@hotmail.com.

图书在版编目(CIP)数据

魅力泉州＝Discover Quanzhou/(美)潘维廉著；潘文功等译．—厦门：厦门大学出版社，2007.7(2019.2 重印)
(魅力·老潘)
ISBN 978-7-5615-2106-9

Ⅰ.①魅… Ⅱ.①潘…②潘… Ⅲ.①泉州市—概况—汉、英
Ⅳ.①K925.73

中国版本图书馆 CIP 数据核字(2003)第 077289 号

出版人 郑文礼
责任编辑 施高翔

出版发行 厦门大学出版社
社　址 厦门市软件园二期望海路 39 号
邮政编码 361008
总编办 0592-2182177 0592-2181406(传真)
营销中心 0592-2184458 0592-2181365
网　址 http://www.xmupress.com
邮　箱 xmup@xmupress.com
印　刷 厦门集大印刷厂

开本 880 mm×1 230 mm 1/32
印张 11.625
插页 6
字数 348 千字
版次 2007 年 7 月第 2 版
印次 2019 年 2 月第 2 次印刷
定价 32.00 元

厦门大学出版社
微信二维码

厦门大学出版社
微博二维码